BEYOND THE NOISE OF SOLEMN ASSEMBLIES

McGILL-QUEEN'S STUDIES IN THE HISTORY OF RELIGION
Volumes in this series have been supported by the Jackman Foundation of Toronto.

SERIES ONE G.A. RAWLYK, EDITOR

SERIES TWO IN MEMORY OF GEORGE RAWLYK

DONALD HARMAN AKENSON, EDITOR

Beyond the Noise
of Solemn Assemblies

*The Protestant Ethic and the
Quest for Social Justice in Canada*

RICHARD ALLEN

McGill-Queen's University Press
Montreal & Kingston · London · Chicago

© McGill-Queen's University Press 2018

ISBN 978-0-7735-5504-4 (cloth)
ISBN 978-0-7735-5553-2 (ePDF)
ISBN 978-0-7735-5554-9 (ePUB)

Legal deposit fourth quarter 2018
Bibliothèque nationale du Québec

Printed in Canada on acid-free paper that is 100% ancient forest free
(100% post-consumer recycled), processed chlorine free

We acknowledge the support of the Canada Council for the Arts, which
last year invested $153 million to bring the arts to Canadians throughout
the country.

Nous remercions le Conseil des arts du Canada de son soutien. L'an dernier,
le Conseil a investi 153 millions de dollars pour mettre de l'art dans la vie
des Canadiennes et des Canadiens de tout le pays.

Library and Archives Canada Cataloguing in Publication

Allen, Richard, 1929–, author
    Beyond the noise of solemn assemblies : the Protestant ethic and the
quest for social justice in Canada / Richard Allen.

(McGill-Queen's studies in the history of religion. Series two ; 82)
Includes bibliographical references and index.
Issued in print and electronic formats.
ISBN 978-0-7735-5504-4 (hardcover). – ISBN 978-0-7735-5553-2 (ePDF). –
ISBN 978-0-7735-5554-9 (ePUB)

    1. Christian socialism – Canada – History – 20th century. I. Title.
II. Series: McGill-Queen's studies in the history of religion. Series two ; 82

HX51.A45 2018   335.'709710904   C2018-904933-2
                                                   C2018-904934-0

This book was typeset by True to Type in 10.5/13 Sabon

*For my graduate students
from whom I have learned so much
– then and since*

*I hate, I despise your feasts,
and I take no delight in your
solemn assemblies.
Take away from me the noise
of your songs;
to the melody of your harps
I will not listen.
But let justice roll down like
waters, and righteousness
like an ever-flowing stream.*
Amos 5:21, 23–24

Contents

Acknowledgments

The community of scholarship that underlies and surrounds a work like this is almost boundless. Summoning the half of it would be an impossible task, but that is not the point of the observation. What is important is the unabashed recognition of the fact, and to bow in gratitude before it. Those to whom I am more immediately indebted will, in their own right, stand in for the rest.

It was in conversation with Marguerite Van Die of Queen's University that the notion of undertaking a collection like this first surfaced. And it is fair to say that without her constant encouragement, helpful advice, and hands-on editing – even the reconstruction of at least one chapter – it would not have seen the light of day. Such commitment can only be accounted a labour of love. I am indebted to Ian McKay, now Wilson Professor of Canadian History at McMaster University, for reading a part of the manuscript and his helpful comments on it. Adrian Zita-Bennett assisted with some early phases of the project. Vanessa Lovisa's exceptional competence as my research assistant and her readiness to help with occasional problems of formatting have kept the work on track. It was Sarah Fick, however, on whose experience in preparing manuscripts for publication I have long relied, who prepared the first full draft sent to McGill-Queen's University Press. Her computer expertise and that of Stephen Madill, backing up this word processing amateur, have resolved many an impasse that threatened my emotional stability. And I need to record with especial gratitude the longstanding friendship and inspiration of Douglas John Hall, the leading Canadian Protestant theologian of my generation, his wife, Rhoda, and their talented family, with whom a visit was always not only intellectually enlightening with respect to the broad issues of religion and politics discussed here, but also a culturally enriching and heartwarming experience.

It will be more than evident in what follows the extent to which the Student Christian Movement, at the apex of its history on Canadian university campuses, was a formative influence in my intellectual development. It was only in its study program that I was led to reflect on the meaning of the university itself. In that respect, it was the magnetic presence of Robert "Bob" Miller who, as national study secretary and founder of the SCM Book Room and later the Bob Miller Bookstore, wielded the greatest influence. His keen interest in modern art and his unerring sense of the leading edge of literature across so many fields was vitally important for me, as for so many. And among the many lively conversations of a lifetime, I need to acknowledge my latter-day appreciation of John Robertson's knowledge and wisdom as a philosopher of religion and science and Richard Rempel's keen engagement with nineteenth and twentieth century British politics, philosophy, and religion, which have enriched my understanding of many of the personalities and issues that lie in the background of a collection like this.

In a similar vein, I feel compelled to acknowledge my profound appreciation of the many dedicated teachers I have studied under. Professor Soward, in my first year at the University of British Columbia, opened up for me the history of the "Twenty-five Troubled Years" that lay in the background of my own growing up. I was privileged at the University of Toronto to be exposed to the liberal, radical, and conservative interpretations of Canadian history under professors Careless, Underhill, and Creighton, respectively, and British and Canadian constitutional history under professors Wilkinson and Martin. Professor Saunders' seminar on the Enlightenment still informs my thinking as few others have done, although Professor Frye's "Nineteenth Century Thought" would be one of those, not to mention his lectures on Milton and Spencer. The then-young Professor Sparshot was a chastening experience in his class on Plato's Republic. He gave my first essay for him the lowest mark of my entire university career – a fifty-three! It was months later, having quickly hidden the embarrassing paper out of sight, that I inadvertently discovered that it was the highest mark in the class!

At Duke University, studying political reform in Britain from the late eighteenth through the nineteenth century under the imperious tutelage of Professor Hamilton was unexpectedly rewarding. Professor Curtis' thoroughly authoritative course on modern Russia since the freeing of the serfs in 1861 was more germane to my reasons for being at Duke. It was Professors Watson and Hallowell, however, who provided the substance of what I required to securely ground the work I wanted to do on the social gospel in Canada – despite the fact that Canada was conspicuous in its absence from the teaching of either of them. An eminently personable and gracious man and an authority on the Progressive Era in the United States, Watson conducted his seminar with a mix of subdued enthusiasm and confident assurance, and he provided me with the insights and perspectives I needed to launch a comparable course in the progressive tradition in Canada. He supervised my dissertation with a characteristic academic rigour and gentility of manner, which I much appreciated. Professor Hallowell in political theory was possibly the lecturer most personally and vitally engaged with his subject of my entire university career. Brought up in an evangelical home, he had gravitated to an Episcopalian (Anglican) expression of Christianity and taught political theory from the perspective of classical Christian and Greek thought, which for me shone a critical light on the liberal theology in which I had been brought up. For Hallowell, the issues of political thought and practice mattered profoundly for the future of humanity. Eric Voegelin and Leo Strauss were polar stars in his classroom, but he was very much his own man. Though I would not follow him in the full conservatism of his position, he was never partisan, was clearly in full command of his subject, and, as will be explained below, provided the basis for my concluding critique of the social gospel in Canada. To have studied under such a galaxy of teachers for whom their subjects mattered immensely has been for me a treasure beyond measure.

I have dedicated this book to my graduate students as an acknowledgment of the degree of mutual learning that is characteristic of that level of "instruction" but is seldom formally recognized and valued at its true worth. The practice of recent years of encouraging their submission of papers to the annual meetings of the Canadian Historical Association (CHA) underlines the point – even if it has rendered the CHA schedule almost unmanageable. Observing and participating in their excited – and sometimes anguished – immersion in original research and writing has been one of the great joys of my life as a historian and teacher.

Returning to the present project, I must acknowledge the unfailing helpfulness and wonderful patience of Kyla Madden, senior editor of McGill-Queen's University Press, with whom I have been in frequent correspondence over past months. Her calm confidence in the completion of the manuscript has kept me from panic over various rising issues, including the prospect of missing deadlines. In short, she has made working with McGill-Queen's University Press a thoroughly satisfying experience, to which Ryan Van Huijstee and Jennifer Thomas added with their consistent helpfulness throughout the copy-editing process. In that connection, I want to express my appreciation of the comments, critical and otherwise, of my peer review readers, which have led, I hope, to a significant improvement in the text. After all is said and done in that regard, however, as author I remain responsible for all errors of fact, textual faults, and such other miscellaneous shortcomings as continue to inhabit the text, including the interpretive positioning taken in its various parts. And I am grateful to Ruth Pincoe, whose interest in the subject and professional skills have created a fine index for readers – and relieved me of an onerous task.

Finally, as with all my projects and pursuits, whether academic, political, or personal, I have enjoyed the devoted support of a precious partner. In mid-2016, as time continued to work its unwanted effects on our health, Nettie declared that she wanted to keep me around as long as possible, only to succumb, herself, to a stroke a few months later. I am doing my best to fulfill her wish.

Preface

1

Beyond the noise of solemn assemblies. The essays and reflections gathered here reflect my long-standing preoccupation as a historian with the interplay of religion, ideas, social formation, and political movements and parties. My first book, *The Social Passion: Religion and Social Reform in Canada, 1914–1928* (1971), was a major attempt to bring those strands together and stands as something of a marker for the arrival of the new social and intellectual history in Canada and the revival of interest in the secular academy of the role of religion as a powerful force in the making of modern Canada.

The first impetus for the present collection arose from complaints of students that some of my published articles were difficult to locate. With the decision to undertake a publication of previously published and unpublished essays, the recognition dawned that, in sequence, they were markers along the way, before and after the writing of *The Social Passion*, and thus bore evidence of changing personal circumstances and the play of new intellectual interests and influences. In short, a thin red line of autobiography that might be of historiographical interest, I thought, could be detected – and with the thinking, the thought began to grow that the collection could, at least potentially, be read at two levels at once, as historical accounts and in terms of their historiography. Thus, ultimately, the end result turned out to be greater than the sum of the parts. Moreover, it also became evident that, taken in sequence, the essays carried forward a narrative line of their own. In the upshot, the project became at once more interesting and more challenging. Whether or not I have been successful, I leave in the hands of the reader, but if some readers find the book rather idiosyncratic, I shall not be surprised.

Such a collection also allows me to accomplish an unfinished aspiration, namely to place within a larger context *The Social Passion*, whose appearance as a second paperback edition was generously promoted by the publisher as "The Reprint of a Modern Classic." My long-standing objective had been to write a volume on the rise of the social Christian movement in Canada in the latter nineteenth century and the first years of the twentieth, and a second on the Radical Christianity of the Great Depression. Neither happened, although the first volume of the Salem Bland biography, *The View from Murney Tower* (2008), went some distance in meeting the first objective. The diversions of thirteen engrossing years in Ontario politics (1982–95) had slowed progress to a crawl. From another perspective, in the big picture, as will become clear, the reasons for my excursion into public life were not unrelated to my teaching. Nor were academic colleagues reticent in proposing occasions that would press me into new explorations, participation in academic fora, lectures public and otherwise, and further publication. Indeed, in the format I have adopted here, these opportunities that I was able to bend to my longer term objectives significantly extended at both ends the intended time frame of the original "prequel/sequel" project.

The essays in this collection are not offered as cutting-edge pieces of current research, although most continue to stand alone and unique in the corpus of Canadian historiography. Of the sixteen chapters, six are, so to speak, "hot off the press," and ten are previously published, among which only one is available online. The first section of four chapters, "The World We Have Known," establishes some starting points of personal background and issues of special interest as I apprenticed my way to becoming a historian. More on that below. Chapters 5 to 16 complement and supplement both *The Social Passion* and *Murney Tower*. As previously noted, they have a narrative line of their own on the emergence and outworking of the social Christian movement in Canada. That narrative begins with an account of the evolution in the nineteenth century of a uniquely Canadian idea of progress from a prevailing providential mindset. It is notable that as that process developed, it was significantly carried forward by skilled trades and labour groups. Paralleling that, but advancing the story, is an account of the diverse strands in the "fabrication" of the early social gospel in Canada. Next is an essay on the classic period of the social gospel, 1890 to 1929, years that anticipated *The Social Passion*. An excursion follows into the distinctive social gospel of the prairie west, with essays on Winnipeg college students in an age of reform, Salem Bland on the new spirituality of the social gospel and the Winnipeg elite, the urban reform work of J.S. Woodsworth, and the social gospel as the religion of agrarian revolt. The narrative line next shifts to Salem Bland and his "New Christianity" in post-Great War Toronto and then to the new social and political radicalism of the 1930s, beginning with the special case of Norman Bethune, whose early religious formation and dramatic career provide an arresting background for the subsequent discussion of the intellectual background and politics of a radical materialist Christianity of the 1930s and 1940s. The penultimate chapter covers the strategically focused ecumenical coalitions of post-Second World War Canada, the End of History debate, and the prospects of social democracy as the Cold War ends. In conclusion, the narrative returns to the Protestant ethic debate with a review/report on the latest phases of the debate (1960–2016) and the significance of Max Weber's concept of the "Iron Cage of Capitalism" for the looming issue of the end of work. A postscript explores the prevalence of myth (in the classic use of the term) in religion and politics as a ground for rethinking the role of religion in the public square in a secular age.

2

The writing of social history is a delicate task that, however disciplined, is also to some degree an act of self-revelation. Canadian historical research and writing has long since abandoned the notion that it was possible to write objective history. The late nineteenth century ushered objective history out the door only to open up the problems of subjectivity in the writing of historical accounts, much as the science of the same period was forced to abandon anticipations of finality and proclaim the "principle of indeterminacy." To remain credibly grounded in reality, however, history as an intellectual pursuit requires disciplined examination of the widest possible range of relevant documentable source materials. But the sources, whatever their nature, have their limitations, as every historian sooner or later discovers, especially when confronted by the blank sheet of paper or the empty computer screen. Fortunately, he/she has come to the documentary encounter not just with important questions but with an invaluable asset – an active imagination at work sensing character and projecting scenarios. Emotions have been subtly touched and sympathies – and antipathies – aroused. They, too, require a certain discipline, but in the process one human being's personal and social experience and cultivated intellect are brought into play. In the upshot, in the finished work, the ingredients will in some measure be evident on careful scrutiny and reflection.

All public writing, not just that of historians, is then to some degree a measure of the author, reflecting something of residual family culture; something of style and temper of personality; something of intellectual culture,
preoccupying interests, and ideological proclivities; something of the feeling
for humanity and/or the world of nature. One reviewer of *The Social Passion*
described it as a memoir, which it was not, but rightly detected an unusual
degree of personal commitment to the subject matter. Another described it
as "semi-idealist," which suggested it was also "semi-materialist." I remain
comfortable with that observation, but I had not set out self-consciously
to write "semi-idealist" history. One scholar, not a reviewer, noted the balanced use of typologies associated with such names as Ernst Troeltsch and
S.D. Clark (church/sect), H. Richard Niebuhr (social sources/Christ and
culture), and Reinhold Niebuhr (moral man/immoral society) – not to
mention others I might add, such as Wilhelm Visser 't Hooft (immanence/
transcendence). Again, these typologies were so integrated into the cumula-
tive world view I brought to the task that they, almost unsummoned, flowed
into the narrative.

It was this experience that also has inspired me to call attention to the
threads of autobiography that a reader might ferret out of the text of this
collection of essays. One of my peer review readers was emphatic that it
was too much simply to leave readers on their own to tease such things
out of the essays without further help from the author – hence the backgrounders that now preface chapters 2 to 16.

If all that has given the collection an idiosyncratic character, I have compounded the effect with the risky decision to include three essays that
reflect pre-professional historical concerns. The first is an undergraduate
contribution to a student periodical that would convey some sense of my
early ideological leanings. Two doctoral essays represent issues with large
civilizational implications that specially interested me as I embarked
upon my formal "apprenticeship" as a historian – and, as it turned out,
would surface in the later essays and autobiographical backgrounders of
this collection. With the growing weight of autobiography in the text, I
was impressed by the need for an introductory piece that would bring a
degree of unity to the separate elements of autobiography that had come
to populate the text. Hence, chapter 1: "Growing Up Religious, Political,
and Historical."

3

Whether idiosyncratic or not, the resulting text underlines the sage advice of E.H. Carr, driven into the minds of successive generations of students of history, that the first task of readers of historical works is to inquire into the person of the author. What follows should facilitate that task for readers of this and other of my publications. I recognize that, in a skeptical, post-Freudian, postmodern age, undertaking a project involving elements of autobiography is bound to arouse suspicion. Be that as it may, one of my more perceptive graduate students later observed that one thing he had learned from me was that one's vocation could also become one's profession. By implication, both could find expression in public life. Growing up Christian and democratic socialist certainly informed my decision to become a historian, as well as my choice of field in which to exercise my professional training, namely the role of religion in the response to the human issues of a new Canadian industrial/urban social order of the 1880s through the 1930s. It also influenced my interest in the complementary issue of how the challenging realities of social change in those decades would erode the ideal categories that religiously based movements brought to the task. The crisis of the social gospel in the 1920s was the result. Radical renewal would be the challenge of the 1930s to prepare the ground for further social and economic advance.

In the 1970s the combined forces of the political and religious right sought to overturn the progressive social advances of the post-Second World War era. These decades, even given their limitations, had registered a significantly more equitable distribution of the country's wealth. In response to the changing political climate I accepted an invitation to contest the 1982 by-election in Hamilton West as the New Democratic Party (NDP) candidate. The Liberal leader, Stuart Smith, had resigned and vacated the seat. There were various issues at play in the election, but my personal intent was twofold: to protest the so-called "restraint" program of the sitting Conservative government that threatened the generations of progressive social advance that was the subject of my teaching, and, in the face of all the media preoccupation with the American religious right and its unambiguous alliance with Reagan Republicanism, I wanted to signal the ongoing presence of a Christian left in Canada. Sadly, the right has prevailed and scales of social justice have turned upside down in this country. I could not then have anticipated that, by some measures, the income gap between the bottom and the top 10 per cent would multiply almost ten times from a multiple of twenty-five to over 200 or that twenty years later the average top CEOs in Canada would earn more in the first working day of the year than the average worker would earn in the entire year. It was already clear in 1982, however, that the relative circumstances of low-income earners were worsening, that an alarming percentage of children were living in poverty, and the prospects of the middle class had plateaued.

This is not the place to recite the many initiatives I undertook in eight years in opposition and five in government. My "maiden speech" as an opposition member of the Ontario legislature was a critique of retrogressive business pressure for supply-side fiscal policies and a defence of the Keynesian demand-side economics that had underwritten post-war Canadian prosperity and achieved a more equitable distribution of the country's wealth. My last major project was the organization of a three-pronged "March against Homelessness and Poverty" to converge on the legislature from Sudbury, Windsor, and Ottawa in the early spring of 1989. The object was to press the reluctant Peterson government to implement the proposals of the Social Assistance Review Committee (SARC), which had been among the conditions required by the NDP for joining in the Liberal/NDP Accord of 1985. The net result was the passage of a $400 million package of progressive social assistance reforms when the legislature next met. John Sweeney, the Liberal minister in charge, sent me a note: "Thank you, Richard." My chief accomplishment in government was the creation of the Ontario Training and Adjustment Board to establish a long-needed training culture in Ontario. This was a long, arduous thirty-month process of mobilizing private and public sector trainers, business and labour groups, and special needs groups into a working coalition. The point of mentioning these initiatives here is simply to illustrate the manner in which my political agenda reflected the issues I addressed in my teaching. My graduate student was not wrong that, for me, what might be called "vocation" and "profession" came together and ultimately found expression in the public square.

4

My other vocation as a historian had also coincided with a period of dramatic change, for in retrospect, the 1970s became the foundational decade of a new history in Canada. The old history of the politics and economics of nation-building, wide-ranging as it was, had reached the limits of its capacity to explain the Canadian experience. The decade witnessed a new interest in the social, intellectual, and religious life of the country, not simply as separate compartments but as interactive elements in the chemistry of national life. It was fortuitous that *The Social Passion* and the "Social History of Canada Reprint Series," published by the University of Toronto Press under the editorship of Michael Bliss, should make their appearance as the decade opened. The social gospel had a recognized presence in Canadian historiography, in the biographies of J.S. Woodsworth, especially Kenneth McNaught's *A Prophet in Politics* (1959) and Stewart Crysdale's *The Industrial Struggle and Protestant Ethics in Canada* (1961), and in writing on Western Canadian farm, labour, and urban reform whose stories Ross McCormack brought up to date with his *Reformers, Rebels, and Revolutionaries* as the seventies opened. A persistent concern over endemic working-class poverty and working conditions that pervaded much of the new social history was graphically represented by Terry Copp in *The Anatomy of Poverty: The Condition of the Working Class in Montreal, 1897–1929* (1974), followed by Mary Vipond on "Labour in Canadian Social Gospel Fiction" (1975). It was not surprising that graduate students and popular historians like James Gray should be drawn to the colourful, conflicted, and symbolic history of moral reform – temperance, prohibition, and prostitution. I had contributed a documentary collection on prohibition in Canada to J.M. Bumsted's *Documentary Problems in Canadian History* (Vol. I, 1969) and followed this up in *The Social Passion*. By the mid-1970s that dramatic story had a first round of telling and was widely read. Ernest Forbes' article in *Acadiensis*, "Prohibition and the Social Gospel" (1971), attributed the wartime success of prohibition not just to the exigencies of war but to the new legitimacy accorded the movement by the rising social consciousness of the social gospel. Michael Bliss in "The Methodist Church and the First World War" (1968) and John Thompson's *Harvests of War* (1978) argued more generally that the social perfectionism of Methodism was a significant component of the wartime idealism and social solidarity that underlay a wartime surge of social reform as I had argued, rather than ending it.

Coincidentally, the 1970s also became the foundational decade of a new intellectual history and the history of ideas in Canada. Carl Berger was a major bridge figure into this new world with his revisionist study of the ideas of Canadian Imperialists in *The Sense of Power* (1970), while his study *Science, God, and Nature in Victorian Canada* (1973) was a clear sign of the new interest in religious ideas in Canada, and his *The Writing of Canadian History, 1900–1970* (1976) was virtually an intellectual history of twentieth century Canada to date. S.E.D. Shortt's *The Search for an Ideal* (1976) explored the mentality of six Canadian intellectuals anxious to find a way through the transitional years before the war of 1914–18. Brian McKillop, in *A Disciplined Intelligence* (1979), closed the decade with a brilliant historical accounting of the emergence of a reigning mentality among English Canadian intellectuals in which a moral imperative stood at the centre of personal and social ethics. With the intellectual legacy and the cultural contours of a "new Canada" mapped for the first time, and the filaments that linked religious, intellectual, social, and political inquiry deftly illuminated, the next two decades would see what might be called a new breed of interdisciplinary historians energetically infilling the cultural geography of English Canada.

It was coincidentally and, roughly speaking, during my years at Queen's Park that the full harvest of the new history began to come in. Introducing the decade of the eighties, if I may co-opt philosophers Leslie Armour and Elizabeth Trott into ranks of intellectual historians, was their hugely enlightening *The Faces of Reason: An Essay on Philosophy and Culture in English Canada, 1850–1950* (1981). Three biographies that took full account of the religious posture of their subjects spanned the seventies and the eighties: Margaret Prang on Newton Rowell (1975) and Michael Bliss on J.W. Flavelle (1978), both prominent Methodist laymen, Rowell a corporation lawyer and politician and Flavelle a big businessman and newspaper owner; and James Greenlee on Sir Robert Falconer (1988), Presbyterian theological professor and president of the University of Toronto. As liberal evangelicals they were comfortable with the new Biblical historical criticism. However, according to their biographers, for all their prominence in public affairs, they eschewed the social gospel. They thus served as markers of Protestant terrain the social passion did not penetrate. *Labour/Le travailleur* opened the 1980s with an excellent review article, "Class and Culture in Recent Religious Literature" (Bruce Tucker, 1980), and editors Gregory Kealey and Bryan Palmer and others like Craig Herron in various of their works recognized the place of religion in the motivation of late nineteenth and early twentieth century labour militants. Unfortunately, a survey I undertook of *Labour/Le travailleur* articles and reviews up to the new century, Quebec excepted, revealed little in the way of follow-up. One exception was Lynn Marks, "The Knights of Labour and the Salvation Army: Religion and Working Class Culture in Ontario, 1882–1890" (1991). The mid-eighties saw the publication of Ramsay Cook's *The Regenerators* (1986), which told the engaging story of a fascinating collection of late Victorian public intellectuals preoccupied with the spiritual renewal of humanity, some of whom were of the social gospel, while others represented another outer boundary of the social gospel among Canadian "regenerators." More sober and mainline was Brian Fraser's *The Social Uplifters: Presbyterian Progressives and the Social Gospel in Canada, 1875–1915* (1988). In these years books on T.C. "Tommy" Douglas began to rival in number those on J.S. Woodsworth as the pre-eminent bearer of the social gospel in Canadian politics. The best of these from a narrative perspective is Thomas and Ian McLeod's *Tommy Douglas: The Road to Jerusalem* (1987), but Lewis Thomas' edition of Douglas' recollections, *The Making of a Socialist* (1982), deserves special mention. Woodsworth would regain some ground with Allen Mills' fine study of his political thought, *Fool for Christ* (1991).

George Rawlyk continued his impressive studies of the evangelical tradition in Canada, but more important, perhaps, was his role in the establishment of the McGill-Queen's Press's wide-ranging Studies in the History of Religion publication program at this time, of which he then became the editor. Three early publications in the series exhibited the rigour of the new intellectual history relevant to the present discussion: William Westfall's *Two Worlds: The Protestant Culture of Nineteenth-Century Ontario* (1989), Marguerite Van Die's *An Evangelical Mind* (1989), on Nathanael Burwash, Canadian Methodism's leading theologian and pioneer of the higher criticism in Canada, and Michael Gauvreau's landmark work, *The Evangelical Century* (1991), arguing that Protestant theological education in Canada, with its focus on historical theology as against the controversy-ridden natural theology in the United States, was very influential in the formation of the more accommodating culture characteristic of this country. Nicely complementing Van Die and Gauvreau was Neil Semple's later masterful biography, *Faithful Intellect* (2005), a study of how the liberal-spirited Samuel Nelles brought Victoria University through a time of intellectual controversy and political turmoil. Van Die would go on to studies and publications on religion, family, and community in Victorian Canada. Bryan Fraser followed Gauvreau with his history of theological education in the Reform tradition at Knox College, Toronto (1995).

Gauvreau had taken up my concluding commentary in *The Social Passion* on the potential secularizing effects of the social gospel, which David Marshall went on to elaborate more broadly in *Secularizing the Faith: Canadian Protestant Clergy and the Crisis of Belief, 1850–1940* (1992), a major oversight in which was the Student Christian Movement of the interwar years, which might have modified his bleak conclusion. That same year, in *Serving the Present Age*, Phyllis Airhart explained how revivalism and progressivism were brought together within the Methodist tradition in the concept of "social evangelism." That would also be a hallmark of the United Church after its founding in 1925, whose history she would go on to write, *A Church with the Soul of a Nation* (2014). In *Remaking Liberalism* (1993), Barry Ferguson recounted the intellectual legacy of four "Queensians" – Adam Shortt, O.D. Skelton, W.C. Clark, and W.A. Mackintosh. However, in casting his account of their new "positive" liberalism as a secularist undertaking, he fails to note the religious language some of them used in their contributions to G.J. Shearer's *Social Welfare*, the publication of the Social Service Council of Canada.

Marianna Valverde's *The Age of Light, Soap, and Water* (1991) reminded readers of English Canadian moral reform activism as part of the International Purity Crusade, 1885–1925, while Sharon Anne Cook, in her history of the Women's Christian Temperance Union in the same period in Ontario, *Through Sunshine and Shadow* (1995), recounted a somewhat more leftward mix of evangelism and reform.

Thomas Socknat carried the social gospel into the international order with his *Witness Against War* (1987). Duff Crerar told the story of *Padres in No Man's Land* (1995) whose post-Great War passion for social reform was soon smothered by the "realities" of church and secular society. Whether intentionally or not, P.T. Phillips brought the focus back to the big picture in 1995 in *A Kingdom on Earth: Anglo-American Social Christianity, 1880–1940*.

In 1996, as I moved on from thirteen years in public life, Lynn Marks enriched our understanding of the interplay of religion and society in the early years of the social gospel in *Revivals and Roller Rinks: Religion, Leisure, and Identity in Late-Nineteenth-Century Small-Town Ontario*. The same year Nancy Christie and Michael Gauvreau returned to the years of *The Social Passion* with an important, somewhat revisionist view of the progressive wing of the social gospel in *A Full-Orbed Christianity: The Protestant Churches and Social Welfare in Canada, 1900–1940*. In a number of fine articles, Christie had demonstrated a keen interest in aspects of popular religion, and the year after *Full-Orbed*, Gauvreau followed her down that road with an article entitled "The World of the Common Man is Filled with Religious Fervour': Labouring People of Winnipeg and the Persistence of Revivalism, 1914–1925" (1997). This focus would be a common theme for the authors over the next years, mixed with a growing interest in gender issues and culminating in their joint editorship of a special issue of *Histoire Sociale/Social History* entitled *Intersections of Religious and Social History* (2003).

In the latter decades of the twentieth century Canadian social history was expanding in all directions. Identity issues had come strongly to the fore, fed in part by a postmodernist rejection of the Western "canon" in literature and grand narrative in history and a penchant for deconstructionism and diversity. At least as influential in the preoccupation with identity issues was the reality and growing force of social diversity in Canada itself, marked by revived interest in immigration history (for which Franca Iacovetta's prize-winning *Gatekeepers: Reshaping Immigrant Lives in Cold War Canada* [2006] can be a stand-in), ethnic studies, urban studies, a more positive appreciation of class, a surging interest in women's history, and with it a keen interest in gender, sexuality, and sexual orientation. Language itself was now under new scrutiny as acquaintance grew with the linguistic theories of Michael Foucault and Jacques Derrida who argued that all language served to promote the power and status of particular groups in the social order. Not everyone was persuaded. Bryan Palmer expressed his doubts about Derrida and discourse analysis in his *Descent into Discourse* (1991).

The new women's history, riding on the shoulders of a rising feminist movement of the time, was perhaps the most aggressive and significant component of identity history. Wendy Mitchinson and Ramsay Cook, in *The Proper Sphere* (1976), published a lively documentary collection of views, 1856 to 1930, on virtually every aspect of women's place in society. Linda Kealey followed with *A Not Unreasonable Claim* (1979), summoning the new writing of early proponents of the new women's history. Joan Sangster began her impressive publishing career with *Dreams of Equality: Women on the Canadian Left, 1920–1950* (1989) and went on to neatly bridge class, gender, and racial (indigenous) identity issues. Her *Earning Respect: The Lives of Working Women in Small Town Ontario, 1920–1960* (1995) lifted working women from historical oblivion to a visible and valued place on the Canadian historical landscape. She noted that, in their search for respect, working women, among other things, associated themselves with church congregations in their community. Sangster would go on to recount the experience of Canadian women running the gauntlet of the country's legal system, the story of women's work in the "Iconic North," and most recently, in *One Hundred Years of Struggle* (2018), a vibrant updated account of winning the vote for women in Canada. Veronica Strong-Boag brilliantly excavated another layer of women's history in her publications on the evangelical Aberdeens at Rideau Hall, especially Lady Ishbel and her passion for social improvement that led her to mobilize the women of Canada into the National Council of Women. Randi Warne's *Literature as Pulpit: The Christian Social Activism of Nellie L. McClung* (1993) claimed McClung for the social gospel. And there was Eleanor Stebner's article "More than Maternal Feminists and Good Samaritans: Women and the Social Gospel in Canada" (2003), rightly taking me to task for allowing so few of a number of eligible women social gospellers onto the pages of *The Social Passion*.

In the background of this preoccupation with identity issues was the rise of liberationist gospels in the Americas in the 1960s and 1970s. The civil rights campaigns in the United States brought a Black social gospel to the fore, bifurcated between Martin Luther King's inclusiveness and James Cone's separatism. In Latin and South America, a Marxist-tinged liberation theology had arisen out of the struggle of Catholic "base communities" to throw off social and economic oppression. Books like Gustavo Gutierrez's *A Theology of Liberation: History, Politics, and Salvation* (1973) attracted considerable attention and brought progressive Catholics and Protestants together in joint coalitions for social action in the United States and Canada. In Canada the principal literary expression of this was the Catholic Bishop's statement, "The Preferential Option for the Poor," which I used my position in the legislature to promote. By 1973 Catholic feminist scholars in the United States had already followed up Simone de Beauvoir's *The Second Sex* (1949) and Betty Friedan's *The Feminine Mystique* (1963) with radical feminist claims based on liberationist theology. Mary Daly in *The Church and the Second Sex* (1968) and *Beyond God the Father* (1973) availed herself of Foucault, Derrida, and Gramsci to argue that language was an identity-forming agency. She repudiated the sole right to "name" given Adam in Genesis and assailed the "phalocentric system of patriarchy." Rosemary Radford Reuther initiated an ongoing pre-eminence among woman liberationists with *Liberation Theology* (1969), staked out her left credentials in *The Radical Kingdom* (1970), and wrote the phenomenally successful landmark feminist systematic theology, *Sexism and God-Talk* (1983), not to mention thirty-some wide-ranging books including *Goddesses and the Divine Feminine: A Western Religious History* (2005) and collaborationist works in the cause of eco-feminism. Janet Forsythe Fishburn, in *The Fatherhood of God and the Victorian Family* (1981) penned an acute intellectual critique of the masculine bias of prominent American social gospellers like Walter Rauschenbusch. American liberationists would go on to link economic democracy, differential identity perspectives of gender and race, ecological politics, and an intense critique of the American imperial ambitions that issued from victory in the Cold War. This rethinking and reawakening of the social gospel in the United States was brilliantly told in Gary Dorrien's *Soul in Society: The Making and Renewal of Social Christianity* (1998). Of Cree descent, Dorrien, as Reinhold Niebuhr Professor of Social Ethics at Union Theological Seminary in New York, would go on to publish widely praised books on the above themes. His most recent work, *The New Abolition* (2016), celebrates the history of the Black social gospel. He charges the historians of the white social gospel in America with complicity in white supremacism for ignoring the history of the Black social gospel in their accounts. Mainline American social ethicists and historians of social Christianity, like John C. Bennett in his *Radical Imperative* (1975), confessed to the slowness of their recognition of the importance of the claims of the liberationists.

It is Ian McKay who best exemplifies the incorporation in a comprehensive work of the multiple perspectives and world views playing upon, and to various degrees influencing, the new history. His prize-winning "reconnaissance" of the history of the Canadian Left, 1890–1920, *Reasoning Otherwise: Leftists and the People's Enlightenment in Canada, 1890–1920* (2008) was a spirited text built around questions of class, religion, gender, and race. McKay's narrative reflected a structuralist concern for viewing ideas within the context of larger systems and structures but grounded his work more firmly on Gramsci's concept of "cultural hegemony," which gave language a powerful role in the legitimation and the critique of systems and structures of power. His earlier "Liberal order" concept did both, and *Reasoning Otherwise*, among other things, provided a language that enfranchised self-proclaimed revolutionaries heretofore stigmatized as "impossibilists."

As the new history swept into the new century, the place of religion among Canadian working people found an occasional place in *Labour/Le travail*. Testifying to the ongoing force of religious conviction among Canadian workers were Melissa Turkstra in "Constructing a Labour Gospel: Labour and Religion in Early 20th Century Hamilton" (2006) and Christo Aivalis in "In the Service of the Lowly Nazarene" (2016), reporting on the Radical Christianity of Canadian labour papers in the 1930s. Such articles rightly claim a place in the context of a traditional concern of Canadian labour historians for the rights of Canadian labour to full cultural and spiritual as well as political and economic enfranchisement. To say so is not to propose annexing them to middle-class cultural pursuits.

James Pitsula's study of society and politics in the city of Regina during the Great War, *For All We Have and Are* (2008), includes an extensive account of the collaboration of Hugh Dobson, a graduate in theology from Wesley College in Winnipeg, and Premier Walter Scott, himself of working-class origins, in the creation of what, for its time, was a progressive social welfare regime in Saskatchewan. As the United Church's Western Secretary for Evangelism and Social Service, Dobson was a major exponent of a liberal social gospel and a force for progressive social legislation in the West in subsequent decades. The new century would also see a major enrichment of the history of the Radical Christianity of the Great Depression with the publication of excellent accounts of the intellectual, religious, and political development and wide-ranging careers of Eugene Forsey and J. King Gordon, founders of the Fellowship for a Christian Social Order and the League for Social Reconstruction: Frank Milligan, *Eugene Forsey: An Intellectual Biography* (2004); Eileen Janzen, *Growing to One World: The Life of J. King Gordon* (2016); and Keith Fleming, *The World is Our Parish: John King Gordon, 1900–1989, an Intellectual Biography* (2015).

5

While the new social, intellectual, and religious history in Canada was sweeping all before it, it would be wrong to leave the impression that it was self-generated. The importance of liberationist gospels of the Americas for Canadian women's history has been noted. Structuralists of diverse stripes and Marxists of various hues in Labour studies leaned on Louis Althusser in France, E.P. Thompson in England, and Antonio Gramsci in Italy.

6

Eric Voegelin, perhaps the ranking philosopher of the twentieth century, has said that to write meaningfully about human affairs one should have what he calls a well worked out "philosophical anthropology," that is, a matured appreciation of the multiformity and the rich complexity of what it means to be human. That undertaking is worth a lifetime of intellectual labour, and few of us meet the measure with a carefully systematized world view of our own. We absorb from many sources with varying degrees of critical capacity, ending, often, with a bias for one or another of the "big options" on offer. Differences of perspective occasion healthy and sometimes heated debate. In the heat of the secularization debate in *fin de siècle* Canada, Carl Berger threatened to abandon Canadian studies for a simpler subject like the politics of Byzantium! Gauvreau and Christie may critique Allen; Palmer may critique McKay; Marks may critique Palmer. When the going gets rough, I turn to the "axial period" of human history, which Voegelin introduced me to several decades ago in his multivolume series, *Order and History* (1956–1987). In the axial period, from the eighth to the fifth centuries BCE, the prophetic imagination and the philosophic mind wrested the exclusive right of access to the divine – that is, to knowledge of what was ultimately true and right about and for human beings and their world – from the imperial and monarchical seats of power. In my own life and work I search out one of the mid-eighth century BCE Hebrew prophets and find there a peasant named Amos who held a mason's plumb line against the crooked structures of power and privilege, whether secular or sacred, that oppressed the people of his day. Like a sheet anchor in high seas, he keeps me headed into the centre of the storm.

Finally, on a technical note, with respect to the essays republished here, I have taken advantage of the opportunity to rephrase the occasional infelicitous passage. And in conformity with McGill-Queen's University Press policy respecting gender-neutral language, I have made appropriate changes in all expressions of my own, but not in the cases of offending quoted matter. To do so, in my opinion, is to falsify history, which is counter to the canons of professional historical research and writing.

Richard Allen
Dundas, Ontario
February 2018

PART ONE

The World We Have Known

CHAPTER ONE

Growing Up Religious, Political, and Historical

1

Cumberland. 1933. A coal mining town on Vancouver Island. I was just four years old and already the primary lineaments of my life were being woven together – the religious, the political, and the historical. My father, Harold Tuttle Allen, was a minister of the United Church of Canada. At his previous charge in the northern British Columbia lumbering town of Terrace, I had experienced two of the emotional drivers of religious response – awe and dread. One day, as winter gave way to spring in 1933, I had watched with rapt attention, checking every short while, filled with wonder at the unfolding of a bud into a lovely leaf. Another day, with my father at Robinson's hardware store in Terrace, feeling an urgent need to relieve my bowels, I was ushered into what amounted to an indoor out-house. I was instantly filled with dread as I stared into the utter unseeing blackness beyond the hole on which it was proposed that I sit. In stark contrast to the engrossing spirit of awe and wonder, I had now encountered a moment beyond fear or repulsion that I would later know as "dread." And biological necessity was instantly overwhelmed.

Now, in Cumberland, the formalities of religion were coming to the fore. St Andrew's United Church, modest as it was, had a Presbyterian style battlemented bell tower. It became my custom to accompany my father on Sunday mornings to the bell tower to help alert the town that it was one hour to church time. On this particular Sunday, convinced that I had served my apprenticeship as a bell-ringer, I slipped over to the church. I had no idea what time it was. As the bells pealed across the town and confusion set in as to the accuracy of household clocks, my astonished father hastily dressed and dashed to retrieve his overly ambitious son. A few hours later, feeling no remorse, the quintessence of the Christianity I was destined to grow up in came to the fore as I stood in line with other little tots, swaying as we sang "Jesus loves me" and "God sees the little sparrow fall."

It was in that same year that my mother, née Ruby Rhoda Reilly, sat me down in front of that talking box they called a radio to listen to my father deliver a political broadcast from a Vancouver radio station – CJOR, I believe. Late in his last year in Terrace, he had gathered a group to consider the growing talk of the need for a new party to bring various socialist, labour, and farmers' political groups together with allies and sympathizers dedicated to replacing a competitive, private profit driven economic order with one founded on principles of economic democracy and social justice. This past summer, he had joined others at Vancouver's Stanley Park to found a provincial branch of such a party, the Co-operative Commonwealth Federation (CCF). With a provincial election looming, he was sought after to run as a candidate, and, having secured the consent of the church board, and a discussion with the sitting Conservative, who was a member of the church, Harold had agreed. He did well – so well, in fact, that the Liberal candidate withdrew to ward off any danger of sending a representative of the newfangled socialist party to the legislature. I understood but little in his broadcast – indeed could put no meaning to the operative word "politics" – but clearly my father was doing something very important.

Cumberland was a town with a history of radical labour militance. A bitter two-year strike under the United Mine Workers of America, in 1912–13, lived on in local memory. Shortly after, the town gained immortality in Canadian labour history when, in 1917, Ginger Goodwin, vice-president of the BC Federation of Labour, was hunted down and shot dead on its outskirts by the Dominion Police for refusing to register for military service under the new wartime compulsory mobilization legislation. A huge parade and protest by workers from across the region had followed in Cumberland. Now, in the depths of a depression that had wiped out more than a third of the jobs in the province, tens of thousands of families were suffering severe hardship. Again there was talk of a strike – their labour power was the only weapon they had. When the union found local meeting venues closed to them, Harold offered the quarters of his church for their meetings. As the planning progressed and a strike bulletin was released, I and others, putting the printed sheet against our chests and running to create the wind pressure needed to keep it there – as we did publicizing local movies – spread the word around town. It was, of course, an act of unknowing, but, in effect, a first step into the grand historical dialectic of opposing classes initiated with the onset of the industrial revolution.

At four, the conditions for growing up religious, political, and historical were already at work, and as it turned out our family time in Cumberland had a dramatic effect in altering the high expectations with which my parents embarked on their chosen mission in life.

2

Harold was descended from the John Smith Yorkshire Methodists who settled in Nova Scotia in the late eighteenth century and established the first continuing line of Methodism meetings in what would become Canada. What Harold did not know was that his own Allen line had descended from liberal Six-Principle Baptists from Rhode Island who joined the Methodists when Nova Scotia's Baptists resorted to a Calvinist discipline to control the damaging irregularities that overtook the New Light Baptist Revival. Harold, himself, had grown up on a fruit farm in the Okanagan where his tubercular father fled, hoping – in vain – to find relief and a cure in the dry air of the BC Interior. The radicalizing influence of a resource extraction economy left its mark on Harold. Attracted by the growing force of socialism in the region and at large, he watched sympathetically when the International Workers of the World – the IWW, the "Wobblies" – attempted to organize a union at the local lumber mill. It was not the Wobblies he would follow, however. Discussing social issues with his Sunday School superintendent, Will Bartlett, he learned rather of the early Christian socialism of Charles Kingsley and Frederick Denison Maurice and the later socialist gradualism of the Fabian Society in England. In the course of his first year at the University of British Columbia (UBC), Harold had his first experience in electoral campaigning, working for the socialist candidate, Thomas Siddaway, in West Point Grey.

Ruby was descended from Irish Methodist Reillys, in turn descendants of French Huguenots. They arrived in Canada during the 1837 Papineau Rebellion in time to witness the horror of British troops setting fire to a church full of French families. Ruby's line moved on to southwestern Ontario and then to the open prairie of southern Saskatchewan where she grew up on a wheat farm in the boom years of the early twentieth century. When in the late war years her father sold the farm and moved with her cousins, the Adams and the Cowans, to Vancouver, she brought with her a background of prairie progressivism. Her mother, an incredibly energetic woman, took on leadership roles in the local church as did her father in local farm affairs and in the Royal Templars of Temperance. He was a close follower of the equalitarian views of Robbie Burns – "a man's a man for a' that" – and the anti-slavery transcendentalist poems of Alfred Russell Lowell.

Harold and Ruby met in Vancouver at upscale Mount Pleasant Methodist Church, and they appear to have fallen in love when, studying at UBC, they were both on the executive of the local unit of the newly founded Student Christian Movement of Canada (SCM). The SCM was the predominant student organization of the interwar years, dedicated to "Building the City of God," as the published record of its founding conference in 1921 announced. It was broadly inclusive, open to all who were prepared to "test the conviction on which the movement is founded that in Jesus Christ are to be found the means to the full realization of life." Countless study groups across the nation studied social gospel texts of Walter Rauschenbusch put out by the American YMCA. "Sharman" study groups were especially popular, in which students studied the gospel parallels in Henry Burton Sharman's *Records of the Life of Jesus* to discover for themselves who this Jesus was. Members boasted of the coeducational character of the SCM and indulged somewhat in the experimental spirit reflected in its cheeky theme song, "Poisoning the Student Mind." Ruby and Harold, both being very musical, joined the UBC Operatic Society. His entire family were great singers. Both brothers became presidents of the Operatic Society at McGill University and a sister, the lead soprano in operatic performances in Vancouver. Ruby was an accomplished pianist who was quite capable of accompanying performances of Handel's *Messiah* in Vancouver's churches.

As undergraduates, Ruby and Harold would complete the Arts program in modern literature and modern history, respectively. Harold would later say admiringly that Ruby had read all of Tolstoy's massive novel *War and Peace*. In the course of pursuing his honours degree in history, Harold consolidated his socialist views within the context of the history of expansive modern Western national cultures of Europe and North America. When his professors failed in their attempts to persuade him to follow a career in history, and he turned to theology and the ministry, he readily accommodated the religious and evolutionary views of liberal theology. He was drawn to the debate over the historical Jesus and the historical critique of the Biblical record. The "higher criticism" was well-established at Vancouver's Methodist theological college, soon to be named Union College with the accomplishment of church union in 1925. Winning all the prizes on graduating that year, he was a marked man as he went off to "probation" back in the Interior. His career and his social hopes were now bound up with a new, national "uniting" church that might harness its social passion to the Kingdom theology of Christian socialism and so deliver a spiritually renewed Canada for the healing of nations so lately at war with each other.

In the meantime, Ruby, having graduated, had enrolled in the Vancouver General Hospital's nursing program to become a registered public health nurse. Letters went back and forth between the two, now engaged to be married: "Dear Boy," ... "Dear Girl," ... Her father questioned the relationship, saying that neither of them had a sense of humour. Harold was the more sentimental of the two, carefully keeping all her letters, while she destroyed most of his. And she had some reservations about marriage. Even late in life she wondered if they should have married; Harold with his total dedication might better have been a member of a religious order. Feeling something of the independent spirit of "the new Canadian girl" of the twenties, she was attracted by the prospects of a career. The feeling became the more intense when the Vancouver General offered her a position as a social service nurse, a new position. Harold was visibly concerned. His probation was almost over, and he longed for her companionship as he took up full-time responsibilities for a congregation. She had so much to offer, with literary interests, her music, and now her nursing credentials. After a time of anguished reflection she decided to partner with him in what she clearly considered would be a shared ministry. They were married in 1928. There was a note of disappointment when he was stationed at McBride, a railway divisional point in the shadow of Mount Robson in the Rocky Mountains. "We will go out," she told Harold, "and work our way back in."

I was born the next February, in 1929. There was something elemental, even heroic, about our – I dare say "our" – first stationings. "McBride" turned out to be 218 miles of lumbering and mining camps and a few pockets of settlement between McBride and Prince George. Harold would be away days at a time, regardless of weather, hiking the rail line, hitching rides on freight trains. In the camps he would hold evening and weekend meetings, usually casual with a mix of talk, Bible reading, song, prayer, and perhaps a "bull session" to follow, which he specially enjoyed. He would bunk and eat with the men and move on. In the settlements he would preach at a meeting place arranged for the occasion – once with the suffocating aroma of the decaying body of a dead horse filling the premises. Normally he would be back in town for Sunday services. Ruby's father supplied her with an Airedale dog named Bonzo for company and a piano to keep her spirits up. When I was born in Vancouver – at her father's insistence – Harold had to hitch a ride north and wade through miles of deep snow to catch a train going south on a different track to see his newborn. For better or worse, they fell out with three or four of the leading women of the McBride congregation who, Ruby declared, would have been a trial for even the most seasoned minister. They moved on to a happier time at Terrace. Harold's experience with men in the camp culture of the province served him well in a town that lived off lumbering. Ruby, who had taken to reading books on training while working with young people at Mount Pleasant, now applied her learning to guide girls through their teens in the United Church's ambitious new Canadian Girls in Training (CGIT) program – training in reverence for life in the spirit of Jesus and in leadership skills for community service. The girls teased me mercilessly, threatening to drown our cat's recently born kittens in the rain barrel. There were summer camps for the girls at Lake Lakelse. And there was time at home for evenings of song with Ruby accompanying Harold on the piano, often ending with the popular love song "Ramona," at which point Bonzo would join them, throw back his head, and "sing" his heart out.

Now secure in his pastoral ministry and preaching in a congenial congregation, and firmly grounded in a theology that informed both his preaching and his politics, it was a confident Harold who, in 1932, joined the BC delegation bound for the General Council of the United Church in Hamilton. En route, he was charged with arranging entertainment for the group. He stopped off briefly in Winnipeg to visit his uncle, Frank Allen, a brilliant professor of mathematics and physics at the University of Manitoba, whom he valiantly but vainly attempted to persuade to abandon his religious conservatism for a more liberal creed. After the Council, he travelled to Montreal, where his brother Stanley was doing doctoral studies in chemistry and physics. Despite the economic distress of the time, Stanley had held on to familial Conservative leanings. After many extended hours of discussions – Stanley was no pushover in political debate, then or later – Harold won him over. Stanley would go on to be a popular CCF member of Montreal's City Council, a member of the League for Social Reconstruction and the Fellowship for a Christian Social Order, and a president of the Quebec wing of the CCF. The General Council meetings had evidently been stimulating. An important resolution was passed calling for the establishment of a commission to bring in a report to the next Council on "Christianizing the Social Order."

Harold returned to Terrace, riding high, bearing clippings from the *Hamilton Spectator* on the Council proceedings, one of which observed that no delegate had made a greater impression on Council than young Harold Allen of Terrace. My parents' three years at Terrace were soon to end and they would be on their way to Cumberland. They were working their way back in.

3

Cumberland was a dramatic turning point in their prospects. In the wake of the election campaign a group of congregants, disaffected by Harold's political venture and the board's allowing him to do so, withheld their financial support. With their future in Cumberland foreclosed, Harold stayed on for a year to recoup the church's finances and put his name before the stationing committee of the BC Conference. There were no takers. No one wanted a "political preacher" – especially if he were socialist. My parents were stationed in Nanaimo, another coal mining centre and a significant port, still on "the island," where they would spend the balance of the depression years on a minimal Home Mission salary, serving several small congregations in the region. There was an attempt to censure Harold for the course and consequences of his recent detour into politics. At the next meeting of Conference such a motion was put by the Rev. A.M. Sanford of the church's college in New Westminster, a move that was effectively quashed when Hugh Dobson, now the United Church's Western secretary for evangelism and social service, declared that he would move a similar motion censuring Sanford for acting as the local "bagman" raising funds for the Conservative party. But for the rest of his pastoral ministry Harold would be effectively blacklisted by the pastoral supply committees of British Columbia's United Church congregations. He was frequently later told by colleagues that, had he not got mixed up with the CCF, he could have had any church in the province he wished. Whether that was not more a condemnation of the prevailing mindset of congregational leadership in British Columbia than of Harold may be debated, but he was not deterred from his course, becoming a respected voice in the BC Conference as chair of its Committee on Evangelism and Social Service and two decades later would become the Western regional secretary for the Lord's Day Alliance. He took on leadership roles in the local CCF riding associations of the towns he served, sat on the party's provincial executive committee, was a regular convention delegate, and served as well, for a time, as provincial organizer. He sometimes confessed to a mission in life to interpret Christianity to socialists and socialism to Christians, a task to which he felt specially called.

Had he had any premonition of the cost of this sort of discipleship? He had read Albert Schweitzer's classic work, *The Quest of the Historical Jesus*, with its arresting conclusion that Jesus was an "imperious ruler" who envisaged another world order and who calls us "to the tasks which he has to fulfil in our time. He commands. And to those who obey him, whether they be wise or simple, He will reveal Himself in the toils, the conflicts, the sufferings which they will pass through in His fellowship, and as an ineffable mystery, they shall learn in their own experience Who He is." Harold had forewarned Ruby before their marriage that they were embarking on no easy journey, that there would be "no flowers and chocolates."

There was no question but that this Jesus was the centre of our life together. Not that we had a prayer-filled or catechetical upbringing. Just as there were no altar calls at our church, so there was no pressure at home to accept Jesus as our personal saviour. On the subject of raising children, Harold and Ruby were in the tradition of Horace Bushnell's *Christian Nurture*, and their practice a reflection of Schleiermacher's view that what was sometimes called "being born again" happened through the natural, gradual process of growing up into Jesus, a view further developed by George Coe, the father of modern Christian education.

Schweitzer's Jesus was hardly fare, however, for children not yet in their teens. But if he was a strange figure and an "ineffable mystery," the Sunday School Jesus, however familiar as one who loved us, we now came to know as a person of another time depicted in a long gown, with flowing hair, and arms outstretched to happy children of many colours. There was something phantom-like about how his love could reach us across the ages – and why would he want to do so anyway? It was at Nanaimo that I would have my first memorable participation in Sunday School at Percy Bunt's downtown church. With my father away much of Sunday and my mother preoccupied caring for my baby brother Philip, my sister Joan and I would walk together to the church on Sunday mornings. Our little assembly would sing songs that told us we were "precious jewels" that "like the stars of the morning" would adorn Jesus' bright crown. We would plead in song for stories of Jesus – "Scenes by the wayside / Tales of the sea / Tell them to me." And they were many: amazing accounts of miracles by Jesus, walking on the sea, feeding 5,000 with a little boy's five loaves and fishes, as he went about doing good. Jesus himself liked telling stories, especially to children, like how, if we loved one another, love would grow and spread like a mustard seed into a large tree. The stories came from a big book called the Bible, but in a digested and, for us, more accessible form. In appreciation we brought forward our pennies, singing, "Hear the pennies dropping / Listen as they fall / Everyone for Jesus / He shall have them all." But it was never clear what Jesus would do with all those pennies. Joan and I had another thought; a penny held back now and then would purchase a penny candy at nearby confectionary to eat on the way home! Then there was the classic "scientific" demonstration in support of temperance. A worm would be dropped into a glass of alcohol – with predictable results. My parents, however, had already upstaged our Sunday School superintendent. Brought up themselves in temperance families, they had already, unknown to myself, registered me as a "Little White Ribboner," pledged never to let a drop of alcoholic beverage pass my lips. It was in that connection that our Sunday School came closest to the spirit of my father's Jesus. We sang "Dare to be a Daniel / Dare to stand alone / Dare to have a purpose firm / And dare to make it known." Daniel, exile in Babylon, punished for rejecting the wine and rich food of Nebuchadnezzar's court, had triumphed in the end. It was only later I learned of Jesus turning water into wine! The song, however, had other applications that began with "Dare to be."

I was by this time aware of "times past." There was a storefront library just down the street. The first books I recall borrowing were a series about prehistoric humanity, the discovery of fire, the making of stone age implements, the invention of the wheel, and so on. When I was eight, my parents gave me a ten-volume set of books, "Junior Classics," each volume running to some 500 pages under the suggestive titles *Fairy Stories and Wonder Tales, Myths and Folk Tales, Heroes and Heroines, Tales of Greece and Rome, Stories that Never Grow Old, Science and Discovery, Stories of Courage and Heroism, Stories of Today*, ending with an index volume. I cannot claim to have read every entry, but I literally lived in those books for what now seems like an age. There were stories from around the world, chronicles of the English and European peoples, the Norse sagas with their pantheon of gods, stories and myths of indigenous peoples of the Americas, including Canada. My literary, historical, and religious imagination was expanding by leaps and bounds – though I didn't have a name for it. In a way, I was being drawn into the worlds of those children gathered around Jesus.

Harold and Ruby were inveterate readers. Their subscriptions to Clayton Morrison's *Christian Century* from New York, the *United Church Observer*, the *Country Guide*, the *Canadian Forum*, and assorted CCF publications like David Lewis's *Who Owns Canada?* kept up a constant flow of liberal theology, urban and rural social progressivism, and left politics and culture into the household. Ruby favoured fiction, though George Bernard Shaw's *The Intelligent Woman's Guide to World Chaos* had a place on our bookshelves. Harold was currently reading G.D.H. Cole on Guild Socialism. He was a member of the Left Book Club in Great Britain, whose usually monthly publications were more than he could keep up with. One of its 1936 selections was a must read: *Towards the Christian Revolution*, the widely praised book-length manifesto of the Fellowship for a Christian Social Order in Canada. Harold was never comfortable without some religious, political, or historical work at hand. He would shortly acquire some of the eleven volumes published as a follow-up to the Oxford Conference of 1937. It was an impressive series, featuring a clutch of the best Christian thinkers of Europe, Britain, and America, reflecting on the new post-war world where, in some places, "the Christian foundations of Western civilization have … been swept away and are everywhere being undermined." Secular and pagan tendencies and the emergence of quasi-religious, all-encompassing states demanding total allegiance had to be challenged, the editors said. Harold was especially interested in the thoughts of the eight contributors to the volume on *The Kingdom of God and History*. Was the Kingdom of God a present reality, realized in the life of the church, or in social forms embodying cultural values, or in the political/economic realm as a social order? Was it an ideal to be striven for on earth, or a way of escaping history to a super-historical communion of saints? How far are events in time manifestations of the Kingdom? Is there a progressive march of redemption in time? If it was Christianity that first brought a sense of unity and purpose to humanity, was there such a thing as history apart from the Kingdom of God? And what was the relationship of history and nature? This was heady stuff! Harold underlined a passage criticizing both Hegel and Marx for projecting the view that history was self-explanatory, and another opposing a relativism that would offer equal justification for each of the contending forces in current debate. A Christian interpretation of history had to insist on "the otherness and transcendence of God" with its corollaries of judgment and grace by which history could be understood to be purposeful and conducive to human freedom. When the twelve-volume *Interpreter's Bible*, incorporating the findings of a century of modern scholarship, began publication in the 1950s, Harold was an instant subscriber.

The contents of Harold's reading, heady as they might be, were not that far removed from the social and economic issues of the present that were laying claim to the attention of a young boy. We sat quietly at dinner as my parents listened intently to the CBC news. The movies I was allowed to see, like *Dawn Patrol* featuring Errol Flynn or *Sabu the Elephant Boy*, always began with a graphic review of world events. I watched passing trains, the tops of their boxcars lined with men heading north to the coalfields in a vain search for jobs. At Lantzville, north of the city, knowing the importance of purposeful activity in maintaining morale, Harold mobilized the unemployed men of the charge to build a small church for their congregation. It was named "Saint Philip's by the Sea" in recognition that my three-year-old brother, Philip, deathly ill with pneumonia, had been spared, thanks to the round-the-clock nursing of my mother and the bold but risky surgery that drained little lungs full of fluid. Immersing himself in work was Harold's typical coping mechanism whenever illness struck the family.

Many of the unemployed were veterans. The Legion Hall, not far from our place, was where they gathered to renew the brotherhood of the trenches, assuage their pain, and boost their morale. Freely roaming the streets, as children in those days were permitted to do, I would hear them singing the songs of what people referred to as the Great War. I didn't understand one of their favourites with a chorus about rolling over in the clover, but "Pack Up Your Troubles in Your Old Kit Bag" had a distressingly present relevance. My best friend, Wilbert Robinson, came to stay with us for a time when his father, a veteran, disheartened by his inability to support the family, abandoned them. His mother fled to a family haven on the mainland to reflect on their future. The appalling tragedy of that war and the emotional devastation it left behind were indelibly etched in my mind when our frail elderly neighbour, whom we seldom saw and was something of a mystery, invited me into her home. She took me through rooms dark with Victorian draperies to a small room, a sacred shrine where she could commune with her only son. The scant evidence of his life and his death in that war was explained one by one: photographs of him as a little boy and as a fine young man in uniform, his helmet, and the small New Testament he kept in the left breast pocket of his tunic, and above all the white cross that had marked his grave – all brought to her by one of his buddies who survived. Now there was talk of another war. Some military generals had seized power in Spain and my mother's adopted brother, Frank, an avid aviator, had gone to Spain to help Republican forces restore democracy in that country. War had broken out between China and Japan. My uncle Stewart Allen was in the midst of it as the medical director and superintendent of the church-sponsored Canadian Hospital in Chongqing, the wartime capital.

Galvanized into action by the crises at home and abroad, Harold had taken the initiative to organize a League for Christian Social Action in

British Columbia, which then was absorbed into the national Fellowship for a Christian Social Order. The drama of Stewart in China, spending endless hours of surgery mending wounded soldiers and rushing into fire-bombed Chongqing to treat and rescue citizens, captured my imagination and engaged Harold's seemingly boundless energy in another initiative of consequence. When a ship loaded with scrap iron bound for Japan docked in Nanaimo's harbour, he organized a group to picket the ship, the first of a number of such protests on the west coast. His action led to a close association and joint action with Nanaimo's Chinese community on both the endemic discrimination against Chinese in British Columbia and the war abroad. When we left Nanaimo in 1939, he was feted with a special banquet by a grateful community. Stewart had teased an early interest in me for things Chinese by sending me a novel on coolies and robbers along the Yangtze River. Then there would be Pearl Buck's *The Good Earth*. Interest in China grew with every letter from Chongqing.

While the Nanaimo years were expansive ones for me, they turned out to be difficult ones for my mother. Harold and Ruby had been pacifists in the 1920s and into the 1930s. He had secured a motion at the BC Conference for the posting of a plaque commemorating the Kellogg Peace Pact of 1928 in its BC churches. The rise of fascism out of the ashes of the war of 1914–18, the years of depression, and the faltering grip of liberal democracy were wreaking havoc with the ability of multilateral agreements, whether under or outside the League of Nations, to keep the peace. Fascist glorification of might and militarism as the key to national morale and meaning was changing the proportions of debate over the relevance of the pacifist option. This debate was particularly hard on Ruby, and, aggravated by other issues, drove her into severe depression. Harold's scattered pastoral and preaching responsibilities had an isolating effect for someone envisaging a shared ministry, an isolation compounded by the extent to which care of a young family fell to her. One incident told it all. Our property, with fenced-off areas, trees, garage, and sheds intended for fowl, fuel, and a goat, was an ideal place for playing cops and robbers, cowboys and Indians, and other quasi-military games, all of which ran counter to her desire to raise a little brood inclined to pacifist ways. "Bang Bang," "Gotcha, you're dead," grated the nerves! My pals had gathered outside the back door, ready for action. Ruby decided to stand her ground and deny me the gun that had grudgingly been bought for me. I stood outside shouting, "I want my gun." Unable to stand it any longer, she opened the door, "Alright, have your gun!" and threw it into the midst of the gang where it landed, shattered into a dozen pieces on the cement sidewalk. And then there was the arrival of Stewart and family, back home on furlough, bent on an extended visit. While Harold and the rest of us revelled in their presence, Ruby was left with the challenge of preparing sufficient fare, limited in these worst of times, unassisted by a sister-in-law accustomed to being waited on by Chinese servants. The time was nearing when we would leave Nanaimo for our new charge. "Leaving is the hardest part," she confided to me. She played the piano hours on end to relieve her depression and ended with stomach ulcers that would plague her for years. There would be several hospitalizations, despite which, a nurse herself, she made herself available for duty as an "extra" in cases requiring intensive care.

4

By the early summer of 1939 we were in Sardis, a village of a couple of hundred people nestled in the shadow of the coastal mountains where they curved toward the Fraser River itself and separated the fertile agricultural lands and the port cities from the rest of mountainous British Columbia. A meandering stream ran through Sardis, which had a grocery store, a gas station, an auto repair shop, a confectionary, a tobacconist who stocked comic books, a feed store for the farmers, a Fraser Valley Milk Producers Association plant, and a public school. This was where we would live out the war years.

Carman United Church, named after the first general superintendent of the Methodist Church of Canada after the union of 1884, was a pretty church with ample grounds and a new, fully furnished manse adjacent. We soon met the principal families: the Pearsons, Greens, Ridouts, Wells, and Newbys, all former Methodists, which may explain why they seemed comfortable with my father being stationed among them. And farmers organized into cooperative producers' associations may have recognized him as one of their own. With the shortage of labour occasioned by the war, he readily joined them from time to time in the fields. There was a small Anglican church where the Scouts met, forbidden to me by parents concerned about the military aspects of the Scouting movement. Our church had Trail Rangers, which never seemed to fulfill the image conveyed by the name. The Conference's secretary for boy's work, Bob MacLaren, preached a gospel of woodworking as the key to the "boy problem," and I was soon equipped with a wood lathe in our basement, working with tools made from old files.

There was a large community of Mennonites nearby, a young family of which, the Dileskis, living in town, were our neighbours. Three miles away was Chilliwack, a city of 3,000 where the principal services, including the regional high school, hospital, and radio station, were located.

In these pleasant circumstances, Ruby could resume the shared ministry she had enjoyed so much in Terrace. With her leadership, musical, and social skills engaged, depression quickly vanished. She would resume her leadership in the Canadian Girls in Training program and become a member of the Women's Auxiliary and for a time secretary of the Conference Women's Work Committee. More importantly, when the organist and choir director resigned, she took on that responsibility. And there were pleasant evenings when she on the piano and the cello-playing rotund farmer, reputed to do his haying in the nude, made beautiful music together in our living room. For Harold, an hour's drive from Vancouver afforded opportunities for collegial contact, especially with Hugh Dobson, and access to the university. It was an agricultural region. We had a large garden, chickens, rabbits, and the occasional bull calf, which, sadly, had to be slaughtered to provision our table. Sardis would have been a thoroughly idyllic experience had it not been for the disintegrating state of international relations and the bullying I experienced from a small gang of older boys led by the Britains and the Jespersons. Not surprisingly, they also turned out to be the town's super-patriots. Our neighbours, the Dileskis, Mennonites, came in for much abuse at their hands. One Saturday evening they stood outside the Dileskis' fenced yard, shouting obscenities and dire threats and telling them to go back to their own country. Harold went out to persuade them to stop and got beaten up for his trouble.

During that first summer, the tension in our household was palpable as the nations teetered on the brink of war. If Great Britain was involved, would Canada automatically follow? If Canada were involved, what should be the CCF response? Midsummer, we had a surprise visit from Harold's brother, Stanley, now active in national CCF affairs. Nationally, party policy as of 1937 had been for neutrality, but that consensus had broken down, with the balance of national leadership now favouring participation. British Columbia and Manitoba, however, still favoured neutrality. Stanley, it appears, had been dispatched by the national office to bring them around. Stanley possessed extraordinary gifts of persuasion, both in manner and substance. "Whose side are you neutral on?" he would ask. Whatever position Harold and Ruby were now prone to, and whatever the nature of the discussion Stanley's visit precipitated, they agreed that, if it came, war in the present case, it would be a tragic necessity. Harold would maintain a long-term relationship with Mildred Farhni and the Fellowship of Reconciliation, but there would be no criticism of the war from Harold's pulpit. A military camp for engineers was established. We would be awakened some nights by the heavy-booted tramping of platoons of new recruits. There would be soldiers at church who would be invited to lunch. One, Clarence, who knew many playful tricks, became a special favourite. And for a time one of the soldiers' wives came to stay with us during his training.

Carman church had a large, well-run Sunday School attended by adults as well as children, where my teacher, Mr Myers, drilled us on the wisdom sayings of Jesus, his parables, and the benedictions and maledictions of the Sermon on the Mount. Stories of modern heroes of the faith were standard fare, like the missionary David Livingstone, in "darkest Africa." There was a modest library where I discovered the Horatio Alger and G.M. Henty books, but more importantly for me, Jack London's *Call of the Wild* and James Fenimore Cooper's Leatherstocking Tales, like *The Last of the Mohicans*, set in the disappearing frontier of the Eastern United States, to which I added, at Ruby's suggestion, all of L.M. Montgomery's Anne of Green Gables books.

Attendance at church followed on the heels of Sunday School, and I would at last be hearing my father's sermon fare. Not that I was specially yearning to do so. It was, however, a significant new fact in my life. For the next eight years, in Sardis and then at our next charge, Fernie, week in week out, I would be exposed to Harold's views on the big questions of God, Jesus, the Bible, the human condition, the Christian life, church and society, and the Kingdom of God and human destiny. He was not a moralistic preacher. We were told at home that we were against lotteries on principle; one should not get something for nothing. But Harold had no problem with my climbing mountains in the coastal range with Chilliwack's best-known gambler, my math teacher, Mr Carroll. If I heard little of personal sins, there was much about our obligations toward each other in a world riven with division and exclusion. There was still individual wrongdoing, but in the complicated impersonal networks of modern social and economic life, the social sins of cutthroat competition, outrageous profiteering at the public's expense, starvation wages, unsanitary workplaces, and adulteration of foods necessitated not just personal admonition but social action and governmental initiative.

On the afterlife, Harold refused to be doctrinaire. That was best left in God's hands. Jesus' account of the last judgment put the issue back where it belonged. As to the miracle stories in the Gospels, he was prone to naturalistic explanations and put in my hands a book, *By an Unknown*

Disciple, that did just that. And he suggested I read a scholarly work in his library by an author I recall as "Wallas" who explained how much the evolution of the Jewish concept of monotheism depended on the vast openness of a desert region and common grazing practices. However, he refused to apply naturalistic explanations to the Easter celebration, despite its location in the cycle of the seasons. When I asked him why Catholics displayed Jesus on the cross but the Protestant cross was empty, he explained that the Catholics emphasized the power of Jesus' death to overcome sin, while Protestants emphasize the new life-giving power of the resurrection. He hastened to add that the new life in Jesus had nothing to do with baby bunnies and chicks! There were those who said he was a powerful preacher. He preached *ex tempore*, and thus, unfortunately, left no written record.

I cannot claim to recall the details of individual sermons and their effect on me. That was more a slow process of absorption, acculturation. The few sermons I have some memory of undoubtedly suffer (or benefit) from the infiltration of others. Cumulatively they left a great impression. One especially impressive sermon was based on the first chapter of Isaiah where God is quoted as saying, "Come let us consider together." For Harold, God was engaged in a kind of dialogue with humanity and eschewed direct intervention in favour of reason. Nothing, Harold thought, could be more relevant to human beings who were constantly being confronted with choices and the necessity of decision as to their personal and social well-being. He, himself, struck a similar posture in his sermons. Another sermon that I recall was equally close to the centre of his religious positioning, was based on Jesus saying, "Seek first the Kingdom of God and God's righteousness, and all these things will be added unto you." "Righteousness" signified the "right way," the way of just relations. This was not in the first instance addressed to individuals but to the collective life of a people, and only secondarily, though necessarily, to individuals. A "kingdom" was a corporate entity, and for Jesus as a Jew, "kingdom" harkened back to the covenant made between God and the Jewish people as a whole. At issue was the manner in which they arranged their common life. It was a matter at once of spiritual and material consequence, for if done according to God's call for justice, the blessings that would follow would be immeasurable. This was, at its very heart, a political matter. The very word derived from "polis," Greek for "city," and concerned the way in which life together in collectivities like the city was arranged for the common good. If there were huge impediments to the realization of such a vision – all the ills, perversions, and corruptions listed by the prophets, ancient and modern,

Harold would point to God's promise in Isaiah: "Though your sins be as scarlet, I will make you whiter than snow." The forgiveness offered in anticipation of repentance, which meant the act of "turning around" from past ways, opened up the possibility of new beginnings for a wayward people. Harold did not preach partisan politics from the pulpit or in congregational affairs, but everyone knew where he stood. If he strayed too close to the line, he would be quickly alerted by Mrs Dr White striking the floor with her umbrella!

I was always impressed by what I would later call a dialectic with the macro dimensions of the historical process that informed the substance of much of Harold's preaching. Just as a well worked out politics lay just beyond the outer limits of some of his preaching, so did a reasoned philosophy of history, as his underlinings in the Oxford Conference volume *The Kingdom of God and History* testify. For someone of a serious historical bent, the coming of a second "Great War" in his lifetime provoked profound questions about the future of Western civilization. He enrolled as an extension student in a Master's program in history at the university. It was excitement itself for me to accompany him on the occasional sally to borrow reading material or consult with his supervising professor. The university cafeteria also had its own allure! Ruby gave Harold a copy of Oswald Spengler's *The Decline of the West* as a birthday present. I took a quick look at the fat volume with Spengler's intimidating face on the cover and misread the title as *The Detective of the West*. Interesting as Spengler was, his almost biological, cyclical view of the growth, maturing, and decline of civilization was for Harold too much of a closed system, like those of Hegel and Marx, and he turned to Arnold Toynbee's *Study of History*, with the more open horizons of a theory of challenge and response, on which to do his thesis. One day, working on the last pages of the thesis, he left his carrel for a coffee break. When he returned, the thesis was gone. It could hardly have been mistaken for trash, with other of his effects still about. Another Master's student was also working on Toynbee and Harold had his suspicions, but no proof. It was too much to begin again.

I was hardly capable at this point in my life of appreciating the more profound levels of Harold's thinking. And there was more to a service of worship than the declamations, explanations, and exhortations of the preacher. There were hymns, whose religious impact was formidable. Originating in different periods of religious experience and theological debate, they could be a source of confusion and contradiction for the thoughtful. They also had a differential appeal across the generations. I inherited Harold's family's love of singing. The hymns he chose had to be selected with one ear tuned to congregational likes and dislikes. I liked the hymns Harold preferred, hymns that encouraged his people to find the meaning of their lives in the struggle for God's Kingdom of social justice, like Harry Emerson Fosdick's "God of grace and God of glory" that pleaded with God to "now renew creation's story" and "pour thy power [on a people] rich in goods but poor of soul / Grant us wisdom, Grant us courage / Lest we miss thy kingdom's goal." There were the great hymns of the Wesley brothers of the eighteenth century Methodist revival that put the same thought somewhat differently for a people poor in goods and stressed in soul, stricken by the ills of the early industrial revolution: "Love divine, all loves excelling / Joy of Heaven to earth come down / Fix in us thy humble dwelling / All thy tender mercies crown." But there were other hymns born of American revivalism that moved some in the congregation, and in the churches of Harold's and Ruby's youth: hymns of retreat, hiding from the storms of life, like "Rock of Ages cleft for me / Let me hide myself in thee." Or clinging to an "Old Rugged Cross" until "at last my trophies I lay down / And exchange them one day for a crown." Or walking alone in "The Garden" with a Jesus who "walks with me and talks with me / And the joy we share as we tarry there / None other has ever known." These tended to be the hymns of choice at the Sunday evening lakeside hymn sings for campers and cottagers around a big bonfire Harold would arrange at nearby Cultus Lake. There was no denying the emotional power of sentimental religion. Good pastor that he was, Harold would lead the singing with conviction, knowing the meaning such hymns held for people tired, burdened with care, and perhaps living lives of quiet desperation. However, they hardly appealed to a mid-teen beginning to understand and sense the challenge and hope of kingdom theology. If one had to sing in that vein, there were hymns of healthier aspect I was more comfortable with, which asked, "Will your anchor hold in the storms of life," and suggested the efficacy of being "grounded firm and deep in the Saviour's love," or a great classic like the Welsh hymn "Guide me, O thou great Jehovah / Pilgrim through this barren land," born of the environmental and social devastations of the coal mining industry in Wales – especially when sung to the self-transcending music of Cwm Rhondda.

Mid-teens was confirmation time; time to make a choice whether or not I wished to become a full member of the United Church. I agreed to attend the confirmation classes Harold would hold, though it did not seem to be a big deal; where else had I been all these years? Again, memory is vague but yields a few grains for reflection. There was a little on the history of church union, consummated in 1925, and an overview of the

Basis of Union, which had since served as a non-binding creed for the church. I think the doctrine of the Trinity came up for discussion, which Harold would explain did not contradict the unity of God, since it was an expression of the primary ways in which we experience God. A discussion of the nature of the Bible could hardly have been avoided. What follows is my best estimate of how, in summary, Harold would have addressed the subject or responded to questions of our class. The Bible was not a textbook of science or history. It spoke in terms of the common understanding of those times. It was a collection of diverse literary forms, story, poetry, legend, myth, chronicle, and legal codes. The biblical story was of a developing people threatened by surrounding tribes and situated between the great empires of the day. They knew victory and defeat, oppression and exile. In their struggle for a unifying identity, they came to believe in a God more powerful than all others. This God set the stage for their liberation from slavery in Egypt, which became the founding story of their nation. Their prophets like Isaiah came to view God as a God of justice who, through his people, was preparing the way for a new stage of history where people would live together in an ideal society of peace and harmony and where pain and suffering would be no more. In the Christian scriptures, Harold would have said, Jesus presented himself as the successor of the prophets and came to be seen by his followers as "the Son of God" (though he preferred to be called "the Son of Man") and after his crucifixion and their experience of the resurrection, as the first Christian communities took shape, they came to see him embodying Israel's role as the suffering servant destined to realize God's kingdom. The church, living in his spirit, was thus the repository of the great prophetic vision, representing it in their life together and dedicated to its fulfilment. That was what our little group was being called to in becoming members of the church.

In the final stage of the confirmation process, we met with the board of elders, where we were expected to make a brief "confession" of our faith so the elders might assess our readiness. I was certainly quite comfortable with – even keen about – what we had learned, but I was having difficulty in putting language to the task. I listened to the others. George Minckler, sitting next to me, made a good effort at doing so. Now it was my turn. After a pause, I simply said, "Same as George." My poor father must have inwardly died a thousand deaths but said quietly, "Richard, you have to put it in your own words." I have no recollection of what I said but, on reflection, I am glad Harold had not loaded us up with simplistic religious slogans for use on such occasions.

5

One of the most infamous pre-war acts of the Canadian government was its refusal to grant refuge to European Jews seeking to escape the pogroms of Russia and Eastern Europe and the mounting Nazi onslaught on German Jewry. And one of its most infamous wartime acts was expropriation of the properties of, and the internment of, the largely coastal Japanese in the interior of British Columbia. On both issues Harold took an active and public stand. He consistently made it clear in his sermons that Jesus was a Jew. And one of his most important assignments by the BC Conference was to act as their liaison officer with the interned Japanese, a few of whom, like the Kabayamas, were United Church ministers' families. I accompanied him on one of his visits to the camp working on the building of the Hope-Princeton highway. He was warmly greeted. We visited their modest but comfortable accommodations, chatted, admired the crafts they worked on in their spare time, and joined a crew at work preparing to dynamite a section of rock. A circle of men with sledgehammers were rhythmically hammering an iron drill into the rock. I was aghast when my father, in a momentary pause in the activity, took one of the hammers and joined the circle. I cringed at the thought of him missing the rhythm, or worse, missing the drill. Much to my surprise and relief, he didn't! I was hugely impressed. Harold would later lead the fight in the BC Conference against the proposed deportation of the interned Japanese, and he personally took the issue directly to the prime minister's office.

Sometime in 1943 there was a knock at our door. A Royal Canadian Mounted Police (RCMP) officer asked if he could come and speak to Harold. He had come to say that he had been instructed to put my father under surveillance. He was not at liberty to give the reasons but said he had too much respect for my father to do so without telling him! I only learned of this later. Had his role as liaison with the internees put him under suspicion? Or was it Harold's continuing activity with the CCF? He was a member of the executive and election planning committee of the Fraser Valley CCF Riding Association, which could hardly in itself have been grounds for suspicion. But in 1943 polls were indicating that the CCF nationally was becoming a serious threat to the reigning Liberals. Coincidentally, Stanley at Sir George Williams College in Montreal was under investigation, along with colleagues like Eugene Forsey at McGill, and both of them would shortly be fired. With an election likely by the spring of 1945, were the Liberals preparing the ground for an onslaught on the CCF? Nothing deterred, when that onslaught came in the form of a vicious literature campaign accusing the CCF of being a proto-communist and implicitly revolutionary party that, if elected, would reduce the country to serfdom, Harold took on the job of campaign manager for the CCF candidate, Henry Tyson, a teacher in Haney, and spoke publicly at rallies on his behalf, exposing the Liberal campaign for the sham that it was. I was now thoroughly politicized myself and was nominated to run as the CCF candidate in the mock election held at our high school. Hopes were high. Saskatchewan had elected a CCF government the previous year, but Tyson and I both came in second, I to the son of an Anglican minister's son representing the Conservative party.

6

1945. Again it was time to move. We had been six years at Sardis. Again there was no call from any congregation, and the stationing committee posted Harold in Fernie in the Crowsnest Pass, far from Vancouver, the Mecca of significant opportunity and action in British Columbia. Again Ruby was feeling considerable distress and retreated to her parents with my young brother Philip for the duration of the move. Fernie was another coal mining town. The United Church there had suddenly become available owing to the election of its minister, Bert Herridge, to the House of Commons shortly before Conference was scheduled to meet. The congregation consisted of the families of miners, teachers, Crow's Nest Pass Coal Company officials, commercial folk, and miscellaneous service personnel. It was a far less dynamic congregation than Carman in Sardis. There was little of challenge for boys my age. I entered a national church essay competition on "Stewardship in the Atomic Age" and won first prize. There were some precious folk like the Thomsons, he an accountant with the Coal Company, and the Biddulphs, a Welsh mining family. Miners in the coal mining regions of British Columbia often migrated from one site to another. In the mining communities of the Crowsnest Pass there were some from Cumberland Harold would meet again, often members of the Labor Progressive [Communist] Party, whom he respected as "warm-hearted family men." He and Ruby were quick to associate themselves with the local CCF riding association. I would be two years at Fernie, revelling in the long winters of skiing. I finished high school there in high style, becoming president of the students' council, singing the male lead in the school operetta, winning the prize in drafting, and giving the graduating class valedictory. In the final province-wide exams I missed by the narrowest of margins winning the lone scholarship offered by the BC government,

edged out by the son of a Japanese family interned in Slocan. Disappointed, but feeling happy for him, it appealed to me that there was something
very right about the result. High school, however, contributed little to a
growing historical consciousness nurtured in a mix of ancient religious
story, classical myth, and medieval romance. I recall nothing of classes in
history or social studies. Mr Evans and Miss Banks, my grades five and six
teachers, did their best to cover what for a young boy were the dramatic
years of West European expansion, Marco Polo overland to China, the great
sea voyages that opened up "new" worlds. I supplemented the history with
romantic fictions of young boys going to sea as cabin boys with the likes
of Sir Francis Drake. Mr Evans stepped backward a few centuries reading
stories of the Crusades to us – very sanitized. It was difficult not to experience a rush of self-conscious identification when Richard the Lion-hearted
came on stage! Miss Banks chaperoned us into Canadian origins: New
France fascinated, habitants, *coureur de bois,* and the fur trade, colourful
governors like Frontenac, the French and Indian wars. Alexander Mackenzie "overland to the Pacific" led into early years in British Columbia and
the rich Indigenous culture of the West Coast. It was all so exciting. Much
of it would later be subject to deconstruction. But somehow, somewhere,
history disappeared for me in high school – or would have, had it not been
for the historical freight carried in other subjects. Miss Fisher, the Chilliwack High School librarian, noting my addiction to Conan Doyle and
Sherlock Holmes, suggested I was reading below my level. She put me
onto the gripping account of Trelawney, an aristocratic literary adventurer
who consorted with the likes of poets Shelley and Byron – especially the
latter in his campaign, literary and otherwise, to free Greece from Turkish
rule. Stanzas of Byron's stirring epic on that subject remain with me to this
day. Ruby kept me growing with books like Martha Ostenso's *Wild Geese,*
which she was reading. At some point I began reading the syndicated
columns of political commentary of Walter Lippman and Dorothy Parker
that were freighted with historical reference and significance. I read John
Gunther's *Inside Europe* – one of his "Inside" series of books – and Theo-
dore White's *Fire in the Ashes,* a description and assessment of the impact of
the war and the potential for recovery. There were other ways of becoming
historical than by high school coursework.

On moving to Fernie, Harold had wasted no time in contacting fellow
Christian socialists associated with the Alberta School of Religion, which
for years had run summer schools under the leadership of H.M. Horricks
of Calgary and fellow United Church minister Arthur Rowe of High
River. As theme speakers they had been able to draw leading American

and Canadian Christian socialists Harry F. Ward and Reinhold Niebuhr of Union Theological Seminary in New York, King Gordon of the Fellowship for a Christian Social Order, and T.C. "Tommy" Douglas, recently elected CCF premier of Saskatchewan. Harold clearly had a felt need to associate himself with the Alberta group, and July saw us encamped at a modest campsite on the banks of the Bow River south of Calgary where, this summer, 1947, the speaker would be the Vermont radical economist, author, and publisher of *The Monthly Review*, Scott Nearing. Nearing and his wife Helen evidently were widely admired as inspiring gurus of a "good life movement" that celebrated the simple, purposive life of self-sufficiency and the role of modern technology in freeing humans to rise to a higher level of being. I grasped something of this in his lectures and in an unusual meditation he did based on the Jeanette MacDonald and Nelson Eddy hit song: "Ah sweet mystery of life at last I've found you ... 'Tis love and love alone the world is seeking."

7

The fall of 1947 saw me off to UBC, enrolled in Arts and Science. The question of a future career had never been a matter of discussion or pressure at home. The first time my father raised the matter was after he learned that I had aced my first-year mathematics exam. Anyone good at math would be good at theology, he said. "You should consider going into the ministry." I had no such intention. The hero in our family was Stewart in China, who, in addition to his medical responsibilities, had been in charge of international relief into China during the war and had surveyed China's medical services for the Red Cross, including those of the Communists in the province of Yenan where they had consolidated their power after their famous "Long March." A medical career had some attraction and had led me to register in biology, chemistry, and psychology. But the son of a father keen on history came under some pressure to include a course in history. At UBC the first-year course was Professor Soward's "Twenty-five Troubled Years, 1914–1939." That course would turn out to be of more immediate use than I could have imagined.

Both Harold and Ruby were keen to see me involved with the Student Christian Movement, as they had been. I tucked the thought away for a future day, but during Frosh Week, when campus clubs were recruiting, there was an SCM table where an attractive, smiling young woman asked, "Would you care to join us for Thanksgiving weekend at Ocean Park?" That took little thought. Ocean Park, south of the city, on a height of sand cliffs overlooking the ocean, was the site of United Church boys camps I had attended in my younger teens. The SCM also had a club room where a full-time general secretary worked and where members and friends could gather, eat their lunches, hear talks, and participate in study groups. The camp was great – until I was asked to do the closing worship. Me. Barely three weeks on campus. This still puzzles me. Had my father, with his desire to see me involved, passed something on to the local general secretary, Frank Patterson?

The presence of many veterans on campus, fresh from the war against fascist barbarism and determined to build a new world order, gave an especially serious tone to extracurricular discussion and debate over social and political issues. Far from being immune to all that, the SCM had a long history of engagement with social concerns. The Western units of the movement still resonated with the political radicalism of the 1930s. Early on someone asked if I had read Karl Marx's *Communist Manifesto*. I hadn't. Did. And was impressed as much by its ethical power as by its revolutionary doctrine. Though a professed socialist, my father had never referred to him in my presence, nor did Marx feature in any of my courses in high school. From a pamphlet in the SCM literature rack I learned to distinguish between Karl Marx, the trenchant analyst and critic of capitalism, and Marx, in the tradition of the Hebrew prophets, the visionary of a coming new age for humanity to be established by a revolutionary working class proletariat. It was in the SCM that I learned the rousing songs of the Spanish Civil War and the powerful hymn of the Second Socialist International: "Arise ye prisoners of starvation ... A better world's in birth."

The SCM at UBC was not an entirely homogeneous group. A degree of polarization in interests, though not of outright conflict, existed between students straight out of high school and local church youth groups and an older group, among whom were those radicalized, like my father, in the BC Interior. And there were those, like myself, progeny of progressive ministerial families. The older group set the tone for the local unit. For some reason they drew me into their midst. The religion of the historical Jesus was "in"; St Paul's religion about Jesus was "out." Tradition was suspect. One of the older group wrote a poetic lament ending: "when orthodoxy rears its ugly head / And turns to palest pink our deepest red." In the course of the year there was a campaign against the proposed deportation of the Japanese. We picketed arms shipments to the Chinese Nationalists. There was a lot fun complementing the seriousness. We were not above schotishing down the middle of Dunbar Street in the wee hours of the morning or lustily singing our most radical songs, sauntering through the business district. An after-exams camp at the YMCA campsite on an island in the Straits of Juan de Fuca featuring the national SCM study secretary, Margaret Prang, rounded out the year.

As the academic year was nearing its end I learned about an opportunity to do post-war reconstruction work in Eastern Europe with the second Beaver Brigade under the sponsorship of the World Federation of Democratic Youth (WFDY) and its Canadian affiliate, the National Federation of Labour Youth (NFLY). When I told my parents of this opportunity, they asked how I had come to be associated with a communist organization. I hadn't. News of recruitment for the group had come to me via the SCM, which, with the early post-war founding of the WFDY, had become the nationally recognized affiliate with a seat on the WFDY executive. Still concerned, they consulted a friend, Donald Faris, a former China missionary now working for the United Nations Relief and Rehabilitation Association, who assured them it would be a great experience. It was. And life changing.

8

The thirty-eight members of the "brigade" represented an interesting cross-section of Canadian youth, with a bias toward East European, Russian, Finnish, and Jewish groups, but also English and French. Four of us were ministers' sons, and one, rather older, Donald "Dusty" Greenwill, was a miner from Cumberland who related stories about my father that were well embedded in local union memory. Arriving in London, it turned out the SCM delegate expected to attend the WFDY council meeting there had not shown up and I was asked to substitute for him. We were in Paris for the Bastille Day celebrations, with a massive parade and rallies chanting "Vive Thorez! Vive Stalin!" while waiting for featured speakers. Thorez was the leader of the French Communist Party. I noted my wariness about cults of leadership in my diary.

Our first work project was to assist in the rebuilding of the Czech village of Lidice, razed by the Germans for the assassination of Reinhard Heydrich, the chief of Security Police for the region, whose extreme severity had earned for him the title "Hangman." The 195 men of the village were summarily executed and the women and children scattered to various destinations. Then there was an International Working Youth Conference in Warsaw where I wandered, stunned at the square mile of rubble that was the Warsaw Ghetto. I was immobilized and awestruck on finding a large section of a wall of glorious mosaic, undoubtedly the remnant of a synagogue, still standing, still defiant. A tour across Poland with conference delegates afforded opportunities to meet and talk, through our own interpreter and multilingual members of our group, with students at the historic university city of Cracow, coal miners' families in Lodz, and industrial workers in Wroclav.

It was at this point that we got some upsetting news. The summer of 1948 was a tense one internationally. With the breakdown of tripartite governance of Berlin, the Russian blockade of the city, and American defiance by airlifting supplies for the beleaguered city, and Yugoslavia's Tito defecting from the Comintern, there was anxious speculation that Europe might be plunged once more into the maelstrom of war. One can readily imagine the anxiety of parents back in Fernie and elsewhere. For us, the immediate effect was the cancellation of our intended next work project in Yugoslavia and, more alarming, our transportation home on a Yugoslavian ship. The Hungarian Youth Organization came to our rescue, lodged us at the university in Budapest, set up tours, scheduled speakers, and arranged visits to hostels for apprentices, factories, schools, the parliament buildings, and the war-ravaged Hapsburg palace across the river in Buda. There were two weeks at a trade union education centre in a former Esterhazy castle at Lake Tata, and then three weeks of back-breaking work digging a canal to link the Danube and Tiser rivers. To our relief, a Polish ship, the Sobieski, leaving from Genoa, would return us to Canada.

As the summer progressed I felt a growing sense of identification with a world in travail and burdened with how to make sense of a civilization that could degenerate so quickly into the madness of massive mutual destruction. That was an historical question. Professor Soward had started me down that road, but that was a mere beginning. And what would make it right? That was a political – and perhaps a religious – question. It was now too late to resume studies. There were a few days in Vancouver, reconnecting with the scm and giving a couple of talks on the experience we had been through.

9

Back home in Fernie, I got a job working in the rail yards for the Crow's Nest Pass Coal Company that winter and spring. Shovelling piles of snow, I found myself making up political speeches. I wrote a series of articles about the trip for the *Fernie Free Press*. I raided my father's library, where I discovered treasures like Friedrich Engels' *Socialism: Utopian and Scientific*.

Thinking back, it remains a puzzle to me that, although a professed social-ist who, I now knew was well acquainted with them, the names of Marx and Engels never passed his lips in my hearing. In the evenings after work by the space heater in our front hall, I read Engels' account of the three stages of history, primitive communism, class division of labour, a final industrial society of plenty where each gave according to their ability and all received according to their need. That, and the concept of an interior dialectic of civilization around the ownership of land or capital by a dom-inant class, lit up the historical landscape like a flash of lightning. Here was an account of the inner workings of the historical process that gave structure, dynamism, and meaning to it all. Its materialist base did not bother me. Although I knew little of Hegel, it seemed a brilliant and sen-sible notion that each socio-economic synthesis, dominated by a power-ful minority class, should give rise to opposition, an antithesis, and ulti-mately to a new synthesis. Nothing in this denied the obligation of working at the common task of providing the means of life, whether material or spiritual.

Harold quickly made me acquainted with the Christian socialists of mid-nineteenth century Britain, Charles Kingsley, F.D. Maurice, and their colleagues, and for good measure put Somerville's abridgment of Arnold Toynbee's *Study of History* in my hands. Reading *Socialism, Utopian and Sci-entific* took me in another direction beyond my earlier exposure to Karl Marx, the economic analyst and social prophet-cum-revolutionary. I was not yet aware, however, of the work being done on the younger Marx and the Feuerbach connection, nor of the issue of how much was philosophy and how much myth in Marx. It was now 1949. Another federal election was underway. The Liberals in a repeat of their 1945 tactics had hired a rabid anti-communist propagandist by the name of Trestrail from Texas to again defame the CCF. One day, a sizeable box from the Liberal national campaign headquarters arrived at our door. Harold had written, saying that if that office could send him 5,000 copies of Trestrail's pamphlet, he could put them to good use. "What do you mean, 'good use'?" I asked. "To help keep the house warm next winter," he chuckled.

10

An SCM Student-in-Industry work camp drew me to Montreal for the summer of 1949. Directed by Alexander "Lex" Miller, author of *The Chris-tian Significance of Karl Marx*, this was to be a special work camp gather-ing senior SCMers to experience industrial labour and consider issues of industrial society at a deeper level than previous such camps had done. Somehow they had accepted my application. For the "in house" study program of the camp I presented a paper on the political implications of the fact that industry was at once a social function and a function of society. Back at UBC in the fall, I attended the SCM western winter conference at Saskatoon, where I was asked to chair Professor John Grant's theme lectures based on Herbert Butterfield's *Christianity and History*. I took with me my father's copy of Paul Tillich's *On the Boundary*. Tillich, who from his post at Union Theological Seminary in New York became one of the twentieth century's greatest public intellectuals, was socialist. He found that the boundary situation between sacred and secular, faith and unbelief, religion and politics, theory and practice, yielded a harvest of insights into the human condition. I was finding myself propelled in a similar direction. I was now convinced that I needed to enroll in the modern history honours program at the University of Toronto, the prospect of which, however, I found quite intimidating. My first essay for Professor McDougall in British history was an attempt at an economic interpretation of the "upside down world" of the Puritan Revolution, 1640–60, in England. When my tutor handed the paper back, I quickly put it in my briefcase. I couldn't read it and feared the worst. Later, summoning my courage, I approached a new friend to look at the mark and tell me what it was. "It's an A plus!" he blurted out. All feelings of intimidation disappeared. I was in the right place. I found the integrated, lockstep modern history program an invaluable experience, and it was excitement itself to be at Toronto when Northrop Frye was decoding William Blake and Milton, Marshall McLuhan was unveiling the mysteries of the medium as the message, and Edmund Carpenter was celebrating the riches of indigenous art, especially the amazing Inuit stone sculptures. And there was a lively political culture, Hart House debates, and the SCM. There would be two more industrial work camps, both under Bob Miller, the new SCM study secretary, recently returned from postgraduate studies in Europe and involvement in Christian renewal projects in Germany. At the National Council of the SCM in the fall of 1952 I was elected national student chairperson of the SCM and was shortly off to Bowling Green in Ohio, as the Canadian fraternal delegate to the annual National Assembly of the student YW-YMCAs in the United States. It was a stimulating time, especially the deeper discussions with students like Dick Schroeder of Dartmouth College, who gave me a copy of Rosenstock Heussy's penetrating book *The Multiformity of Man*. However, the highlight may have been finding a copy of Paul Tillich's *The Protestant Era* in my room. I read late into the nights, deeply impressed by his arresting chapter, "The End of the Protestant Era," which title he had wanted for the book itself, but the publisher refused. Another chapter, "Historical and Non-Historical Interpretations of History," explained the different understandings of time and history in Hebraic and Greek religion. In the former, history was driven by a will to justice working in and through the processes of social development and prophetic judgment within the temporal order, and therefore full of hope, while in the latter, the Greek, humanity was bound up in the cycles of the natural and cosmic order where fate and fortune ruled. In Hebraic myth the world was created by God and declared good, while in Greek mythology the world being created by subordinate demi-urge was imperfect, compromising all efforts of fulfillment in the natural and human order of things. Hebraic prophetic religion could be political through and through anticipating a time when justice would be done. Time was linear; it had a beginning and an end. For the Greek, human destiny was bound up in the endless natural cycle of life, death, and rebirth necessitated by the inherent imperfection of the created world. For Hebraic religion and its Christian and Islamic offshoots, the salvation religion promised was possible within the order of history, while in the Greek, it had to be found beyond and outside of history. Hence, "historical and non-historical interpretations of history."

It was not Tillich's intention to carry the story forward into the influence of Greek religious ideas upon the early Christian church as it expanded into the Greco-Roman world, elevating concepts of body-soul dualism and the immortality of the latter over the bodily resurrection mythology of Judaism. Much of that was recovered with the return to Biblical roots with the Protestant Reformation and the re-evaluation of the religious significance of the secular and the profane.

For me, this further encounter with Tillich was hugely important. With the help of Tillich and others, I was now becoming self-consciously aware of the subtle co-inherence of the religious, the political, and the historical in the Protestant Christianity of my upbringing. You could say that at Bowling Green I finally grew up.

CHAPTER TWO

Christians and the New Post-Second World War Regimes in Eastern Europe

BACKGROUNDER

In 1949 the Student Christian Movement of Canada (SCM) sent three senior students, David Busby, Donald Evans, and Mary McCrimmon, as delegates to the World Youth Festival in Budapest, sponsored by the World Federation of Democratic Youth. Summary reports of their experience and impressions were published in a fall issue of the SCM's national journal, The Canadian Student. *They reported a gloomy, oppressive mood in the city, reluctance to converse, and hints of secret police operations. No doubt they were faithful to what they had heard. Whoever and whatever all this was based on, it contrasted sharply with my own experience of a city, country, and region in which I had spent four months the previous summer. Everywhere a mood of liberation prevailed and gratitude to their Soviet liberators. Everywhere there was an optimistic spirit of renewal and rebuilding. Eastern Europe seemed populated with youth choirs and dance groups. Several members of the group I was with were fluent in local languages and knowledge of English was widespread; people had no hesitation in talking to us. It was true that the wartime alliance was breaking down at the time. The media over the past couple of years had devoted much space to the reconfiguration of Europe in the wake of the war of 1939 to 1945, with a perhaps understandable partiality for the West European regimes and severe hostility to those in the East that ended up well within the orbit of Soviet Russia. The recent reports of Busby, Evans, and McCrimmon, unfortunately, seemed to partake of a polarization that was important to resist. In the early post-war enthusiasm for building a new international order, the SCM, as a national student organization, had joined the World Federation of Democratic Youth and the International Union of Students, both of which were now finding it difficult to survive without succumbing to one side or the other in the ideological great powers standoff that was disintegrating into a Cold War. In these cir-*

cumstances, I felt compelled to respond, not just with facts but to question their historical and political speculations and present another, different perspective. In retrospect, both would seem to have had merit and warranted consideration. Tony Judt, in his much-praised book, Postwar *(2005), noted that East Europeans, in these first years after liberation, were eager to take up where they left off before the war. A decade earlier they had developed social programs well in advance of those in the United States. The war over, the revered Czechoslovakian leader Edouard Benes had declared the importance of getting on with building a socialist society. Life in the shadow of the Union of Socialist Soviet Republics did not appear to be cause for alarm, and Matyas Rakosi, a long-standing and respected figure on the Hungarian left, was for most a leader they could follow in building a socialist future in their country, whatever capitalist America might think. But that was early years, and in the light of the first comprehensive review of six decades of studies of developments in the East, 1945 to 1953, the* SCM's *trio of observers may well have detected ominous signs of change. Anne Applebaum, in* Iron Curtain *(2012), relates how the exigencies of an emerging Cold War would lead to a Russian stranglehold on the region's resources to fuel its part in the* MAD *(mutually assured destruction) competition of two superpowers. By 1953 a combination of Stalinization, re-emergent anti-Semitism, and widespread corruption had overtaken the politics of the region.*

An important question for me on my return from Europe was what attitude and strategy Christians should adopt toward the new regimes in the light of their history and their prospects within the Soviet orbit. The thesis that I developed in this article was that there was only one alternative for Hungary (as for most of Eastern Europe) at the end of the war, and that the constructive course for Christians was support for the new regimes, working to help their better features prevail.

CHRISTIANS AND THE EAST EUROPEAN REGIMES[*]

Nature of the New State

Power in the new state is based on social ownership of the means of production and is concerned with their use for the common good. As a result, social securities add as much as 40 per cent to the value of wages, and the standard of living is higher than ever before. In keeping with social

---

[*] First published as "Christians in Eastern Europe" in *The Canadian Student*, March 1950, 69–71. Courtesy of the Student Christian Movement of Canada.

ownership, real participation by workers in the management of industry is encouraged. The value of work is reckoned in terms of social utility.

This situation is the result of a revolution that, as most revolutions, is characterized in its aftermath by absolute power and pressure to conform. It has involved the rejection of, and control over, those who previously held economic and consequently political power in their hands. That there have been abuses of this power, and that innocent people have been ostracised is not to be doubted. The reports abound with examples of them. Such abuses, however, do not exist for the large part of the population. Although the government enjoys substantial popular support, counter-revolutionary forces, such as the Roman Catholic Church, remnants of the old wealthy classes, the American secret service, and even members of the communist party, corrupted by its long period of illegality, are strong. Thus, four years after the war, power is vested to an even greater degree in the government. Pressure to conform is well manifested in the cult of state worship and hero worship, which seems widespread.

Alternatives to Old Regime

Between the two wars, Hungary was ruled by the combined power of the landholders, the industrialists, and the Catholic Church. It is essential to an understanding of the nature of any possible alternatives as well as to an understanding of the role of the Catholic Church in Hungary today, to realize the extent of its power in pre-war times. Sixty-five per cent of the population belong to the Catholic Church, including the largest percentage of landowners. Hence the Church was guilty in the existence of three million landless peasants. It controlled ninety per cent of the schools. The degree of intellectual freedom was certainly as limited as it is now, and the percentage of school attendance not nearly as high. For 900 years this church has been allied with the State (which hardly dared openly defy it). In that time the Hungarian crown became an important symbol of Apostolic Succession. Our history texts speak of the Horthy regime as "White Terror." It was absolute, and being such, the only way to bring reform was by revolution and absolute power.

Mr Evans in his report tries vainly to thrust a third alternative into the situation. I think facts prove that József Cardinal Mindzenty [the head of the Roman Catholic Church in Hungary] was attempting to restore the old regime. At any rate it is logical that he should attempt to do so. In his report, Mr Evans speaks of the alternative Mindzenty advocated, as giving more freedom for reform. It is significant that in pre-war Hungary political freedom decreased, rather than increased. In another part of the report it can be inferred that this is recognized by recognition of Horthy as being co-responsible in the non-existence of a third alternative. Then indulging in a bit of illogical reasoning, "showing" Fascism often to be a result of Communist agitation, he lays the blame equally at the feet of Matyas Rakosi [long-time leading figure in the Communist party in Hungary and now premier]. Evans argues that in a state "where Communists are weak and the ruling class allows some degree of civil liberties, a non-absolutist, middle way of reform is possible." Then he says that "as Communists grow in strength they make Fascism the only probable alternative and exclude the possibility of a third way." It is a fact that, where conditions have permitted a third way, the Communists are weak. Why, then, in our hypothetical case have they grown in strength? Either because the middle way was not efficient, or more likely, because the possibility of reform existed only as long as it did not threaten the security of the ruling class. Fascism is not the result of Communist agitation. Let us go beyond immediate causes and ask why Communism? This latter pattern describes the nature of the old regime in Hungary and explains why there was no middle way.

Is there any ground for believing that appropriation by America as a "sphere of influence" would create, or would have created, more desirable conditions? Although this is and was an impossibility, without precipitating a major conflagration in the world, it is a thought that seems to be cherished by a great many people. The anti-communist policies of the United States would cause the reinstatement of much of the old leadership. Italy, which seemed to me to be much more a police state than Hungary, is a good illustration of the future of a Hungary under the United States. There, under the facade of popular government, and in the face of dire economic conditions, a large part of the social democrats have sided with the communists. The rest have little influence. A return to this in Hungary would merely pave the way for a new, more violent revolution, as it is doing in Italy.

As I see it, there was no alternative that was both preferable and practicable to the forces that took power in Hungary following the war. Nor is there any now, which, from the Hungarian point of view, would be more desirable.

A Dilemma?

The fact that a particular social order was inevitable by the nature of the forces at work in the field does not, however, say that it warrants

Christian support, for if it did, might we not say that fascism in Germany deserved that support? Are we in a dilemma?

We Christians often think of justice and power as abstractions, forgetting their historical setting. And in attempting to judge between degrees of these things, we often seem to face "impossible social alternatives." Yet there are Christians who choose. Josef Hromádka [a pastor and theologian in Czechoslovakia] sees his task as working within the new order; Cardinal Mindzenty sees his as working for the old order of things. The former is criticized because he is forced by his position to impose his ethic on others. Surely Mindzenty must be criticized on the same ground. If we insist on dealing in abstractions, we find ourselves facing two mutually exclusive and equally undesirable positions – between which Hungarian Christians and ourselves must choose, for not choosing is, in reality, choosing the status quo.

The Way Out

To extricate ourselves we have to recognize a few things: first, that whatever choices we make we impose our standards on others, and second, that we Christians have to work within the slow-moving processes of history. We have to recognize that each politico-economic system by its own shortcomings names its follower. The rising social forces of any day come from the disinherited of the system. It was with the latter that our Lord mingled and from whom chose disciples. The ideology of the disinherited (a unique combination of justice and self-interest) is very susceptible to and, in many respects, similar to the Christian ethic. Here it is that we find the distinction between our impossible social alternatives. We have to distinguish between those forces that are truly new and creative and those that arise as an attempt to perpetuate the old, decadent order, and the security of those identified with it. In the latter category lies fascism, and the old regime of Hungary.

In respect to Hungary, all this means understanding the significance of, and praying for the efficacy of the new, more just relationships of individuals around the means of production [to generate a more democratic political morality throughout the state]. In taking part in all this and, wherever possible, helping change the more undesirable aspects of the present regime, Christians are not jeopardizing their right to preach the gospel and are making a positive contribution to the triumph of the just over the unjust.

CHAPTER THREE

The Great Protestant Ethic Debate:
The First Phase, 1905–1960

BACKGROUNDER

This essay and the next were both written for John H. Hallowell, professor of political theory at Duke University, where I was a doctoral candidate, 1961–63. In 1961, after four years as the general secretary of the Student Christian Movement (SCM) unit at the University of Saskatchewan, and the completion of a Master's degree in history, I found myself being sought after to fill top positions in the Australian and British SCMs. I had taken a somewhat innovative role in Saskatoon. Taking my cues from Irenaeus, one of the great early church "Fathers," that the aim of Christianity was "Man fully alive," I saw the university in any agency of that same purpose and worked at a mix of programs that would help the university fulfill its high calling. There would be lecture/profiles on modern prophetic figures like Darwin, Marx, Kierkegaard, Dostoevsky, and Niebuhr; Proftalks over lunch on current research; displays and sales of leading-edge books (there was no campus bookstore); agnostic weekends; lectures on Christianity and science and ethical issues in medicine; and so on. Finding university culture at once congenial and challenging, I put Australia and Great Britain aside in favour of an academic future. I had begun my explorations of the social gospel in Canada in my Master's thesis and was attracted to Duke where Shelton Smith, reputed to be the leading authority on the social gospel, was located, only to find on arrival that he had left on a two-year leave. But bad luck turned to good fortune. I would work under Richard L. Watson, Jr, on the Progressive Era in the United States, in which the social gospel was a central feature, and with Hallowell in the history of political thought. Hallowell's text Main Currents in Modern Political Thought *concluded with a substantial chapter,* "Christianity and the Social Order." *Both were excellent teachers. Watson kept me solidly grounded in the progressive tradition, while Hallowell was* a critic of "progressive immanentism," following Eric Voegelin in viewing progressive theory as a form of gnostic heresy claiming secret knowledge of the end toward which history was moving. He was my "big picture" man. They were wonderfully complementary.

Academics aside, I had become aware of a very personal and family issue involved in the Protestant ethic debate. My parents' experience as Christian socialists at the hands of United Church boards and their Pulpit Supply Committees should early have alerted me to a problem at the heart of Protestant Christianity. It was not until 1949 at the Montreal Student-in-Industry Work Camp, where someone put R.H. Tawney's Religion and the Rise of Capitalism in my hands, that I awakened to that troubling fact. Of course, I was now familiar with Marx's famous apparent write-off of all religion as the opium of the people, and I was aware that the association of Protestant individualism and free-enterprise capitalism was at the root of a long-term drift of working classes from the churches of Western Christendom. Reading Walter Rauschenbusch's seminal social gospel work, Christianity and the Social Crisis, about the same time, I was persuaded by his argument that the Christian church, over the centuries, had abandoned the religion of Jesus, rooted in the Jewish prophetic tradition. Tawney's thoroughly documented conclusion was persuasive that, historically related though they were, and symbiotic as they would become, Protestantism and capitalism were separate phenomena; neither was the origin of the other. But what of that other earlier classic that Tawney was responding to, Max Weber's The Protestant Ethic and the Spirit of Capitalism? I read it. I was puzzled by Weber's use of the figure of Benjamin Franklin as a prototypical modern capitalist. Soon enough I learned that this was not a historical work but the projection of an "ideal-type" that could be measured against historical reality to test its validity. That was quite intriguing, but for the time being I left it at that. The issue, however, was fundamental. A Protestantism that contributed to the advance of capitalism, or let itself be captivated by it, was not my parents' Protestantism. Weber's famous thesis and the great controversy it ignited was essential background to the rise of the social Christian movement. It was also, and more importantly, from a larger perspective, fundamental to an understanding of the convulsions of the world I had inherited and whose history I was devoted to studying. This chapter covers the controversial first phase in the reception of Weber's thesis. The more discursive phase that followed, 1960 to the present, is the subject of the final chapter in the book.

THE GREAT PROTESTANT ETHIC DEBATE

1

In 1904–05, Max Weber, the brilliant and versatile German sociologist at the University of Heidelberg, published his controversial essay *The Protestant Ethic and the Spirit of Capitalism*. Part of the larger debate on the origins of capitalism, in which the major figure was Karl Marx, Weber's essay was easily interpreted as an alternative hypothesis to the historical materialist account of Marx. Just as Marx has often been crudely simplified by idolaters and detractors, so has Weber. What was intended as a highly particular study of an aspect of the development of capitalism has been looked on as an explanation of the whole phenomenon on a spiritual basis.[1] This and other misunderstandings, even on the part of some of the most notable contributors, have vitiated much of the debate the essay engendered.

Two concerns permeate the work of Max Weber, the emergence of rationalism in Western culture and the triumph of capitalism. Early in his career he became alarmed at the impact of *hochkapitalismus* upon the structure of the German state and society. That capitalism developed so rapidly in Germany in the latter nineteenth century is suggested by Tawney as a reason why this debate over "religion and the rise of capitalism" began where it did, rather than in England where the process was spread over a much longer period.[2] That fact gave Weber's work a contemporary relevance which kept his name circulating in German politics.[3] Furthermore, it contributed to the emphasis he placed upon the nineteenth century as the period of the triumph of capitalism.

The problem Weber addressed in his essay was essentially a simple but fundamental one: What enabled capitalism to dominate Western society? He recognized that capitalism as a systematic pursuit of profit involving a rational organisation of labour had existed in other civilizations and antedated the Reformation in the West. Nowhere, however, owing to the restraints morality and religion placed upon economic gain, had capitalism dominated a whole society. Furthermore, in traditional societies, Weber felt that economic pursuit was rationally attuned to meeting the physical needs of life and/or the station in life accorded by society. How did it happen, not only that traditional restraints gave way so completely in the West, but also that highly systematic and rational means were devoted to the irrational end of unlimited accumulation?

Weber did not discount the role of precious metals from America, the growth of trade, the adoption of Arabic notation or double-entry book-keeping, the secularizing of the state, and other influences in the development of capitalism but felt they were insufficient explanations of the momentous revolution that such a development implied. If these factors were determinative, why did not the influx of precious metals, for instance, bring a triumphant capitalism to Spain and Portugal? Had not trade increased and waned before? Why did Arabic notation and book-keeping not lead to capitalist domination in their place of origin? Such factors were undoubtedly necessary to the development of widespread capitalism, but they provided the occasion and the means rather than the substance or driving force of modern capitalism.

In all societies, Weber observed, religion played a predominant role in the restraint and direction of conduct. This being so, was it not possible that not only the decline of restraints upon the acquisition of wealth, but also the dedicated, almost religious spirit in which the capitalist conducted his enterprise without regard to personal ease and enjoyment had deep religious origins and was developed under religious sanctions? This pervasive attitude of irrational self-denial among the agents of this socio-economic system denoted "the spirit of (modern) capitalism."[4]

The origin of this "spirit of capitalism" was suggested by statistics that appeared to show the predominance of Protestants in business occupations and among skilled workers, and in the tendency of Protestants to seek a utilitarian rather than a classical education for their children.[5] The impression imparted was reinforced by the long history of observations of the coincidence of commercial prosperity and Protestantism in general and Calvinism in particular.

Historically, whatever concessions the Catholic Church may have made to the growing capitalist practice in the fifteenth and sixteenth centuries, that practice had at best been tolerated. Although the attitude of Luther and Calvin was not perceptibly different, they broke down the dualism of Catholic ethics by translating secular occupations into vocations for the service of God. Luther's conservatism, his monastic experience, and his theology prevented the secular vocation from developing the ascetic, perfectionist character in which, under Calvin's auspices, the old monastic discipline entered the daily affairs of others. Not only Calvinism, but Methodism, Pietism, and the Baptist sects evinced this character.

It is important to note that Weber did not attach great significance to the moral teachings of the churches. Similarity in their teachings could lead to great differences in conduct because of the different theological and religious contexts of the various churches. The critical factor, to Weber, was the rigorously logical theological system based on the idea of predestination developed by Calvin, "which provided the underlying power of the Reformed moral awakening." On the one hand, its insistence that salvation depended in no way on merit provided a tremendous assurance that vitalized the Calvinist enterprise of fulfilling God's will that human society should glorify God through obedience. At the same time, a concern about one's election to grace undoubtedly created an anxiety that the Calvinist system, stripped of all sacramental means of grace, could only allay by counselling presumption of election and unceasing labour to the glory of God. An important, further implication of Calvinism was that it completed the process begun by Judaism of driving magic from the world and making it a reliable and purposeful sphere for work and conquest. It accomplished this through the system of predestination and insistence upon a total trust in God alone that not only reduced the meaning of sacraments but even minimized reliance upon friends. Not only was a strong individualism fostered thereby, and a sense of love of neighbour through impersonal community service, but also, another spur was provided for the assuaging of anxieties in work. Such to Weber were the dynamics of the "Protestant Ethic."

Since God's will was served in one's "calling," success in this world could easily be thought a part of God's predestination. Weber is clear that this was a later development after the great struggles of the sixteenth and early seventeenth centuries had ended, and strict dogmatic formulations had lost their centrality (though not their psychological impact).

Weber gives little attention to the historical characteristics of original Calvinism, since he was more interested in the period subsequent to the mid-seventeenth century when the business pursuits of "Calvinists" began to compromise their more explicit teachings about work and wealth, without, however, affecting the psychological dynamics that underlay their activism. Weber relied heavily on Richard Baxter, whose writings were most influential through the latter seventeenth century among various denominations influenced by Puritanism. While Baxter stressed the dangers of wealth, the point, upon further examination, Weber suggested, was the moral objection to relaxation under the security wealth provided: "Even the wealthy shall not eat without working."[6]

In his essay, Weber did not attempt to set forth a historical interpretation of the rise of a Protestant Ethic and its interplay with a new middle class who were to become the bearers of the spirit of capitalism. Rather he sketched some correlations of characteristics (he eschews the word "cause") and concluded with an outline of the extensive program of study required to validate what he had presented as a tentative hypothesis.[7] Before his death in 1920 he had worked out part of the program, a comparative study of the relation of economic life to the great world religions.

Although he was aiming at historical truth, Weber's method was not historical. Having once framed the objective of the investigation and having decided the significant components, his method was to keep each component constant in turn and analyze its relation to all the others. This done, it would presumably be possible to assign each its due weight in an "ideal construct" that could then be tested by historical reality.[8] Historically, the method has the double problem of presuming too much initially and forfeiting the dimension of complex chronological interaction. It has been a source of confusion to critics – and apparently for Weber, who sank briefly into despair over the bleak prospects it offered humanity, as though it were reality itself.[9]

2

The Weber thesis immediately became a subject of controversy, which, despite the observation that it had the sound of the rattling of old bones, remained the most fascinating discussion in economic history in the twentieth century.[10] No doubt this is because of the fundamental nature of the issues it raised regarding the nature of historical knowledge, the role of ideas and religion in history, and the sources and nature of life lived in contemporary culture in the West.

Contributors to the debate are legion, and the survey that follows is based on some fifty items easily available in English. That number could probably be doubled without moving to another language.

The controversy has gone through four stages. In the first place it was subjected to severe criticism by Continental scholars, few of whose works have been translated. Secondly, in the second and third decade of the century, it slowly entered the field of British debate where it received a general acceptance, culminating in R.H. Tawney's brilliant exposition and modification of the thesis in his book *Religion and the Rise of Capitalism* (1926). Tawney initiated the third phase in which the thesis was popularized through numerous expository articles in academic journals. The translation of *The Protestant Ethic and the Spirit of Capitalism* in 1930, and of a major supporting work by Ernst Troeltsch, *The Social Teaching of the Christian Churches* in 1931, assisted in spreading the discussion and providing a firmer base for it. A number of national and denominational studies were undertaken with various results. Three authors, an economic historian, a Catholic economist, and a church historian in major works, and a historical materialist in an article, substantially rejected the thesis. Finally, the fourth period opened with two articles by an economic historian and a sociologist analyzing the controversy thus far, pointing up frequent misinterpretations and the limited nature and purpose of the original essay. Several new contributions were made in this last period. A more temperate and judicious spirit seemed to prevail. If the authors seemed to be engaged in tying up loose ends, that impression may either be sealed or dispelled by late contributions possessed of a new vigour.

3

The first round of the controversy on the Continent seems to have broached most of the objections to which the thesis was to be subjected in more or less detail later. Felix Rachfahl made light of the distinction between capitalism and the spirit of capitalism, played down the significance of ethical-religious motivation, and observed that, among trading cities, Antwerp had always been Catholic and Amsterdam retained Spanish allegiance longest of all Dutch cities. However, he felt, that on balance, Protestantism had a liberating and stimulating effect on economic life, part of the reason for which was the concept of a calling.[11] Lujo Brentano, an economist from a Catholic family that in the eighteenth century had moved its business operation from Italy to Germany, launched a fundamental attack on Weber. He contested the novelty of Reformation teaching about calling, doubted Puritan affinity for business, and argued that their moral teaching was part of the common currency and that, if there was anything that could be called a "spirit of capitalism," it was simply the animating drive for the highest possible profit. The sanctions for the practical affairs of capitalists, he argued, derived from neither Catholic canon law nor Protestant discipline, which were both hostile, but from Roman law and the Stoic concept of the harmony between nature, reason, and the existing order.[12] Werner Sombart, in contrast to the foregoing, defended throughout his extensive writings on the history of capitalism the idea of a spirit of capitalism. He viewed capitalism as a strictly separate culture, much in the same way Spengler viewed civilization.[13] The spirit animated the whole and was expressed through all the parts. Hence his work abounds with suggestive approaches but provides much less system and documentation than the case requires. In contrast to Weber, he suggested that Judaism was the source of the capitalist spirit. This made it possible to account for the emergence of capitalism prior to the Reformation and to lay emphasis on the Reformation's elevation of the Bible with its Old Testament Jewish scriptures, especially the Calvinist use of the same. Sombart seems to have done as much to confuse as to enlighten, for few later writers refer extensively to his works.

Probably the strongest support for Weber came when Ernst Troeltsch, a close associate at Heidelberg, published a two-volume work, *The Social Teaching of the Christian Churches*. This pioneer study of the interaction between Christianity and social life endorsed Weber to the hilt. He stressed the fact that because Calvin had to deal with the practical life of a commercial city, "capitalism was able to steal into the Calvinistic ethic,"[14] though under strict controls. Although Calvinism became bourgeois in time, this was entirely in line with certain elements in its spirit that were bound to become secularized in time. Troeltsch also notes English Christian socialism from the turn of the century as being essentially Calvinist in origin. Thus, he concludes, "in these Christian circles and in them alone, was it possible to combine modern economic activity with Christian thought."[15]

The weakness of Troeltsch's contribution lay in its lack of original research, which was obviously required by Weber's thesis. Rather, Troeltsch relied on the best secondary works in existence. This, and his preference for the Enlightenment as the great modern watershed in Christian history, has left him open to considerable criticism.[16] Nevertheless, he has had a great influence.

One of the severest critics of Troeltsch and Weber was Karl Holl, who until recently has not enjoyed an English translation. Holl was a highly original and scholarly church historian at the University of Berlin. In lectures prior to the First World War, he vigorously contested the conservative interpretation placed on Luther. He also suggested that, for the English Puritan, isolation of the individual and concern for signs of election were the result of the failure to achieve an orderly ecclesiastical constitution in contrast to Calvinists elsewhere.[17] But even there, he noted, Puritan hostility to the taking of interest was equal to that of Continental Calvinists, of whom, he argued with persuasive examples, it could be said that "till the middle of the seventeenth century ... no church has fought capitalism as persistently."[18] Nevertheless, overcome by the barbarism brought on by war and expanding business, the Calvinist's civil virtues produced in extreme cases a kind of business enterprise "which is not unjustifiably called a model of contemporary capitalism."[19] As to the general state of the controversy over Weber's thesis, Holl scored the "vulgar applications that his theories have received from theologians and secular historians ... Thus, everything is happily mixed up." He wished that Weber's replies and qualifications would be universally noted and called for "the examination of particulars."[20]

Thus, the early Continental phase of the debate, if it made both plausible and effective criticism of some of Weber's particulars, seemed to conclude, despite misunderstandings, that there was merit in Weber's thesis. But it should be noted that, in general, the criticisms were documented, whereas the assent was not, and seemed to rely upon general impressions.

4

The second phase of the controversy seems to have begun in Britain with the publication of two expository articles by the Congregationalist theologian P.T. Forsyth, in the *Contemporary Review* in 1910.[21] Three years later, Hermann Levy in *Economic Liberalism* echoed Weber and cited Puritan individualism as one of the components of that movement, which culminated in an unadorned industrial egoism and led both to "the highest industrial success and the most absolute surrender to uneconomic desires."[22] In 1904, William Cunningham, a member of the Anglican clergy and an economic historian of some note, proposed that secularization and the breakup of papal power are critical factors in the triumph of capitalism. Calvinism was not at all mentioned.[23] However, ten years later, in his work *Christianity and Economic Science*, Cunningham espoused the thesis advanced by Weber and Troeltsch. Although interested chiefly in economic theory, he devoted some pages to an application of Weber to Scotland – an omission for which Weber had often been scored. Cunningham's undocumented conclusions were positive, even though internally unconvincing.[24] Another economic historian, W. Ashley, writing at the turn of the century, editions of whose work continued to be published until 1922, and whose concern was not with the modern period, found the different attitudes of Luther and Calvin to usury an adequate explanation of the economic differences between their followers. He did not credit religious influences with great significance in the development of capitalism, however.

The most extensive discussion of the issue in Britain prior to R.H. Tawney was that of George O'Brien in 1923. O'Brien, although he subscribed to Weber's general thesis, indulged so liberally in a Catholic-bias as to make his work useful principally for exhibiting that tendency. Protestantism, the worst of heresies, provided the spiritual force for both the emergence of capitalism and socialism.[25]

R.H. Tawney, an Anglican economic historian with Labour sympathies, in 1926 published what in most respects has been the most brilliant contributions to the controversy. He has been described, on the one hand, as providing a Marxian interpretation in which religious attitudes were the victim of economic forces[26] and on the other as concluding that Calvinism was the decisive factor in the triumph of the capitalist spirit.[27] Perhaps more a study of economic thought than of economic action, his study, *Religion and the Rise of Capitalism*,[28] is nevertheless based on extensive knowledge of the economic practice of the time. Although his interpretation of the "capitalist spirit" is broader than that of Weber – "the temper which is prepared to sacrifice all moral scruples for profit"[29] – the scope of his investigation is somewhat narrower, confined primarily to the English case, but perhaps the more definitive, given the significance of the industrial revolution in England.

Weber would agree that the capitalist spirit, as defined by Tawney, was "only too familiar to the saints and sages of Middle Ages,"[30] whose economic attitudes he outlined in his first chapter. Tawney examined with care the critical phase that Weber observed, but whose problems he bypassed: the long period of a century and a half in which Calvinism gradually became sufficiently moderated to be noticeably hospitable to capitalist practice. Like the established church in the sixteenth century, the Puritans in the seventeenth century tried to hold the line against the advance of capitalism with conservative teaching. Even from the influential Richard Baxter a more prudential note began to sound, and in the expansive days of the Restoration the circumstances of economic opportunity drew out the individualistic, methodical, and ascetic spirit embedded in Calvinism. A new "identification of labour and enterprise with the service of God" thereby nourished "the magnificent energy which changed in a century the face of material civilization."[31] Thus, although at times Tawney slightly misinterpreted and oversimplified Weber, his dialectical interpretation of the Protestant ethic and the spirit of capitalism amounted to the same thing in the end. Granted it was not the ethic but the progressively secularized character of English Puritanism that entered the typical alloy of the modern capitalist mind, and in a sociological if not a doctrinal sense, that was of Calvinist making.

The later transformation of the Puritan mind in England, however, is not documented other than through a few pamphlets of the early eighteenth century. Tawney thus leaves us still asking what evidence there is for assuming a high correlation between Puritans in particular or Protestants in general and business occupations, or for assuming they were relatively prominent among the successful entrepreneurs of the age.

5

The years 1926–30 were ones in which the Weber thesis became more widely disseminated in preparation for the third – and most fruitful – phase of the debate in the 1930s. Weber's *General Economic History* was published in English in 1927, containing in its last chapter a brief summary of the relevant findings of his studies in the world religions.[32] The revised original essay was translated by Talcott Parsons, an American sociologist, and published in 1930. As we have noted, Troeltsch's major work was translated the next year. Kemper Fullerton, an American Old Testament scholar well known in German theological circles, published an article faithfully interpreting Weber in the 1928 volume of the *Harvard Theological Review*. He sealed his assent to the thesis by observing that "after all, however blind economists may be to the fact, metaphysical convictions are the only ones which have the power absolutely to dominate men's lives."[33] In 1928 and 1929, Talcott Parsons contributed articles on Sombart and Weber to the *Journal of Political Economy*[34] about the same time as F.H. Knight surveyed the chief figures in the debate to date in the *Journal of Economics and Business History*.[35] While Parsons' articles were simply interpretive, Knight's were frankly sympathetic to Weber and Sombart. Earl J. Hamilton of Duke University, writing on "American Treasure and the Rise of Capitalism," however, was not convinced.[36]

A process similar to that in America must have been proceeding in other countries as well, for in the 1930s several national and denominational studies were undertaken and a number of more general works written. E. Bein in 1931 published a study of the economic views of the Dutch Reformed Church between 1565 and 1650 in which he failed to find any support for Weber's thesis.[37] His dates may be somewhat early for significant results. Without attempting any proof, a fellow compatriot, W.F. Van Gunsteren, expounded Weber's ideas in a general way in a work in 1934.[38] In 1933 Amintore Fanfani published his dissertation on *The Origins of the Capitalist Spirit in Italy*, in which, in judging from his later book, he found little or no trace of religious influence.[39] Scandinavian studies came somewhat later, in 1940 and 1947. W. Clemmenson, in the former year, published a study of the Weber thesis as it applied to Denmark. Although he apparently studied only religious literature, he rendered a positive verdict for Weber on the basis of the failure of the Lutheran State Church or the

Pietist movement, not being Calvinist, to encourage the development of the capitalist spirit.[40] A rather more adequate piece of research was conducted by Christen T. Jonassen in Norway, where a Methodist type of revival made an extensive impact between 1796 and 1824. Not only did the revival create the type of worldly ascetic attitudes Weber described, but its leader, Hans Nielsen Hauge, founded a number of businesses in what was still a pre-capitalist economy. Population pressure on the land stimulated alternative business pursuits and by mid-century a capitalist economy was growing, much of whose spirit was provided by "Haugians." Unfortunately, no population analyses or case studies support the last step in Jonassen's argument and the case must be held open.[41]

In the realm of denominational studies, Georgia Harkness, in her study of John Calvin in 1931, devoted considerable space to Weber's thesis, which she clearly understood. She suspected that Weber had never seriously studied Calvin, pointing out that the distinction between the Lutheran and Calvinist interpretations of "calling" was not justified. She suggested that a "good work" did not necessarily apply to industry or business, nor did "worldly asceticism" necessarily bring economic efficiency in its train. However, with the balance of the thesis she concurred.[42] R.N. Carew Hunt two years later in England accepted a similar view.[43] W.J. Warner in a study of British Methodism lent strong support to Weber in his portrayal of the evolution of Wesleyan economic ideals and practice.[44] What is never said in the book is that the Wesleyans were only one part, granted the largest, of the Methodism.

Isabel Grubb, however, in a study of *Quakerism and Industry Before 1800* (1930) discounted the suggestion that Quakers exhibited special competence in business matters. She could find no evidence that business success was fostered by religion, but some to the contrary.[45]

In 1929, H. Richard Niebuhr, American Protestant theologian and noted church historian, published *The Social Sources of Denominationalism*, in which the influence of both Weber and Troeltsch was evident. Although the volume did not purport to apply the Weber thesis as such, Niebuhr commented that the thesis was "one of the most enlightening contributions made to church history by sociologists and economists ... Despite overstatements it is not possible to disagree with their fundamental contention."[46] However, further examination of American Christianity led him to disagree that the Protestant ethic ever became identical with the spirit of capitalism. In a book that surveyed the idea of the Kingdom of God in its various expressions as the American equivalent of the Vision of God of Medieval Christianity, he wrote that "the failure to organize economic life [according to Christian principles] was not due to hypocrisy but rather to the fact that the capitalism of the seventeenth and early eighteenth centuries was a relatively modest and harmless thing whose growth toward an absolutism like that which church and the state had exercised could not be foreseen."[47] "The faith in the kingdom did not demand that an unconverted humanity's lust for power and gain be liberated, but rather that it be brought into willing subjection to the rule of God. Atheism of the practical sort found in Deism needed to intervene before this idea could be confounded with economic liberalism."[48] Niebuhr concluded that "the spirit of capitalism and the spirit of Protestantism remain two wholly different things."[49]

These various denominational and national studies, with the exception of Warner, suggest that Weber's thesis may be plausible (Harkness), but that denominational studies alone do not support it and suggest a continuing Protestant tradition existing over against the capitalist spirit. An indirect relation through psychological attitudes carried within the stream of economic action via apostasy, however, remains possible and is not opposed to Weber's essential position.

That conclusion is what is demonstrated in the remaining major studies of this third period. Amintore Fanfani, a Catholic political economist, strongly opposed to capitalism and a premier of Italy (1962), published a keenly analytical work in 1934, *Catholicism, Protestantism and Capitalism*, which was translated into English the next year.[50] He dealt with the perennial problem of whether the spirit of capitalism could be divorced from any capitalist enterprise by stating that it was "spirit" in the sense of a dominant social attitude with which the discussion was concerned. That was clearly a post-Reformation development. However, neither the ethics nor the idea of "vocation" or "calling" in Reform theology could be held responsible, being essentially extensions of Catholic background. Rather, the growth of trade and increasing mobility through the fifteenth to seventeenth centuries, typically of such eras, loosened social ties and the restraints of faith. Protestantism's contribution to that and the freedom implicit in its doctrinal separation of nature and grace were its only (minor) positive influences in the rise of capitalism. The spirit of capitalism was not a consequence of new Reformation theology but of the decline of faith.

H.M. Robertson, in the lead book of the Cambridge series on economic history, *Aspects of the Rise of Economic Individualism* (1933), was highly critical of "Max Weber and his school," whom he accused of attempting a psychological determinism. He tried to show, agreeing with Fanfani, that there was little novelty in Calvin's doctrine of calling. He suggested that the spirit of acquisition was sufficient motivation for advancing capitalist practice and argued at length that Jesuit casuistry was much more lenient with such a spirit than Calvinism. If capitalists needed rationalization they would be able to find it in the pagan concepts of natural law. For encouragement, they could turn to the secular state. The formation of this rational spirit depended upon the development of secular science – in fact, Robertson argued, it would be very easy to substitute systematic bookkeeping for the Protestant ethic as the origin of the capitalist spirit. Robertson's work is a frank attempt to show that the spirit of capitalism arose "rather from the material conditions of civilization than from religious impulse."[51] Calvin's rationalism is allowed some small part, but any effective contribution to capitalist development required accommodation to its secular spirit.

J. Broderick of the Society of Jesus effectively showed that Robertson was at two or three removes from most of his sources on Catholic teaching, that his incriminating evidence regarding Jesuit practice came from Jansenist sources unchecked against other evidence, and that he had not read his sources widely enough to secure a balanced view. Broderick was most particular in citing cases and developing them.[52] His criticism of Robertson was continued by Talcott Parsons, who commented that Robertson's attack missed the point. It dwelt on the official teaching and discipline of the churches and said nothing whatsoever of the character they produced, nor of Weber's central concern as to the origins of the "disinterested ethical discipline in modern economic life." Weber was not proposing a search for the origins of capitalism by confining the inquiry to the works of several Calvinist divines, Parsons urged, but rather an examination of ascetic Protestantism to discover whether it was the source of a particular and important trait of modern capitalism.[53]

Supporting Robertson, however, and drawing on further Continental research, Albert Hyma, in a rather contentious work, *Christianity, Capitalism and Communism* (1937), maintained that Calvinism resisted the erosions of capitalism later than most acknowledged. He also observed that capitalism declined subsequent to the entry of Calvinism into Hungary, and like others, he accused Weber of reading into Continental developments from British evidence. He, too, however, relied too heavily upon official church writings. Although in his support of Robertson he was susceptible to the same misconception of Weber's purpose, Hyma added considerably to information about the situation in the Netherlands where the Calvinist tradition was strong.[54]

Closing the third phase of the controversy was a critique of Weber from another point of view. Gordon Walker, in an article entitled "Capitalism and the Reformation," pushed Robertson's materialistic explanation one step further in explaining the Reformation. The Price Revolution that coincided with the Reformation and dramatically affected the circumstances of the commercial classes called forth the peculiar Calvinist doctrines, which, once in existence, "played an important indispensable part in the triumph of European Capitalism."[55]

Thus, if the Weber thesis ended its second phase riding high on the crest of R.H. Tawney's brilliant efforts, it encountered heavy seas in the 1930s. Several able and a few exceptional works resulted from the debate. Most, apparently unable to find either appropriate sources and/or methodologies to cope with the subtlety of Weber's thesis, reinterpreted it in some way in order to answer it. In the process, Weber largely escaped.

6

The fourth and latest phase of the Weber controversy opened auspiciously for Weber but closed with the most systematic and devastating attack to date. F.L. Nussbaum in a historiographical article, "The Economic History of Renaissance Europe" (1941), declared that the thesis "remains the most interesting single question in the field of economic history"[56] and suggested three steps to clarify the discussion: first, it would be recognized that religion is not merely the utterances of priests and preachers and that Calvinism is not merely the taking of interest; second, religion and economic life should be envisaged as two among several factors in European cultural life necessarily integrated with the whole and each other, and not two separate entities operating on each other externally; and third, it should be realized that in every present there is future and past implicit.[57] Ephraim Fischoff, an American sociologist, attempted to clarify the debate in *Social Research* in 1944, much in the manner of Talcott Parsons above, but seemed to put the discussion beyond the competence of historians by defining the purpose not as a search for a causal influence exerted by Calvinism on the evolution of capitalism but for the "genesis of a psychological habit which enabled men to meet the requirements of early modern capitalism."[58]

Despite Nussbaum's advice, Benjamin Nelson wrote an extensive work, *The Idea of Usury*, tracing through usurious practice the breakdown of the traditional ethical dualism between tribal brothers and strangers.[59] Useful in many respects, especially bibliographically, the central role Nelson gave to Calvin seems misconceived.[60] Irwin G. Wyllie, in a study of nineteenth century American clergy as eulogizers of capitalism, concluded that Weber should have pressed the Protestant origins of the capitalist spirit further forward in time. Injecting a note from the recent developments in the history of science, W. Stark concurred with Weber's main thesis and proposed its application to the emergence of a rational scientific worldview.[61]

On another front, Milton Yinger, in *Religion and the Struggle for Power* (1946), accepted Weber's thesis in general and added some refinements to account for the evolution from early "pure" to late "corrupted" Calvinism by applying Weber's own notion of the sect to church process in religious movements.[62] His argument had a Marxist flavour as well, when he argued that the commercial and industrial classes would have found a religious sponsor in any event but allowed that, without Calvinism, capitalism would have developed along somewhat different lines.

American Protestant church historians were much less favourable to Weber's thesis in the 1950s than the foregoing or than their predecessors in the 1930s. Harold J. Grimm saw Calvinism long acting as a brake upon capitalist development.[63] Roland Bainton dismissed many of Weber's key arguments as exaggerations and maintained that the only demonstrable connection was the impetus that Calvinists gave to any form of activity in which they engaged.[64] Winthrop S. Hudson, in an article in 1949, showed the extent of Weber's and Tawney's misinterpretation of Richard Baxter but acknowledged that post-Restoration Puritanism quickly declined into something that did violence to the whole Puritan intellectual system.[65] John T. McNeill, in an excellent study, *The History and Character of Calvinism* (1954), adduced evidence to show that characteristics attributed to Puritans were common to all churches in the early eighteenth century.[66]

In a second article, Hudson in 1961 made a very simple but effective point. He observed that Weber's central assumption that capitalism was essentially irrational and counter to natural human instincts posed a false problem. This misreading of the human situation had been accepted by Troeltsch and Tawney and never explicitly attacked by opponents. A Biblical perspective on human nature would have expressed quite a different view, with its illustrations of the perennial ingenuity of humanity's endeavour to hide the nakedness of self-interest behind a cloak of religious pretension. It might be that Calvinism, strong in the towns, was more exposed to the attrition this entailed.[67] Leo Strauss, an eminent conservative American political theorist, in a comment accompanying the Hudson article, noted the influence of Nietszhe in the assumption of the "profound remoteness" of the capitalist spirit from all natural instincts, even from what we may call the natural vice of avarice. Looking for an irrational source, Weber overlooked the fact that the capitalist enterprise throughout was justified by reference to the common good. This association, he suggested, may more appropriately be traced to the Renaissance line of thought that leads from Machiavelli to Bacon, Hobbes, and other English compatriots who exerted an influence on later Puritanism. Weber had rejected this train of thought because he thought the Renaissance purely an attempt to restore classical antiquity. For Strauss, Fanfani, and Hudson, the "waning of faith" was a necessary condition for the emergence of the capitalist spirit, but it was not a sufficient condition. "The sufficient condition is the attempt at a new understanding of social reality – an understanding which is 'realistic' in the sense that it conceives of the social order as based not on piety and virtue but on socially useful passions and vices."[68]

7

By the time this fourth phase of the controversy was reaching its close, the most important question looming through the debate was: What, after all, was the evidence upon which the Weber thesis rested? Some damaging evidence had been brought against it, but often within the frame of alternative theses equally questionable, associated with misinterpretation of Weber, and presented by authors who took the position that the thesis might well be sound though outside the field of their special competence. On the other hand, most of its supporters had either reiterated the thesis or, like Tawney, subtly assumed it at crucial points in their argument. Kurt Samuelsson, a Swedish economic historian, decisively placed the controversy on a new basis by asking: "Did such a clear correlation exist between Protestantism and economic progress that there is any reason to inquire into cause and effect at all?"[69] In the most careful and closely argued book in the debate, *Religion and Economic Action*, Samuelsson carefully examined the different types of evidence used by Weber and rejected the thesis that any of them necessarily or particularly related Protestantism in general or Calvinism in particular with the rise of modern capitalism. In capitalist ideology, mercantilism, the Enlightenment, and Darwinism were most prominent. Mercantilism spread the "middle class virtues" through whole populations. Emancipation from Rome was largely independent of religious codes. Protestant and Catholic both long fought for low interest rates, which, after all the debate, may have been more significant for capitalist expansion than high ones. The figures Weber used for the economic propensities of Protestants and Catholics demonstrably implied quite other conclusions than his. Furthermore, no adequate correlation could be made between Protestantism and national prosperity as Weber argued.

In the face of Samuelsson's keen demonstration of the inadequacy of the foundations of the Weber thesis, the fascinating mystery in its central proposition, that "Calvinism with all its renunciation of personal gain, is so tremendously practical" in the multiplication of wealth, disappears. The valid observation based on the continuity of culture that Protestantism has had an influence upon modern economic life does not mean that that influence was significantly different from that of Christianity in general. Future proponents [post 1960] of the Weber thesis must contend with the latest positions dug by Hudson, Strauss, and Samuelsson – which, in effect, means that they must begin again at the beginning with new evidence or not at all. Whether that would be the case is the subject of the final chapter of this book.

CHAPTER FOUR

The Origins of Totalitarianism:
More than a Problem of Interpretation

BACKGROUNDER

The word "totalitarianism," as best I can recall, first swam into my ken in 1945. The Second World War was ending. With the Co-operative Commonwealth Federation (CCF) party gaining on the ruling Liberals, a federal election had been called and a bitter propaganda campaign was being waged against the socialist menace. A centrepiece of the campaign was Friedrich Hayek's The Road to Serfdom, *which would become the Bible of the neo-liberalism of the Cold War and after. With fascism all but routed, communist totalitarianism was now being widely bruited to be the great danger of the hour to liberal democratic rights and institutions. Private property in capital, Hayek argued, provided an essential defence, as much for the propertyless as for the propertied. Indeed, Hayek declared, any limitation, or regulation, of private property in capital was dangerous. To strive for an "unachievable utopia," even in its gradualist versions, was to establish institutions and practices that would make it easy for power-hungry totalitarians to accomplish their evil ends. Hayek's* Road to Serfdom *would become the foundation work of a growing neo-liberal movement. My father, then campaign manager for the CCF candidate in the Fraser Valley riding, took to the platform at a large rally in Chilliwack to refute Hayek's argument. Hayek's urgent campaign to revert post-war to laissez-faire capitalism was the real danger before Canadians, not totalitarian communism. As the CCF candidate in our high school mock elections, I read the book and totalitarianism was now part of my political lexicon. Five years later, like everyone else, I was reading George Orwell's* Nineteen Eighty-Four *and* Animal Farm. *Arthur Koestler's* Darkness at Noon *followed and* The God That Failed. *I read Edmund Wilson's* To the Finland Station, *Sydney Hook on Lenin in* The Hero in History, *and Bertram Wolfe's* Three Who Made a Revolution.

Enrolled in the doctoral program at Duke University in 1961, I returned to the totalitarian question in courses on modern Russia with John Curtis and in political theory with John H. Hallowell. Hallowell's first book, The Decline of Liberalism as an Ideology *(1948), was an inquiry into why totalitarian politics triumphed so easily in Germany in the 1930s. Hallowell documented the fatal erosion of public commitment to the liberal institutions of civil consent in the Weimar Republic. After the war, the intellectual world in the West devoted an enormous amount of time and energy to the attempt to understand the origins and nature of the totalitarian phenomenon. It was for Hallowell that I wrote the following essay.*

THE ORIGINS OF TOTALITARIANISM

Totalitarianism is the spectre that haunts the twentieth century. The events to which the word points are seared in memory. A few have struggled to encompass the phenomenon as a whole and lay its meaning clearly before us. Those who have made such attempts have written with a sense of urgency and warn us that, far from being immune, all nations are afflicted to some degree with the conditions of mind and body politic from which totalitarianism has sprung. The very word "totalitarianism" both suggests much of the meaning of this spectre and points to the methodology required to investigate and elucidate its full meaning. Theologians, philosophers, historians, political scientists, economists, sociologists, psychologists – what science has not attempted to come to grips with the totalitarian phenomena? Yet there seems to have been no extended interdisciplinary study undertaken. Paul Lehman, at a symposium that revealed the division of opinion on the subject engendered by specialization, pointed to the need for "a new sense of cultural community" to confront "the prolonged shadow of totalitarianism" and suggested an effort at a "symbolic interrelation of theological and non-theological images in a 'developmental construct' of totalitarianism."[1] Eric Voegelin, in a searching review of Hannah Arendt's *The Origins of Totalitarianism*, has made much of the same plea in pointing to the need of a well-developed philosophical anthropology to categorize the political phenomenon[2] properly. Such approaches are fraught with problems. Quite apart from the difficulty of communication across academic lines, and the issue of what view of humanity is most adequate to the task, there would be many radical inductionists who would hardly concede the appropriateness of the methodology.

To say the foregoing is not to say that individual studies to date are unhelpful. The different viewpoints and methods have been instructive and give rise to questions such as the following: Can one single feature be established as the mark of totalitarianism? Or must description fall back upon a "syndrome" approach? Is totalitarianism unique, or is it another form of a historically recognizable polity? Is totalitarianism a secular religion? What is the role of ideology and terror in the totalitarian state? Is there any particular personality pattern or economic structure essential to totalitarianism? Are there inherently disintegrating features in the totalitarian system? The list could go on; the answers vary.

Among the notable contributors to the discussion are those who see the key to the political phenomenon in the psychology of the individuals concerned, emphasizing the elements of self-alienation and authoritarianism.[3] Some, like Hermann Rauschning, have seized upon the nihilistic dynamism of the Nazi movement as the clue to its meaning. Others, like Drucker and Kahler, see, not unhopefully, the end of an era and the turmoil and uncertainty of a transition period. Ernst Cassirer views totalitarianism as a regression from the tradition of Western rationalism into forms of mythical thinking, prepared during the nineteenth century but called forth by the extreme crisis of the First World War and its aftermath. On the other hand, William Barrett would credit the furies of totalitarianism to the dissolution of traditional Western values by the abstractions of rationalism. J.L. Talmon concerns himself with left-totalitarianism, stressing its common Enlightenment origins in the pragmatic liberal creed and selecting the Babeuvist "conspiracy of equals" as the beginning of a continuous movement seeking the embodiment of an exclusive perfectionist creed in the political order. Talmon's is a religious history in the broad sense that "the concrete elements of history, the acts of politicians, the aspirations of people, the ideas, values, preferences and prejudices of an age are the outward manifestation of its religion."[4]

Like Talmon, Hannah Arendt begins her analysis in the eighteenth century. However, she is less concerned with intellectual history and groups Bolshevism and Nazism together, tracing their emergence in European society after a century and one-half of anti-Semitism and fifty years of imperialism that had alienated, vulgarized, and pulverized all major segments of the population. She can find nothing in Western philosophical tradition that can bring meaning out of the totalitarian phenomenon. It is a "radical evil" that "breaks down all the standards we know" and that has "emerged in connection with a system in which all men have become equally superfluous."[5]

Eric Voegelin, using a different principle of order than simply those facts and events that the historical stream throws up (a criticism of Arendt), portrays the totalitarian outburst as the climax of a long secular trend beginning with the immanentist sectarians of the medieval world. Talmon saw some foreshadowing of totalitarian democracy in these groups but felt there was no continuity into modern Europe. Arendt dismisses the hypothesis, seeing no signs of totalitarianism in them at all, and implies that it is an attempt to explain the new and distinct "through drawing some analogies or reducing it to a previously known chain of causes and influences."[6] Voegelin, however, does not say these sectarians are totalitarian but that the major modern political movements had their inception in and received their dynamic from the immanentist placement of the kingdom of the spirit within the unfolding process of history. This directed the energies of humankind into "civilizational activity" as a "mystical work of self-salvation," a work bound sooner or later to collide with the realities of existence and reveal its inner bankruptcy. This collision occurs in totalitarianism, defined as the existential rule of Gnostic activists."[7]

Taken together, this group of viewpoints on the meaning of totalitarianism clearly raises the many problems involved in discerning the meaning of historical events, particularly those of the scope of the totalitarian phenomena of our time.

To illustrate the problem more specifically: Hannah Arendt makes the sound observation that the coincidence of the threats to both authority and freedom in the twentieth century suggests that freedom and authority are so intimately interconnected that the validity and understanding of the one is compromised once the validity of the other has been lost. She states that a genuine experience of authority is almost impossible in the modern world. Rather than draw the clear conclusions, she sidesteps into the view that authority not only linked but chained human beings to the past. As discussed, "It could be that only now the past will open up to us with unexpected freshness," and although the loss of authority has created "a Protean universe where everything at any moment can become almost anything else," this "does not entail, at least not necessarily, the loss of the human capacity for building, preserving and caring for a world that can survive us and remain a place fit to live in for those who come after us."[8] Is authority then not requisite to freedom after all? And does the loss of our respect for the works of our parents not undermine our faith that our children will nevertheless respect ours? Such an anomalous conclusion suggests that, for Arendt, meaning is more than the sum total of her profound insights, and that faith in the inherent meaning of events has clouded (brightened?) her conclusions. We can hardly credit her with candour when, contrasting her methods to that of Voegelin, she says: "I proceed from facts and events [whereas he proceeds from] intellectual affinities and influences."[9]

Erich Kahler is perhaps more consistent in indulging in the same wish to see history working creatively in the phenomenon of totalitarianism: "the historical function of national socialism is to make a clean sweep ... unmasking all the rotting institutions, slogans, pretenses of modern times," and by its defeat to open the way for a "new, common and humane order."[10] He concludes his chapter on National Socialism, "Nihilism and the Rule of Technics," with the words, "This is the world in which we live." Yet these are also the "conditions which man has produced," the "creation," not the creator, from which an individual's directives come now that he/she has "come of age." This is possible for Kahler to say because he believes that "in today's technological situation is hidden the same human significance that was revealed in the word of God, only that today the idea is no longer separate from matter ... and so, it may have the prospect of materializing."

Not Kahler's idea of the new humanism but "the course of events [will bring people] to see that without human community and fraternity they are all lost together."[11] But if, as Kahler suggests, the premises of national socialism are given in all countries and in all movements, why would not humanity react in a global totalitarian state as Ernst Juenger's German young people did with their "high organisational capacity and complete color-blindness toward values, faith without content, and discipline without justification"?[12] There would seem to be no historical reason other than that "destructions are followed by reconstructions, and mass killings by high birthrates."[13] But on this basis, the implied meaning of history is that of cyclical recurrence and suggests a return to the wisdom of the ancients that there is nothing new under the sun, advice which Kahler's vision of humankind hardly reflects.

Although in the first edition of her book Hannah Arendt remarked on the possibility that the failings of totalitarianism may have been due to the lack of global dimensions to the experiment, she also faced the real possibility "that one fine day a highly organized and mechanized humanity will conclude quite democratically ... that for humanity as a whole it would be better to liquidate certain parts thereof." Her response is to point to Plato's dictum: "Not man, but a god, must be the measure of all things."[14]

To make such an observation is to be close to the Christian faith that the fulfillment of history is in the hands of God, who has given the measure of humanity in Jesus Christ. Karl Löwith has traced the gradual disappearance of this faith in the historiography of Western civilization. It is surely more than coincidence that following the reduction of history to bare continuity in Burkhardt, there should appear in human history the first consistent political experiment in the total malleability of humanity – and hence of history.

The problem of the meaning of totalitarianism, then, presents at the same time the problem of the meaning of history. The order ascribed to it is commensurate with the order of truth that is brought to it. It is indeed difficult, as Voegelin has reminded us, to categorize phenomena of spiritual disintegration without a theory of the spirit, or to cope with major political crises in history without taking political principles to the point where they meet with the philosophy of history.[15]

The phenomena of totalitarianism exist as a control upon the theory that would account for it. At the same time, as the problem of politics is that of the order of society, which, perhaps only semi-consciously to its artisans, represents some order of truth, it should be possible to infer something of that truth from the system itself.

Among the phenomena of totalitarianism is the "totalitarian dictator." Friedrich and Brzezinski, in their study of this feature of totalitarianism, concluded that the office is in possession of more nearly absolute power than any other previous leader and that the totalitarian dictator fits none of the traditional categories of leadership. They suggest that this individual is a compound of mystical identification of the leader and the led, buttressed, even created, by propaganda, terror, and organizational manipulation.[16] The will of the leader in effect becomes the constitution. At least in Hitler's case, he accepted responsibility for all the acts of his followers, thus depriving them of the necessity of being accountable for their actions and identifying himself as the source of all action. Although the inner councils were not taken in by the propaganda directed at members of the party and the population at large that he was infallible, yet his persona was essential to the whole machinery. Although some have questioned the efficiency of this kind of leadership,[17] Hannah Arendt points to the suicidal loyalty it engendered, which held the lines of command together in Germany to the end of the war in 1945. Stalin did not assume this kind of position until he withdrew into inscrutable mystery as the "leader with faith in the people" in the 1930s.[18]

The character of the totalitarian movement (and progressively of totalitarian society as a result) is that of a secret society with its elaborate ritual and its successive layers – sympathizers or fellow-travellers, general membership, the elite, and the inner council. Each layer obscured for the layer outside it the true character of the core and kept the one inside it from coming too severely into contact with the world outside it. This device blunts the edge of the totalitarian claim that the world is divided into two gigantic hostile blocs: "Protected against the reality of the non-totalitarian world, (members) constantly under-estimate the tremendous risks of totalitarian politics."[19]

The structure of the totalitarian state, however, is far from monolithic. Stephen H. Roberts, in *The House that Hitler Built*, observed that "even an expert would be driven mad if he tried to unravel the relationships between Party and State."[20] Prior to taking power the Nazi party had a parallel organization to that of the state. In power, Hitler duplicated and triplicated not only the offices in the administration concerned with identical or similar functions but also the various organizations for each profession. This apparent extravagance made possible a high degree of secretive preparation of alternative courses of action and hence sudden shifts from one policy to another. At the same time it made both espionage and sabotage difficult in the extreme. Demotions could be made in the guise of promotions. The "structure" further reflected the conspiratorial mentality in which an enemy could turn up anywhere. It was well to be prepared with alternative offices, personnel, and policies. This kind of structure is, in effect, that of the Soviet Union as well, with its three separate organizations – the state, the party, and the NKVD, each with its department of economy, political department, ministry of education, and so on.[21]

The prominence of the secret police and the use of terror accompany such regimes as an inevitable corollary. To the dismay of early sympathizers, the use of such means increased as internal opposition diminished. Given the premises that there is a decaying, hostile world infecting, subverting the bringers of the new order, any major problems were the work of "objective enemies" who had to exist by definition. Those who were, "in principle," enemies of Hitler tended to fall into biological classifications of race and health, and those of Stalin into ideological or class character. In practice, anyone could become the target. Some observers suggest that periodic uses of terror are necessary to the totalitarian system to keep the population fragmented and suspicious of others.[22]

Two marks characterize the totalitarian economy: its total planning and its disregard of strictly economic objectives. Although the old capitalist order seemed to remain intact in Germany, in fact, private profit had lost its autonomy as a goal of economic activity and was diverted from the non-managing partners to the state.[23] Ideological considerations replaced

the economic ones in both Nazi Germany and Soviet Russia: full employment, conspicuous consumption of certain kinds for the lower classes, the
German *wehrwirtschaft*, production medals, division of workers by piece-
work, and the Stakhanovite system, elimination of minorities that were
not economically useful, and so on.[24] Communist and National Socialist
policies differed chiefly because of two factors: first, the former had to
develop, whereas the latter inherited, an advanced industrial system, and
second, economic centralization is a much more basic part of the Communist than the Nazi ideology. Nevertheless, both were marked by non-
utilitarian approaches to economic life. To both Hitler and Stalin, their
primary resources were the elites or cadres of the party.[25] As to material
resources, the eventual triumph of the totalitarian system would bring the
resources of the world to their doorstep.[26]

In the realm of law, the Nazi government left the Weimar constitution
intact, and in 1936, Stalin had the constitution of the USSR drawn up. It
was clear within a short time that, in usual constitutional terms, neither
meant very much. The Führer's will virtually became the constitution
(even the military did not dare question Hitler on military matters, according to Rauschning), and within two years, Stalin had liquidated all those
who had composed the constitution. The attitude this reflected was not
merely expediency but a view of law as that which a society realizes at any
given time. The fundamental concept is that of society immanently realizing justice in fulfilling the historical or natural law of its development. No
tension between justice and law is possible. No constitution is possible,
which is not dated the day after it is signed. Stalin explicitly believed this,[27]
and Hitler certainly behaved as though he did. In fact, Hitler was even able
on this basis to see validity in regulations not made public: "the total state
must not know any difference between law and ethics."[28]

The question of totalitarian law brings us inescapably to that of ideology. Undoubtedly this is the critical element in precipitating many of the
foregoing elements of totalitarianism. Most observers point chiefly to the
negative character of the totalitarian creed – particularly in its fascist and
national socialist forms, with their total rejection of the past. However,
creed and ideology are not quite identical. The latter's primary quality, as
Arendt so clearly points out, is its element of logic, which, in its compul-
sive force, ends up devouring the interest the idea was meant to serve.[29]
For its followers, it takes on the quality Cassirer ascribes to myth, that of
binding the emotions and the mind even as it "frees" them.[30] It is perhaps
significant that after a certain point, Marx's thinking can be characterized
as mythical, in that it projects upon an outer world the ethical conflicts of

the self.[31] In any case, the fictitious world of ideology when brought to bear upon the political life of the real world runs into "formidable obstacles. The series of critical situations thus created give rise to the swift enlargement of power and the totalitarian radicalization of the means of control; in the course of this process, the totalitarian dictatorship comes into being.[32] The tension between the ideology and reality sets in motion what has been called the "permanent revolution" of totalitarianism. On the one hand, the fictitious world must be established as a tangible workaday world in a limited area, and on the other, must be prevented from becoming normalized as one order among others, thus compromising the global and totalitarian aims.

The social and historical context in which the totalitarian phenomenon appeared is too complex and problematic for any extensive discussion in this paper. No amount of detailing of circumstance, however, should be allowed to override the fact that totalitarianism was not inevitable, that it was a choice made by human beings. On the other hand, no single individual and perhaps no single generation may be held entirely responsible. When we describe circumstances, we are falling back on the choices of others, re-enacting the Genesis story, paraphrasing Adam: "She gave me to eat." The context does not explain fully or give the significance of an event. The necessity of context to the understanding of an event is due to it being part of it.

Undoubtedly the critical conditions following the First World War had a great deal to do with the emergence of totalitarianism. The folly of unconditional surrender, impossible peace terms, the inability of capitalist organization of the economy to cope with mass production and distribution, unemployment in most sectors of the population, inflation undermining savings – these and other major problems created countless personal crises that reduced people to desperation. One might add Peter Drucker's observation that the failure of communism placed the last straw on the idea of economic individuals, but although this added to the crisis for many, the failure of communism was marked by the emergence of totalitarian characteristics in its regime.[33] The observation then begs the question, as does the whole "post-war crisis thesis." Was Western culture so rotten that in a dozen years the structure came tumbling down? Any answer must look in totalitarianism, not only for signs of breakdown, but also for evidence of the culmination of certain forces within the civilizational development.

The obvious moral deterioration of the gentile population, marked by the horrific slaughter of the Jews in the Third Reich, has often obscured their own significant involvement in the emergence of the modern state, their equivocal role as pariah and parvenu, their own inner deterioration as a community, and the degree to which they themselves fostered elements of the racial myth, none of which can lend justification for the Holocaust that followed. The apparent collectivism of totalitarianism is usually looked upon as the breakdown of individualism, whereas perhaps more than anything else it is the culmination of individualism in a mass of individuals divested of any inherent sense of order and therefore prepared, in Drucker's phrase, to substitute organization for order. One hears echoes here of Ortega y Gasset in his *Revolt of the Masses* (1930) where he sees individualism being eroded by the ubiquitous use of new technologies whose esoteric physics are not understood and are therefore treated as an alternative nature.[34] What appears as irrationalism in the fictions of the totalitarian ideology may rather be the culmination of the abstractions of a rationalism that three centuries earlier proclaimed a method by which humankind might become the rulers and masters of nature. The breakdown of liberal nationalism was occasioned primarily by the dynamic expansiveness of capitalist industry as well as by the "tribal" movements of Pan-Germanism and Pan-Slavism. The breakdown of law derived from traditional natural law concepts was, on its obverse side, the result of the tradition of autonomous persons in combination with the growing concept of an immanent natural law of development. The religious breakdown symbolized by the willing followers of the German Christian Church was not only the result of the collapse of the Christian conscience but the climax of theological traditions, which, on the one hand, had so separated God and nature that God was superfluous and, on the other, had so identified God and history that God was but the seal and guarantee of human accomplishment.

It is more significant than is often allowed that this array of breakdowns and culminations should have occurred at the point when modern technology had reached the degree of perfection of which Promethean humanity had long dreamed. Technically, virtually anything was becoming possible. Totalitarian terror, propaganda, and state military power were possible only due to the advanced state of technology, as, of course, is a centralized industrial economy worked by a mass of labour and controlled by powerful interests. The dimension of advanced technology would seem to be a key factor separating totalitarianism from traditional forms of autocracy, whereas the dimension of terror seems to be a key factor separating totalitarianism from Western democracies. Where unlimited means are at hand, the intentions of power are unequivocally apparent. In this respect, totalitarianism may stand as the symbol of certain fundamental choices that have lain at the root of much of modern Western civilization.

Two basic, intertwined characteristics of totalitarianism seem to obtrude from this brief survey: the condition of uprootedness and orientation toward the future. Despite the distress occasioned by the former, the mental set of modernity is so overwhelmed by ideologies of development and by technological accomplishment that a sense of rootedness essential to the human spirit is lost. Yet, without its satisfaction, every attempt to realize the possibility of the future is imperilled.

The bias toward the future in the culture of the modern West is part of its Christian heritage. But separated from belief in God as the ground of existence and the source of order, the judge and redeemer of orders – and hence the source of future hope – this bias toward the future by itself takes on the attitude of leaning over an abyss. In this perilous position, ideology and organization allied with technology leap in to offer temporary stability, but also gadgetry, consumerism, and in totalitarian regimes the pursuit of "objective enemies" for divertissement. Opponents of the ideology and the organization become threats to the "security" of life thus offered and to the promise of new order held out by ideology and reorganization. The bias toward the future is no longer sustained by the life of faith but is motivated, and hence really destroyed, by the fears of uprooted civilization.

The choice that lies at the centre of such cultural phenomena, and hence, perhaps, the "truth" that totalitarian order represents, is the idea of human autonomy or self-sufficiency. The insufficiency of this "choice" is reflected in the inherent expansiveness of modern civilization – contradictorily seeking an ever larger base upon which to "secure" its self-sufficient existence. The failure (and the success) of autonomous human beings finds its logical expression in a society whose orders have collapsed, whose individuals have no common interest (Arendt), whose order and direction have degenerated into a *perpetuum mobile* of organization. Where the cultural breakdown and culmination have not been so severe, the growth of "heteronomous man" (Töllich) or "other-directedness" (Riesman) has been observed. Perhaps this could be called a "soft" version of totalitarian society. Both autonomy and heteronomy represent the loss of genuine selfhood, found in the life of faith.

If totalitarianism is the sign of the loss of Christian belief, in large populations of the West, it is also the sign that a post-Christian era requires a new articulation of the meaning of Christianity. As Dietrich Bonhoeffer suggests in his *Letters and Papers from Prison*, for a world that does not need God to cope with natural evil, to assuage the fear of death, or to explain away what still lies beyond the bounds of human knowledge, but needs God primarily to save humankind from itself, God must be understood anew as the transcendent One in the midst of life,[35] inspiring mercy and compassion, and a quest for social justice, without which the ills that beset modernity will ensure our continuing susceptibility to the temptations of totalitarian solutions.

Arendt, in replying to Voegelin's review of her book, commented that it was difficult to see what difference belief in God could possibly have made in totalitarian Germany.[36] It would, of course, have been idle and irresponsible to promote belief in God as a *Deus ex Machina* who resolves the political crisis. A crisis made over centuries is in no respect solved in a day, nor by a simple exhortation to believe. It is significant, however, that it was the Christian church and Jehovah's Witnesses who provided the most widespread resistance that Hitler encountered.[37]

Totalitarianism, as a present danger, is not simply a matter of interpretation for specialists or a problem for Christianity but a profound issue for humanity. A radically renewed faith is one possible answer among others to the problem. The danger will not be met by simply proposing that everyone become Christian or religious in the customary sense of the words. But surely a beginning may be made on the ground beyond nihilism staked out by Albert Camus, where "all may indeed live again ... but on the condition that they shall understand how they correct one another, and that a limit, under the sun, shall curb them all. Each tells the other that he is not God."[38]

PART TWO

From Providence to Progress

CHAPTER FIVE

Providence to Progress:
The Migration of an Idea
in English-Canadian Thought

BACKGROUNDER

Late in April of 1984 I received a call from William Westfall, co-chair designate of a conference on religion and culture in Canada to be held four weeks hence at the Ontario Institute for Studies in Education. Fernand Dumont from Quebec City and Northrop Frye from Toronto were to be the lead speakers, each of whom had a formidable literary output, stood at the very apex of the coterie of top-ranking intellectuals the country had produced, and were recognized internationally for the depth and breadth of understanding they brought to cultural studies. Frye had had to withdraw for personal reasons. Would I stand in for him? To say I was floored by the suggestion would be a massive understatement. I had taken courses from Frye and like most students stood in utter awe of him. What did Westfall know that I did not? To my surprise, after a momentary hesitation, I found myself assenting to his intimidating proposition. I was now two years into representing Hamilton West in the Ontario Legislature. However, three years earlier I had put together a course on the history of ideas in English Canada from Bishop Strachan and William Lyon Mackenzie to Northrop Frye and Marshall McLuhan – or so I conceived it. It never reached its destination, but perhaps there was an appropriate theme I could pull out of it for a conference on comparative religion and culture. I decided to tackle for English Canada what was commonly seen as a unique feature of French Canada within the Canadian mosaic, the sense of providential mission, and to explore its relation to the emerging idea of progress that would become a generalized mindset of English Canadians as the nineteenth century unfolded. Strange as it may seem, I guess I was so preoccupied with gathering up my resources for the occasion that, up to the time of delivery, I was actually unaware that I would be sharing the platform with Fernand Dumont, opening the conference.

Coincidentally, however, to round out the paper I had returned briefly to the case of Quebec and noted the important public role of Dumont in Quebec in the search for a new Canadian social democracy. As I concluded he strode across the platform to shake my hand – a very gratifying gesture!

PROVIDENCE TO PROGRESS
IN ENGLISH-CANADIAN THOUGHT*

From Providence to Progress. In European terms, the transition in modern thought that runs from Bossuet to Condorcet, from Bishop Ussher to Charles Darwin, has long been a commonplace. Canadians, if they have any acquaintance with the subject, have taken it after a fashion as their story, too, without being very concerned to clothe it in Canadian garb. Providentialism, we have long known, was central to the dramatization of what being French and Catholic in the valley of the St Lawrence was all about. But until this past generation, it has been possible to read Canadian history as though English Canadians had avoided that apparent irrationality. We were above all that. Now we know better. Sidney Wise, Goldwin French, George Rawlyk, Jack Bumsted, William Westfall, John Grant and John Moir, to mention a few who have explored the ideas of the reigning clerical intelligentsia of our formative decades, have focused a shaft of light on God's other peculiar peoples in British North America.[1]

Providentialism was the Hebraic-Christian theory of God's care for creation, of the superintendence of nature, of offering guidance throughout human history, and of provision for the needs of humankind, whatever the adversity they might experience. The model was always the chosen people of Israel – chosen not because of any merit or special power, but to be a vehicle for the restoration of errant humanity.[2]

There were at least three major versions of the providential idea in British North America – one French, one Maritime, and one Upper Canadian. All were intimately linked to the new world of the Americas. The

---

* First published as "Providence to Progress: The Migration of an Idea in English-Canadian Thought," in "Religion/Culture: Comparative Studies," proceedings of a conference sponsored by the Association for Canadian Studies and the Graduate Centre for Religious Studies, University of Toronto, 23–26 May 1984, eds. William Westfall, Louis Rousseau, Fernand Harvey, and John Simpson, *Canadian Issues/Themes canadiens* 7 (1985): 33–46. Courtesy of the Association of Canadian Studies.

French model with its elaborate parallels to the Biblical story told of a people with their patriarchs led to a new land where they would be a beacon of hope to the old civilization. Believing the hand of Providence, in the form of the British Conquest, had spared them the ravages of the French Revolution, they came to think of themselves as the bearers of a purified Catholicism to an apostate Christendom.[3]

The most accessible Upper Canadian version was articulated by John Beverly Robinson in that little-attended classic, *Canada and the Canadian Bill*, published in 1840. A superior intelligence had ordained that the Americans should rebel before their continued growth in numbers and trade would have enabled them to sweep all the British North American colonies into revolt and independence. Geography providentially precluded the further union and independence of the British North American colonies. Hinged around the St Lawrence system with its beauty, utility, and salubriousness, the British North American colonies were "happily situated ... for the purpose of perpetuating British dominion in North America, 'enjoying' a constitution and laws better calculated than those of any other country to secure the best interests and provide the happiness of the human race."[4]

Robinson, of course, was the student of John Strachan, Bishop of Toronto, whose complete providentialism was spread through the region by his clerical cadre. Strachan, like most of his contemporaries, believed in a great chain of being which, with its hierarchy of creatures, each of which found fulfillment in its own station, was a metaphor for society. Restless striving beyond one's level brought anxiety and distress. Whatever befell individuals and nations was a product of human action and God's moral governance, and should be accepted for the lessons taught. A person's best duty was to attend to the practical matters and reciprocal obligations of an organic and hierarchic society. To concern oneself with the future outcome of events was evidence of doubt, not faith. Although Strachan could anticipate material and social improvement, there was no redemption or perfection toward which history moved.

Strachan's thought, however, was caught between the Greek assumptions of the chain of being that perfection lay beyond time, and the Hebraic assumptions of providentialism that God's will would somehow prevail. He could not refrain from concluding, therefore, that the British were God's chosen nation, in "whose written institutions are contained elemental principles for the gradual regeneration of mankind and the purification and extension of true religion." In the wake of British influence, a "Universal Empire of Religious Opinion," Strachan thought, would replace the present "Universal Empire of Arms."[5]

The Strachan/Robinson providential view of British North American history may be taken as the classic English-Canadian version of that great idea. It was shared by Bishop Mountain in Lower Canada and Bishop Inglis in Nova Scotia – and by the followers of both. It was essentially a static conception of both nature and society, an expression of those who, if they were not wholly satisfied with the world as it was, were engaged in a momentous struggle to preserve an established – and to them – proven sense of order in a world of revolution and rumours of war.

Its elements were reasonably clear: a transcendent God as the source of order; the cosmos as a great chain, which, after Alexander Pope, one link broken, the whole collapses; history as God's design; the constitution an ideal balance of King, Lords, and Commons; society a hierarchy; the individual subordinate to class; state oversight of economic life; and the whole superintended and suffused by an established church legitimating all and charged to instruct governors and governed alike in the propriety of this old whig cum Tory arrangement.[6] Tory providentialism, as we know, would not – and could not – last as the reigning model of British North American development. Glance forward to the progressive world view a century later and all seems to have changed; yet on closer examination the imprint of providentialism is clear in the latter-day progressives – a testimony to the resilience and adaptability of central religious concepts in Canadian history.

Transformation there was, however, and it began in *some* respects on the ground inhabited by Strachan and Robinson themselves. *All* was not *stasis* in their great scheme. God insisted on meddling in details; the chain of being assumed a creativity that filled the earth with beings of every possible description; God's will was reflected in history; the balanced constitution was not yet worked out, for both Strachan and Robinson struggled with the problem of a natural aristocracy in a new land, and laid that mantle on the middle class, whose aggressiveness they vastly underestimated. The North American environment, they knew, threatened their sense of settled social order on every side, and Robinson was already, in the 1830s in the face of religious diversity, projecting the establishment of religion in general rather than a single church.[7]

It could be said that these sidelights of the classic version were to become the beacons in the great transition from Providence to Progress in Canada in the nineteenth century. Central to that transition, however, was the evangelical revolution, which in Canada did for the industrial middle class (but not them only) what Calvinism had done for the commercial class of the seventeenth century.

English and American Methodists in the Maritimes and the Canadas, Free Kirk Presbyterians from Scotland, and Baptists from New England provided the base of the evangelical challenge to Tory providentialism. What is at first confusing is that they too espoused a providential world view. This is most explicit in the case of Henry Alline and the New Light movement of the 1770s in Nova Scotia. Their exodus from New England twenty years earlier was viewed as a providential act separating them from an erring people whose many signs of infidelity were now capped by resort to arms. The British were equally judged, and an outbreak of revival in Nova Scotia was viewed as God's transference of the mission of New England to a new visible community of the faithful. This would be a sign to the nations of the way ordained by God, a centre of order in a disordered world. In the reflected light of revival, all Nova Scotia was seen as a "people highly favoured of God."[8]

Egerton Ryerson's Upper Canadian Methodist loyalism was also cast in terms of a dynamic and uninhibited Providence. Despite a flirtation with William Lyon Mackenzie, in outward form there would be little he would change in Robinson. As the son of Colonel Joseph Ryerson, former High Sheriff of Norfolk, he – like Alline – did not contest the social hierarchy of the time, distinguished between masses and classes, and issued no challenge to the social structure. He delighted in the Old Whig traditions and spoke of educating youth "to fulfil aright the relations and duties in society assigned to them in order of Providence."[9]

The ethos of Alline's and Ryerson's religious movements, however, abridged those explicit teachings by intensifying the immediacy of God's governance and grace for the individual believer, and elevating scripture and personal religious experience (as confirmed by fellow believers) over the authority of church and tradition. Religion was essential to the social health of the State, but only as it was a clear response to the moving of the Spirit of God. Church establishment was quite unnecessary to that.

The evangelicals' sense of the nearness and availability of God – "joy of Heaven to earth come down"– together with their intensity of awareness of the moral perils of existence and "their intention to press on to perfection," brought a quite new dimension to Canadian providentialism that was especially congenial to the enterprising of town and country. That all this was available to every human being and beyond the control, even the mediation, of church or state, was the essence of the evangelical revolution – and the beginning of the disruption of Tory providentialism in Canada. It is no wonder that bishops Strachan, Inglis, and Mountain all agreed that the evangelicals were "a set of ignorant enthusiasts whose preaching is only calculated to perplex the understanding and corrupt the morals, to relax the nerves of industry and dissolve the bands of society."[10] The chain was being broken, hierarchy implicitly levelled, and, it seems, Providence contested. William Lyon Mackenzie, the reformer's firebrand, his republic of the common individual, and his rebellion, represented for the bishops the logical conclusion to evangelical religion. Whatever the truth of that view – and Mackenzie had at once his evangelical followers *and* his falling out with evangelical leaders like Ryerson – preserving the purity and immediacy of God's spirit in the conscience of the common individual was so important to Mackenzie that he devoted the first four clauses of his new constitution for Canada (1837) to that end. Mackenzie, himself, had no formal church ties, but only so could the common individual be a true agent of God's will in history. Mackenzie's estimate of the social implications of the "order of providence" were very different than those of both Strachan and Ryerson, but his views make him an important forerunner of those providential cum progressive attitudes found in the labour and farmer movements later in the century.[11]

After 1837, however, the battle lay between Strachan and Ryerson, and the history of nineteenth century denominational growth makes it plain whose version of providential theory was the more relevant to the time. Between 1842 and 1881, when the population of Ontario multiplied four times, Methodists multiplied over seven times, Presbyterians five and one half times, and Baptists over five times, while Anglicans multiplied only 3.4 times – less than the rate of population growth.[12]

The evangelicals drove through the breaches of established providentialism, swept away Strachan's favourite class – prosperous yeomen, skilled tradesfolk and the commercial groups of the mid-century Canadian city, and offered them an immanent deity to warm their hearts, direct their earnest strivings, and hold out the hope of heaven. Their prosperity they attributed to Providence, and through their prosperity, the country would be blessed. In them, Providence did not provide so much an ordered structure as an orderly process – maintained by a proliferation of free churches and state-run schools.

It is not surprising, therefore, to see the political works of the business nationalists of 1867 formulated in terms of a providential post-millennial prophecy: "He shall have dominion from sea to sea, and from the river unto the ends of the earth." The spread of gothic monumental style, in the 1860s, financed largely by businessmen of the mid-Victorian city, spoke not so much of the alternative beats of sacred and secular at the time but of a broad unity of religious aspiration and economic action.[13]

The force of an immediate, uninhibited Providence was evident to Victorians in the triumph of technology and science, which were so closely allied to the advance of commerce. But technology and science, themselves, in turn hastened the transformation of the English-Canadian idea of Providence in an immanent and progressive direction.

T.C. Keefer's popular essay of 1849, *The Philosophy of Railroads*, celebrated the march of improvement and upward mobility the railway portended. In a lecture to Montreal skilled tradesmen, or "mechanics," in 1854 he explained how Roman roads permitted the expansion of Christianity and how the railway was "a necessary and indispensable forerunner – to that second great moral revolution, the Millennium ... Wherever a railway breaks in upon the gloom of a depressed and secluded district ... the pulpit will then have its grateful listeners, the school its well filled benches." "Those huge drivers," he added, paraphrasing Whittier, "will yet tread out the last smouldering fires of discord."[14] Keefer rightly sensed an element of heresy lurking in his rhetoric, but his railroad represented the application of the Newtonian, highly Protestant universe to the Canadian countryside: motion supersedes rest, and an ubiquitous God at once animates and maintains order.

There was, in this preoccupation with the moral force of technology, not just a little of Francis Bacon, who, with Samuel Smiles, was a patron saint of the Mechanics' Institute in Canada. Indeed, Keefer's career bore an uncanny resemblance to Bacon's in his disillusionment with the political order and his search for an alternative vehicle for the social good. Keefer helped found the Canadian and American Societies of Civil Engineers and the Royal Society of Canada and was the only person to become president of all three. By professionalizing the engineer, Keefer appeared to hope that the high priests of a beneficent technology would acquire the discipline and collective force to play their regenerating role.

For Keefer, like so many others of his day, it was the quickening pace of knowledge that lay at the core of his hope. Everywhere one encountered, as in Keefer, the quotation from the book of Daniel in the Old Testament referring to the last times, "when many shall run to and fro and knowledge shall increase."[15] Ironically, the original reference was to the corruption of original Judaism by the invasion of Greek culture, but it was taken, in the nineteenth century, in post-millennial fashion, as a condition that heralded the millennium and was clearly of God's providing.

Knowledge, for Keefer and for mid-century mechanics, was not just neutral information. It was power. It was, said J. Dallas, lecturing at the Mechanics' Institute in Barrie in 1865, that which pre-eminently distinguished individuals. Knowledge was won from nature, and "rightly viewed and properly investigated" leads us to "that great Being, who with matchless wisdom, unbounded benevolence, and transcendent greatness, guides, governs, and preserves his creatures."[16] One could only conclude that knowledge as power also partook of the moral qualities of its ultimate subject. In a world where Providence was passing into Progress one could almost say that science thought God's thoughts not after God but with God.

Whether consciously derived from Bacon or not, this regenerating sense of knowledge was in type. Bacon distinguished between the loss of innocence as a consequence of the Fall of Humanity and the loss of dominion over nature. Religion's role was to restore the former, but it was the role of science to restore the latter. Bacon's subtle suggestion that science was uncorrupted by the Fall and may even be a means of restoring something of humankind's pre-lapsarian innocence by re-establishing dominion over nature was a heady notion that Canadian mechanics appear to have subscribed to in their own way.[17]

Is it too much to see in Keefer's engineers and in aspiring mechanics the arrival of another chosen people at a critical juncture when politicians appeared to be failing the nation with their pork barrelling and their sinecures? The rituals of lodges like the Ancient Order of United Workmen made much of the analogy of the divine artificer and the mechanic, and one could be pardoned for thinking that a new meritocracy, at least, was in the works. One speaker, addressing the mechanics, hastened to assure the upper classes that the intellectual advancement of the lower classes put them in no danger – adding, however, that a well-informed, working population would necessarily create a well-informed aristocracy – and concluded that, when the millennium arrived, the movement toward it will be seen to have been "from the least to the greatest": surely as neat a transvaluation of social role as one is likely to encounter.[18]

The skilled trades worker's consciousness of his/her providential role, however, went into crisis in the 1880s with the advancement of a new technology that devoured the worker's skills and the rise of large-scale industrialization that threatened the labourer's status – not to mention livelihood.[19] Some, advancing as entrepreneurs, carried the old ideology into the business worker's rationale regarding the control of capital and labour.[20] Others, their skills in jeopardy and their self-understanding in crisis, transferred their providential ideology to the nascent labour movement and looked ahead to a new age of just reward for productive labour.

The Canadian labour press from 1880 to 1910 abounds with evidence that labour spokespeople viewed their movement in religious terms. They criticized a "churchianity" whose spirituality was corrupted by its alliance with wealth. They professed to follow a Jesus who was as concerned for workers' bodies as for their souls. Moses was the great prototype of a labour leader, and the exodus the legitimation of the strike. Whether in Rowe's *Palladium of Labour* in Hamilton (1883–86), in Puttee's *Voice* in Winnipeg (1896–1918), or in *Cotton's Weekly* in Cowansville, Quebec (1908–14), a pervasive sense of the Biblical nature of creation and the conditions under which one applied one's labour to it informed their commentary. Like the Israelites in the wilderness, they sought a promised land. The quest was not less Christian because it rejected bourgeois spirituality in favour of an earthy Biblical materialism. The labour movement, rejected by the builders of the current economic order, said Phillips Thompson (borrowing Biblical language) would become the headstone of the corner of a new civilization.

The providential world view was apparently alive and well, and living in late-Victorian Canada. But was it Providence, or was it Progress? Indeed, what was the difference? The Evangelicals, radical reformers, technology and its pamphleteers, business people, mechanics and the labour movement, all had forced the doctrine into a more immanent mould and disrupted in varying degrees the concept of a settled and divinely ordained social hierarchy. The central and substantial change, however, was in the perceived mode of divine activity in nature and history. More than anything, that change rested finally on the triumph of uniformitarian modes of thought, evolution, and idealism in Canada in the latter half of the century.[21]

Traditional providentialism presumed intervention by God in the natural and historical order. Catastrophism had reigned in pedagogical theory as in Biblical story. By the 1830s, however, William Paley, famous for his watch analogy, had convinced many that the uniform workings of nature were a manifestation not only of the power and wisdom of God but also of God's goodness. Natural design was evidence that God's attention was bestowed on the minutest of objects. Paley therefore concluded that the structure of natural law and Providence were compatible. "We have no reason to fear, therefore, our being forgotten, or overlooked, or neglected."[22]

Hugh Miller's widely read reconciliations of Genesis and Geology popularized an extended time scale that made change the result of gradual accumulation rather than catastrophe or intervention.[23] If not as comforting as Paley, he established for a succession of science teachers in the church colleges of Canada a lasting conviction that science and religion only conflicted when one or both were misunderstood.[24] Both Paley and

Miller were well known in Canada. They were congruent with Keefer, they were influential names among the Mechanics' Institutes, and they were read by such prominent Canadian intellectuals as Victoria's Nathaniel Burwash and McGill's William Dawson.

When Egerton Ryerson as first principal of Victoria College said, "If one branch of education must be omitted, surely the knowledge of the laws of the universe and the works of God, is of more practical advantage, socially and morally, than a knowledge of Greek and Latin,"[25] he was thinking not only of the world of work but of social order. To say so was to celebrate with the young Burwash, in 1858, the year before the monumental *Origin of Species*, a Providence that had so designed the mind of individuals and nature that mental enlargement and social good might result from the study of nature.[26]

William Dawson had high praise for Miller and went to great lengths to affirm that the notion of uniform cause in nature was thoroughly Biblical.[27] Hebraic monotheism reached across Greek polytheism and medieval barbarism, he thought, to affirm with modern science the unity of God, the unity of nature, and the unity of humankind. In his struggle with Darwin, Dawson's limitation of species to a minimum allowed the acceptance of natural selection to explain variation; but the necessity of design prevented, for Dawson, entire abandonment of special creation at a few specific points. Creation, however, he declared, was a matter of law not fiat.

Dawson refused to let uniformitarian hypotheses run roughshod over induction. Evolution had not resolved the problem of the gaps, and he was probably the first to warn against an unscientific application of uniformitarian geology to anthropology. Ironically, his qualifications of uniformitarianism were intended to maintain some final ground of unity and design for science and religion – and not least for society. Without the conviction of a designing Providence, Dawson saw only social chaos. Dawson's God was, after all, a God of law and orderly progress. Providence was not abandoned in Dawson, even if interventionism was massively abridged.

Others more distant from the scientific scene – poets, pastors, and professors – more readily accepted an evolutionary outlook as the century closed – often by bypassing the central issue.[28] Principal Grant of Queen's University said it was just a question of replacing a creation that was direct and all at once with one that was indirect and took place over time. Young clergy in the 1880s and 1890s, like Charles Gordon and Salem Bland, struggling with the blind fatalism of natural selection and early Social

Darwinism, were rescued by Henry Drummond, Prince Kropotkin, and Benjamin Kidd, and in the process the transformation of Providence into Progress took another step.[29]

With the decline of "interventionism" came the retreat from the drama of conversion. Nurture – not nature – became the watchword. Religious education's rapid rise in the 1880s asserted that God's chosen mode throughout history had been an educative one. The transactions between humans and God – as between humans and nature as well as between God and nature – were increasingly viewed as matters of mind and consciousness.[30]

Mind was the ground on which Canada's pre-eminent idealist philosopher, John Watson, finally tackled Darwin in the 1870s. One had to posit something more than matter in motion in the form of natural selection, he thought, for the process always to resolve itself in ever higher, more complex forms. He could not imagine, he said, an ordering mind emerging in an absurd universe. Watson's influence was immense, but he was far from alone in spreading the attractive unities of idealism through Canadian colleges and universities and beyond.[31]

"The course of human history," Watson declared, "is the process in which the individuals forming the Spiritual organisms of humanity rise to self-consciousness of the Principle which gives reality to them all." "Every advance in science," therefore, he saw as "preparation for a fuller and clearer conception of God; every improvement in the organization of society as a further development of that community of free beings by which the ideal of an organic unity of humanity is in process of realization."[32]

It was a conception that suited turn-of-the-century Canada. In various applications it would be carried by some like George Parkin into the geopolitics of Empire,[33] and by others into the expanding prospects of the prairie west. It was used to interpret the significance of the business combinations of the age – even by critics like Salem Bland who predicted that sooner or later business people would adopt the altruistic ethics implied in the organic nature of their enterprises. It could be seen in Phillips Thompson's explanations of the significance of the labour movement. Everywhere it spoke of reform.

The Christian spirit seemed not just to overflow the church but to be independent of it. Preachers turned to novelists and poets for the new ethical standards of the age, and single taxers – even socialists – were lauded for their practical Christian enthusiasm. Immanent and uniformitarian categories set some to studying Spinoza once more. Thoughts of pantheism came fugitively to the thinking individual of today, said William Osborne of Wesley College, Winnipeg.[34]

Clearly a world of relative calm had been replaced by a world of bursting activity and, even more, a world that yearned for settled tranquility had been replaced by one that embraced change with brimming enthusiasm – though not, one would have to say, without an anxiety the new doctrine of progress served to assuage.

North American geography, middle-class ambition, and business expansion, the triumphs of technology and the aspirations of skilled trades workers, a nascent labour movement, uniformitarian science with Darwinian revisions, and idealism – all conspicuously accompanied by an increasingly urbane evangelical spirit – all had their way with the idea of Providence in Canada in the course of a century.

If the transcendence of God was not forgotten, immanence was emphasized. The chain of being had become the river of life, and interventionism in nature and history was transformed into the gradualism of mental relations. With these large changes, conceptions of social hierarchy had largely disappeared, and socially active churches and public schools mediated the values that ordered change. If the architectonics of grand design in history yielded to more fluid conceptions, there were still large purposes in time associated variously with the labour movement, Canada, the British Empire, and the Kingdom of God (or all of these), for which it was necessary to struggle and even sacrifice. Evil was still in the field, and every paean to progress was accompanied by a litany of the ills still to be overcome. Progress, at least in this English-Canadian variant, did not mean subordinating self to impersonal social forces. Labour persisted as a dominant value as in Robinson, Ryerson, and Mackenzie and, whatever the awkward realities, the individual was viewed as free of class and enjoined to seek self-realization under the direction of conscience and reason. Nor was the individual less alone than under Ryerson's superintending Providence, for, in George John Blewett's elegant idealist metaphor, God was the home of persons.[35]

Indeed, Progress in Canada did not become the entirely secularized vision it was in large parts of Europe, Britain, and in some measure in the United States. In Canada, one did not talk of "increase taking place in the nature of things" as though God were not somehow both in and beyond the process. Progress in Canada was Providence updated. And so it remained for much of this twentieth century, even surviving the experiences of war and economic collapse.

Despite the tragedies and dilemmas of our own time, traces live on in the hopes of those like Fernand Dumont, late in the annals of another providential tradition, that some fine day a people like us will be able to invent an original form of democracy that springs from our peculiar experience, and "bring to the surface questions and answers that richer and more knowledgeable countries [as well as poorer and less knowledgeable] need in order to bring some shadings to their lefts and their rights."[36] That would indeed give meaning to a long survival – and to an old idea.

CHAPTER SIX

The Background of the Social Gospel in Canada

BACKGROUNDER

Having just published The Social Passion *in 1971, I turned my thoughts to organizing a national conference on the social gospel in Canada. I was encouraged in this by Dr Ronald Faris, Director of Studies in the Department of Extension at the University of Regina, who saw the logic of holding such a conference in Regina, capital of a province where the social gospel had been a hallmark of its religious and political identity and site of the first Canadian government led by a Christian socialist premier. The result was a conference drawing together still-living representatives of the movement to tell their own story and those engaged in interpreting the social gospel from different disciplinary perspectives. The conference took place 21–24 March 1973. This essay, with some modification, was my introductory lecture and represented my efforts to date to retrieve a past that* The Social Passion *had leapt over in focusing on the crest and crisis of the movement. My intent, also, was to introduce some recent critiques of the social Christian movement at large. Beatrice Brigden opened with her tireless efforts as a social purity reformer educating prairie women on sexual hygiene, after which she would join A.E. Smith in the Brandon Labour Church. Fred Tipping explained how religion had figured in his evolution as a labour reform figure in Winnipeg. Ethel [Dodds] Parker recounted her role in the founding of Presbyterian settlement houses. King Gordon detailed the important role of Christian socialism as a radical critique and extension of the social gospel in the 1930s. And Harold Allen presented "the view from the manse" on the social gospel and social crisis in British Columbia in the 1930s.*

BACKGROUND OF THE SOCIAL GOSPEL*

Introduction

In 1968, when I embarked on a first publication on the social gospel and the reform tradition in Canada, I wrote that "the earliest expressions of the social gospel in Canada may still lie in sources untouched by historians' hands, and in those sources the rise of the social gospel may be obscured by the gradual nature of its separation from older forms of Christian social expression." Even four years later that statement still largely holds true, and holds true for both parts of it. Even for those of us who have looked at some of those sources it remains true that the process of transition from older forms of Christian social outlook into the new was a slow one and the steps are not always easy to discern. However, it is now possible to provide an initial sketch of those transitional conditions and of the encounter of somewhat contrasting and yet complementary intellectual movements that fed the nascent social gospel in Canada.

The Social Gospel Defined

In the first place, let us remind ourselves what it is we are talking about. It is possible to use that phrase, "the social gospel," to refer rather broadly and vaguely to any and all efforts of Christians to express their faith in the social context, and sometimes even to encompass any movement that offers a hope of social regeneration. However, what we are here concerned with is not that broad conception of the social gospel, but with the movement of Christian social thought and action that arose in the last decades of the nineteenth century in the context of a society becoming increasingly collectivized under the impulses of industrialism and urbanism.

The social gospel used the word "social" advisedly to distinguish itself, because not all approaches to social problems by Christians have had an

---

* First published as "The Background of the Social Gospel in Canada," in Richard Allen, ed., *The Social Gospel in Canada*, papers of the Interdisciplinary Conference on the Social Gospel in Canada, 21–24 March 1974, at the University of Regina. Mercury Series (Ottawa: National Museum of Man, 1975), 2–34. Courtesy of the National Museum of Canada.

explicitly social character. The generations immediately preceding the social gospel held conceptions of humanity and society that were intensely individualistic. They thought that the social problems of their time could be solved by harnessing individual energies and individual wills. It was not that they did not see a social problem, but that they saw it largely resting upon causes that lay within individuals. Insofar as they attacked institutions, it was to remove impediments to individual action – obstacles to the will and affections renewed by evangel preaching and conversion, to the mind equipped by education, to energies geared to useful enterprise. The social gospel that arose in the latter years of the nineteenth century, however, developed under influences that encouraged a social concept of humankind and underlined the social dimensions of the gospel, so that the solutions that appeared to be most useful were those that had an essentially social character. The social gospel addressed the whole problem, not just of individuals, not just of informal social groups, but of institutions and institutional relationships in society. Therefore, it became very deeply involved in virtually every promising reform of the time. The social gospel was not just incidentally social religion; people in its ranks could be heard muttering that the real Holy Communion, after all, did not take place in the church but happened daily in the homes and farms and workshops of the nation.

Interpreting the Social Gospel

Before reviewing the early years of the social gospel's emergence in Canada it is useful to glance briefly at some of the interpretations scholars have provided of the social gospel at large. Like most historical phenomena, the social gospel has been viewed in a variety of lights. Most research and writing on the social gospel has been done by American scholars, which has reinforced the view of earliest scholarship that the social gospel was a uniquely American movement. The first American efforts to account for the history of the social gospel were undertaken in a mood very sympathetic to it. Historians such as C.H. Hopkins and H.F. May and biographers such as D.R. Sharpe themselves shared a progressive cast of mind. They interpreted the social gospel as arising out of a stimulus–response situation, in which theologically liberal, progressive-minded Christians responded to the challenges of industrial/urban society. Their works, written in the 1940s, usually abandoned the story between 1915 and 1917 and left the impression that the social gospel would decline with the blow the war of 1914–18 delivered to the progressive tradition as a whole. Between

1956 and 1960, however, several historians, notably Paul Carter in *The Decline and Revival of the Social Gospel* (1956) and R.M. Miller in *American Protestantism and Social Issues* (1960), demonstrated the continuing force of the social gospel between the two world wars. It was, however, a more sober, radical movement they portrayed, affected by the experiences of war and depression, a belated encounter with Marxist thought and the influence of neo-orthodox theology that took sin, or human alienation, more seriously than had the progressive tradition. Carter, especially, manifested the influence of these movements on his own thinking, and the beginnings of a critique of the earlier social gospel was evident in his work.

The work of revision was carried further by Timothy L. Smith in *Revivalism and Social Reform* (1957) and Donald Meyer in *The Protestant Search for Political Realism* (1960). They shifted the focus away from what was being responded to – the industrial/urban crisis – to the mental and religious conditions out of which the response was being made. Smith showed how much the social gospel owed to the revivalist movement of the middle nineteenth century. He revealed that the revivals had not only popularized a slogan "saved for service" and spawned a variety of social works but had also fostered a quest for personal perfectionism that readily spilled over from the personal to the social sphere and allied itself at one level with utopian communities and at another with the search for a righteous America. Meyer was prepared to say that the real issue with regard to the rise of the social gospel in North America, or elsewhere, lay in where one placed the locus of religious hope and how one undertook to resolve the conflict between ultimate hope and the limitations on present action. The social gospellers, he claimed, had tended to lose touch with reality and interpreted their world too much in terms of religious wish fulfillment. The implications of those works were rather hard on Christian liberals, but early European assessments of the social gospel in the United States had made similar points. Fine studies like *The Background of the Social Gospel in America* (1928), by the Dutch scholar W.A. Visser 't Hooft, however, had been largely ignored outside the seminaries until the 1950s. The same can be said of the early American work of H. Richard Niebuhr, often described as a theologian's theologian, who in 1929 published *The Social Sources of Denominationalism*, a social approach to religious formation. A decade later Niebuhr reversed his ground and adopted a religious approach to social formation in an important work entitled *The Kingdom of God in America.* He viewed the social gospel as the last stage in a peculiarly American religious theme, namely the vision of the Kingdom of God, beginning first of all in the Puritan Commonwealth with the notion of the absolute sovereignty of God over humanity, then moving through the period of the great awakenings to the notion of the Kingdom of Christ in the human heart, and then finally emerging as the social gospel's Kingdom of God as an ideal social order. Visser 't Hooft, in what is probably still the most suggestive study of the intellectual background of the social gospel in the United States, likewise began his account with Puritan beginnings and included the influence of revivalism. However, he also sketched the role of Enlightenment thought and the influence of the natural and social sciences and undertook as well an analysis of the underlying theology of the social gospel. Quite naturally the new interest in the history of ideas in the 1950s and 1960s brought such works into circulation alongside those of Smith and Meyer.

As the study of the social gospel moved into the realm of ideas and religion as the proper sources of the social gospel in the United States, it began to be much more apparent that the ideological and religious elements of the movement were more than just American. They were part and parcel of a vast North Atlantic triangle of culture and religion. Consequently, the latest studies of the social gospel have begun to develop that approach. Canadian students of the social gospel have found it much more difficult to ignore the trans-Atlantic influences, partly because Canadian historiography places such stress upon that factor in our national development, but more because the British influences are so obvious.

Moving on from that general historiographical background into the Canadian case, it should be clear that to try now to understand the origins and background of the social gospel in Canada it will be necessary to take a multi-faceted approach. Complex phenomena have complex origins. As well as material conditions arising from new technologies affecting not only conditions of life and work, it will be necessary to go back into those years when religious currents of revivalism were still prevalent on the Canadian scene and when new ideological influences were having an impact on Canadian minds, setting up mental and religious tensions calling for resolution.

Material Conditions

The social gospel in Canada, like the variants of social Christianity elsewhere, was undoubtedly a response to the challenge of the social and economic conditions precipitated by an emerging industrial/urban order. That would be to adopt a materialist approach and fashion it in terms of a Toynbeean challenge and response thesis. Whether that constitutes a sufficient or complete explanation, we will shortly examine, but that there were challenges of immense proportions resulting from the social impacts of industrialization in the years of the rise of the social gospel in Canada, from the 1880s to 1914, was more than obvious. By the end of the 1890s conditions of factory labour and escalating conflict between capital and labour called for the attention of a Royal Commission. Its report could hardly be said to have stayed the current of industrial unrest. A few years later, there would be a strike of several hundred Valleyfield Cotton Mill workers, with the militia called out to suppress it, and a still-wider strike would ensue. About the same time, the Grand Trunk Railway workers tied up the whole eastern Grand Trunk Railway system. The company tried to break the strike with imported Italian labour from New York and patrolled the rail lines with guards armed with carbines. In 1902, the year of the great Pennsylvania Coal Strike in the United States, which virtually brought the economy of North America to a standstill, 2,000 Crowsnest Pass miners went out on strike, 8,000 miners went out on strike in Nanaimo, and 1,500 street railway workers went out on strike in Montreal.

The depression in the late nineteenth century, particularly the worst of it in the early nineties, left working families in pitiful conditions and struggling for survival. Furthermore, there was the dislocation caused by industrial consolidation in the form of trusts and combines. American monopolies like Rockefeller's leviathan, Standard Oil of New Jersey, was devouring Canadian independent oil dealers, and homegrown industries were combining into larger scale enterprises. And then there came all those staggering problems that followed in the early years of the new century with rapid urban growth and western development. Toronto almost doubled in population between 1901 and 1911; Winnipeg tripled; Vancouver multiplied four times; Regina, ten times. The problems? Housing for a growing working class and a flood of immigrants, sewage, water, light and gas, issues of health and disease, safe milk and food supplies, transportation, not to mention law and order, alcohol and prostitution. All of these demanded new structures of urban governance, and the problems were complicated and compromised by a limited property-based electorate and the special interests of a dominant commercial elite. Farmers feeling the loss of children to the city were anxious for the future of rural life, which they saw as the wellspring of the nation. They, like factory labourers, had to adapt to new technologies, but they were also confronted by large marketing issues, especially in the movement of grain staples to international markets, in the course of which they had to battle transportation and elevator monopolies. The solution: state assistance and new cooperative marketing structures, the creation of which, as in the case of labour and the city, called for a new social ethic.

Religious and Intellectual Background

In the face of all that, one would say that a social gospel would be expected to emerge in response; that what developed as the social gospel was what one would expect of the Christian conscience, if believers were true to their calling; and that if there had been no social gospel it would be necessary to invent one. There would be a considerable truth in such observations. But the story of the emergence of the social gospel in Canada is not that simple. It did not originate just as a response; the response arose out of a complex of attitudes and ideas that were part of a cultural milieu. It is necessary, in the first instance, to explain the social gospel in Canada primarily as a religious and intellectual movement. We do not take too seriously explanations of major economic phenomena such as depressions based upon psychological dynamics; nor should we be very happy with explanations of religious movements based primarily upon economic or social factors, significant though they may be. And so, without ignoring the importance of the economic context, let us turn to the religious and intellectual background of the social gospel in Canada.

The crucial years are the 1880s and 1890s. Canada, eastern Canada in particular, but the West as well, was still caught up in the last of the series of awakenings and revivals that, through the previous century, had pulsed through North American society, Britain, and various parts of Europe. The decade of the eighties has been labelled by S.D. Clark as the great revival of the Canadian city, but as one looks at the evidence for that revival it becomes apparent that it was a revival of country and town as well. It was countrywide, and it caught up the bulk of the population. There was a plethora of homegrown evangelists: the Misses Birdsell and Mason, the Dimsdale sisters, Mr Meikle, and the Salvation Army, which came with their marching bands in 1883 first to London, Toronto, and Kingston and then to most of the towns and cities of the country. In response to them, Anglicans had their Church Army and Methodists drummed up their gospel bands, touring the towns and countryside. There were the great evangelists of the age, Moody and Sankey, and their Canadian counterparts, Crossley and Hunter. What was their impact? It is not easy to measure, but it must have been very substantial coming on top of the earlier runs of revivals in the country and on the continent. The press response to the arrival and the conduct of Moody and Sankey in Toronto might be indicative. In the relatively small *Globe* of those days were eight and nine columns per day every day devoted to the revivalists as long as they stayed in the city.

The impact of revivalism was to evangelicalize Canadian Protestantism as far as it would go. What did that mean? It meant, first, that the revival spread the idea that radical change in life was possible; that human beings were not bound inside a closed system of predestination; that they could take the initiative in approaching God. Second, it popularized the idea that God was after all an immanent being, available and working in the process of reformation. And in the third place it fostered the image of the revivalist as a crucial mediator, equally arousing personal repentance and God's grace for restoration. Each of these elements was readily trans- formable into social terms in the context of an increasingly collective age. The urgent call for the salvation of this individual now could very quick- ly, under appropriate circumstances, become an urgent call for the salva- tion of this society now. Likewise, the notion that God was involved in the process of personal transformation could very easily be developed into the idea that God was involved in the social processes of change. The revival- ist could readily provide the pattern for the social activist calling society to repentance and evoking a passion for social reform, reorganization, and reconstruction.

Another of the immediate results of the late nineteenth century revival in Canada was the renewal of old organizations and the creation of new, a development that was combined with a new sensitivity to a variety of groups in the Canadian community. For instance, in the midst of one of the revivals in Toronto, a man by the name of B.F. Austin, in 1884, wrote a book entitled *The Gospel to the Poor*. He argued that, if the churches were going to mean anything to the poor of Toronto, it would be necessary for them to get rid of their system of pew rents. But he was not just intent on getting the poor into church; the volume contained a striking attack on poverty and the system of society that produced it. The principals of the Methodist colleges, Principal Jabez Jacques of Albert College and Principal Alexander Burns of the Hamilton Ladies College, became ardent writers on behalf of women's rights.

Women, themselves, began their advance in church organizations, orga- nizing, in those years of revival, groups like the Women's Missionary Soci- ety and Women's Christian Temperance Union (WCTU), both of which became powerful national organizations with an ever-broadening reli- giously motivated social mandate. Under the leadership of Frances Willard in the United States and Letitia Youmans in Canada, the WCTU went on to embrace a good many reforms beyond temperance. Frances Willard tried to work out alliances of various kinds with labour unions, called herself a Christian Socialist, and was very much a woman to be reckoned with in the social reform world. It was not because she had no influence in Toronto that there was for many decades in downtown Toronto a building called Willard Hall.

Men's organizations began likewise to be part of church structure when the Brotherhood movement crossed the Atlantic at the end of the 1890s. They brought with them the British "Pleasant Sunday Afternoon" program, in which men gathered to hear speakers on issues of social concern. Their British counterparts set a clear example in sending a delegation to support strikers in southern France and the first meeting in Canada heard their minister denounce the Industrial Pharoahs of the age and predict an uprising of the people in the new century. Young people's organizations came to the fore with tremendous zeal and enthusiasm. The Young Men's Christian Association (YMCA) was revived and began to take their tents into downtown areas of the cities, there to encounter the conditions that they had been insulated from in their local YMCA organizations. In trying to spread the gospel they met a criticism that we do not often hear of the Ys any more, that they were improperly taking on the religious functions of the churches. The Methodist Epworth League, the Baptist Young People's organization, the Presbyterian Young People's organization, and Christian Endeavour, the great interdenominational youth organization of North America, all had their origins in this period or were galvanized to new vigour. Their conferences were beyond belief in terms of numbers. Attendance at Christian young people's conventions usually ran into the thousands and ranged as high as 50,000 at special conventions. Of course, they were devoted in the first instance to the idea of personal holiness, but in a moment we will see that they did not stop there. Sunday Schools, an old institution, also experienced a revival, and provide perhaps the best example of the sequences that can be traced through these years as the social idea and the social gospel emerged out of these earlier forms of renewed Christian life. In 1884 one of the ladies of Metropolitan Methodist Church in Toronto, touched by revival and much concerned about the problem of downtown street urchins, decided to set up a Sunday School. She got a room on Jarvis Street and began her work. Across the street stood the Model Boarding House. In the course of soliciting for children and canvassing for support, she and her helpers had occasion to meet the people who inhabited the boarding house. When they got inside it, they discovered that each evening there would pour into the basement of that building, about 50 feet by 150 feet in dimensions, scores of men seeking a night's lodging. There were shelves arranged, several tiers of them, at a slight slope to the wall. No bedclothes were provided, and the men slept in their clothes with about a foot and a half of space each. Sleep would be interrupted as still others came in, some of them drunk, some of them still drinking, arguing, and fighting. And then, as the cold morning dawned, they would get themselves out of the uncomfortable quarters and walk the streets of Toronto. It was an eye-opener for a lady who had never before observed such conditions. She went back to her church, secured some funds, bought a warehouse, and redecorated and furnished it to provide both more comfort and privacy and some opportunity for relaxation and enjoyment. Very shortly she put the Model Boarding House out of business. No doubt it was not appreciated by the owner of the boarding house, but that warehouse went on to become Fred Victor Mission, financed by the wealthy Massey family.

The sequence continues. Hart Massey when he died in 1894 had a small eulogistic pamphlet written about him called *Why Save Money*. Why should one save money? One should save money to follow in the steps of a man like Hart Massey. What had Hart Massey done? As a child he had driven grain to market, he had worked on his father's farm, and he had gone about "doing his father's business." The last phrase was deliberately taken from the New Testament. It was Jesus' answer to his parents explaining his dilatoriness in the Temple. The pamphlet went on to cast Hart Massey in terms of the Gospel of Wealth. As such men under the influence of revival took up social causes, the Kingdom of God surely would not be long in coming. That someone so using their wealth could hasten the coming of the Kingdom of God was a rather staggering conception that clearly had some affinity with the ambitious social activism of the social gospel. We have been often told that J.S. Woodsworth, a principal figure of the social gospel in Canada, had his first introduction to downtown urban slum conditions when visiting Mansfield House in east London, which he visited in the winter of 1899–1900. But in actual fact, Woodsworth had his first contact with slums in downtown Toronto at this very Fred Victor Mission. And so the line of sequences develops. Woodsworth, himself, mirrors the same sequence if he is followed through the 1890s, beginning with the first fruit of revival, namely, the eliciting of a pure and holy life. In his diaries he recounts how he went through three stages in the decade: first, he wished to devote his life to that totally holy and blameless condition of existence that he thought the gospel called him to; then he thought that the great calling of his life ought to be in missionary work; finally he reached that third stage where he realized that the concerns of Christian social ethics would be his lifework. But the experiences of the nineties were telescoped within him, each one continuing to inhere in the others. Woodsworth became the head of All Peoples' Mission in Winnipeg and developed it as a work of civic and social reform of national significance. But that, too, had begun precisely as had the Fred Victor Mission, out of Sunday School extension in the wake of revival.

Another sequence. The Epworth League, the organization of Methodist Young People, was brought to Canada in 1889 in the wake of this surge of revivalism. Again the first impulse of the organization was to personal holiness and the second was to the development of missions. But by 1905 and 1906 the Epworth Leagues began to turn their attention to city problems. Many of them stood staunchly behind James Simpson in Toronto, once a popular and articulate Epworth League president, when he campaigned as a socialist candidate for city offices, eventually becoming Toronto's first socialist mayor. Clearly, then, the revivalism of the eighties fostered conceptions, set up inner religious dynamics, and initiated sequences that led directly into the social gospel in Canada.

A National Gospel

The third crucial element in the background of the social gospel in Canada was the emergence of the Protestant churches as major national culture-building agencies in precisely these same years of revival.

The churches had made a great contribution to nation building prior to Confederation and had got involved in ambitious programs of expansion in the years of Confederation and after. That called for consolidation of enterprises, and between 1874 and 1884 both the Methodists and Presbyterians brought their several variants together in unions that made of them national territorial churches. A great deal of propaganda had to go into the building of those nationwide churches, and the vision of national churches from sea to sea had been energized by a quest for national righteousness. Such a quest, originating in the revivalism of the time, produced a species of evangelical nationalism that a host of preachers took unto themselves to propagate among their people across the country. The upshot of it all was churches taking on new responsibilities for social well-being that often had political and economic implications. George Monro Grant, Presbyterian principal of Queen's University, was volubly publicly denouncing political corruption. Albert Carman, general superintendent of the Methodist Church, castigated charity as an evasion of social justice and advocated the single tax on land values to eliminate poverty.

It would be a mistake, perhaps, to overemphasize the national component in this emerging evangelical nationalism, so as to annex it primarily to the pervasive gospel of nationalism itself. In the first place, evangelicalism has always carried a powerful international component, and part of the new national posture of Canadian Protestantism meant undertaking responsibilities for overseas missions. Missions easily became involved with imperialism, and especially with the social imperialism born of a wedding with social reform. But the primary impulse through it all was evangelical; if there was a mission to the nation or by the nation it was not primarily nationalist but evangelical.

Indeed, as the Protestant churches were embarking upon their new national roles, a heady mood of anticipation overtook them. At the International Sunday School Convention in Toronto in 1881, a Dr Dorchester gave a thrilling account of how evangelicalism had prospered over the previous 300 years. Later in the year when his book on the same subject appeared, W.H. Withrow, in a review in the *Methodist Magazine*, responded with considerable excitement to the prospects held out by the book's evidence of the geometrical rate of evangelical growth. Certainly evangelicalism had never been stronger in Canada, and its major bearer, the Methodist Church, was not only the fastest growing church in the land but in the 1890s became the nation's largest Protestant denomination.

Changing Views of Childhood

The development of national structures and the enthusiasm of evangelical accomplishment combined to provide a powerful impetus to the development of a conscious culture-building role among Protestants that helped to prepare the way for the social gospel and remained part of its complex of attitudes. The panoply of organizations recently established for all age groups and both sexes initiated a new form of institutional cradle-to-grave Protestantism that gave the churches a powerful purchase upon Canadian society. In this context, it is difficult to overestimate the significance for Protestant culture building and the social gospel of the changing attitudes to childhood that marked these same decades. It was also important that, in a society little touched by Enlightenment thought, those changing attitudes arose out of Canadian evangelicalism itself.

For most of the century, it would seem, the general attitude toward childhood was that children were little adults, born in original sin and requiring baptismal rite and a mature conversion experience to equip them for living new lives of purity and love. In an overwhelmingly

Christian land this might not – and for many did not – constitute a problem for social reform, and evangelicalism in the full flood of its optimism had its own hopeful answer on that score. However, it not only was an inhibiting conception as far as the possibilities of secular social reform were concerned, but it also limited the possibilities of the social gospel. It was more than a little significant for the emergence of the social gospel, therefore, that there were those who, for reasons of conscience and theology, were concerned about the eternal fate of children dying in infancy and anxious about the state of limbo in which current conceptions left young persons prior to conversion.

Among these evangelical reformers of attitudes to childhood in Canada was Henry Flesher Bland, Salem Bland's father. In 1875 he preached a sermon, later published as a pamphlet, *Universal Childhood Drawn to Christ*, in which he argued that children could be considered, Biblically, to be born in original goodness and might indeed remain in that condition, given proper nurturing. He suggested that it was possible for non-Christians to maintain such a state if they remained faithful to the light that was within them. To say less was to put the grace of God in doubt. Shortly after mid-century Horace Bushnell in the United States had promoted such ideas through a widely read work, *Christian Nurture*. However, it seems to have been British and not American sources that helped develop Henry Flesher Bland's original ideas on the subject. In any case, he gradually won over large numbers of his fellow pastors in the face of opposition, so that in the 1890s and after, the gospel of Christian nurture for children became widespread in the church at large. But the main point here is that the idea of original goodness provided a more hopeful basis for Christians to engage in "secular" social reform.

Christian nurture, it also turned out, could have quite explicitly radical uses. Henry Flesher Bland's son, Salem, in the 1890s, was frequently called on as a popular young minister to give Sunday School addresses. Not only did he use the occasions to popularize the Biblical critics and their applications, the new social ideas of the age, and advise Sunday Schools to help the poor, but before the decade was out he was counselling Sunday School teachers to arouse among their young children new aspirations and goals that would cost money, thereby pressing the wage earners who would come out of those Sunday Schools to seek higher wages to satisfy the needs of the higher life that was their right. That was a heady proposal to be making to Sunday School teachers in the 1890s! In the hands of those who thought like Bland, the Sunday Schools, re-invigorated by revival, were pressed further into the social gospel. Original goodness encouraged the possibility of a social gospel; Christian nurture could provide the population to demand and sustain reform.

Some critics of Henry Flesher Bland observed that the end result of his ideas would be a culture religion. If that were so, then there were other initiatives in that direction giving evidence of new cultural breadth in some Protestant quarters. For instance, in 1875, when W.H. Withrow proposed to the Methodist Church that it should found a literary, social, and scientific magazine by the name of the *Methodist Magazine*, he was poohpoohed by Methodists with the argument that the church did not have enough culture in it to support that kind of an enterprise. But such criticism ignored the increase in wealth, education, and sophistication of a new urban Methodism. Withrow went on through the 1880s and 1890s to edit the longest lived Canadian literary magazine of that period.

There were other signs of a broadening spirit and advance beachheads in a changing world by a new breed of evangelical Protestants. For instance, in 1859, by a marvellous section of beach on the southern shore of Lake Ontario, at Grimsby, there had been established one of those vital institutions of Methodism and evangelical religion called the camp meeting. For years the midsummer weeks had rung with the exhortations of the preaching fraternity who were bringing souls out of despair and into glory, the wails of those who were in distress, and the shouts of triumph. But by the 1870s and 1880s, Grimsby was in the throes of change. Large numbers of permanent cabins had been established, there was a dock for steamers, and the summer was partitioned into a variety of social and religious activities. It was necessary to establish regulations to keep people from becoming too lax and secular, but, on the other hand, there were many who defended this new kind of evangelical summer resort, arguing that times were changing. A relaxed agricultural society was giving way to one of urban intensity, and it seemed no longer appropriate to bring people to a camp meeting, work them up, and send them back full of energy as though they were returning to slower paced agrarian communities. Rather, the time had come for relaxing people, for providing places where the bow could be unstrung and people could take their ease. Centres like Grimsby were duplicated across the land and eventually grew in numbers, in the West as well. Places like Rock Lake in Manitoba and Lumsden Beach in Saskatchewan became centres for summer schools for gearing the newly organized laity of the church to new ways and new ideas, including the new social conception of the gospel.

Broadening Influences from Abroad

The churches had experienced the renewing spirit of revival with its implications for changed living; church organizations and initiatives had multiplied; the heightened sense of mission in and to the nation as national churches had produced a new sense of the church as a culture builder; expectations of the coming victory of evangelicalism created not only a mood of high anticipation, but also an alertness to new ideas and experiments abroad. It was of immense significance for the development of the social gospel in Canada that important new voices in Christian social thought and action in the western world at large were beginning to be heard at this critical juncture. Emerging leaders of the social gospel listened with increasing excitement. Through the 1880s and 1890s, for instance, Methodist eyes were focused intently upon innovative programs like Hugh Price Hughes' Forward Movement, which galvanized Methodism around the world from his base in West London, England. Hughes published a paper called the *Methodist Times* and became deeply involved in political and social comment, so deeply, in fact, that someone commented that it would be too bad if anything serious ever happened to London when Hugh Price Hughes was out of it. Hughes could be very direct about the social obligations of Christians and counselled his following across the world that Christians had no higher duty anywhere than to turn out corrupt corporations wherever they might be. In 1891, when William Booth's *In Darkest England and the Way Out* appeared, it got a heavy readership in Canada. It seemed to be advising the churches as they were undertaking their new culture-building roles that perhaps it might be necessary to build a state within a state in order to cope with the social problems of the time. Booth outlined a program he was determined to follow if he could secure the funds: model suburban villages, model agricultural villages, model industrial works, employment agencies, summer resorts – in short almost a state within a state. There were many who called it socialism and there were others who called it plain Christianity and followed Booth along the way.

For some, the visions of Hughes and Booth were radicalized by figures like Henry George and Tolstoy. George was perhaps the most significant North American Protestant social reformer of the age and was an ideal mediator between the old individualism and the new socialism. He was a classical economist and thought that the economy should continue on classical entrepreneurial lines. He argued, however, that classical economics had become distorted by private landholding. Land, after all, like water and air, was a gift from God to humankind. Why should any individual hold it in his/her own name and for his/her own profit? His followers went on to popularize the single tax as a means of taking land rent out of the hands of private proprietors and putting it at the disposal of the community. For all his desire to refurbish classical economy, Henry George's approach to land reform entailed a major governmental involvement in economic affairs in the name of community. It was more this major intervention of common Christian morality in economics than George's more explicit proposals that was his greatest contribution to the age – and to the emerging social gospel. Moses, who led his people to a land of their own, was George's hero, and his work teemed with pointed Biblical allusions.

Tolstoy followed, apparently securing a good press in the Canadian secular and religious journals in the eighties and nineties. It was not the Tolstoy of *War and Peace* or of *Anna Karenina*; it was the Tolstoy who had gone through a deep religious crisis and had come out of it with the conviction that the personal and social problems of the time could only be met by the adoption of the absolute ethics of the New Testament. He began to cart manure around Moscow, make shoes with his hands, and give away his wealth. He began writing books like *My Religion* and short stories like "How Much Land Does a Man Need?" reinforcing the growing Georgite and other reform movements and inspiring Canadian leaders of the social gospel.

To mention Hughes and Booth, George and Tolstoy is not to do justice to the many-faceted reform movements welling up on both sides of the Atlantic in the last decades of the century. A variety of enterprises, secular and religious, sprang up to confront social, political, and economic ills: the daily and weekly press and church publications carried a surprising amount of information on them, which cannot be documented here. Subscriptions to British and American publications were common, visits to both countries not infrequent, and immigration following the mid-nineties all hastened the spread and absorption of new ideas and experiments.

Darwin and the Social Gospel

Amid the ideological ferment, however, were elements that were of such importance in the background of the social gospel in Canada that they require further comment: reform Darwinism, Biblical criticism, and a new positive view of the state.

Christian Nurture might well have been called a peculiarly non-Darwinian application of environmentalism. But a Darwinian revolution of significance for the emergence of the social gospel was also underway in Canada in the 1890s. Darwin had documented the importance of environment in fostering or impeding the emergence and development of certain characteristics in species. That suggested in turn the importance of social environments in personal development, and Christians, who had clear ideas as to the kind of person they themselves aimed at, readily saw the uses of environmentalism – although often it issued in little more than the legislation of certain features of human behaviour out of existence.

The contribution of the Darwinian revolution to the social gospel, however, went far beyond such limited uses of scientific environmentalism to the provision of scientific grounds for more far-reaching Christian social hopes. Initially, the application of Darwin to society by Herbert Spencer and others had been in terms of the notion of a struggle for survival of the fittest. There were two problems with this Spencerian formula, which were being explored in the 1880s and 1890s. The first was that an individual could not be adequately presented in terms of a natural model alone, since he/she was such a powerful actor upon the environment. The artificial, not the natural, was the human mode, as Lester Ward in the United States pointed out so clearly. But a second related yet contrasting issue with more significance for the emergence of the social gospel was the dawning awareness that Darwin was not talking about a struggle for survival by individuals but about the origins of and survival of species. As philosopher-scientists like Henry Drummond and Peter Kropotkin observed, the patterns of behaviour by which species survived, however, did not so much involve competition as devices of cooperation and mutual aid. From the lowest plant levels of symbiosis in which plants coexisted by living off each other through to the more advanced patterns of social life of animal species, and, indeed, into the species known as *Homo sapiens*, it seemed that nature and evolution undergirded the social graces. The very Christian ethics the Church had taught for so long seemed to have the endorsation of the latest discoveries in natural science. Surely society was moving toward a thoroughly cooperative order; and could not Jesus Christ be presented as summing up in human form the final meaning of evolution, the first fruit of a perfected humankind? Few who were attracted by such ideas asked whether they were consistent with the preconditions for morality, but boldly incorporated moral striving as part of the divinely implanted evolutionary urge. The new reform Darwinism began to be discussed in the 1890s in summer assemblies that Canadians attended at Chautauqua in upstate New York, in the Niagara Assembly, in the newly founded ministerial institutes, at Queen's and Victoria College alumni conferences, and so on.

The Higher Criticism and Prophetic Politics

Rather unpredictably, the controversial Biblical higher criticism of the time also served to foster the social gospel in Canada, particularly through its elevation of the role of the Biblical prophets of the eighth century before Christ. In the older tradition they had been viewed as predictors of the coming of the Messiah, but when the Biblical critics went to work on the Old Testament, analyzing, comparing, and reorganizing its parts, it became apparent that these individuals were the giants of insight and the pivotal figures of the whole Old Testament story. They had been individuals who had got their revelation of God through alertness to the signs of the times. Their vision of a God who wanted justice, not religious ritual, bade them to hold the plumb line against Israel's practice. They got involved in politics and public affairs and sometimes suffered most heavily for it. If that was the way of God's revealing then, some began to say, why was it not the way of God's revealing now? Why should not preachers become like the prophets of old? Why should not they hold the plumb lines against the nations of their own day? Why should not they criticize commercial wrong and industrial injustice? So a new kind of social fare began to creep into the pulpits of the land in the 1890s as the Biblical criticism began to be absorbed. Its arrival could not have been timed better to coincide with the circulation of new social hopes, theories, and schemes.

From Laissez-Faire to the Positive State

The transition from *laissez-faire* conceptions to the idea of the positive state is a much better known story than the foregoing, but its significance for the social gospel went beyond the common understanding of that transition. Negative ideas of the state were bound to give way before the late-century surge of environmentalism, rising ethical concerns about the human implications of classical political economy, and new social conceptions. Perhaps the most potent influence upon attitudes toward the state, however, was the spread of neo-Hegelianism. Early in the century the German philosopher Hegel had formulated a most impressive philosophical system, which viewed history as a progressive expression of the eternal idea, or Reason, culminating in a social state in which authority and liberty were resolved. Here was a philosophy that could catch up many of the currents of religion and thought sketched above. It was congruent with the evangelicals' immanent sense of divinity in the processes of change. It linked human intelligence with the divine intelligence, thereby offering a harmony of religion and all phases of human culture, and readily endorsed the reform Darwinists' notion of the social evolutionary purposes exhibited in nature. It had played a vital part in the emergence of the new synthesis in Biblical understanding effected by Julius Wellhausen in the mid-1880s. It provided much of the foundation on which Edward Caird constructed his concept of progressive revelation. It was the substance of De Witt Hyde's *Practical Idealism*. With all of these potent neo-Hegelian influences upon many of the very constituents of the background influences in the formation of the social gospel, it was doubly significant that it had been neo-Hegelians like T.H. Green in England who had formulated the philosophical basis for the new positive state in idealist terms so appealing to increasingly liberal Protestant aspirations in Canada. It is not surprising, then, to hear Salem Bland, a pioneer of the social gospel in Canada, attributing to Hegel the synthesis in his own thinking in the 1890s.

Conclusion

By the end of the nineteenth century, then, these diverse material, religious, and intellectual ingredients were being stirred together in various proportions: economic dislocations of the new industrial/urban order; the revivalist emphasis on the need and possibility of a radical change in life; an evangelical theology of the immanence of God in the processes of change; a belief that the application of Christian energy could arouse social repentance and the will to challenge nefarious social, economic, and political structures; the establishment or revitalizing of a host of new religious organizations creating a new institutional cradle-to-grave Protestantism at the very time the churches were adopting a broader culture-building role, developing a sense of national mission, and anticipating the coming triumph of evangelicalism; the development of more hopeful views of childhood, opening new possibilities for secular social reform; a belief that evolution itself not only affirmed the social graces, but called humankind to new patterns of co-operative living; the renewal by higher criticism of the prophetic tradition that God required not burnt offerings but justice; and the beginnings of a new appreciation of the positive uses of the state. The mixture could obviously be a heady one, and it is readily apparent why, in their exalted states, some referred to their new commitment as a "social passion."

It is impossible at this point to trace in detail the complex historical interaction between so many elements comprising the background of the social gospel in Canada. However, it is important to note that their interaction was underway at the same time that the challenge of the urban/industrial order was mounting for all Canadians. The resolution of religious and intellectual problems on the one hand, and social and economic problems on the other, was proceeding at one and the same time; the one did not give rise to the other, related though they were, and intertwined as they were to become. The challenge of each elucidated the issues of the other, and the contribution of the social gospel to the reform movements of the next generation was the result.

CHAPTER SEVEN

The Social Gospel and the Reform Tradition in Canada, 1890–1928

BACKGROUNDER

Like The Social Passion, *this essay has assumed somewhat classic proportions as the first short statement of the centrality of the social gospel to a surging Canadian reform movement of the 1890s into the 1920s. It is the only essay in this collection available online. In a preliminary form it was delivered as an invitational lecture at the University of Alberta. The essay owes much to Richard L. Watson, Jr, a noted authority on the Progressive Era in the United States, who supervised the dissertation from which the essay derives. However, it was under John Hallowell that I came to appreciate a troubling element in social gospel progressivism that would provide the core of my conclusion to this essay as well as to the final chapter of* The Social Passion. *In part this was due to Hallowell's interest in the Christian realism of Reinhold Niebuhr, then the reigning public intellectual in the United States. For Niebuhr, the various collective entities of the social order, including those movements for justice that the social Christians were called to support, were fundamentally engaged in a power struggle driven by self-interested motives. Christian social activists were not confronted with absolutes of good and evil, but choices between the greater good or the lesser evil. Over time, to the degree that success attended chosen causes, Niebuhr counselled, the more the elements of self-interest and a drive for power in the established order would predominate. For Niebuhr, that meant that the quest for the kingdom of God's justice had to be renewed in each new generation. It was at this point that Hallowell's interest in philosopher Eric Voegelin came into play. Voegelin saw in all varieties of progressivism a gnostic tendency to advance theories of history that assumed a secret knowledge of an ultimate end purpose in which the temporal process would culminate. Hallowell, himself, put it this way: "[The contemporary] crisis is the culmination of modern man's progressive attempt to deny the existence of a transcendent spiritual reality and of his progressive failure to find meaning and salvation in some wholly immanent conception of reality [such as] the Class, the Race, or the State."[1]*

The tension between transcendence and immanence in Christian thought was not new to me, and I had read a similar critique in Wilhelm Visser 't Hooft's The Background of the Social Gospel in America *(1928). The problem of immanence for the social gospel advocates was not the total abandonment of a transcendent spiritual reality (God), but a refreshing, if overwhelming, emphasis on the presence (immanence) of God in the temporal order, in the movements and agencies for social justice that social gospel activists espoused. Niebuhr's critique of the social gospel was that in so identifying God, they were in danger of slighting the ongoing judgment of the social order implied in the transcendence of God, and thus short circuiting a clear-headed recognition of the hard realities they were dealing with and ending, if not in promoting some new tyranny, at least in disillusionment at not having fully achieved the end they sought. The social gospel in Canada was not inclined to the surrogate religions of "Class, Race, and State" with which Hallowell was preoccupied, but it would be students of the likes of Niebuhr who would rescue the social gospel from its disillusionment in the latter 1920s, take the lead in combatting the monstrous evils of the 1930s, and chart a new course for the future.*

THE SOCIAL GOSPEL AND THE REFORM TRADITION*

The literature of social reform has not been extensive in Canada even though a sizable movement of reform was abroad in the land from the 1890s through the 1930s, a movement that was found in church and in secular society, and at municipal, provincial, and, progressively, federal levels. In the last chapter of his *Progressive Party in Canada,* Morton sees the decline of that party as a result in part of the waning of the impulse toward reform in society as a whole. Underlying and accompanying the movement toward reform through the political system had been the social gospel, a movement of which the most important function was to forge links between proposed reforms and the religious heritage of the nation, thus endowing reform with an authority it could not otherwise command. At the same time it attempted to create the religious and social

---

* First published as "The Social Gospel and the Reform Tradition in Canada, 1890–1928," *Canadian Historical Review* 49, no. 4 (1968): 381–99. Reprinted with the permission of the University of Toronto Press.

attitudes thought necessary for life in a world reformed. But the world proved too intractable for the realization of the movement's high socio-religious hopes, and in the wake of the frustrating experiences of the early 1920s, supporters of the social gospel, and other reform movements, took different paths; some withdrew from politics, some retreated to pragmatic politics, some transferred their enthusiasm to other causes (notably peace movements and personal religion), and others moved toward a new radicalism. The reform movement may be viewed from many standpoints, but only when it is looked at as a religious manifestation, a striving to embed ultimate human goals in the social, economic, and political order, is its success and failure fully appreciated. The history of the social gospel in Canada is an account of that process.

The social gospel rested on the premise that Christianity was a social religion, concerned when the misunderstanding of the ages was stripped away, with the quality of human relations on this earth. More dramatically, it was a call for individuals to find the meaning of their lives in seeking to realize the kingdom of God in the very fabric of society. It was a measure of the radicalism implicit in the social gospel that the Methodist church in 1918 called for complete social reconstruction by a transfer of the basis of society from competition to cooperation. It was a measure of the conservatism inevitably associated with such a call that even some of the most radical supporters of the social gospel believed that in the family as they knew it, and in the political democracy of their time, two essential elements of the society toward which Jesus pointed individuals were already in existence, or virtually so. Such a reduction was necessary to apply a pan-historical and transcendent concept to immediate needs. And without such reduction the reform movement would have enjoyed considerably less power.

The Protestant background out of which the Canadian social gospel had to emerge was one dominated overwhelmingly by the Anglican, Methodist, and Presbyterian churches. The similarities and disparities in the social outlook of these churches prior to the onset of depression in the late nineteenth century may be suggested by their reactions to a strike of the Toronto Printers' Union in 1872. The Anglican *Church Herald* condemned the labourers for usurping the role of the employer and blamed the strike upon "the insidious whimperings of a foreign-born league." *The Presbyterian Witness* argued that labour's campaign "strikes at the very root of ... personal independence and perpetuates their social demoralisation ... No man ever rose above a lowly condition who thought more of his class than of his individuality." The Methodist *Christian Guardian* declared a profound sympathy with all honest working individuals and a sincere desire for their betterment, but went on to say: "we seriously question the wisdom and advantage of this movement – especially the strikes to which it is likely to lead."[2] When news of Henry George's Anti-Poverty Society reached Toronto in 1887, the other two churches would probably have echoed the response of the *Christian Guardian* on 29 June: "We have no faith in the abolition of poverty by any laws that can be made in legislatures ... The best anti-poverty society is an association of men who would adopt as their governing principles in life, industry, sobriety, economy and intelligence." Such an individualistic ethic was unable, however, to withstand the combined onslaught of extended depression, the rapid growth of industrial urban centres, and the spread of new social conceptions.

It has been argued that the social gospel in Canada was an indigenous development.[3] Although it is possible that a Canadian social gospel might have developed simply in response to domestic urban and industrial problems, it did not in fact happen that way. To be sure, the earliest expressions of the social gospel in Canada may still lie in sources untouched by historians' hands. And in those sources, the rise of the social gospel may be obscured by the gradual nature of its separation from older forms of Christian social expression characterized by a concern for church–state relations, education, political corruption, and personal and social vice. But almost all evidence regarding the emergence of the social gospel from this tradition points to currents of thought and action that were sweeping the Western world, none of which originated in Canada. To trace this "North Atlantic triangle" of culture and religion underlying the social gospel at large and its transmission to and development within Canada is a worthy but massive project. In this paper, only a description of some of its salient features can be attempted.

The inspiration of the pioneers of the social gospel in Canada and the origin of some of its prominent institutions reveal the extent of its indebtedness. W.A. Douglass in the 1880s expressed his disagreement with individualistic methods of social regeneration by tirelessly campaigning for Henry George's panacea of the single tax.[4] Salem Bland, later to become the philosopher and mentor of the movement, was an omnivorous reader, and in the decade of the 1890s when he seems to have first formulated a social gospel outlook, he was especially influenced by Carlyle, Tennyson, Emerson, Channing, and Thoreau, by the historical critics of scripture, and by Albrecht Ritschl, the great German theologian whose optimistic theology played a great role in the emergence of a social gospel theology. At least as significant for Bland was the literature of evolution.[5] The notes for his first socialist lecture, "Four Steps and a Vision," acknowledge various works of Darwin, Drummond's *Ascent of Man*, and Kidd's *Social Evolution*, as well as *Fabian Essays*, Arnold Toynbee, Edward Bellamy, and Henry George.[6]

Canadians had attended the three great interdenominational conferences in the United States on social problems in 1887, 1889, and 1893, and one follow-up conference had been held in Montreal in the latter year.[7] Institutional vehicles and expressions of the social gospel such as the Brotherhoods, institutional churches, settlements, and labour churches derived ultimately from British models, although American mediation and modification took place in some instances. This pattern of influence continued throughout the life of the social gospel in Canada.

The optimism of the social gospel drew on more than a generalized sense of progress, and even on more than the influence of evolutionary concepts. One of the more significant religious developments of the nineteenth century was the expansion of evangelicalism – expressed variously in German pietism, the Methodism of the English-speaking world, the missionary movement, and American revivalism. As against the reformed tradition of Calvinism, evangelicalism stressed free will, an immanent God, religious emotion, and a restrictive personal and social morality that made its followers formidably austere. Among its doctrines was a belief in the possibility of personal perfection beyond the temptation of sin. In the course of the nineteenth century it made an immense impact on all Christian traditions, especially in North America. As evangelicalism became more diffused in the latter half of the century and awareness of the social problem arose, the individualism of the evangelical way seemed to be less and less appropriate to many.[8] The demand "save this man," now became "save this society, now," and the slogan "the evangelization of the world in our generation" became "the Christianization of the world in our generation."[9] The sense of an immanent God working in the movement of revival and awakening was easily transferred to social movements, and hence to the whole evolution of society. Thus Josiah Strong in the United States could speak of the "great social awakening," and many could come to view secular social action as a religious rite.

Such combinations of ideas and impulses were apparent in a sermon given to the first Brotherhood group in Canada on 14 April 1895. Speaking on "Social Resurrection," J.B. Silcox argued that Jesus' "resurrection means that humanity shall rise ... into higher, nobler, diviner conditions of life." He joined several British thinkers, preachers, and writers, he said, in predicting a worldwide revolution for the people in the twentieth century. According to Silcox, "This uprising of the people is divine in its source ... God is in the midst of it ... To the ecclesiastical and industrial Pharaohs of today, God is saying, 'Let my people go.'" He concluded by calling for "a political faith in Jesus" based on the charter of the Sermon on the Mount.[10] C.S. Eby in *The World Problem and the Divine Solution* (1914) was somewhat more philosophical in expression. Jesus Christ was the "type of coming man on this planet." The ultimate reality of which Christ was the revelation was in and through all things: "the universal spirit of Christ would reconstruct man and mankind." Trade unionism, socialism, and business organization were a work of this spirit developing a new social order.[11] On this basis Eby built his Socialist church in Toronto in 1909.[12] Many influences from the world of letters, science, religion, and reform were held in solution in the social gospel in various proportions. Few distilled the solution as did Douglass, Bland, Silcox, and Eby, and while they might be more radical than most, their thought represented the tendency of the movement as a whole.

The pressures of the last years of depression in the early 1890s precipitated a quickening interest in new forms of social thought and action among a growing group of Christian ministers and lay people. One of the most important centres of this interest was the Queen's Theological Alumni Conference, instituted by Principal G.M. Grant in 1893. At its annual meetings, the conference discussed papers on such topics as Biblical criticism, economic development, the problems of poverty, socialistic schemes, the single tax, social evolution, interpretations of modern life by modern poets, studies of the prophets, Tolstoy, the relation of legislation and morality, and Christianity in its relation to human progress. As a Methodist minority among Presbyterians, Salem Bland was probably the most radical of the regular members.[13] At the beginning of the decade, a pirated edition of General William Booth's *In Darkest England and the Way Out* was selling vigorously.[14] Booth's scheme, involving the establishment of labour exchanges, farm colonies and industrial towns, model suburban villages, paid holidays, and an intelligence service for processing useful social data, was branded by some as socialistic, but encouraged others to view social action as an essential part of true religion.[15] Two Canadian ministers, S.S. Craig and Herbert Casson, taking their cue from John Trevor in Manchester, attempted to found labour churches. Nothing more is known of Craig's venture in Toronto,[16] but Casson's attempt at Lynn, Massachusetts, lasted from 1893 to 1898, after which he became a well-known socialist lecturer in Canada as well as the United States.[17] A Congregationalist layman, T.B. Macaulay, in 1894 brought the Brotherhood movement from England to Montreal, whence its "brief, bright and brotherly" meetings, which mixed gospel songs with social reform, spread across the nation.[18]

Among social problems, those of slums and immigration prompted the larger part of the institutional response of the social gospel within the churches. Again, it was in the last decade of the nineteenth century that the more ambitious innovations were undertaken with the establishment of St Andrew's Institute in 1890 by a Presbyterian, D.J. Macdonnell, and the Fred Victor Mission in 1894 by a Methodist group under the impetus of the Massey family. Together providing facilities for night school, library, savings bank, nursery, clubrooms, gymnasium, medical centre, and restaurant, they reflected ventures pioneered in England, Scotland, and the United States in the previous decade.[19] Further institutional response to urban problems came after 1902 with the development of settlement houses by Miss Sara Libby Carson, working under the Presbyterian church. By 1920 there were at least thirteen settlements in Canada, probably all of them formed under the impulse of the social gospel.[20] Where Miss Carson was not involved directly as organizer, she was often associated as consultant, as in the cases of the Toronto and McGill University settlements (1907 and 1909, respectively), which grew out of social concern in the student YMCAs. When the University of Toronto opened its Department of Social Service in 1914, the University Settlement provided the framework for practical work, and Miss Carson and the Rev. F.N. Stapleford of the Neighbourhood Workers' Association, among others, were recruited as lecturers.[21] Under J.S. Woodsworth, the settlement approach to the problems of North Winnipeg became a more potent spearhead of social reform, and the beginning, for Woodsworth, of an ever more radical formulation of the social gospel.[22]

In the 1890s, the churches were deeply involved in a mounting campaign against "drink." This was rationalized by leading figures such as F.S. Spence as part of the great gospel of liberty.[23]

Significantly, however, a rude sort of environmentalism was creeping into the "ideology" of prohibition, placing it in the context of a reform program based on the strategy of reform Darwinism: that the way to reform the individual was through alterations in his/her environment. As a wider array of social problems began to engage the minds of clergy and lay people alike, new committees and church structures were required. The Methodist Committee on Sociological Questions from 1894 to 1918 presented to general conference ever more progressive and comprehensive reports for church guidance. By 1914 committees or departments of temperance and moral reform became full boards of social service and evangelism. The social task had been placed alongside that of evangelism in the official hierarchy of concerns of the Methodist and Presbyterian churches, and committees of social service were common in the other denominations. In 1913, when Methodists and Presbyterians combined in a program of social surveys of major Canadian cities (and some rural areas), a systematic attack, chiefly upon the complex environment of the cities, was in the making.[24]

In the background of this escalation of social gospel enterprise was an ambitious effort at institutional consolidation. The Church Union movement, initiated in 1902, was making headway, and in 1907, an alliance of church and labour groups, having won the Lord's Day Act, blossomed into the Moral and Social Reform Council of Canada, jointly headed by J.G. Shearer and T.A. Moore, social service secretaries of the Presbyterian and Methodist churches, respectively. Although until the middle of the second decade the provincial units of the council were largely engrossed in temperance campaigns, for several years thereafter they promoted a broad program of social reform and community action that won the praise of young radicals like William Ivens and William Irvine.[25] In 1913 the national organization changed its name to the Social Service Council of Canada and further broadened its perspectives.[26]

These years were exciting ones for progressive church individuals. Not only were they advancing their campaign to win the churches to what they called sociological concepts, but they were also making significant progress in liberalizing the restrictive personal disciplines of their denominations and gaining ground for historical criticism and a reformation of theological curricula.[27] During and after 1908 a lively discussion on the relation of Christianity to socialism developed. The subject was kept alive by a small group among whom were Bland, the Rev. Ben Spence, the socialist-prohibitionist who in 1904 managed A.W. Puttee's campaign to win a second term as a labour MP,[28] A.E. Smith, who endorsed labour candidates in successive pastorates at Nelson, British Columbia, and Winnipeg and Brandon, Manitoba,[29] and the Rev. W.E.S. James, who was general secretary from about 1905 of the Christian Socialist Fellowship in Ontario and organizer in 1914 of the Church of the Social Revolution in Toronto.[30] A wave of millennial socialism in Britain after the election of 1906, the controversy surrounding R.J. Campbell's *New Theology*,[31] and touring lecturers such as Keir Hardie (1908 and 1912) and the Rev. J. Stitt Wilson (1909 and 1910), who preached the message of socialism as applied Christianity, undoubtedly spurred discussion in Canada.[32]

Both socialists and clerics picked up the theme. In 1909 W.A. Cotton, editor of the Canadian socialist journal *Cotton's Weekly*, developed the notion that Jesus had been the original labour leader.[33] In 1910 a large meeting in Montreal heard an exposition of socialism based on the Bible, and the prominent socialist from British Columbia, E.T. Kingsley of the Socialist Party of Canada, declared Christianity and socialism to be identical. The current did not run all one way, of course. A group of Toronto socialists in November 1910 devoted at least one evening to the subject, "Why a Socialist Can Not Be a Christian."[34]

After 1908 professed socialists in the churches seemed to not have been so isolated or so peripheral. In that year the Rev. Dr D.M. Ramsey in Ottawa described socialism as "carrying into economic regions the Christian doctrine of human brotherhood."[35] The Rev. Elliott S. Rowe organized socialist leagues in Sandon and Victoria, British Columbia.[36] Bryce M. Stewart in his survey of Fort William in 1913 found a considerable number of Christians sympathetic to socialism, and observed, "It is beyond question that in purity of purpose, ethics, and scientific reasoning the socialist position is far beyond any other political organization, and should appeal especially to the Christian."[37] In the same year, the Rev. Thomas Voaden of Hamilton, in a series of lectures later published, presented the thesis that socialism was the effect of Christianity forced outside the churches.[38] However, this socialism that was not entirely outside the churches was becoming more and more apparent. In a survey of London, Ontario, in 1913 by the Brotherhoods of that city, it was found to be common opinion in the churches that neither unions nor socialist groups threatened or interfered with the church's work and, further, individuals of both organizations were found among the church's workers.[39]

Given the groundswell that seemed to be building up for the social gospel as the twentieth century entered its second decade, it was not surprising that when the Social Service Council called a national congress on social problems for March 1914, the response was overwhelming. For three days over 200 regular delegates from across the nation, representing welfare organizations, churches, farm and labour groups, municipalities, provinces, and the federal government, were subjected to a barrage of social statistics, social conditions, social challenges, and social exhortations.[40] Most of the forty Canadian speakers were from central Canada, and although the rural problem was considered, speakers overwhelmingly represented urban areas: social workers, city judges and politicians, city doctors, labour leaders, college professors, and city clergy. Although city oriented, the world of business management and ownership was conspicuous by its absence.

This was primarily a conference of professionals. Its social sources lay outside and below the centres of power that were forging the new Canada. The lines of sympathy were clear in the enthusiastic response to the claim of a visiting speaker that "there is so much religion in the labor movement and so much social spirit in the Church, that someday it will become a question whether the Church will capture the labor movement or the labor movement will capture the Church."[41] Not all the speakers gave evidence of the social gospel, but when their concerns were related to other information about them, the inferences seemed clear: Dr Charles Hastings, Toronto's medical health officer, was a Presbyterian elder, a past chairman of the Progressive Club, and a member of the Public Ownership League;[42] J.O. McCarthy, Toronto city controller, was a leading figure in the Canadian Brotherhood Federation and a member of the Methodist Board of Social Service and Evangelism;[43] James Simpson, vice-president of the Trades and Labor Congress, was a Methodist local preacher, a lecturer for the Dominion Prohibition Alliance, a vice-president of the Toronto branch of the Lord's Day Alliance, and a perennially successful socialist candidate for offices of city government in Toronto who was consistently supported in his campaigns by the Epworth League, the Methodist young people's organization.[44] In short, it seemed that to scratch a reformer at the congress was to find a social gospeller.

So popular were the evening open meetings that the *Ottawa Citizen* could not recall any recent visiting theatrical production to rival them and, when the tumult had subsided, concluded on 6 March that the congress had been "one of the greatest assemblages ever held in Canada to grapple with ... social and economical problems." The congress represented the social gospel entering a crest of influence. C.W. Gordon (Ralph Connor), writing the introduction to the report, was excited by the challenge thrown down to the "economic and social conditions on which the fabric of our state is erected." He may not have been aware of the hint of incongruity in his conclusion that "there is in our nation so deep a sense of righteousness and brotherhood that it needs only that the light fall clear and white on the evil to have it finally removed."[45] Was reform to be won so cheaply? An unevangelicalized Calvinist might have been pardoned his doubts.

During the generation of its ascent, from 1890 to 1914, the social gospel front remained remarkably united. One could now discern three emphases or wings beginning to crystallize, however. The conservatives were closest to traditional evangelicalism, emphasizing personal ethical issues, tending to identify sin with individual acts, and taking as their social strategy legislative reform of the environment. The radicals viewed society in more organic terms. Evil was so endemic and pervasive in the social order that they concluded there could be no personal salvation without social salvation – or at least without bearing the cross of social struggle. Without belief in an immanent God working in the social process to bring God's kingdom to birth, the plight of the radicals would surely have been desperate. Between conservatives and radicals was a broad "centre party" of progressives holding the tension between the two extremes, endorsing in considerable measure programs of the other two, but transmuting them somewhat into a broad ameliorative program of reform. The harmony of these wings was not to last. Between 1914 and 1928 the social gospel enjoyed and endured at one and the same time a period of crest and of crisis. Its growing differentiation in church, interdenominational, and secular organizations multiplied its impact on Canadian society and at the same time initiated interaction between the various modes of its expression. These were the conditions of its potency. They were also the conditions of its crisis, for the encounter with social reality was the true test of social gospel concepts, and the very complexity of that reality and the conflict inherent within it inevitably set one wing of the social gospel in conflict with another. This involved process culminated in the years 1926–28, and the movement generally entered a period of weariness, reaction, and reconsideration.

The war of 1914–18 was the occasion, and in considerable measure the cause, of a crisis in relations between the radicals and the church. Over the course of the war, four radicals, then or later of some prominence, lost their professional posts: William Irvine, J.S. Woodsworth, Salem Bland, and William Ivens. The situation of each individual was complex, but while they all believed their fate to be the result of increasing commercialism in the church and growing reaction in the state, and while Professor McNaught adopts the radicals' arguments as to what happened to them, the thesis is hardly acceptable.[46] It can only be maintained by slighting a number of facts : the acceptance of their radicalism, either prior to their appointment or without protest during a considerable period before severance of employment; the obvious support all had in the courts of the church; the complicating factor of pacifism in two cases; a host of evidence that Bland was more likely a victim of retrenchment in Wesley College; and most important, the growing progressivism of the churches throughout the wartime period.

The evidence of church progressivism from 1914 to 1918 is more than substantial. All churches were dismayed by the outbreak of war, and the Methodists and Presbyterians at least condemned the profiteering that accompanied it. The Methodist general conference in the fall adopted the strongest reform program to date and promised a further instalment in four years.[47] The Presbyterian Department of Social Service in 1916 regarded with hope the increase of nationalization and social control of industry in allied countries and took heart in new Canadian legislation on prohibition, female suffrage, worker's compensation, and protective legislation, the beginnings of provincial departments of labour, government encouragement of fishing co-operative societies in Nova Scotia, and the establishment of a bureau of social research under Woodsworth by the prairie provinces.[48] The Social Service Council sponsored regional congresses carrying on the spirit of its Ottawa success, added several more secular affiliates to its roster, and just prior to the war's end established the first national social welfare publication.[49] The church declarations of social policy in 1918 were further left than the manifestos of any major Canadian party and approximated the British Labour party's program for national minimum standards.[50] The Methodist call for a complete social reconstruction received international circulation, and, as stated in the *New Republic*, placed that church in the vanguard of reform forces.[51]

Radical social gospellers like Ernest Thomas of Vancouver, Bland, and A.E. Smith[52] played an important role in the formation of these church resolutions, but for the radicals, the most important consequence of their mid-war crisis with church and state was the impact of their association, and hence of the social gospel, on agrarian and labour movements. J.S. Woodsworth was to be found addressing meetings of the Federated Labour party in Vancouver and writing in the *British Columbia Federationist*. William Irvine became a leading figure in the Non-Partisan League in Alberta, editor of its journal the *Alberta Non-Partisan*, and a key individual in the Dominion Labour party in Calgary. William Ivens in 1918 undertook an organizing tour in the prairie region for the Dominion Labour party,[53] stepped into the high priesthood, as the *Voice* put it, of labour forces at Winnipeg by founding a thriving labour church, and became editor of the *Western Labor News*.[54] From 1917 to 1919, Salem Bland contributed a regular column to the *Grain Growers' Guide*, and during the summer of 1918 he addressed tens of thousands of westerners (with Henry Wise Wood) from the Chautauqua platform. Adding their voices to the journalism of reform were two more radicals of the social gospel, A.E. Smith as editor of the *Confederate* in Brandon[55] and James Simpson as editor of the *Industrial Banner* in Toronto.

Despite the wartime crisis, the progressive and radical social gospellers had by 1918–19 reached a position of considerable power and consequence in the Canadian reform movement. And in the conservative wing, the progress of prohibition was startling. The war economy aided the cause, and in 1918 a government order-in-council prohibited further manufacture and sale of liquor until a year after the war's end. But it must be admitted that the temperance forces won a national consensus on the subject. By 1919 only Quebec held out as a province, and it was at least two-thirds dry by local option. The farm organizations for some time had officially endorsed the reform, and now labour was finding near prohibition a stimulus to union membership.[56] Anglican publications joined other church journals in declaring that if prohibition was good in wartime, it was good in peace as well.[57]

There can be no doubt that the unrest, and especially the great Winnipeg strike of 1919, dealt the social gospel a rude jolt – and yet the impact can be easily exaggerated. The radicals, of course, were in the midst of it, sometimes carried to enthusiastic excesses of rhetoric that could easily be misunderstood. Their social millennialism undoubtedly contributed to the élan and discipline of the strike but also to an element of unreality in which it was shrouded.[58] The Labour church provided its focus and strove as eight continuing churches in Winnipeg to maintain the essential unity of the left and the religious sense of labour's purpose that had been generated.[59]

The critical question, however, was how the progressive social gospel at large reacted to the events of 1919. The problem was complicated not simply by the growth of conservative reaction inside and outside the churches, but by the complex of attitudes in progressive minds to employers, unions, and social conflict. Generally sympathetic to labour, and persuaded that the spirit of Jesus was in social unrest calling on the church's true function as a defender of the oppressed,[60] they nevertheless believed that the "day of club and bludgeon is gone by," as Creighton described it in the *Christian Guardian*.[61] Misreading the face of power in industry, they were often, as was H. Michel in the *Canadian Churchman*, as pleased with the ending of a strike with improved conditions and shop committees as with recognition of a union and bargaining rights.[62] Nevertheless, the social gospel's position held remarkably firm. Of the church's press that inclined toward the social gospel was the *Presbyterian and Westminster,* attacking the Winnipeg general strike outright.[63] The *Western Methodist Recorder* sympathized with labour and strike action but attacked the most radical element of strike leadership.[64] The *Churchman* reluctantly conceded the case in the face of government charges of sedition.[65] But the *Christian Guardian* and *Social Welfare* supported the strike throughout.[66] Clergy in and out of Winnipeg frequently spoke out on behalf of the strikers and questioned the government's interpretation and intervention. While the strike was on, numerous church conferences were in progress across the land, and it is difficult to find a case where social policies were modified in the face of unrest – quite the opposite.[67] S.D. Chown, general superintendent of the Methodist church, in many addresses urged members to continue to cry out against injustice and to consider the social gospel the voice of prophecy in their time.[68] He has been charged with pronouncing a "ban" on the strikers.[69] He did not, but he was concerned that there was an indiscriminate injustice in the general strike weapon that he could not sanction and believed that if labour continued such tactics the church might have to be more reserved in its support.[70]

Three events taken together served to heighten that reservation, however, to stalemate the progressives' program for industrial peace and to perplex the social gospel. Even radicals of the social gospel had long argued that the very collective organization of industry bore out their arguments about the nature of society and hence the nature of the ethic required of modern individuals.[71] The business people and industrial owners would surely come to recognize this. However, when in September 1919 the government gathered a national industrial conference with representatives from management, labour, and the public, it was almost a total failure.[72] But when the churches conducted an immense Inter-Church Forward Campaign in the winter and spring to equip them for their enlarged social role in the new era, it was an immense success.[73] Some, like Chown, saw in the success a new alliance for progress – the socially minded clergy folk and the "new businessman."[74] For some months, the Methodist social service officers had been aware of a small flood of enquiries from business people asking guidance as to how to apply the church's policies to their business operations.[75] J.G. Shearer in *Social Welfare* was astonished at the number of plants that had instituted joint industrial councils, although he was suspicious that some at least were intended to forestall unionization.[76]

The dilution of progressivism such developments entailed was completed for many by the printers' strike of 1921, in the course of which the church publishing houses, the Methodist in particular, experienced at first hand the hideous complexities of industrial conflict. The Methodist house encouraged union membership. Depressed business conditions of 1921 precluded meeting all union demands. Nevertheless, with most other printing establishments in Toronto, it was struck on 1 June. Its manager allowed himself to be drafted as chairman of the employers' anti-strike committee and soon found himself in the midst of an outright open-shop campaign. The union, on the other hand, not only rejected reasonable offers, but turned on the Methodists with special fury because they seemed to not be living up to their progressive declarations of 1918. Despite an outcry from Methodist summer schools, and frantic negotiations by Ernest Thomas of the Social Service Department, there was little that could be done. Neither the church nor any other business could now live on the terms of the envisaged economic order of social gospel prophecy.[77] Creighton concluded that strikes were simply stupid and had no constructive word for labour in the great British Empire Steel and Coal Company conflicts of the mid-decade.[78] The Social Service Council drifted from its celebration of the significance of labour in its Labour Day issues to its calm notices of the day at the decade's end.[79] The United Church's pronouncement on industry in 1926 simply launched the new church on a sea of ambiguities, which many recognized, but which none could chart more accurately.[80] The bright vision of the social gospel seemed to be going into eclipse.[81]

For a time, the upward course of the agrarian revolt and the Progressive party offered new opportunities. From the earlier days of E.A. Partridge, the social gospel played an intimate role in the theory and practice of the agrarian movements.[82] The churches had attempted to foster social life and community ideals through institutes, conferences, and summer schools.[83] The *Guide* promoted the notion of the church as a community centre.[84] Farm leaders like Drury, Good, Moyle, and Henders were prominent members of social service councils.[85] Bland and the Congregationalist D.S. Hamilton worked closely with S.J. Farmer and Fred Dixon in Winnipeg on behalf of the single tax and direct legislation.[86] Henry Wise Wood counselled his farmers to look to the church for a social saviour, for it was just now beginning to recognize Jesus as a social leader as well as a personal saviour.[87] Wood's whole program of civilizational reform was built on the theological assumptions of the social gospel.[88] Since 1903, from Wesley College, Winnipeg, Salem Bland had been sending out young ministers of the social gospel who frequently became members of local units of the Grain Growers' Associations.[89] By 1919 the social gospel had become, in effect, the religion of the agrarian revolt,[90] and its continued involvement in the process of party and policy formation was such that Norman Lambert, secretary of the Canadian Council of Agriculture, observed that religion and social work were inextricably linked with the farmers.[91]

The victories of the Progressive party can, then, be viewed in part as victories of the social gospel. But equally, the failure of the Progressives in 1926 must be weighed on the social gospel scales. In brief, it must be conceded that the social gospel belief that in the rise of such movements true religion and genuine democracy were triumphing together in the modern world contributed to the Progressive party's sense of being something other than a traditional party and of fulfilling something more than a political role. This non-politics of hope was inevitably ground to pieces in a parliamentary world where alliances were necessary, but compromising, where decisions were mandatory, and where the better alternative was seldom clear.

At mid-decade, although the great accomplishment of Church Union brightened the horizon, that victory had been won at some cost. The drive to consolidate social service in the new church had worked to the disadvantage of other expressions of the social gospel. Support was withdrawn from the Brotherhood Federation, and the Social Service Council ran afoul of church financing and personal animosities. The former collapsed completely, and the latter, also hit by depression conditions, the counterattacks against prohibition, and the death of its secretary, J.G. Shearer, lived on in a maimed condition.[92] The campaign for a national church made church social service leaders more hostile than they would otherwise have been to the labour churches that had spread to at least ten other cities before collapsing in 1924–25.[93] T.A. Moore of the Methodist Social Service Department had, for three critical years of their life, played a dubious role with the Royal Canadian Mounted Police (RCMP) in its investigation of the churches.[94] The labour churches, however, died chiefly of their own inadequacy as a religious institution. After 1924 they followed their logical course, with a transfer of religious commitment and zeal to the creation of a more radical reform party via Woodsworth's Ginger Group, and in A.E. Smith's case, one might observe, to the Communist party.[95] Not only did Church Union further drain progressive social gospel energies in the task of institutional reconstruction, but on the morrow of Union, the critical battle in defence of prohibition had to be fought. One by one after 1920 the provincial temperance acts had gone down to defeat. In 1926 the last main stronghold, Ontario, was under attack. The church that was to rally the forces of social righteousness was already fighting a rearguard battle.

At stake was the survival of the conservative social gospel. In the aftermath of defeat the temperance forces were shattered beyond repair.[96] "Old Ontario" has died, declared Ernest Thomas as he launched a careful critique of temperance strategy.[97] The consensus, carefully built up over the years, had disappeared, just as the association of social work and religion, so long nurtured under the social service formula, was now giving way to secular organizations quite outside, and often severely critical of, the churches.[98]

It was no coincidence that the crisis in the social gospel coincided so nearly with the crisis in Progressive politics and in the reform movement at large. The categories in which they all worked, and the divinities that moved them all, lay shattered. Nevertheless, the lessons of the encounter with reality were not easily absorbed, in part owing to the ease with which the social gospel could transfer its passion from one cause to another. Partly as a positive expression of the social gospel, but also, one suspects, as a sublimation of frustration, much progressive zeal in 1923 transferred itself to a resurgence of pacifism, and after 1926 to a more broadly conceived peace movement.[99] Only among a few individuals like Ernest Thomas and leaders in the Student Christian Movement were penetrating questions being asked about the adequacy of social gospel concepts.[100] Prosperous church expansion in the later 1920s was accompanied by religious introversion and by small fellowship groups.[101] But out of the latter, the reconsiderations of the more critically minded, the struggles of the survivors of the political wreck of Progressivism, and a growing dialectic with more radical forms of socialist thought, was to come a new thrust of a reconstructed social gospel in the 1930s.

PART THREE

Consciousness, Crisis, and Consequences

CHAPTER EIGHT

Children of Prophecy:
Wesley College Students
in an Age of Reform

BACKGROUNDER

Having given some prominence to the Student Christian Movement in The Social Passion *as an important bearer of the social gospel in Canada in the 1920s and having been a student activist myself, I was naturally curious about the social attitudes and commitments of college students of a previous generation. The 1890s through the 1910s had seen a rising movement of social prophecy and concomitant social reformist activity among Winnipeg's clergy and the college professoriate. How did Winnipeg students, and especially the students of Wesley College, the primary site of social gospel activism in the West, respond to the prevailing context of social reformist thought and action? Did they simply reflect and follow the lead of their professors and local clergy, or were they originators and initiators, if indeed they were responsive at all to the reformist mood of the times? It was such reflections that prompted me to offer the following paper at the Red River Valley Historical Society meeting in Winnipeg in 1974.*

Wesley College was an interesting case. Isolated at mid-continent, it was far from metropolitan centres of culture. However, in the mid-1890s, set in a region just beginning to be taken seriously as fit for settlement and with barely 100 students and six professors, it had already had a visit from the legendary John R. Mott, rallying Christian students worldwide for "the evangelization of the world in this generation." From one perspective this was the tail end of the phenomenal nineteenth century international missionary movement. From another, it was little short of a global reform movement entailing educational institutions, hospitals, agricultural reforms, and even elements of women's liberation. Two years later Wesley students, in a presentation at a YM-YWCA meeting, adopted the language of solidarity used by modern sociologists to describe the challenge of the hour to get out on "the broad plain of the world in aid of our stricken brothers." There was "no such thing as purely individual salvation," the presenter concluded. The students of colleges and universities in North America, mobilized in a far-reaching YM-YWCA *network of student units – of which Wesley College was one – were already in the vanguard of the social gospel and social reform as early as the 1890s. The next two decades would seal that compact.*

CHILDREN OF PROPHECY*

Despite the fact that student and youth movements underwent a rapid expansion in the age of reform in both Canada and the United States (1890–1918), they have largely been ignored by historians. This lack of attention is unfortunate for, though student or youth movements may simply be aspects of wider social movements, they are – as contemporary history of the 1960s would seem to show – particularly important as sensitive resonators of new and exciting ideas and attitudes. The students of Wesley College, Winnipeg, from the 1890s to 1918, are a case in point.

Wesley College was established in 1888 as the central outpost of Methodism on the Canadian prairies. Pushed by the movement of its people into the region and drawn by the challenge of building a new Western society, the church created the college to provide higher education for its children and ministers for its circuits. The college was established during the early years of a period of social reform, and its first principal, J.W. Sparling, the former president of the church's Montreal Conference, was sympathetic to the reform stirrings. Sparling's first choice for faculty was Salem Bland, a brilliant young preacher at Kingston who was very popular among Queen's College students. Bland, then in the first flush of infatuation with the ideas of Henry George, refused Sparling's offer but accepted another one in 1903.[1] This pursuit of Bland symbolized Sparling's reform inclinations: in twenty-four years of vigorous leadership of the College, he attempted to build an institution that would inform and reform the substance of prairie society. His faculty generally seconded his purposes, and from among his students came a constant flow of graduates aware of the challenge of social conditions in this "sociological era of the

---

*   First published as "Children of Prophecy: Wesley College Students in an Age of Reform," *Red River Valley Historian*, Manitoba Edition (summer 1974): 15–20.

world";[2] some of them, in fact, would devote their lives to the cause of social reform.

Throughout most of the 1880–1918 period, Wesley College offered matriculation for university preparation, a three-year and (after 1900) a four-year Arts program, a five-year diploma course in theology, and a three-year Bachelor of Divinity program. From three students and two professors in 1888, it rapidly grew to over 100 students and six professors in the later 1890s. After the turn of the century, enrolments leapt ahead and Wesley surpassed Manitoba College (Presbyterian), its chief rival. In 1902–03 the enrolments stood at 189; six years later they were at 308; ten years later they peaked at 430. The number of faculty increased at a somewhat slower rate; in 1901 there were nine faculty members (excluding Sparling), a large enough number to ensure a reasonable student–faculty ratio; in the next decade, however, the faculty grew by only five members, increasing the student load considerably.[3]

Students were at Wesley in the first instance to study, of course, and that, by all the measures of the time, they came to do quite well. Impressed at first by Manitoba (Presbyterian) College, the student body led all colleges in the province in academic awards from 1897 to 1900, and in most years it won over half the provincial medals between 1900 and 1914.[4] Wesley's students more than held their own in winning Rhodes scholarships and gaining access to top-ranking institutions like Harvard for postgraduate study.

Despite the successes, life at Wesley did have its problems. As enrolments climbed, overcrowding – especially in 1912–13 – resulted.[5] Only time and more buildings could resolve that particular difficulty. As for individual student problems, the faculty did their best to keep students at their books by exercising a close paternal oversight and by insisting that students in difficulty limit their attention to certain classes, perhaps by dropping others. In serious cases, the faculty interviewed parents or wrote letters to them, such as the one informing the parents of a Miss Waddington of "her parlous state in regard to her work."[6] Similarly, some student problems were eliminated by prohibiting the taking of arts and theology courses concurrently, while others were dealt with by the enforcement of class attendance regulations. However, when in November 1906, the faculty decided to impose a 90 per cent class attendance rule, the students responded with a peremptory note stating that they would attend no more classes until the rule was cancelled. The note was simply returned because of its tone, although a delegation with a request for a 75 per cent rule was entertained.[7] The boycott of classes continued for a week but the faculty held firm and the matter was referred to the Board, which gave the students at least some relief the following year.[8]

It was perhaps not surprising that the attendance question should have been a touchy one: while some classes were quite lively, others were apparently based on the recitation of prescribed texts and were so mechanical that bored teachers had able students act as occasional substitutes.[9] From time to time there were also problems with examinations set by the University of Manitoba,[10] which was at first the college's examining body. In general, however, these disputes did not mean there was basic disagreement between faculty and students over the discipline of studies and college life. Although educational reforms were in the air, few agreed with suggestions for "the abolition of examinations and the curtailment of lectures." Along with the editor of the *Manitoba Free Press*,[11] the faculty and students of Wesley seemed to think them necessary for the development of proper mental discipline.

Student extracurricular life was a feature of the college from its earliest days and, as numbers increased after the turn of the century, blossomed into considerable richness not to mention considerable frivolity. In Wesley's second year a soccer club was organized, followed by a variety of athletic groups, a rink, tennis courts, and field days. A literary society was formed in 1891, with debates, dramatics, and choirs added in subsequent years. In 1893 a YMCA was organized during a visit by John R. Mott, who was building an international student Christian movement, and it was followed shortly thereafter by a YWCA group. In 1894 student piety, dedication, and ambition sent James Endicott to China and sustained him there as a representative of Wesley College among Methodist missionaries.[12] In contrast to such sobriety, quite a different note was struck in the organization of initiation rituals and Halloween celebrations. The former entailed such antics as bouncing each freshman in turn on the ground inside a giant, rubbery telescoping tube known as the Esophagus Wesleyana. The faculty had little success in suppressing this particular ritual, so a group of fearful freshmen purloined the dreaded Esophagus and hid it in the secluded Bird's Hill area.[13] Faculty did manage, however, to tame the destructive Halloween parades of the 1890s and turn them into singing, cheering processions to the homes of J.H. Ashdown, chairman of the Board, and Principal Sparling. The faculty was successful in this instance partly because they bribed the students with lunches at the Ashdown's and Sparling's and partly because they encouraged the male students to conclude the day with taffy pulls with the "Lady students" back at the College.[14]

With the establishment of residential quarters for the men on the top floors of the Wesley College building, a new kind of discipline was added: making beds, sweeping rooms, and putting out sweepings and slops for the janitor before 9:00 a.m. Residence, however, brought some new problems of "indiscipline" – "room-bumming" and water fights between juniors (third floor) and seniors (fourth floor).[15] With the institution of mock parliaments came pranks with a more serious purpose: for example, one debate on annexation with the United States was resolved when two opposition members were called home to their missions by urgent but faked telegrams.[16]

Restraining student ebullience was sometimes a problem, not simply at initiation and Halloween. One year, Manitoba students, participating in Wesley classes on a reciprocal teaching arrangement, proved so rowdy as to require exclusion en masse from their privileges.[17] There were also occasional incidents like the throwing of a chair from a balcony into a class below.[18] However, with the student body of considerably less than 400 students for most of this period, college life was close-knit. Faculty worked and played with students in the full range of activities from the "Lit" to the football field – sometimes at considerable hazard, as the *Vox Wesleyana* reported: "Professor Jolliffe ... began the season by freezing his feet on the football field, followed it up by letting his nose get consolidated at a hockey match, and finally almost lost his life through exposure while teaching second year Latin in class room D."[19]

This closeness of faculty and students may have had something to do with Wesley student interest in social reform.[20] Students obviously had a great respect for Dr Sparling and were close to young instructors, notably W.J. Rose, recently returned from Oxford, and M.C. Rowell, daughter of the Ontario Liberal party leader. The most influential professors, however, were W.F. Osborne and Salem Bland, whose political activism troubled Wesley's Board Chair, J.H. Ashdown. Osborne was a very popular English professor whom the press sometimes referred to as Manitoba's Methodist lay orator.[21] He was a radical Liberal, deeply involved with the Manitoba and North-West Conference of his church, and he used his influence in the Committee on Temperance and Moral Reform to promote a "political Christianity."[22] At the 1906 General Conference of the Methodist Church he was co-author of the avant-garde "Report on Sociological Questions" that was subsequently much in demand by church bodies across the continent. It described the current laissez-faire profit-driven economy as "semi-barbaric" and claimed for the community its rightful share of the wealth it produced.[23] In 1910 he resigned from the staff to campaign with the Liberal party for political office, but he returned in 1911, having lost the election. His undertaking earned for him the only rebuke of a faculty member in the minutes of the Board of the College. The rebuke hardly lessened Osborne's popularity with the students and he was frequently and favourably referred to in the *Vox Wesleyana* throughout his teaching days.[24]

Salem Bland, finally succumbing to the blandishments of Sparling, joined the faculty in 1903. A quiet, incredibly well-read man who loved discussion, he had an immediate impact on the student body, partly because of his lively, richly reflective manner in the classroom, but also because of the thoughtful way he dealt with the personal and social issues of the Christian life at Sunday morning YMCA Conferences.[25] Coming to the West with social reform sympathies already well developed, he became progressively more radical as the years passed, associating himself with the major figures of the prohibition, single tax, direct legislation, free trade, public ownership, woman's suffrage, and labour reform movements headquartered in Winnipeg. From Sparling's death in 1912 until his controversial dismissal in 1917, Bland was undoubtedly not just the most popular professor with the students but also the most prominent public figure at Wesley.

Although Osborne and Bland had great influence upon Wesley's students in a variety of ways, the springs of social reform in the student body had deeper sources than individual influence and encompassed Osborne and Bland and the rest of the faculty, too. Those sources included the worldwide evangelical movement, religion conceived as a culture-building force, the stimulus of evolutionary thought and the new social sciences, the challenge of immigration, and the social issues that came with rapid urban growth and industrialization. In many ways these sources interacted with each other, but their separate inspirations can be readily discerned.

The visit of John R. Mott in 1891 and the sending of James Endicott to China were but two obvious signs of the involvement of Wesley students in the international evangelical and missionary movement. Mott's aim through his student groups was the evangelization of the world in that generation. Endicott was the first living symbol of Wesley's response. The conception entailed more than the mechanical conversion of millions of heathen. Evangelicals had long talked of the "gospel plan for the improvement of the world," and that led directly to the brink of social reform. As a student paper for a union YM-YWCA meeting in 1898 put it: "We are knit together in a common brotherhood [in a world] ruled by the Creator on a system of reciprocity. [Missions means lifting] our voice in behalf of our

stricken brother, [which in turn] lifts our own hearts to a higher plane ...
Let us get out on the broader field of human interest and affection, where
we feel the world's anguish and hope and strivings ... 'Social Solidarity'is
a maxim now of sociologists. There is no such thing as purely individual
righteousness."[26]

The paper clearly rang with the clarion call of the social gospel, then a
rising force in American Protestantism, although that may not have been
every student's rationalization of belief in these missions. On whatever
ground, Wesley's students went on to participate in the great Student
Volunteer (for Missions) Movement conventions in Toronto (1902),
Rochester (1909), and Kansas (1914).[27] YMCA programs for the time struck
such themes as "Satisfaction," "Self-Control," "Glorying in Christ," and
"How I Study the Bible,"[28] but in the light of Methodist readiness to see
in "scriptural holiness" a mandate for reform,[29] it is wise not to judge such
titles too hastily. Soon the language and the content became more congruent as Dr Elliott in 1908 and after led Bible studies on "The Social
Significance of the Teachings of Jesus."[30] Professor Rose, now teaching at
Wesley, proclaimed the gospel to be a statement of "the solidarity of
humanity."[31] Bland announced to the YMCA that the future belonged to a
church that accepted the social ideas of Jesus.[32] That such subjects were
recapitulated on the pages of the student paper while others were rejected, testifies to their impact on the student mind. From 1908 on, in fact, a
host of articles in *Vox Wesleyana* suggest the ascendancy of the social
gospel among students at Wesley.[33]

The Christian social mission also had its home front. Wesley College had
been founded as the central outpost of Methodism on the prairies, and one
of its goals was to build a Christian society in the West as the heart of a new
Canada. Students and staff alike were caught in a tension between enthusiasm for rapid growth and an anxiety over the implicit dangers that might
hold for the Western spirit. Materialism loomed as a constant enemy. Convinced that Wesley College had a mission to provide an alternative focus
for prairie life, and believing that "Christ was the greatest of Social Reformers," the editors of the *Vox Wesleyana* decided in 1899 to write seeking
advice from Hugh Price Hughes, a well-known British Christian socialist
and leader of the Methodist Forward Movement. Hughes replied, envying
their opportunity of building a new country, but pointedly warning them
that, as in the United States, "pioneers, settlers and colonists may be so
absorbed in their own prosperous business life, and in looking after their
private religion, that they may grossly neglect their public duties," leaving
"Mammon and all the vices to capture the political machine, and to

demoralize local government." Christ came, he urged, "not to save individual souls, but to organize a Christian church" that would work "to reconstruct human society ... and to recover for all men their divine birthright
of a noble life."[34]

In this spirit, the *Vox* editor, A.W. Kenner, lifted the sights of his journal
beyond local and college matters and pointed fellow students to their part
in "shaping the destiny of the age."[35] Editors and contributors in succeed-
ing years went on to criticize the imbalance between expenditures on education and subsidies for railway monopolies: "None too soon are the people of Western Canada comprehending the nature of corporations and
construction companies."[36] Student writers advocated art collections,
wrote pleas for Canadian literature, and proposed College extension programs as means of countering preoccupation with material development.[37]

There was evidently much discussion among students about the human
type emerging in the West. J.W. Shipley, *Vox* editor in 1908–09, tried to put
the debate to rest by scoring the attempts of idealists to reduce differences
to types, and pointing to the obvious unlikelihood of a representative
character emerging in the foreseeable future out of such heterogeneous
elements.[38] The discussion, however, was more a product of hope and fear
than of fact. On the one hand, it appeared that "Wesley is easily keeping
pace with the giant strides of her native West,"[39] and on the other, it
seemed as urgent as ever to bring the whole life of the people into "a higher more spiritual atmosphere than the one that tends to predominate in
our Western country."[40] Both observations worked together to propel students into a variety of social causes.

The coming of the Boer War encouraged the student reformers in their
first full bloom of social consciousness. A.W. Kenner unhesitatingly called
it "Our War" and spoke of "a great nation forced to war in the cause of
humanity," even while he urged students on in the work of reform.[41] The
College followed closely the adventures of "our Scout in Transvaal," a Mr
Daykin who enlisted with the Strathcona Horse.[42] At the same time, the
Vox featured articles on "competition vs. cooperation" and on the need for
a new reform party.[43] The blending of Imperialism and the social gospel
was further demonstrated in 1907 when Rudyard Kipling visited Canada.
A.O. Rose, *Vox*'s literary editor, was moved on that occasion "to an unexpected and scarcely explicable enthusiasm" when Kipling, the poet of
Empire, spoke of Canada as the greatest of colonies and bade his hearers
listen to "the tread of empire as it moves ever westward" onto the vastness
of the prairies.[44] Imperialism, too, was a call to rise above self and
parochial and material pursuits.

Perhaps the most immediate circumstance of concern to students and impelling many of them into reform activities after the turn of the century was immigration. The inundation of the prairies from every quarter between 1900 and 1914 challenged student convictions respecting the universal message of the gospel, the destiny of Canada and the West, and British imperial culture. Church conferences and publications after 1902 gave regular attention to the problem. Immigration was constantly debated in the Methodist young people's Epworth Leagues, in which many students were involved. At Wesley College the question was first seriously broached by Professor Blewett in 1902 in an address to the YWCA group on Rhodes scholarships: "in view both of the newness of our life and of the foreign elements which we have to assimilate, it might very reasonably be urged that no part [of the Empire needs more to be] brought into contact with the highest academic life of England and with the 'larger ideals of Anglo-Saxondom' than our own North-West."[45]

No one, however, did more to focus student concern on the larger aspects of the immigration problem than J.S. Woodsworth. Woodsworth, who had been "Senior Stick" at Wesley in 1897–98, had gone on to graduate studies in Toronto and Oxford at the very time his fellow students were asking counsel of Hugh Price Hughes. In Toronto and London he encountered urban slums on a large scale for the first time and came to admire the work of Oxford students in the Mansfield Settlement House among the poor of London. Back in Winnipeg, in an address considered somewhat unusual in 1902, he prodded students with a picture of "What Others Are Doing."[46] At that time he made no reference to immigration apart from the problem of poverty; rather, he emphasized bridging the economic and cultural chasm in society through programs sponsored by the privileged, notably medical advice, legal aid, more educational opportunities, social clubs, and simple friendship. When in 1907 Woodsworth became head of All-Peoples' Mission in Winnipeg's immigrant quarter north of the tracks, students in considerable numbers were among his regular workers.[47] In 1912 the students, through the intercollegiate YMCA, organized their own settlement in North Winnipeg, consisting of four or five male students living in and directing the services of about twenty others teaching English and running boys clubs.[48]

There were other ways of responding usefully to the problem of immigration. Some students spent summers with the Reading Camp Association, the forerunner of Frontier College, working with immigrant construction labour by day and organizing classes and recreation for the men's leisure hours.[49] And no one will ever know how many female students spent long summers teaching school in immigrant districts: they were legion, and Wesley College contributed its share. One of these reported on her experience among immigrant children with both affection and urgency: as voters these young ones would be future rulers – ambitious and persevering, they know that "the man who is morally and mentally weak will not rise." Further, she believed that, with trained minds and healthy bodies, they may be trusted to help make Canada great.[50] In short, immigrant children were to be viewed in the same light as the young of older Canadian stock.

Vox Wesleyana was notably free of alarmist nativism. The Japanese were described as a "superbly qualified and able" people who could only be met on their own ground.[51] Ralph Connor's book, *The Foreigner*, was given a critical review,[52] deploring its sensational and false portrait of Galicians, though one of its themes, that immigration and the mixing of peoples was contributing to the development of an improved Canadian race, was echoed elsewhere on the pages of *Vox*. Commentators, moreover, were not above pointing out questionable characteristics of Anglo-Saxondom.[53]

Inevitably students varied in their choice of arena for the exercise of practical altruism, and only a minority of students would press their reformism into the more radical forms of social criticism. At least by the late 1890s, however, some students at Wesley were beginning to recognize that there were fundamental problems in the economic and social structure itself. In 1899, visits by radicals like Mr Douglas, Mr Reade, and Eugene V. Debs caught student attention.[54] Articles soon appeared on "Competition versus Co-operation";[55] A.E. Vrooman, a philosophy student and later lawyer, called in 1900 for a new party of reform and in 1903 urged government ownership to bring responsible power to industry.[56] *Vox* editorials scored Carnegie, the American steel magnate and philanthropist, arguing that individual wealth was "largely accidental and should revert to the people."[57] Socialism as such was, however, an infrequent subject. C.V. Coombe, shortly to be a reporter with the *Tribune*, contributed the first substantial Christian defence of socialism on the pages of *Vox* in 1909. On at least one occasion, in 1914, students organized a formal debate with local socialists Percy Chew, W.H. Stebbings, and Moses Baritz,[58] And, in 1917, criticism of socialist doctrines by the political economy professors in the colleges prompted the organization at Wesley College of a socialist club that allied itself with the intercollegiate Socialistic Society.[59]

Before the end of the war, however, the socialist option (except in the most generalized use of the term) attracted few students. Political comment in *Vox* was rather as varied as the components of the reform move-ment itself. In 1908, the editor criticized a growing practice of "American style" graft in Winnipeg civic politics.[60] W.D. Bayley, the religious editor, scored the same phenomenon in the provincial campaign that followed.[61] Liquor traffic was attacked as "the greatest stain on the character of man as a rational, moral being." No letters to the editor attacked the preferred solution, prohibition.[62] Children's welfare and juvenile courts came in for comment, and, in 1914, as a broad reform alliance was on the verge of win-ning power in Manitoba, pleadings for non-partisanship in politics could be read in the student paper.[63] On balance, Wesley's students were proba-bly still within the Liberal fold, which was the chief inheritor of the pre-war impulses of reform in Manitoba. However, it should be remembered that E.M. Michener, a Wesley graduate in theology, became leader of the Alberta Conservative party in 1910; Harold Daly of Arts 1908 became head of the Winnipeg Young Conservative Club; and J.T.M. Anderson, later Conservative premier of Saskatchewan, was a graduate in 1911.[64]

Wesley's student reformers took their cues from many sources. The essence of their missionary program, their concern for the future of the West, the challenge of immigration, the problems of industry and the city provided potent stimuli for reform sentiment. The recognition of the need of reform, however, was aroused and sustained in many ways. The Literary Society devoted many evenings to Canadian, American, and Eng-lish authors: Wildred Campbell's verse attacked the bartering of franchise and begged "heaven strike, or send a holier dawn / to Canada";[65] Walt Whitman's lines urged the ultimate goodness of all things and the redemption of the world by comradeship;[66] Dickens' immense popularity sustained an altruistic concern for the poor and the oppressed.[67] Student debates, both collegiate and intercollegiate, covered the whole gamut of social problems of the time. In 1910, for instance, students of some later significance for the social gospel – men such as W.D. Bayley and Samuel East – won their cases that the socialist tendencies of the age ought to be supported, that the government's railway policy was not in the best inter-ests of Canada, and that oriental immigration ought to be approved.[68]

The height of reform sentiment among Wesley students probably had a direct relation to the numbers preparing for work in the church, espe-cially after the turn of the century. Between 1900 and 1914, the number in the Bachelor of Divinity program increased from six to fifty-seven. Pro-bationers in the Arts program and in diploma theology increased star-tlingly after James Woodsworth's successful annual recruiting ventures in Great Britain from 1906 on. In 1908–09 there were 76 probationers and 100 diploma students, and in 1912–13 93 and 101, respectively.[69] With over half of the Arts students preparing for the ministry, it is not surprising that Wesley was dominated by a moral earnestness that was not quite so characteristic of its chief rival, Manitoba College.[70] Moreover, the "Woodsworth boys," while by no means all committed to advanced social conceptions, added to the infusion of a substantial portion of British reform spirit into the reform tradition at Wesley. Following the careers of students like William Ivens, William Irvine, H.D. Ranns, A.E. Whitehouse, Samuel East, A.E. Cooke, George Dorey, Harry Dodd, Walter Metcalf, and Herbert Fewster, among others, demonstrates the powerful presence of the social gospel in the developing mentality of Wesley's students throughout this period.[71]

Student interest in social reform was still more systematically fostered after 1907 by the inauguration at Wesley College of the first classes in sociology offered in the prairies. At first given for theological students, student and faculty demand for more instruction related to the "living issues" of the time led to a course in 1909 by J.S. Woodsworth, then to a full-time lecturer, A.G. Sinclair, in sociology in 1911, and further classes in subsequent years.[72] Some of the theologs in particular pressed this campaign. William Ivens, future founder of the Canadian Labour churches, celebrated the addition of Rauschenbusch's work, *Christianity and the Social Crisis*, to the curriculum and went on to provide a further reading list for private student study.[73] H.A. Fewster argued for practical work for theological students so that they might become "the companions of the working man."[74] From 1915–16, the course of study for probationers in theology required a study of the social, moral, and religious conditions of their fields.[75] Gradually the spirit of reform at Wesley was being given institutional form.

Until the outbreak of the war in 1914, the student reformers at Wesley seem to have felt little if any sense of conflict within the college tradition that had itself caught up so much of the variegated reform movement of the time. However, Wesley College, committed to combating the materialistic spirit of rapid Western development, was throughout the period heavily influenced, if not dominated, by men who whether in law or business owed their considerable material prosperity to Western expansion. Most men on the Executive Board were associated with Grace Methodist Church, possibly the wealthiest Methodist congregation in the West, and Wesley's largest single supporter by far.[76] J.H. Ashdown, Winnipeg's hardware magnate, and mayor, 1907–08, as chairman of the Board from 1900, was the chief of the representatives of Winnipeg's commercial elite in the oversight of the college's affairs. It was an intimate kind of oversight, as he and Sparling would together investigate such mundane matters as problems in the college plumbing system.[77] To give Ashdown and his colleagues their due, they were undoubtedly in their own way also concerned about crass materialism and the spiritual development of the West. They were not immune to the impulses of reform. It was under Ashdown's mayoralty, for example, that public ownership of Winnipeg power was implemented,[78] and as mayor he actively worked with J.S. Woodsworth and others in the rationalizing of the city's welfare agencies.

However, there would come a time when social criticism in the college (and at large) would turn from attacking the manifestations of materialism to its sources in the economic system itself. Ashdown and the commercial elite, Methodist or not, could not fail then to be implicated. By 1912–13 two sources of student inspiration, J.S. Woodsworth and Salem Bland, had undergone that transformation, and students were following in their wake. In 1912 Principal Sparling died and early 1914 saw W.F. Osborne and Bland presenting radical critiques of the churches and the political system, respectively.[79] A conflict within the college appeared to deepen from that point, not at first much involving the students, though a patronizing note could be seen in the *Vox* editor's reference to "our socialists." For the students, as for the whole college, the conflict culminated in the celebrated dismissal of Bland in June 1917.

Ostensibly a case of discharge owing to retrenchment in College finances, the affair was immediately transformed into an issue polarizing the more ameliorative and radical reformers and threatening to alienate Wesley College from its large Western constituency. Salem Bland's popularity was still waxing in 1917[80] and with his dismissal, students organized in defence of their hero and called for his reinstatement, while the Board sought to explain its actions. The students remained up in arms for much of the next year. Bland later charged that the Board had subjected the students' protest committee to a severe grilling, which failed to budge them.[81] However, the complexity of the issue clearly dissuaded some and unnerved others. Either the Board or the new principal, J.H. Riddell, pursued the students by letter to their summer residences, even suggesting the wording of a letter that they might return, stating their change of mind on the issue. At least two responded with but slight variations on the text.[82] Restoration of College unity both among staff and students became the prime objective of the principal and the Board, together with recouping College finances. Both objectives called for severely curtailing the publication of the student journal. Ironically, no subsequent issue (nor any faculty minutes) ever referred either to the affair or to Salem Bland. It was not the end of student reform at Wesley. That would arise again in later years. Student generations change quickly, and social problems remain. But for the moment the College tradition lay shattered, a victim of the separation and collision of two approaches to social reform implicit from the beginning in the conception of the role Wesley College was to play in the new West.

For a generation, Wesley's students to a degree evidently unique in the Canadian prairies – and perhaps in the country as a whole – reflected the spirit of the age of reform and became agents of its dissemination. They were children of prophecy, and their visions encompassed the world, the nation, the West, and Winnipeg. It would be a long time before one could again hope so highly and dream of so much.

CHAPTER NINE

Salem Bland,
the New Spirituality of the Social Gospel,
and the Winnipeg Elite, 1903–1913

BACKGROUNDER

When Dennis Butcher asked me in 1984 if I could contribute a chapter to a book celebrating sixty years of the United Church on the prairies, I was loath to say yes. Travelling across Ontario with the legislative committee holding hearings on the extension of funding for the last two years for Catholic education was absorbing a lot of time and energy. On reflection, however, I had accumulated ten years of further research on Salem Bland in the West that I had nowhere reported on. And I had been wanting for some time to respond to the frequent criticism in some quarters that the social gospel was simply a matter of this worldly amelioration of the human lot and had little to do with the core spirituality of Christianity that, in the view of the critics, was a personal faith aimed at reconciling individual sinners and God and ensuring their souls a place in the heavenly kingdom.

I knew that what I wanted to do with Salem Bland in his first decade of teaching and preaching in Winnipeg and the West would articulate the claims of the social gospel to be a new spirituality resonant with the core teachings of the Jewish and Christian scriptures. Wesley College students had already glimpsed that vision and seen the necessity of moving beyond a purely personal gospel (see chapter 8). There was plenty here to fuel a response to the critics. However, some years previous I had read an article by Thelma McCormack that I had wanted to do something with. Entitled "The Protestant Ethic and the Spirit of Socialism,"[1] it seemed nicely congruent with my intentions for Bland in this essay and germane to a response to the critics. In her essay McCormack had leaned heavily on Karl Holl, author of The Cultural Significance of the Reformation *(1959). Holl's argument was that Luther had never intended his concept of the "priesthood of all believers" to be rendered in the terms of religious individualism it came to adopt. Rather, Luther intended the more social "you are each other's priests." To be a "priest" was not to have right of direct access to God for personal ends, but to mediate God to others in a community of believers, liturgically, pastorally, and prophetically, witnessing God's intentions for the world at large. The commercial and later industrial entrepreneurial classes had taken Luther's phrase in a self-serving direction Luther had never intended. Max Weber was not wrong in his celebrated thesis in* The Protestant Ethic and the Spirit of Capitalism, *which was based more on Calvin (see chapters 3 and 16), but insofar as the Protestant ethic was grounded on Luther, it should more properly be paired with "the Spirit of Socialism." That was where Bland's reflections and activism were taking him over the decade. Clearly, the corporate elite of Winnipeg would not be comfortable with this formulation. Latter-day critics could disagree, but a case had been made for the new spirituality, and latter-day scholars would amplify the argument. My purpose in the essay was not to dwell at length with the critics or McCormack, but to let the Bland story carry that freight. Somewhere I found the time to write – and the following chapter was the result. [Note: After several attempts to locate the Holl book, it turned up in the citations and the bibliography of Gordon Marshall,* In Search of the Spirit of Capitalism *(1982), which I used as a principal source in the recent writing of chapter 16 as the last full chapter of this book.]*

SALEM BLAND
AND THE NEW SPIRITUALITY OF THE SOCIAL GOSPEL*

The social gospel has been seen by its critics as a superficial movement, concerned only with meliorating social relationships, confusing the redistribution of wealth with the coming of the Kingdom of God and generally divesting the gospel of its spirituality. In the same vein it is easy to view Salem Bland, the Methodist mentor of the social gospel on the prairies, simply in terms of his role in the more obvious moral and social reform causes of the period between 1903 and 1919, his expanding rela-

---

*   First published as "Salem Bland and the Spirituality of the Social Gospel: Winnipeg and the West, 1903–1913," in *Prairie Spirit: Perspectives on the Heritage of the United Church of Canada in the West*, eds Dennis I. Butcher, Catherine Macdonald, Margaret E. McPherson, and A. McKibbon Watts (Winnipeg: University of Manitoba Press, 1985), 217–32. Courtesy of the University of Manitoba Press.

tionship with urban and rural progressivism, and his increasingly radical politics after 1913.[2]

Salem Bland's struggle to fashion a social gospel for the Canadian prairies, however, was nothing less than a quest for an appropriate spirituality in an age of great collective undertakings. The quest was an urgent one and led from the nature of the soul to the meaning of culture, from devotional life to the arts, from academic study to social action. Life was lived in relationships; grace was everywhere. What Bland fashioned, in effect, was an alternative Protestant ethic, best described by Luther's admonition, "you are each other's priests." The critical years in that quest lay in the ten years that followed his arrival in Winnipeg in 1903.

A Prairie Vision

On 17 September 1903, as newsboys in Winnipeg's dusty streets hawked the Monday afternoon papers with their announcement of his imminent arrival, Salem Bland was near the end of a long serpentine journey across the Laurentian Shield.[3] Three months before, sitting in the study of Eastern Methodist Church in Ottawa, rereading the Pastoral Address of the recent Montreal Conference, he had underlined these words: "The North-West has special demands upon us ... Methodism has there the opportunity of its history. A springtime has come."[4] He did not know that at summer's end, Dr J.W. Sparling, principal of Wesley College, Winnipeg, would be standing in that same room demanding that Bland come to his college to teach church history and New Testament. He had asked before. This time he had come in person and would not be denied. In a matter of days, Bland was on his way.

Remarkably well read and an exceptionally fine preacher, Bland at forty-four was widely regarded as one of the brightest ministers in the Church. He was also radical, a single taxer, a defender of labour's right to organize and a proponent of extensive state provision of cultural amenities and social schemes to equalize conditions in society. He believed that business combinations would nurture a more social spirit but urged cooperation and public ownership as congenial vehicles for that spirit. Bland had been active in prohibition campaigns. He was the president of the Ottawa Lord's Day Alliance and advocated a union of Protestant churches. He was also – and this may have been the nub of Sparling's determined arguments – immensely popular with young people. The decision to teach at Wesley College had been made, and now he was heading for the open prairie.

Already the prairies had found a place in his vision of an ultimate Protestantism that he was convinced would emerge from the spiritual strife, the intellectual debate, and the material struggles of the new century. The immensity of the land ahead conjured for him the image of a pure faith that could exist without reliance on external authority; it would be a faith dependent only on the grace of God. Surely such a country would grow not only great crops but also men and women of large stature and spirit, and a society fresh in its purposes and uncommonly responsive to human need.[5]

The Protestant Ethic and the Commercial Elite

The earliest preoccupations of Europeans on the prairies had, of course, been furs – and then wheat. Church individuals in the West had expressed uneasiness about the all-consuming passion that each of these staple commodities evoked. A Presbyterian colleague of Bland's, Charles W. Gordon, alias Ralph Connor, declared that "the West had not to fight against agnosticism so much as love of wheat. Let a man get filled up with wheat, and you could get nothing else into him, tho' you offered him heaven."[6]

Wheat brought settlers. Following Bland's train into the Winnipeg Canadian Pacific Railway (CPR) station was the 147th immigration train of 1903, bearing 140 Hungarians and Galicians.[7] Wheat brought the expansion of the rail system, land speculation, and the transformation of the prairie commons to private property. It also brought banking, insurance, investment and marketing services, machinery dealers, and hardware chains. Wheat, in short, brought the revolution that incorporated the West into the modern world of commercial and industrial capitalism and subordinated it to the driving centres of investment in central Canada and across the Atlantic.[8]

Bland was not long in meeting the primary agents of this revolution. J.A.M. Aikins, his host during his first weeks in Winnipeg, was founder of the most prestigious law firm in the city, counsel for the Western Division of the CPR and the Department of Justice, solicitor for several banks, and a director of the Imperial Bank and the Great West Life Assurance Company. At the College Board, if not around Aikins' table, he would have met J.H. Ashdown, board chair and hardware prince of Western Canada, who held bank and mining directorships and was a founder of the city and of the Board of Trade. R.T. Riley's successful business career had won him the presidency of the Board of Trade and numerous directorships. Rodmond Roblin, the Conservative premier, was on the College Board too, and, because he promoted elevator companies and organized the Ranching and Grain Growing Company, he was legitimately considered a grain merchant.[9]

These men were the patriarchs who brought Ontario to the banks of the Red, Assiniboine and Souris rivers, overturning the bicultural institutions of a society delicately balanced between English and French, Protestant and Catholic, the "bloods" and the "breeds." The victories of municipalities and school districts over parishes, of the old Liberal formula of "rep by pop" over communally based constituencies, and the establishment of public nondenominational school systems had all been their victories.[10]

And these were the men to reckon with in prairie Methodism. Well-schooled in Protestant concepts of the use of time, talent, and treasure, they devoted themselves to church, Sunday school and college, to advancing the YMCA and YWCA, to assisting charities, hospitals, and Children's Aid. They listened attentively when James Henderson of the Missions Department declared that "the money-power of the world is greatest in Christendom, just because Christianity has given man the best possible control of himself and of the forces of nature around him." But Christian men and women had to Christianize that money-power by imitating the self-giving sacrifice of God: "Your wealth is yourself," Henderson said, and he thought that the secret of the larger life and of greater prosperity was to give more.[11]

As a group, these men were by no means motivated by simple greed or hindered by narrow vision. Aikins, if he can be allowed to speak for them, was concerned about how children could acquire a sense of identity and destiny and become the breed of strong-minded citizens that would "mould the nation in righteousness."[12]

The Methodist commercial élite in Winnipeg, however, in the early 1900s, were heirs of highly individualized doctrines of justification by faith and the priesthood of all believers, the Protestant slogans that denied the right of any power to stand between an individual and God. Transformed by the commercial classes of the seventeenth century, the Protestant ethic came to justify the individual manipulation of property and fuelled the expansion of the spirit of capitalism. The priesthood of all believers became, in effect, a priesthood of property. It now justified a structure of economic relations that Bland increasingly considered unchristian, and it generated a type of spirituality that, if it satisfied ambitious burghers, was quite inappropriate, he thought, to a new social age.

He was not long in saying so. In the course of three notable and highly acclaimed addresses a month after his arrival, he predicted that prairie society would become one of catholicity and reconciliation, congenial to the new social ideas pushing their way forward in the churches. The older parts of Canada had grown up in an age of individualism, an expansive era that had seen the "crackling and peeling of old restrictions." Liberal freedoms had been a great advance, but many old tyrannies had vanished only to make way for new ones. The palms had gone to the strong and the powerful, and it had been a hard time for the less able. Was it too much to think, he asked his new public, that, on the prairies, common people should come into their own?

God's word, spoken in the fellowship of prairie churches, he suggested, would lead them to church union. But the spirit of reconciliation could not end there and leave an economy that separated people from each other and divided society into the propertied and the unpropertied. The prairies should be a land of public ownership. He was quite explicit: private enterprise had undertaken what the public had been either too timid or stupid to do, "but we deserved to be fleeced and were great fools if we placed human nature any longer under such circumstances."[13]

The point did not arouse open protest. Perhaps it was lost in the general acclaim for the three addresses whose ideas ranged broadly over the West and the nation, continent, and empire. Perhaps the remarks were heard in terms of current sentiment that had created in Winnipeg the first publicly owned asphalt plant in North America. The Winnipeg business community was already eyeing the possibilities of making electric power publicly owned as a way of reducing costs. But Bland's intent clearly went far beyond local business concerns.

He was little concerned with the materialism or petty immorality of the time, which he put down to passing boom conditions. Such behaviour was too easy a mark for successful religious and humanitarian people who otherwise ignored the unchristian network of relationships they were committed to in the world of commerce and industry. Material pursuit was vital and urgent, Bland observed, and a true spirituality did not reject it, but was concerned with the way in which the pursuit of wealth was ordered. Whether or not Bland's point was taken up at the time, his debate with the commercial élite of prairie Methodism had begun.

The New Spirituality at Wesley College

Bland's heroic attempt to fashion an alternative religious vision for the prairies was played out in a number of forums – in the classrooms and extracurricular activities at Wesley College, in the programs of the Ministerial Association, at the Manitoba and Saskatchewan Conferences of the

Church, at summer camps, and through hundreds of speaking engagements throughout the West.

Bland early established a reputation among students for his Sunday morning YMCA conferences at the College, and he was in considerable demand as a speaker at the popular Literary Society meetings, not to mention the Church young people's organizations.

Wesley College students had already been introduced to the social gospel, probably through their YMCA and YWCA organizations which brought them in touch with North American and British student movements. One Wesley College student, in 1898, explaining the significance of missions, touched most of the bases of the new spirituality: "We are knit together by a common brotherhood [in a world] ruled by the creator and a system of reciprocity. [Missions means lifting] our voice in [sic] behalf of our stricken brother [which in turn] lifts our own hearts to a higher plane ... Let us get out on the broader field of human interest and affection where we feel the world's anguish and hope and strivings ... 'Social solidarity' is a maxim now of sociologists. There is no such thing as purely individual righteousness."[14]

That student's view was entirely consonant with the conviction that Bland himself had struggled to secure for himself, that "culture is an enlargement of experience. It is the power gained ... to enter into other lives and modes of thought foreign to our own."[15] He cautioned students that if there was anything to be learned from human experience, it was the readiness to foreclose the future, to lower the shades of life, to settle for some little idolatry.[16] They should not let the great gift of self-consciousness arouse an anxiety that could build walls around the self and dam up the tides of life. Nor should they indulge in the "evil dreams of our separateness" from which arose all sorts of oddities and incongruities.

Whether he spoke on the arts, on prayer or on the nature of the soul, Bland sought to convey a sense, both realistic and mystical, that life was lived in relationships. The arts were designed to enlarge human sympathies. The painter drew individuals into his/her feelings, the novelist engaged with the afflictions of others, and the dramatist expressed the personal and social dilemmas of life.[17]

The devotional life, in Bland's view, did not consist simply of two or three seasons of prayer or a half hour of daily Bible readings. Instead, prayer opened the individual soul to the soul of life itself. And reading the great spiritual testaments of the ages opened the mind to the choicest of spirits from Augustine to Wesley. Devotional life entailed fellowship, because God's truth comes in fragments and people need to share these fragments with each other. The condition Jesus laid down for his presence was that two or three be gathered together. Bland emphasized that this should not be limited to a cozy circle of like-minded friends, because in principle "individuals can never be complete until they have embraced the Russian, the Oriental, and the African philosophies."[18]

Every dimension of life, Bland claimed, offered help in the nourishment of Christian life. Every mood of nature and the body, even social life and athletics, could be means of grace. And academic study prompted the humble obeisance of the mind before the ordered structure of other minds and of God's world.[19]

God's own strategies were social, Bland claimed. In God's plan for the restoration of humanity, God chose a people and a church to nurture the way of reconciliation in the world at large.

Bland was prepared to concede that personality was a separate source of will and action, and he preserved a sense of mystery about the nature of the soul. But he insisted that the soul was not a separate entity like a boiler one could take out, repair and polish, then replace. The soul was not separate from the body or its environment. Salvation, he had long claimed, entailed full health and wholeness of life.[20] It was a false and unchristian spirituality that simply counselled a personal quest of individual blessedness.

Bland was not alone in developing these spiritual dimensions of social Christianity among Wesley College students. Others among the faculty, like William Osborne and W.J. Rose, and local preachers, like A.E. Smith and J.S. Woodsworth, amplified the vision. James Elliott and George Blewett, in Wesley's Chair of Philosophy, systematically drew out the full implications of the vision. Both men were philosophical idealists: Elliott, like Bland, was schooled in his idealism by John Watson at Queen's, and Blewett studied at the great centres of idealist thought in Britain and Germany. "God," Blewett said, "is the home of persons." Individuals become persons as they laboriously struggle for a larger consciousness of the good of others or, in other words, as they take up the tasks that affirm membership in the family of God. To do otherwise was to be alienated from the source of one's own life and growth.

Blewett's ultimate vision, like Bland's, was therefore a society in which the attainment of the good by one "consists in its attainment by others, and in the last analysis by all."[21] It followed that social institutions which obstructed that objective were inimical to the spiritual quest of Christians and merited not submission, but transformation or repudiation. To undertake the task of social change was to find one's proper relation to the larger mind of God. Christianity, in a broad sense, was as inescapably political as it was spiritual.

If this disturbing conclusion led to attacks that charged the social gospel with abandoning a proper spirituality, the evidence remains that Bland and his colleagues were fashioning a spiritual quest on high Christian grounds.

Biblical Foundations for a Western City

Outside the College, Bland's first areas of action were the Methodist Ministerial Association and the Manitoba and Saskatchewan Conferences. His involvement in the Ministerial Association after mid-1904 was possibly the critical – though not the only – element that transformed what had been desultory gatherings into a breaking ground for new thought and a clearinghouse for concerted action. All the denominations had been scouring the country for a cadre of preachers whose prophetic ministries would indelibly imprint the new West. The Methodist Ministerial Association in Winnipeg in 1904 reflected the results. With the ranking states people of the Church in Winnipeg and College individuals like Bland and Blewett joined with forceful middle-aged and younger figures like J.H. Morgan, Robert Milliken, J.S. Woodsworth and A.E. Smith, the intellectual level of the Association's proceedings leapt dramatically upward. At the end of 1904, theological students were permitted to join student ministers at Ministerial meetings, and the meetings were never the same again.

The range of interest among the group was wide: Bland demonstrated critical methods in the study of Galatians, Blewett spoke on Christian mysticism, and Woodsworth reviewed varieties of religious experiences. There were papers called "Labour Organizations and Labour Ideals" and "Socialism and Individualism in Christian Work." Sometimes serving on the program committee, occasionally drawing on his students for reviews, often making presentations, always forcing the pace of discussion, Bland became the dominating presence in the Association for the next half dozen years.[22]

In mid-1904 Bland joined the central figures of this group in launching a western Methodist weekly paper. For some reason the church's official paper, the *Christian Guardian,* had never taken hold in Winnipeg.[23] Other Methodist publishing ventures were sprouting in Victoria and Assiniboia, but the self-consciously progressive Methodist clergy of Winnipeg felt the need of a paper that would chronicle their remarkable growth, monitor Western development and articulate the challenges of advanced Protestant thought and reform in the West. With Milliken and Morgan as editor and associate, and Bland contributing and supporting, a twenty-page publication was soon reaching most Methodist homes in the district. Although it eventually lost out to the Victoria-based *Western Methodist Recorder*, the paper vigorously pressed Winnipeg Methodists to "go into the city" and engage themselves with its deepest problems.[24] The city, of course, was Winnipeg.

Few if any of the clergy in Winnipeg had ever experienced the tumult of rapid urban growth that the Western boom precipitated in their community. The problem of the city was on all their minds: it was the great collective of the modern age to which they had to address their gospel. On the one hand, urban social problems caused most of them to shift away from preoccupation with a personal gospel, and on the other, the reality of urban divisions challenged central tenets of Bland's social gospel.

The railway had long since split Winnipeg in two, but Bland's arrival coincided with the great CPR expansion that irrevocably divided the city, separating the foreign immigrants and English working-class districts from the middle classes around the business centre of the city and the wealthy along the riverbanks. Industrial conflict escalated as Winnipeg's commercial and industrial base expanded. The immigrant working class was badly abused by housing speculators, employers and by the *Free Press*, which lightheartedly approved of CPR police disciplining them whenever they caused trouble.[25] Civic elections were fought over police efforts to contain "social vice" in the red light district; utilities and transportation barons fought with advocates of public ownership for control of power, gas, and street railways; and debate on private property rights impeded the sanitary reforms necessary to keep smallpox, diphtheria, tuberculosis, and especially typhoid at bay.

Despite the reality that confronted him, and despite the agrarian bias of many of his co-religionists, Bland held a large and hopeful view of the city. It was easy, he thought, to see the city only in terms of its darker aspects. But the existence of homes, hospitals, schools, and missions had to be acknowledged as well as the squalor, illness, ignorance, and immorality, and the most delicate refinements of culture along with slums and taverns. The city was the centre of the greatest intensity and variety of relationships and of the greatest intellectual activity of the land. It was "the birthplace of reforms and revolutions, the fountainhead of change." Ultimately, the city was not so much a product of economic acquisitiveness as it was of human sociability, in which people ministered, however imperfectly, to each other's needs. The Bible could be cited to legitimate such views. It declared that the highest wisdom "uttereth her voice in the streets; she crieth in the chief place of concourse, in the opening of the gates." The Jews left the villages for the cities of Capernaum and Jerusalem, Bland observed. Indeed, although the Biblical drama began in a garden, it ended in the city.[26]

In 1905, as Bland stepped up the pace of his public activity, he enlarged on the challenge of urban reform thrown out by the new Methodist paper. In Moose Jaw, Winnipeg, Carman, Emerson, and Portage la Prairie he sketched the characteristics required of the new "saints for the age" and outlined the evolutionary roots of and prospects for a cooperative social order.[27] Before a Christian endeavour youth rally in Winnipeg, he presented his mandate of Christian socialism and laid out a comprehensive program for an urban reform administration that included reservation of parks and river bands for the people; sanitary reform and municipal ownership; additional and better schools, hospitals and asylums, municipal art galleries, libraries, and free concerts; and adequate wages for workers and recognition of trade unions.[28] Not surprisingly, the Winnipeg Labour Council soon asked him to address them. By mid-1905, when the Union of Canadian Municipalities met in Winnipeg, Bland launched a series of sermons about the city.

The urgency of civic social action inspired the Manitoba Conference of the Church in June; the Winnipeg District called for support for the new newspaper, for institutional urban church work, and for putting All Peoples' Mission on a proper legal basis so it could get on with the formidable task of serving Northern Winnipeg. William Osborne and Robert Milliken organized a committee to develop a movement for municipal political action based on the activities of the Epworth Clubs and the Young Men's Clubs of the Church.[29]

While Bland associated himself with Osborne's Municipal League, which at the end of 1905 went into action on the issue of prostitution, he was quick to castigate the middle class for its "out of sight, out of mind" position on prostitution and berated segregationists who wanted to restrain the police on the issue of prostitution but who would, at the same time, unleash the police on the slightest perpetrator of a crime against property.[30] At St Stephen's Young Men's Club, amid the December campaign, he said that it was the great disparity of wealth that was the central economic issue facing the city, called once more for the widest possible extension of public ownership, and declared that an inspired people, in company with God, would remake the city in terms of its own underlying cooperative spirit.[31]

The inspiration that prompted these quests lay, for Bland, in that foundation of radical monotheism in Western culture, the Bible. At both the

Manitoba and Saskatchewan Conferences, therefore, he established a year-round program of modern Bible study for members. The topics for discussion, the readings, and the approach bore directly upon the cause of reform: Amos holding the plumb line to crooked structures of power; the Sermon on the Mount with its reversal of priorities of the present age; James on the perils of private wealth for the soul; Paul on the unity of spirit amid a diversity of traits and talents. All were critical to mounting a reform campaign of broad, basic, and durable proportions in Winnipeg and the West in the decade prior to the First World War.[32]

The Relevance of the Kingdom Of God

For Bland, himself, as his teaching progressed and as he tried to encompass a larger reality, the search for Biblical foundations for the social gospel was an ongoing quest of huge proportions. He read voraciously on New and Old Testament themes, in church history and apologetics, in philosophy and social criticism, not to mention general history, biography, and fiction.[33]

Once a devotee of Paul, Bland had come to appreciate how far Paul's rigorous training as a Pharisee in Hebraic law, the peculiar nature of his conversion, his long, fierce conflict with the Judaizers of the early church and the Colossian heretics had deeply influenced, and limited, his articulation of the gospel. Up to a point, Paul's Christology could be harmonized with an evolutionary world view, with which Bland's generation was absorbed. Paul's lack of interest in the life and teachings of Jesus, however, his fascination with the death of Jesus, his struggle with the Judaic law, his clear separation of divine and human natures, and his elaborate theology all ran in another direction.

For a time, the fourth Gospel, the Book of John, provided a more congenial theological ground on which to gather social Christian arguments. It was indeed quite natural that the evolutionary idealism that so much impressed Bland in the mid-1890s should lead him into long and serious study of the Book of John, with its theme of life-giving incarnation. John portrayed Christ as springing from the original source of life, which he so fully represented that Christ was the source of abundant life. More than Paul, John read the character of Christ back onto God, so that God was clearly seen as self-giving love. Moreover, John's naturalistic images of vine and branches nicely fit social themes and an evolutionary scheme. Not only was all this more congenial to Bland's purposes, but John himself, like Bland, had undertaken to render the gospel in new clothing for a new generation. The appeal is not surprising. John's words were addressed to the neo-Platonic idealists of Asia Minor. In short, John appeared to be the relevant gospel for the new century. But Winnipeg, the labour movement and the writings of Adolph Harnack, the great German scholar, changed that in 1905.

The hard reality of social problems in Winnipeg sat in such utter contrast to John's elegant metaphor of the word becoming flesh that by 1906 Bland was speaking of him as walking the world on tiptoe.[34] Bland's encounter with the Winnipeg Labour Council in 1905 was his first engagement with serious Marxists. He was asked to present his reform Darwinist address, "Four Steps and a Vision," and the effect of the resulting debate was such that he did not deliver the piece again.[35] Although the he never fully adopted historical materialism, he maintained an ongoing respectful relationship with the Labour Council that encouraged the growing realism and radicalism of his religious and social thought. From that point on he appears to have joined the growing debate over the adequacy of idealism as a master philosophy for the age.[36]

It was Adolph Harnack, however, who shifted the centre of Bland's New Testament interest from John to the "historical Jesus" of the synoptic gospels with their recurrent metaphor, the Kingdom of God. Bland read Harnack's immensely influential book *What is Christianity?* In 1905, and in early 1906, in an exciting address, he harnessed Harnack's concept of the Kingdom of God to the cause of urban reform.[37]

By 1900, New Testament scholarship had isolated the parables in Matthew, Mark, and Luke as the core of the teaching of Jesus – and the idea of the Kingdom of God as the key to the parables. The parables were immediate and earthy. They dealt directly with the daily interpersonal encounters and expressed God's sovereignty.

Bland's excitement over the connection of a political analogy like the Kingdom of God with the heartland of Jesus' teachings is evident in the ideas that tumbled over each other in his addresses to the Ministerial Association and the Saskatchewan Conference in 1906. This clearly biblically based idea thereafter displaced reform Darwinist arguments in his promotion of Christian social reform. This shift to a more Biblical apologetics of the social gospel was widespread in North America at the time, but Bland articulated it directly from its European roots and not from its American branches; the Canadian social gospel was not just a reflection of its American counterpart.

Bland was not above creating his own parables addressed to the clashing movements of the time: "Watch the big press in the *Free Press* basement – so complicated, things moving in all directions at once, yet with no clash, no check, no destruction." God's kingdom was an organized world, Bland declared, and the teaching that proclaimed it was a "doctrine of social Christianity summing up all schemes of social reform, all municipal and national action, gathering them up into one organic whole, rooting them in Christ."[38]

Bland's reading of Harnack's works did not, however, cause him to adopt Harnack's rather courtly moderation in social reform. For one thing, Harnack "arrived" in Winnipeg on the eve of the street railway and Vulcan Iron Works strikes that initiated twelve years of intense industrial conflict in the city. But quite apart from that radicalizing development, unlike Harnack, who largely disposed of the Old Testament, Bland maintained his footing in the prophets even while he kept his eye on the New Jerusalem of the Book of Revelation. The result was a growing radicalism of which Harnack would hardly have approved.

Nonetheless, there remained in Bland's character and in his thought – and hence in his teaching of the social gospel – an unresolved but engaging tension between the spacious concepts of the "larger consciousness" born ultimately of Greek idealism and the temporally urgent ones born of Hebraic prophecy and apocalyptic. Those varied moods of cultural reflection and social compulsion endured to enrich the Christian social movement in Canada.

The Renewing Spirit and Prairie Politics

The Winnipeg campaign for civic righteousness – which saw Protestant clerics and lay people involved in moral and sanitary reform issues, conciliating industrial conflict, and campaigning for public power, women's suffrage, and reform of civic government – merged in 1905 with provincial politics. The Roblin government, whose liquor policies were increasingly unacceptable to moral reformers, would have to eventually face the electorate, and clerical activists and their principal lay supporters were soon in the thick of a political battle. Critics wondered whether political preachers were not betraying historic Protestantism, sowing discord in the church, and compromising themselves with political entanglements.

The issues for Bland – as for many – went well beyond temperance concerns. Roblin's one attraction was his interest in public ownership of utilities, but his penchant for selling land to individual and corporate speculators, rather than selling directly and cheaply to settlers themselves, opened up yawning possibilities of corruption (which indeed marked the rest of Roblin's years in office). Bland attacked Roblin in an open letter, and his name was blazoned in the headlines; Aikins made an abortive effort to have Bland removed from his post at the College.[39] Whatever the influence of Bland's intervention in the campaign, Roblin won handily.

By 1906, Bland was in heavy demand as a speaker throughout Manitoba and Saskatchewan. His graduates were now fanning out across the prairies. They claimed that Bland was the single most influential person of their college years and were always forceful in duplicating his message. They and others called for his presence, and he responded until time and energy gave out.

"Come if you can, Doctor," wrote John Lane of Swan River in May 1907, "we do not often have college men come to the frontier points."[40] E.S. Whittaker of the Moose Jaw YMCA importuned Bland to lead Bible study at a young people's summer school being inaugurated that summer. Local preachers lacked the power to inspire young people, he said, and "if we can have a part of the good things the East is enjoying all the time, we will be happy." Would Bland come and "help us launch this new order of Christian culture for the West?"[41]

So the requests came in: people were hungry for inspiration, full of hope as to what the West might become if it were shaped properly. Many requests had to be refused. Since 1904 Bland had been accepting almost fifty invitations a year to speak and preach. In 1907 requests came from Moose Jaw to Toronto, and in 1908 they came even from the West Coast.

Some of the Western brothers in the Methodist ministry – Wellington Bridgeman at Neepawa, for example – were affronted by the elements of modernism creeping into the Western pulpit and expressed their "frustration and anger when faced with things arising out of metropolitan sophistication."[42] The heavy demand for Bland's services, however, suggests that it was not the predominant mood of the pre-war prairies to beat a retreat before the modern world. Bland's promotion of church union, a major part of his message to the gathered congregations at prairie points, was a case in point. He spent no time on the economics of multiple congregations in small towns, but linked the prairie experience to the mixing of creeds and cultures throughout the world. Comprehensiveness was necessary in the church as never before, and with it a new receptiveness to other traditions. Where oriental or immigrant cultures were consistent with Christianity, it was necessary to endorse them, he suggested, and he cited historic and Biblical authority.

The task, Bland said, was to discover what was "vital – common – universal – always – and around this to gather the educated and the simple of every class and race." In linking this task with "the spirit of these broad-flung prairies," Bland presented the church union movement as part of the destiny that called his listeners to be both prairie people and modern men and women. It was a compelling challenge. That he thought them capable of it was a flattery they could hardly ignore.[43]

Whether it was at Crystal City, Cypress River, Stonewall, Neepawa, Holland, or Carberry, local presses sang the praises of his captivating style and the substance of his message: "The popularity of Dr Bland is sure to draw large congregations," the *Selkirk Weekly Record* announced;[44] *The Killarney Guide* observed that "as a speaker he is bright, attractive, forceful, and profound"; "The Doctor is known throughout the West," it added, "as a great student of social and political problems."[45]

Bland's widespread preaching engagements brought him into extensive contact with local leaders of the Manitoba and Saskatchewan Grain Growers' Associations, which expanded rapidly between 1903 and 1913. Their mounting power, their rootedness in prairie Protestantism, and their indefatigable promotion of the cooperative ideal tempted Bland, as it did others, to think in terms of a new party that would regenerate politics in Canada. Invited to address the provincial conventions in 1912 and 1913, he came close in Saskatchewan to provoking a decision to initiate a third party.[46]

While both church union and the "new politics" would have to await the conclusion of the First World War, both projects were symbols by 1913 of the desire for an institutional break with the past that Bland's social and religious visions helped to generate. The new spirituality of the social gospel was in search of new wineskins.

A Time for Decision

In Winnipeg and at the College, other developments were pressing Bland to a break of a similar order. The social problems of Winnipeg multiplied with the forced pace of rapid growth. If the "instant duty of Christianizing the social, economic and political order," as he put it in 1908,[47] was not to be dissipated, solid information and clear social thinking were urgent. In 1907, addressing the first convocation of the University of Saskatchewan, Bland called for courses of sociological study in the new institution. The next year, the issue became a live one at the Manitoba Conference of the Church and Bland was soon involved in setting up such a program at Wesley College.

A great laboratory for the study of social problems lay at hand in the North End. Young J.S. Woodsworth, who was assigned to All People's Mission just north of the tracks in 1907, was already involving students in social studies, urging them to go on and form a social settlement, live among the immigrants, learn their language, and help them fight their battles. Such an immersion would lead to critical examination of the structure of society – and to its reconstruction.[48] Bland was close to Woodsworth from 1907 to 1913, when Woodsworth left All People's. He was frequently at the Mission and shared with Woodsworth an increasingly warm attachment to the Winnipeg labour movement.

In 1910, when another provincial election was anticipated, Bland called for a new workers' party in the province.[49] In May, when the Manitoba Labour Party was formed, it very nearly won a seat with Fred Dixon as candidate but went into decline thereafter.

The extent of Bland's association with labour in Winnipeg was not entirely clear, but his growing interest in farm and labour politics coincided with a declining participation in the Methodist Ministerial Association. In a significant sermon, delivered early in 1911, entitled "The Christ without the Camp," he suggested that one of the essential ideas of Christianity is that "Christ is ever outside the settled places and practices of society, and in every age calls followers into the lonely unknown places of which it is only known that Christ is there."[50] A new note of anxiety appeared in Bland's sermons, that is, that the Church had become too settled, too encrusted – even too heavenly (heaven, too, could become one of those settled places, a habitual category) – to respond to the call of the spirit. The Church had to come down from the clouds and break out of its institutional confines to regain its vitality.[51]

It was now evident to Bland that, to become a movement again, Christianity also had to disentangle itself from the existing economic order, many, if not most, of whose protagonists sat in the pews of the churches. Among those property owners who refused to share civic political power with non-property owners were some prosperous church members. They were prominent among those who contested the attempts of working people to organize and bargain collectively, without which workers were forever divided against each other in a "free market" of labour. And there were some wealthy members of the big churches, as Woodsworth's experience in North Winnipeg made plain, whose prosperity was bought at the expense of Winnipeg's newcomers, who were charged exorbitant rents for confined, insubstantial, and unsanitary quarters.

In 1903, on coming to Winnipeg, Bland had asked "whether the evangelical churches are going to show a spirituality strong enough for the strain that is coming on them. [They] have to accommodate the greater number of the wealthy and official classes, which they never had to do before. Will they remain true to their traditions of spirituality?"[52]

By 1913 the answer was reasonably clear: it was time for plain speaking and confrontation. The question was not just whether there would be further social progress, but whether the Church would be part of it. Clear divisions were the order of the day.

Asked to preach at Grace Church, Winnipeg's wealthiest Methodist congregation, in August 1913, Bland unleashed an uncompromising assault on the state of the Church. Using Winston Churchill's recent novel, *The Inside of the Cup*, he held up the mirror image of a congregation generously supporting good causes – missions, charity, hospitals – while their daily economic actions dispirited, deprived, and diseased the poor. Shocked by the recognition that his church largely represents forces opposed to real Christianity, the minister in the novel turns from inoffensive orthodoxy to militant revolt. The church, Bland declared, was still the hope of the world – but novelists, not preachers, are stating the new ethical standards of our age, and socialists and single taxers are exhibiting the enthusiasm Christians once had. All Christians had to share the blame for allowing economic conditions to become so corrupt that "you cannot expect a businessman to live a Christian life today ... We must begin the great work of attacking all the cruelties of our commercial life, all the rascalities of high finance, all the abominations of our political system."[53] Bland's subtitle made the issue entirely clear: "Religion no Substitute for Justice." The point was not that religion was superfluous, but rather radical monotheism to which Bland subscribed elevated justice above the trappings of religion.

There is no record that Bland was ever invited to preach at Grace Church again. But it was not because the radical social gospel that Salem Bland had fashioned in his first ten years in Winnipeg had abandoned Christian spirituality for entirely secular schemes and superficial nostrums. It was rather because a rich and profound spirituality, at once traditional and modern, would not permit him to speak other than he did. Whether or not the commercial élite of Winnipeg would be overthrown, they had at least met their match, and an alternative Protestant ethic in Canada was well on its way to becoming the spirit of Canadian socialism.

CHAPTER TEN

J.S. Woodsworth
and the Crisis of the Canadian City

BACKGROUNDER

Among the early books Michael Bliss, as editor, chose for the Social History of Canada Reprint Series were two pioneering books on major social issues in Canada by J.S. Woodsworth. It might well be wondered how Woodsworth managed to research and write Strangers Within Our Gates *(1909) and* My Neighbor *(1911) between 1907 and 1911, when he was expanding All Peoples' Mission into a major social service agency working out of multiple sites in North Winnipeg. Woodsworth was a graduate of Wesley College in Arts, Victoria College in Theology, and Oxford, where he imbibed the progressive Christian idealism of Edward Caird. After a stint working among London's poorest at Mansfield House Settlement, he returned to Canada, hoping to teach social ethics at a university. Failing that, however, he would be a lifelong teacher, whether in his role as a social worker, an urban reformer, a Member of Parliament, or the first leader of the Co-operative Commonwealth Federation (CCF) party in the 1930s. The titles of both of his books were taken from the Judeo-Christian scriptures. Those not Biblically literate might easily misread them. According to Jewish law, the Torah, strangers were to be offered hospitality and provision made for them. There were elements of immigrant political and religious culture that concerned Woodsworth, but he disagreed with R.G. McBeth in* Our Task in Canada, *who feared a permanent infection of the Canadian blood pool, and Professor E.W. MacBride at McGill University, who, believing in a genetic determinism, foresaw a permanent corruption of the Canadian gene pool.*

Woodsworth was, by contrast, optimistic about immigrants' ability to adapt to new ways in their new country. Given the impact on Canadian cities of massive immigration, 1900 to 1911, it was important that My Neighbor *was written with that more optimistic view in the background. Had it not been so, North*

Winnipegers would hardly have elected him to Parliament consistently from
1921 to 1942. The second title, My Neighbor, *derived from Jesus' parable of the*
Good Samaritan, makes the point that the neighbour in the evolving
urban/industrial collectivities on whom one's well-being depended would not be
the tinker, tailor, grocer or retailer known, as of yore, for personal uprightness,
but strangers along a chain of suppliers of goods and services. E.A. Ross, in
Sin and Society (1908), had made that point with great eloquence. For
Woodsworth, the modern city could only be made livable if the public came to
understand the lessons of social solidarity: the necessity of a new social con-
science governing one's own place in the whole, and the need of political and
economic structures and regulations ensuring accountability on the part of all
those distant agents of production and suppliers of goods and services. Reliance
on the personal ethics that made the exchanges of the local markets of town and
village reasonably accountable was now quite outdated.

Woodsworth was not entirely original in his arguments and many proposals
in the book. He was widely read in the British and American literature of urban
reform, surveying, analyzing, and proposing solutions, including journalistic
exposés. All, however, were marshalled with the progressive reform of the Cana-
dian city in view. For Woodsworth this was far more than a secular crusade. My
Neighbor was written in the belief that there was a gospel – good news – for
society. Social solidarity was the watchword of "the new day"; there was no such
thing as "purely individual salvation."

J.S. WOODSWORTH AND THE CANADIAN CITY*

"In Canada, the city and its problems are only beginning to require serious consideration," wrote J.S. Woodsworth in 1909.[1] An observer of the
1970s might comment with too much truth that the city and its problems
are only now beginning to receive the attention they merited half a century before. In 1911, Woodsworth went on to write *My Neighbor,* a pioneering study of Canadian civic pathology and an impassioned plea for
urban reform. Despite the problems of the city under the double impact
of industrialization and immigration, he was able to write with considerable optimism. Ironically and tragically, the sprouting urban conscious-

---

* First published as "Introduction" to J.S. Woodsworth, *My Neighbor: A Study of*
  City Conditions, Social History of Canada Reprint Series, ed. Michael Bliss
  (Toronto: University of Toronto Press, 1972), vi–xix. Reprinted with the per-
  mission of the University of Toronto Press.

ness that he observed, and did his best to nurture, was soon to be stunted by an overgrowth of provincial and national concerns.

At the time that Woodsworth wrote, the budgets of the three largest Canadian cities were roughly equal to those of the provinces in which they were situated. However, the waging of two wars, overcoming a prolonged depression, the making of a welfare state, forging a universal public education system, and the maintenance of national unity all conspired to augment national and provincial status and displace the burgeoning concern for the emerging city. More recently, continuing urban growth, prolonged prosperity, an enlarged sense of the ecological interdependence of individuals and nature, renewed concern for the quality of life, and a flowering of the arts, despite budgets that no longer rival those of the provinces, have reawakened the early century's consciousness of the city. With remarkable contemporaneity, Woodsworth speaks across the half-century eclipse of the Canadian city.

Both the lapsing and the renewal of urban consciousness make the reprinting of My Neighbor a matter of importance. The book stands at the confluence of political science, economics, sociology, history, and religion. When it was written, most of these fields of study leaned heavily on the issues raised by city and industry. In the interval, none of these disciplines has provided Canadians with a literature on the city, preferring the "macro" concerns of province, region, and nation. Even in religion, while the social gospel escalated its concern to the social order – or even the international order – as a whole, others turned beyond the beyond to the "wholly otherness of God." Urban studies are only now beginning again with some force, and not only is My Neighbor an essential source in the background of that enterprise, but it remains one of our few accessible routes back to the era of the rise of the modern Canadian city and the first urban reform movement.

It was not quite correct of Woodsworth to observe in 1908 that only then were city problems beginning to require serious attention. As early as 1851, Toronto discovered over 3,000 children in its midst, living with neither education nor familial restraint, and promptly ended opposition to free schools. Clerics in the late 1880s became aware that poverty and the class structure of the city were impeding the propagation of the gospel and began innovations of which Woodsworth was the heir at All Peoples' Mission, Winnipeg. The struggles of labour and capital were intense enough to require the appointment of a royal commission in 1886. Civic corruption in Montreal had led a Montreal businessman, Herbert Brown Ames, to write a statistical analysis of social conditions in Montreal, *The*

City below the Hill (1897), and to embark on a campaign of reform. Municipal ownership of the great civic franchises was already a warm issue in the 1890s, as was the remodelling of city government.

In the meantime, the less partisan but more sensational press, particularly the *Star* in Montreal, the *Telegram, World,* and *News* in Toronto, the *Journal* in Ottawa, the *News-Advertiser* in Vancouver, and the *Sun* in Winnipeg, provided a regular fare of urban conditions and reform, which the more established papers were reluctant to indulge.[2] A substantial part of such news and commentary derived from the British and American scenes. The conditions of English cities as revealed in Henry Mayhew's *London Labour and the London Poor* (1851), William Booth's *In Darkest England and the Way Out* (1890), and Charles Booth's *Life and Labour in London* (1893) were familiar to many Canadians. Then (as now) the condition of the American city heightened the measure of concern Canadians gave to their own circumstances. The press religiously fed the public the latest and most lurid events in the travail of the American city – and not infrequently pointed a monarchist moral. Some undoubtedly knew Loring Brace's *The Dangerous Classes of New York and Twenty Years' Work among Them* (1880), and others the highly readable works of Jacob Riis, *How the Other Half Lives* (1890), *The Children of the Poor* (1892), and *A Ten Years War* (1900), and Lincoln Steffens, *The Shame of the Cities* (1904). Church editors, like W.H. Withrow of the *Canadian Methodist Magazine,* kept substantial readerships abreast of the Protestant response to urban America with articles on city missions, institutional churches, deaconess orders and lay workers, and reviews of the works of Joseph Cook, Washington Gladden, Lyman Abbott, and other pioneer social gospellers.

There were probably few in the 1880s and 1890s who felt the shame of the Canadian city, but a growing company, including W.D. Le Sueur and W.A. Douglass and their Georgite Anti-Poverty Societies, pointed out that signs of an urban crisis in the making were not wanting. If problems were not as severe as in the larger American cities, that was no reason for complacency. Canadian cities had not reached the monstrous proportions of New York or Chicago, but the census of 1901 revealed that, while in the previous half-century the population of Ontario had doubled, Toronto had grown six times over; the province of Quebec had almost doubled in numbers, but Montreal almost five times. Especially in the 1880s many lesser centres had grown well in advance of the general population increase. By 1901 almost one out of every four Canadians was living in a town or city of 5,000 or more.

After the turn of the century, concern intensified as Canadian Clubs, Empire Clubs, church groups, women's organizations, and associations of young men and young women with increasing frequency secured lecturers on the subject of the city and its problems. The churches, the YMCAs and YWCAs, and the universities, after 1902, spread a network of city missions, social settlements, and institutional churches across the country and propagandized their constituencies for their support. Municipal governments sponsored magazines like *Municipal World* and the *Western Municipal News*, and other journals like the *Canadian Magazine* carried articles on urban reform with increasing frequency. In 1907, S. Morley Wickett edited for English Canadians a collection of such articles in *Municipal Government in Canada*; three years later French Canadians were offered a broad scheme of civic advance by G.A. Nantel in *La Métropole de demain*. When the newly founded Canadian Political Science Association held its first conference in 1913, municipal government was the focus of attention. Participants were probably surprised to hear W.B. Munro of Harvard conclude that Canadian city government was based more on the American than the British model, with a system of separate boards, commissions, and officers all deriving equally from the sovereign electorate, frustrating unified administration and impeding reform. The growing urban middle class, however, was probably more concerned with problems of sanitation and food supplies than with theories of government and willingly supported campaigns such as that of Dr Charles Hastings, later Toronto's medical health officer, for pure milk in 1908. More impressive still were the occasional threats to civic peace and order, as when a Toronto streetcar strike exploded on 22 June 1902 into a violent confrontation of strikers and the militia. That, too, was a time to recall many events in American urban history – and to ponder deeply.

In the first years of this century the concern for urban affairs mounted, as it had in the early 1880s in the United States, in direct response to the phenomenal growth of urban populations in conjunction with an astonishing increase in, and a shift in the source of, immigration. Between 1901 and 1911 the urban population of the country increased 62.28 per cent. Whereas in 1901 there had been fifty-eight cities with a population of over 5,000, in 1911 there were ninety. Four cities, Montreal, Toronto, Winnipeg, and Vancouver, then numbered over 100,000; Montreal was approaching the half-million mark. More alarmingly, Toronto and Montreal very nearly doubled in the decade, Winnipeg multiplied four times over, and Vancouver nearly so, while newer prairie cities like Calgary and

Regina grew by ten times and more.[3] Had the influx been of one language and nationality it would have placed intolerable burdens on civic development; but it was almost as varied in language and nationality as it was possible to imagine. While the Canadian government avidly promoted the flood of immigration, Canadians of all classes grew anxious over the social consequences. Serious social problems were obviously in the making when steamship companies scoured Europe eager only for the price per head; when minor potentates like a self-styled "King of the Italian Workers" in Montreal arranged the arrival of hundreds of Italians with neither jobs nor resources; and when the occasional agency did a brisk business supplying strike-breakers for Canadian industries in the throes of labour disputes.

In spite of the number and diversity of immigrants between 1901 and 1911, the proportions of British and French in the population declined only three and two percentage points, respectively, in the decade.[4] The statistical averages, however, hardly gave the full picture, since the immigrants were not evenly distributed. While two-thirds of Ontario's immigrants in the decade were British born, the number of foreign-born immigrants was double that of immigrants of British birth in Saskatchewan and Alberta, and whereas recent immigrants constituted only 20 per cent of Ontario's population in 1911, in the four western provinces they composed about 50 per cent.[5] It was not more alarming statistics but the concentration of population that made the social problems of immigration so much worse in the cities.

In 1908 Woodsworth wrote *Strangers Within Our Gates*, an important early study of immigration. As that first book was being prepared for reprinting, the manuscript of *My Neighbor* was on its way to the publishers. It, like his first book, had in the first instance been conceived and requested by F.C. Stephenson as a textbook for his Young People's Forward Movement for Missions and reflected the course Methodist young people's interest and study had recently been taking. Since Woodsworth not only derived his personal financial support from the movement but also found his largest original audience for his books through its agency, Stephenson and his Young People's Forward Movement merit more than passing mention. At the end of the century, when the missionary movement was reaching its height and North American churches had far more applicants than they could finance, Stephenson had met a blank wall in his efforts to join the ranks of overseas missionaries. Unwilling to accept refusal, he had devised a simple but ingenious scheme of self-support by canvassing and pledging Methodist young people's groups (Epworth

Leagues) in his region to finance him directly by means of a small monthly levy per member. The notion proved contagious and in 1894 Stephenson soon found himself at the centre of a development spreading through Methodist and other young people's organizations. It leapt the border into the United States in 1897, and Woodsworth himself carried the idea to Britain shortly thereafter. So valuable had Stephenson's work become that, by 1904, now a fully trained and ordained medical missionary, he was persuaded to stay at home and become a full-time secretary to the whole enterprise in Canada.[6]

The scheme was much more than a mindless gathering of pennies and shipping of missionaries. Stephenson assiduously promoted intensive study in the organizations touched by it, and informative inter-communication between missionaries (home and foreign) and their group supporters. Young people's groups had already shown an interest in the social gospel, and Stephenson was concerned both to enhance their interest and deepen their knowledge. As much as any single person, he was responsible after 1904 for rearing, especially in the Methodist church, a generation of members prepared to walk a considerable distance with the social gospel. He established summer schools to further the work and was soon in the midst of a substantial publishing enterprise comprising a monthly bulletin of letters from missionaries, pages for several periodicals, and textbooks.

In 1901, a conference of church youth leaders in New York decided to project a series of Forward Mission study courses for the Canadian and American movements, each to focus on a textbook. By 1911 at least eighteen texts had been published, including *Aliens or Americans* (1906) by H.B. Grose and *The Challenge of the City* (1907) by Josiah Strong. However, there was no Canadian on the editorial committee, and the results were painfully obvious. Strong's book had precisely one sentence for Canadians: "Canada must face the double problem of the city and her own great Northwest" (p. 265). A chart in the book erroneously suggested that Canada was more urban than the United States in 1891 and 1901.[7] Stephenson could hardly have been satisfied with the series. Despite pressure from his superiors on the Mission Board to use the American inter-denominational series where possible, he began and continued the publication of a separate series of Canadian texts for Canadians.[8] Woodsworth's books were texts five and seven, respectively, in the Canadian series.

The circulation of any one of Stephenson's texts is difficult to calculate, but in 1911 he wrote that in the previous three years he had circulated over 20,000 textbooks. Perhaps half of them were from his own series. It was curious that William Briggs, the church's publisher, never listed them in his advertisements, but Stephenson had his own captive market and, more as an educator than salesman, wrote, "The fact that these are studied and discussed in YP [Young People's] meetings is much more important than that they are sold."[9] The Epworth League and the other Canadian Methodist young people's groups at whom Stephenson chiefly beamed his literature alone had memberships totalling 62,085, with an additional 18,395 in Junior Epworth Leagues.[10] Carefully worked out programs stressed social subjects one week in each month. Given sections of the prescribed text were assigned and related activities suggested. Special series of articles to complement the text were arranged in the *Epworth Era*, the *Missionary Outlook*, and the *Christian Guardian*. Beyond the young people's groups, Women's Missionary Societies and Men's Brotherhoods used Stephenson's texts. Programs prepared for over 200,000 members of Methodist Sunday Schools rehearsed some of the basic information the books contained.[11] And for the use of all of these, Stephenson's department prepared lantern slide lectures and resources for pictorial displays, one of the results of which is the excellent photographic collection on social problems of the period now in the United Church Archives. One of Stephenson's books, C.B. Keenleyside's *God's Fellow Workers*, became something of a runaway international best seller in mission circles. There is no evidence that this happened to either of the Woodsworth works, but with twenty-three summer schools across the country in 1911 introduced to *My Neighbor*, and the foregoing machinery geared to promoting its use, the book, and even more the burden of its contents, must have had an impressive circulation among Methodists alone.

Whether other churches used the book is not clear. The Presbyterians had also been moving more deeply into sociological studies and in 1911 published a textbook edited by W.R. McIntosh, *Social Service: A Book for Young Canadians*, containing a chapter on the city by O.D. Skelton. But neither they nor any other church issued a work comparable to *My Neighbor*. A Maritime Presbyterian reviewer urged it on all the churches, describing Woodsworth as "a citizen of every Canadian city and a contributing member of all the churches."[12] Dr A.P. McDiarmid, president of the Baptist Church's Brandon College, agreed, finding it "exceedingly suggestive and stimulating, as well as broadly informative."[13]

The extent of the book's circulation outside the churches is a matter of some speculation. Dr John MacLean, of another Winnipeg city mission, who followed such matters, noted that it had met a hearty response in the public press and on the platform.[14] Winnipeg reviewers in the *Manitoba Free Press* and the *Telegram* greeted the book warmly, noting its special value for "the complex civic life developing here," and approved its central message of social solidarity. They appreciated its "point and directness and practical force." "Ivanhoe" in the *Telegram* found no reason to criticize Woodsworth's subscription to gradualistic socialism, and "The Bookman" in the *Free Press* added: "It is a book to trust."[15] Fellow social workers, J.H.T. Falk in Winnipeg and F.N. Stapleford in Toronto, were pleased at last to have a sociological work with Canadian content. The prominent Winnipeg reformer F.J. Dixon hoped it would shame Canadians into realizing that "in the realm of progressive legislation this is one of the most backward countries." One editor found it a useful medicine for those like C.H. Cahan who, incredibly, was urging Canadian Clubs to prepare to defend waterways and railways against a possible American invasion; reading *My Neighbor*, he prescribed, would make it clear that the real dangers to this country were ones common to both countries, and Boston and Montreal, Buffalo and Toronto, should be helping each other solve them. Only an American reviewer found fault with the extensive quoting of some British and many American authorities. From one standpoint this was a weakness in the work, but most Canadian reviewers were more than thankful to have so convenient a short course through the best literature on the subject of urban sociology. The book had other uses as well. The *Woman's International Quarterly* in London, England, prescribed it, along with Woodsworth's earlier study, as an antidote for highly coloured immigration advertisements. At the same time, the journal expressed its sympathy for the civic agony of a young nation being invaded by contingents of forty-one nationalities.[16] The book evidently found its way to quite a diversity of reviewers and, if the reviewers are any guide, to a considerable and admiring general readership.

It was not simply as a compilation of matters of fact and commentary, however, that the book made its mark, but by two apparently contrary characteristics: eclecticism and single-mindedness. Woodsworth readily confessed to the former, and undoubtedly his enthusiasm for most of the reform programs of the day broadened the range of his appeal. It was as easy to accept the book as an application of the parable of the Good Samaritan, from which the title was taken, as it was to hail it as an outline of the next steps toward a socialist commonwealth. There was, however, a guiding idea behind his eclecticism that accounts for the subdued intensity that pervades the book. That was the idea of social solidarity. Whatever Woodsworth touched he viewed in its light and, despite his disclaimers of literary pretence, his style not infrequently becomes genuinely eloquent as the subject matter moves closer to this centre of his thought.[17]

The book was clearly of national importance, and many agreed that Woodsworth was the man best prepared to write it. It could hardly have been written by him or by anyone else much before 1911. Brandon, in which he grew up, and Winnipeg, which he experienced as a student in the 1890s, were still, like most Canadian cities, focused more upon their rural hinterlands than upon themselves. He had experienced the problems of British and European cities, and some of the responses to them, during his studies and travels of 1899–1900, but the pertinence of the experience was not yet apparent to him. Back in Canada, he was happy with the consoling observation that the Canadian poor were still honest and independent. In 1905, when an assistant minister in a large Winnipeg church, he teamed up with Salem Bland of Wesley College in a series of sermons on the city, but in 1907 he could still write as though the countryside and its virtues provided the final solution to the problem of the city.[18] What happened to the Canadian city after 1901, and what happened to Woodsworth, thrust in 1907 into the worst of Canadian civic problems as superintendent of All Peoples' Mission, Winnipeg, changed all that.

Like the Fred Victor Mission in Toronto, All Peoples' began some years before as a Sunday School class, the network of whose little lives had slowly involved church workers in ever-widening circles of social activity. By 1911, Woodsworth created a multi-faceted institution with several bases in Winnipeg's north end. Institutes, settlements, and neighbourhood houses provided religious services in foreign languages; men's, women's, and children's associations and clubs; language, industrial, and household science classes; concerts; lectures; libraries; gymnasiums; baths; community and hospital visiting; and relief. There were, of course, assistants: an ordained man, eight deaconesses, three theological students, four "kindergarteners," a director of boys' work, two students training for special work with language groups, two young women in training for settlement work, and some hundred volunteers from Wesley College and the city generally. The miracle was that any book, let alone two pioneering studies, was written in the midst of such a development. But Woodsworth found time in these years to become one of the most widely read Canadians on social and civic subjects and, as well, to become the centre of efforts to rationalize city welfare agencies in Winnipeg, to serve on the civic playgrounds commission, and to act as a Ministerial Association representative on the Trades and Labor Council. Through the last, he became labour's representative on the provincial Royal Commission on Technical Education from 1911 to 1912. The years 1907–1911 had been ones of total immersion in the city problem.

Woodsworth was not only engaged across a broad front of action, and reading widely, but, as a stream of articles in the secular and church press testify, he was almost constantly reflecting on the nature of the social problems before him. That was probably one reason why a reporter could note, "He has no sense of humour – he really hasn't." But another result was that he broke out of his agrarian bias to become both personally attached and committed to the city, and an authentic spokesman of urban reform.[19] He recognized what few other urban reformers realized, that, with continued mechanization, the growth of the modern city was becoming a self-sustaining phenomenon. The city was the future of civilization. Still more, he presented the clearest and most pointed articulation of the proposition that the fundamental interdependence of the city required total rather than piecemeal solutions. There was an implied collectivism in the proposals of most urban reformers – indeed of most reformers – of the time. That was an extension of the late nineteenth century's reharnessing of the state for social efficiency and the public good. But Woodsworth's social vision went beyond the agencies of the state and high-level civic planning and reorganization to embrace the development of a lively social consciousness and cooperative solutions by voluntary groups. The publication of *My Neighbor* marked as clearly as any event the arrival of a time for Canadians to engage in a large revaluing of their traditions. "Our British ancestry, our Protestant traditions, our frontier training," he was to write in 1913, "have developed a sturdy independence, but have left us 'short' on those elements which are essential to the cooperation involved in our complex modern life which finds its highest expression in the city."[20] It was significant that whenever Woodsworth turned to rural problems after writing *My Neighbor*, his proposed solutions reflected the social values he saw implicit in the city.

Woodsworth's thoroughgoing social approach to the city was not simply compounded of observation, for he was, after all, his father's child, a son of a Methodist moralism that made it not difficult to see self-interest and economic greed in every influence corrupting the city. He was a member of a denomination with a long tradition of practical idealism and a doctrine of personal perfection in love in this life. Such elements from his past had been subjected to the transforming influence of the social gospel, rising about him in these formative years, and a testimony to whose influence upon him lies in the remarkable number of its works cited in his chapter references. His anticipation of a "new social revolution" was predicated upon a belief that "more and more the altruistic in aim is predominating in the efforts of men," and that social perfection was the proper goal of humanity.[21] The social gospel provided the hopeful context not only for his appreciation of urban problems and his solutions, but also for his total conception of the city and its significance. With the writing *of My Neighbor,* Woodsworth himself became a major exponent of the social gospel. For him, faith was now supremely expressed in the spirit of social service and the city was not only its testing ground but, by the designs of a providential social evolution, the agency and the scene of its ultimate demonstration.

The city, however, was not to remain the centre of Woodsworth's career. He was to spend two more years at All Peoples' and in 1913, the year of his resignation, under commission from the Methodist and Presbyterian churches, he undertook social surveys of several Canadian cities along with Bryce Stewart and W.A. Riddell. Social welfare and research continued to preoccupy him, along with much travelling and speaking, until the middle of the war when the collision of his pacifism with wartime patriotism disrupted his life and drove him closer to the labour movement. Following the Winnipeg general strike of 1919 his avowal of labour politics led him back to North Winnipeg, but now as a Member of Parliament representing the people he had laboured for so earnestly at All Peoples'. The building of a national farmer-labour party, the task that occupied the rest of his life, was consummated in 1933 with the founding of the Co-operative Commonwealth Federation (CCF), the forerunner of the New Democratic party. He presided over its early growth as leader until, in 1939, his pacifist convictions led him to part company with party policy. He died in 1942. Although urban conditions remained a central part of his concerns, his farmer-labour politics and federal position caused him to later bypass the city as an arena of social action and concern. As in the life of the nation, the city suffered an eclipse in the life of J.S. Woodsworth.

Scattered through *My Neighbor* are a half hundred proposals comprising a broad program for urban advance. Many have been implemented; others, like state responsibility for the health and legal defence of its members, are still being worked out. Some reforms are now themselves in need of reforming. After half a century of bureaucratic civic development, spurred in part by reformers like Woodsworth, some may prefer a more individualistic ideal than his (though he was never a statist by temperament or intention and the social consciousness he believed necessary to the continuance of reform was advocated as a completion and not a denial of individual freedom).

The new urban reformers of the 1970s will find some of his proposals too simple and his faith too confident, but much remains to link them.

Woodsworth's lack of dogmatism makes his work more approachable than it might otherwise have been. His concern for driveways, parks, civic centres, playgrounds, ultimate community ownership of land, universal and humane minimum standards of life, the socializing of education and medicine, the personalizing of social welfare, rapid transit, the extension of galleries and museums, and the cultural enfranchisement of the masses all have a distinctly contemporary ring. He could urge, as present reformers do, the bypassing of established civic political organizations, and the mobilizing of people in the wards. He and the new reformers share a driving hope for the future of the city, and there are anticipations in his book of their fear that the city might instead become the citadel of an inhuman technology, a tangle of transportation systems with meaningless destinations, a morass of information without communication. He remains "a citizen of all Canadian cities," and whether Woodsworth's ideal city ever exists, the true urban reformer will live in no other.

CHAPTER ELEVEN

The Social Gospel as the Religion of the Agrarian Revolt in Western Canada

BACKGROUNDER

In an article whose notes are lost somewhere in my files, a colleague wrote that I was the only historian of my generation to propose a new category of interpretation for Canadian historiography, namely "religion." He undoubtedly had the following article in mind and perhaps my conclusion in The Social Passion Religion and Social Reform in Canada, 1914–1928 *about the fate of the Progressive party in the mid-1920s. In this essay, I not only recounted the role of religion in a major political event in Canadian history but also went on to suggest that the agrarian revolt, itself, could not be fully understood unless it were seen as a religious phenomenon seeking to embed ultimate hopes for humanity in the temporal order, and therefore subject to religious categories of interpretation.*

My intent was not to sideline other interpretive perspectives that were legitimate in their own right. This is not an unusual argument in religious studies, and it has ancient roots in Judaic monotheism with its proscription of idolatry – even the naming of God. More recent articulations, including my own, derive from the wave of existentialist thought after the Second World War. Sartre and Camus in their literary works and Tillich in his theology, philosophy, and sermons looked out on a humanity burdened with anxiety over the meaning of their lives in a world where accepted norms and traditions had either dissolved or were in dissolution. Sartre saw "no exit" from this condition, other than taking one's life in hand and acting with decision, and creating one's own path through this trackless world. Camus, in effect said, Yes, but we needed to remind ourselves and each other that we are not God. Tillich's response to this existential crisis was his runaway best-seller, The Courage to Be. *In it he distilled for the public the essence of his landmark systematic theology. Tillich identified among the sources of anxiety plaguing moderns a metaphysical anxiety arising from alienation from the "ground of being." Failure to deal with this on its own terms, Tillich said, leads to the erection of some "ultimate concern," devotion to which takes on trappings analogous to those of religion, but which cannot satisfy because they do not address the central issue. However, in failing its role as a surrogate "God," the object of "ultimate concern" demands further indulgence to assuage the loss, a trap it becomes difficult to escape. Difficult because the ultimate concern is an attempt to escape the realities of fate and death, guilt and condemnation, and meaninglessness and emptiness – all of which arouse a dread of "non-being." Tillich's "courage to be" counsels a bold self-affirming confrontation of these phases of "non-being" in the faith that one's being ultimately rests in the "ground of being" – the God beyond God, accepting that for all one's "imperfections" there is a self-renewing acceptance. Tillich's theological reflections provided the basis for his widely influential "Principle of Correlation," bringing cultural and religious phenomena into mutual dialogue.*

A contemporary example of the application of this concept is Harvey Cox, The Market as God (2016). Cox describes how the Market God has its temples, priests, prophets, missionaries, holy scriptures, doctrines, and congregations where the faithful gather to renew their faith in the mystery of the "hidden hand" and the consuming power of continuous acquisition to alley besetting ills and insecurities.

In the conclusion to the article below, I did little more than sketch a hypothesis, using only the aspect of a double alienation driving the agrarian revolt – the regional alienation from the national system compounded by an existential alienation from "the ground of being." This double alienation, I suggested, fuelled among Western agrarians a spirit of revolt – a collective act of self-affirmation – whose object was recognition as a mature and equal partner in the confederated nation.

THE SOCIAL GOSPEL
AS THE RELIGION OF AGRARIAN REVOLT*

Between 1916 and 1926 Ontario and prairie farmers mounted a concerted attack upon the political and economic structure of the nation. Known to history as the agrarian revolt, it toppled three provincial governments, strengthened the agrarian hold on one other, routed one federal party and government, and made the life of its successor a tenuous one. Provincially and federally the farmers secured legislation affecting freight rates, tar-

---

* First published as "The Social Gospel as the Religion of Agrarian Revolt," in *The West and the Nation: Essays in Honour of W.L. Morton,* eds Carl Berger and Ramsay Cook (Toronto: McClelland and Stewart, 1976), 174–86.

iffs, credit, and marketing. They secured a modicum of electoral and social legislation and were instrumental in ending federal control of the natural resources of Saskatchewan and Alberta. In the upshot, the agrarian revolt achieved a greater measure of equity for the farmer, and for the prairies in particular, but the balance of its program – indeed the Progressive party itself – died a lingering death after 1923 amid the crosscurrents within the party and the legislatures of the nation.

The agrarian revolt in the West, like its predecessors, and successors, had obvious political, social, and economic roots. Politically, the farmers had been under-represented in Parliament. The West had been the stepping stone of nation-building, yet it stood on the sidelines of the federal power structure. Socially, the older agrarian regions were experiencing a march for the city and to the newer ones, immigration from Europe, Britain, and the United States had brought a new fare of reform ideas to feed discontent. Economically, farmers in the West were disadvantaged by policies of industrialization that forced them to buy in a protected market and sell in an open one, far from the site of production and through agencies entirely unaccountable to them. It was a debtor region. The varied phenomena of the agrarian revolt can be and have been largely accounted for in such terms. However, all of those conditions were perceived and evaluated in terms that were both explicitly and implicitly religious. It was under the impress of religion that the farmers were rallied to the cause, chose their tactics, and explained their purposes. And religious considerations played a notable role in both their success and their failure.

No individual lives by bread – or wheat – alone, and movements with ostensible economic beginnings invariably find themselves clothed with ideas and hopes that provide frameworks for action not reducible to economics or even politics. Patterns of behaviour, both individually and collectively, emerge that sometimes owe more to religious concerns of alienation and reconciliation, of guilt, justification, redemption, and ultimate hope than to the cold rationalities of economic interest. The two impulses meet in a framework of ideas, or an ideology, combining self-interest and ultimate aspirations by which a group, class, section, or nation explains to itself and to the world what its problems are, how it is approaching them, where it is going, and why. To a remarkable degree, the social gospel and the ideology of the agrarian revolt coincided.

The identification of Western agrarianism with religious motives was even closer than the foregoing implies, for both the leadership and the membership generally espoused religion with a will. Henry Wise Wood,

the great Alberta agrarian leader of the time, though not an active churchman in his Alberta days, was a very religious man who viewed the United
Farmers of Alberta as a religious movement.[1] The Regina *Leader* described
the Saskatchewan Grain Growers' Association (SGGA) as "a religious,
social, educational, political and commercial organization all in one, and
in the truest and deepest meaning of these several terms."[2] W.R. Wood,
secretary of the Manitoba Grain Growers, wrote that "we are practically
seeking to inaugurate the Kingdom of God and its righteousness"[3] and
Norman Lambert, secretary of the Canadian Council of Agriculture, suggested that the aim of the Progressive party was "to give 'politics' a new
meaning in Canada," and "hand in hand with the organized farmers movement on the prairies has gone religion and social work."[4]

Such remarks were in the first instance a consequence of the formative
influence of the churches in the years of prairie settlement. Even allowing
for the ease with which members were lost in those vast expanses of plain
and parkland, the church had been a major educative influence. The leaders of the Grain Growers were often (though not always) church folk of
note and even clergy; and most of the participants were church members
who could sing "Onward Christian Soldiers" with great vigour and conviction.[5] Furthermore, many with aspirations to the ministry, others with
some theological training, religious workers, and clergy took up positions
of influence in one or another of the farmers' organizations: Henry Wise
Wood, Percival Baker, Norman Smith, William Irvine, Louise McKinney,
G.W. Robertson, R.C. Henders, W.R. Wood, R.A. Hoey. Not infrequently,
clergy joined their lay people as members and officers of Grain Growers'
locals. Rev. P. McLeod, Presbyterian minister of Baldur, Manitoba, at the
1916 Convention, tried to move the organization from political independence to support for a farmer-labour party.[6] Rev. W. Kelly was vice-
president of the Wellwood local in Manitoba in 1919 and had experience
in Australian farmers' movements. Revs. A.C. Burley, Harold Wildings,
and J. Griffiths were delegates to the Saskatchewan Grain Growers' Convention in 1920[7] and in 1921. Rev. Hugh Dobson, Western Field Secretary
for Methodist Evangelism and Social Service, was a member of the inner
policy group of the Regina constituency organization of the Progressive
party. In addition, a number of ministers dared to take unto themselves
the controversy of running for political office as independent or Progressive candidates with farmer support.[8] The church was not, however, exact-
ly of one mind about such clerical involvement. None of the denominational hierarchies discouraged such social action, but locally it was

sometimes a different matter, as one young Presbyterian minister wrote: "Several of the old party men have left the church because of my active association with the Grain Growers' Movement."[9]

This interpretation of agrarian and church leadership, especially in the period of the agrarian revolt, was not of itself, however, only a consequence of the past services of the church in the settlement process. It was more a reflection of the impact of the social gospel in prairie Protestantism and the farm movements themselves. As the prairie farmer faced the gargantuan task of marketing an ever-growing grain crop in the complex, impersonal international market, the agrarian myth of the virtuous individual "yeoman" wresting dues from the soil by his/her own skill broke down. Only in combination and cooperation could farmers cope with the forces arrayed before them: elevator companies, railroads, grain exchanges, even political parties and governments. They were in need not only of new organizations and techniques but also of a new social faith. The social gospel supplied it.

The social gospel had been rising to the surface of Canadian Protestantism in the decade previous to the founding of the great prairie agrarian organizations. To one degree or another all the mainline Protestant church colleges in the West – Wesley College, Manitoba College, Brandon College, Regina College, and Alberta College – became disseminators of the social gospel. Wesley College was chief among them with individuals like W. F. Osborne and Salem Bland on its faculty and was the first prairie institution to offer a course in sociology. As teachers, preachers, and lay folk, the college students carried the message back to the communities of the West. The flow of the social gospel into the West was multiplied by the migration of British and American Midwestern farmers and then multiplied again when the churches were forced to turn to British recruits for the ministry. Many of them had already been influenced by both the labour movement and the social movement in the British churches and readily confessed that they were already primed for the message of a professor like Salem Bland at Wesley College.[10]

Bland himself was probably the most vigorous exponent of the social gospel in the West. A cripple, an avid reader, an engaging teacher, and a powerful preacher and platform personality, he typified the many connections of the social gospel with prairie reform movements. He had been an ardent prohibitionist. He was on the executive of the Free Trade League and was honorary president of the Single Tax and Direct Legislation Association. He was a representative of the Ministerial Association on the Winnipeg Trade and Labor Council. He was a favourite guest speaker at Grain

Growers' Conventions in Saskatchewan and Manitoba. On his first appearance before the former in 1913, he proved to be rather in advance of the leadership, though not of all the members, when he proposed the establishment of a third party led by the farmers. When he was dismissed from Wesley College under controversial circumstances, the *Grain Growers' Guide* secured his services as a regular columnist, proclaiming: "There is no abler champion of the principles for which the organized farmers stand." His column "The Deeper Life" related resources of Christianity and, in particular, the social gospel to a broad spectrum of agrarian needs and aspirations. The Chautauqua movement employed him (as well as Henry Wise Wood) in 1918 for its second summer of educational and entertaining programs in prairie communities. In 1919, the SGGA used him to spearhead the call to political action that the association leadership now considered unavoidable. And the next year, when the *Saskatoon Star Phoenix* reviewed his book *The New Christianity*, it pronounced it to be "a concentrated form of the message which ministers are sending forth from pulpits today" and "just what [one] has thought all his life but lacked the power of expression to put it into words."[11]

But it was not through the formal agency of Canadian Protestantism alone in the West that the social gospel reached its place of eminence in the agrarian revolt. Agrarian leaders had minds of their own; many of them read widely; and the agencies of press, journal, and book brought the world to their doorsteps. The *Grain Growers' Guide*'s book section publicized and sold many of the books like Henry George's *Progress and Poverty* and Edward Bellamy's *Looking Backward* that had made such an impact on the nascent social gospellers of the previous generation. The *Guide* occasionally leaned on the American social gospel, reprinting articles like Lyman Abbott's "My Democracy?"[12] In 1916 it used articles by Washington Gladden to provoke discussion of the role of the church in prairie communities.[13] The prairie press at large carried news of notable developments in social Christianity elsewhere. The Regina *Leader* commented favourably upon the proposal of R.J. Campbell, English author of *The New Theology*, that it was the business of the church to profess the religion of Jesus that "was in its inception a social gospel" and by helping erect a socialist Christian state "sweep way those existing conditions which throw a pall over the lives of the larger proportion of our people." And when, in 1912 and 1913, the "Men and Religion Forward Movement" was underway in the United States, the *Leader* carried a weekly column entitled "Religion and Social Service."

Primary farm leaders manifested the social gospel early. E.A. Partridge, the greatest agrarian radical of the early 1900s and the most innovative farm leader of the period, came to the West in 1883 with a Ruskinian socialist outlook already formed. It was not necessary to go much farther than Partridge in looking for a definition of the social gospel. In 1909 he wrote, as editor of the Grain Growers' Guide: "Christ wasn't trying to save his soul for the next world ... but was trying to serve humanity by showing men the truth about the proper relations to set up between themselves and God and themselves and others."[14] Therefore, he said, it was necessary to "take your love of God, which in its practical form is love of your neighbour, into politics. Practical religion is for every day, but more especially for Convention day, Nomination day, Election day until our legislative halls are purged of those who represent the most heartless and selfish instincts of the race."[15] Such applications of Christianity were of ultimate significance, because the emphasis on wealth and competition in the present system "checks the march of civilization and indefinitely delays the coming of the Kingdom for which Christ so earnestly laboured."[16]

Henry Wise Wood was not a member of any church in Canada but brought a liberal-leaning religious outlook from an upbringing and training under the Campbellite church in Missouri.[17] Wood was an assiduous reader, both of the Bible and works in social theory, and produced, out of elements of cooperative and socialist thought, social Darwinism, and Scripture, a comprehensive social philosophy for the agrarian movement that can only be categorized as social gospel. Wood held that, over the centuries, humankind had been held in subjugation by the spirit of animal selfishness, expressing itself in autocratic regimes of government or industry, competition between individuals, businesses, and states, and a quest for profit that was nothing less than a worship of mammon. Scripture, the Prophets, and Christ taught another way of social unselfishness that expressed itself in the alternatives of service, cooperation, and democracy. The fulfillment of the social spirit was synonymous for Wood with the achievement of the Kingdom of Heaven.

Tactically, Wood considered that the social spirit was best nurtured in those realms of life where individuals were closest to each other, namely in the economic realm of occupational groups. In this light, the United Farmers of Alberta (UFA) and the Wheat Pool were as much religious institutions as the church. The primary task of the time, therefore, was to organize those groups on a cooperative democratic basis, and once so organized, to maintain them in the true way. Government might then be built upon the self-government of the groups, and second, upon a legislature and executive representative of all occupational groups. These tactics entailed serious problems in the transitional period when not all groups

were organized on a democratic basis, but Wood must have looked hope-
fully upon the widespread advocacy of industrial democracy after the
Great War, when he was advancing his theories.

Because so much was hanging in the balance, not just economically or
politically but religiously, Wood was insistent that farmer politics must be
UFA politics, and that UFA politics must not aim primarily at winning
elections but at developing principles. Hence Wood's radical emphasis
upon group politics. But he had no doubts about the outcome. How
would God, who had allowed the perfection of lesser creatures in the natural order, allow God's supreme creation to fail? The Supreme Power had
this work in hand.[18]

It was possible, then, for the agrarian leadership to appropriate the
social gospel and give it forceful expression without a sustained contact
with the prairie pulpit, although few were without its influence at some
stage in their careers. Either way, they sought the support – and sometimes rehabilitation – of the pulpits of the West, and in 1917 they created UFA and Grain Growers' Sundays as formal occasions on which to celebrate the social gospel. Not all ministers and locals took up the
opportunity, but the farm leaders left little to chance. The SGGA asked
ministers to preach on the principles of the association, in the belief, as
George Langley put it, that "bringing into prominence ... our human
interdependence will lift us into closer relationship with the Divinity
that is the centre of our common brotherhood."[19] Henry Wise Wood was
even more explicit in two forceful circulars on the subject. He advised the
ministers of the province not to preach on "orthodox things," personal
resistance to temptation, or an outdated Biblical view of farming. Rather
"tell them that the only thing Jesus ever taught us to pray for, was this
reorganized, regenerated perfect civilization. Tell them that this regeneration deals with every element of civilization ... and that all that cannot
pass through the refining fire ... must be consumed by it." To the UFA
members, Wood wrote that if the church in the past had only offered
them a personal saviour it was because they had asked for nothing more.
Now, however, the Church was beginning to recognize Christ as a leader
who offered the great social deliverance that individuals were seeking.
Only on these lines could the farmers and the church find a path through
their perplexity. As Wood maintains, "Is Christ to develop the individuals
and Carl [sic] Marx mobilize and lead them? Is Christ to hew the stones
and Henry George build them into the finished edifice?"[20] Wood's advice
was followed, and in 1920 the *Edmonton Free Press* observed that these
Sundays had become established institutions providing an occasion to

examine Christ's social teachings, and other press reports of the services convey a similar conclusion.[21]

The more traditional holy days were also occasions for the *Guide* and the agrarian leadership to put their activities in religious perspective or to call on a sympathetic cleric to rehearse the social gospel. For example, J.B. Musselman's Christmas message in 1918, as secretary of the SGGA, observed that "'Peace on Earth and Goodwill toward men' must ever remain a myth while men think of Christ and His teachings only as the means of their personal salvation."[22]

Although at one level the adoption of the social gospel by the farm leaders brought the agrarian organizations and the church closer together, their heightened religious sense equally provided a severe critique of traditional organized religion. That message could also be read in Wood's circulars in Alberta, in Musselman's deliverances in Saskatchewan, and in W.R. Wood's articles in Manitoba.[23] William Irvine, who was later to become the chief systematizer of Henry Wise Wood's political ideas, urged with respect to the UFA Sundays that there might be more point in "Church Sundays" on which the true spirit and expression of Christianity might be communicated by the UFA to the churches of Alberta.[24] When only one of the ministerial delegates of the SGGA convention in 1919 turned up for a discussion of church union (the others no doubt sick of the subject and eager to discuss headier matters of farmer politics), it was suggested that it was up to the farmers to form a Grain Growers' Church of their own along union lines.[25] Even in the ranks, it would seem, an increasing number were viewing their movements as peculiar sources of social, even religious, regeneration and expressing in practice what William Irvine was shortly to write in *The Farmers in Politics*: "The line between the sacred and the secular is being rubbed out" and "everything is becoming sacred." First and foremost in that process was the organized farmers' movement.

The social gospel, then, was a power to be reckoned with as the Western farmer figuratively took up arms against the national system. But for all that the social gospel could be described as a new development in the religious culture of the agrarian West, once the farm organizations were baptized by the social gospel with the Holy Spirit, it was possible to make even the resources of the older evangelicalism do service in the agrarian revolt. Were not the farm organizations themselves now the centre of revival, calling the nation to repentance and conversion? Musselman's reaction to the astonishing electoral victories of the fall of 1919 in Ontario and at Cochrane, Alberta, was to quote a hymn that had echoed from revival and camp meeting: "Lo, the promise of a shower; / Drops already from above; / And the Lord will shortly pour / All the pleasure of His love."[26]

And so it seemed as the following three years saw a remarkable harvest of constituencies, legislatures, and governments.

Insofar as the Western farmers were in need of a social faith for the new commercial age that was upon them, they found it in the social gospel, and it provided for them not only a great manifesto of social justice but also the promise of a great deliverance and the coming of a new time. To say so much, however, and to document it, is not to exhaust the significance of that development. It is necessary as well to ask certain questions: How did the social gospel relate to the enduring ideology of the agrarian myth? What role did it play in the internal problems of the Progressive party, and how did it affect its political tactics? Finally, how much was the social gospel of the agrarian revolt a part of the rampant English Protestantism of the second decade, which won prohibition in the West with one hand while it virtually wiped out foreign language instruction in the schools with the other? Definitive answers to these questions still await substantial research and interpretation, but at least some suggestive inferences can and ought to be drawn from what is already known.

Richard Hofstadler has made much of the inappropriateness of the agrarian myth of the "virtuous yeoman" to the situation of the Western American farmer, whom he views rather as a large-scale producer and land speculator, given to an indulgent identification with the common individual in times of depression but assuming his/her entrepreneurial mantle when the going was good. Depending on the season, he/she ran with the hare *or* the hounds. Without going into all aspects of the applicability of this image to the prairie farmer, it is evident that in season and out, the social gospel sought to strip away the individualism of the agrarian myth – and did so with some success. Nevertheless, what was lost for the individual was gained for the group, and, one might almost say, for the region. While the cartoons of the *Guide* still appealed to the beleaguered individual farmer, they taught just that, that the farmer as an individual was no match for the world. In stressing the virtues of association and the common humanity of farmers, however, the social gospel was far from detracting from the commercial realities confronting them. Each new triumph of organization from 1901 to 1923 was at one and the same time a celebration of the progressive march of Christian social ethics, the arrival of a new breed of virtuous cooperators, *and* an advance in the farmers' commercial sophistication. This enduring sense of common humanity and the moral superiority of the farmers' response to their world, however, could hardly do other than compound a sense of alienation within the nation in the political and economic crisis of 1918–21.

At the same time, in an apparent contradiction to the social gospel's emphasis upon the brotherhood or sisterhood of humankind, the overwhelming bulk of the agrarian leadership and a majority of their following were obviously deeply committed to the continuing surge of Anglo-Protestant culture religion, expressed in campaigns for "national schools" with English-only language instruction, prohibition, and church union; the social gospel of the agrarian revolt was closely associated with all of this, as can be demonstrated in a number of ways. UFA support in Alberta was strongest – almost unshakeable – in the older settled region of the province south of Red Deer, populated largely by those of British, American, German, or Scandinavian extraction, and devoted to commodity production. This was where those campaigns on behalf of moral righteousness, which the UFA embraced – prohibition, social reform, direct democracy, and smashing the "interests" – had their strongest support. By contrast, these causes – and the UFA – were much less popular in the more recently settled northern area with its heavier concentrations of French-Canadians and Ukrainians.[27] In Saskatchewan, in 1919, the provincial legislators among the ranks of the Grain Growers' Association were with one exception Protestant: half were Presbyterian, a fifth Methodist.[28] And in a study of the Progressive party's middle leadership in 1921 in Saskatchewan, all of those on whom significant data could be found were Protestant.[29] In Manitoba, using still another measure, Salem Bland was most frequently called to speak and preach in the English Protestant region west and south from Winnipeg, which was most constant in its support of prohibition.[30] Perhaps, on the one hand, what the association pointed to is obvious. It is not possible to link all social gospellers of the agrarian revolt equally to the status politics of Anglo-Protestantism in the West, but it is not surprising to read of the rousing reception given by the SGGA in convention in 1918 to the call for English only in the schools by Dr J.G. Shearer, head of the Social Service Council of Canada and the pre-eminent Presbyterian social gospeller in the land.

What then does one say about the virtuous cooperator of the social gospel of the agrarian revolt? Simply that one individual's redemption is another individual's alienation? That is not an uncommon pattern with ideologies as the identities of self-interest within them become clearer, and it is evident in the dynamics of the agrarian revolt as well. But that its character can be entirely ascribed to status politics and nativism in the face of new urban – and even rural – groups and classes occasioned by a combination of industrialism and immigration is not entirely fair or accurate. At a time when it is recognized that there was not, after all, that much to be feared from the maintenance of immigrant cultures, Western agrarian Anglo-Protestants ought not to be belaboured too heavily for wanting to maintain *their* culture. One might assume that immigrants were seeking a better country – as were the social gospellers and the agrarian co-operators – and were they not offering them its best? In the catalogue of responses to immigration, it cannot be ignored that it was the UFA that provided the House of Commons with its first Member of Parliament of Ukrainian descent in 1926, or that the SGGA began early on using immigrant languages in its publicity and developed a Foreign Organization Department whose staff was able to use languages other than English, or that the Women's Section of the SGGA showed a considerable and continuous concern for the welfare of immigrant families in prairie communities.[31] The culture religion underlying the social gospel did not speak an unequivocal word in response to immigration. If in the upshot that response was a mixture of inclusiveness and exclusiveness, it cannot be put down to simple negativism and nativism. Certainly that would not do justice to the literature that Protestant agrarians read on the subject – whether church papers, novels like *The Foreigner*, or texts like *Strangers Within Our Gates* – all of which were marked by a complex ambivalence.

If the agrarian's response to immigration was somewhat paradoxical, there was also an irony in its appropriation of the social gospel. Clearly, the social gospel of the agrarian revolt first derived from urban rather than agrarian responses to industrialism. Its framework of thought derived from urban universities, urban civil servants, and urban pastors, and it was popularized by urban-based presses and urban-trained preachers. It could be described as a metropolitan concoction that the hinterland came to share. It provided common ground for farm leaders and urban professionals, whether journalist, cleric, or social worker, and – to a lesser degree and in the right season – labourer. It is not surprising, then, that when the social gospel came to prescribe for the countryside, its proposals were extensions of the amenities and social features of urban life.[32]

The social gospel had no criticism of the agrarian drive after the turn of the century for the businesslike practice of agriculture. The problem was not with business *per se* but with the misuse of corporate wealth and power. What the social gospel of the agrarian revolt proclaimed was that the agrarians had found a way of handling business, wealth, and power, consistent with democracy and Christian social ethics.

Inevitably, the religious dimensions of the agrarian revolt made it more difficult for the movement to function in the given world of Canadian politics. The Progressive party refused to function as an opposition party on behalf of all Canadians – which exposed that it was, after all, an agency of group interest. Progressives who alone voted overwhelmingly in the federal House against racetrack gambling and for church union could hardly be expected to make up their minds between Conservative high tariff iniquity and liquor-corrupted Liberal administration in 1925–26. The one affronted their group economic interest and the other their Anglo-Protestant culture religion, both of which were incorporated in the social gospel of the agrarian revolt, even while they were in some measure transformed by it.

The inner problems of the party were likewise an expression of religious sensitivities. From the beginning the UFA representatives had been the bearers of the pure doctrine. They had refused to concede formal organization as a party; they had early separated out, constituting the majority of the "Ginger Group," associating themselves with the Labor "group," Woodsworth and Irvine; and they survived the debacle of 1926 almost intact. In religious terms, of all the Progressives, they had, under Wood's tutorship, came closest to forming a new cult. It should come as no surprise that where post-millennial politics had been most intense, but had failed to avert the disasters and dispel the demons of the 1930s, a virulent pre-millennial politics of the second coming should take its place. The fundamentalist reaction of the 1920s, of course, had intervened and helped that process along.

In embracing the social gospel, the agrarian movement wedded a universal religious perspective to the particular problems of its own condition. The tensions inherent in that marriage were difficult to resolve and revealed themselves most clearly in the crisis of 1925–26. The tension, however, was a sign of the creative, transforming process of true religion · at work. The depths of human alienation from the source of being underlay the experience of agrarian alienation from the national sources of well-being. The enduring human urge for ultimate reconciliation hovered over the desire to be more fully a part of the national community. The perception of alienation and the identification of hope in the particular circumstances of the West, in turn, victimized some and excluded others, but in the process, the West became a new, mature society, notable for its cooperative structures of business and for what were almost non-partisan service state governments, within a federal system committed to equal opportunity for all regions (however difficult that has been to realize in practice). The universal perspectives of the agrarian revolt helped move Canadian society to a greater measure of justice. The social gospel of the agrarian revolt had done its work.

CHAPTER TWELVE

The New Christianity in Post-Great War Toronto

BACKGROUNDER

It was a startling but pleasing discovery. Several years into my work on the Salem Bland biography[1] I learned that, as students, my parents had met and heard Bland in 1924 when he was at the University of British Columbia, completing a cross-country speaking tour. As he had failed to secure a pastorate that year, the Department of Evangelism and Social Service had commissioned him to cross the country speaking and holding workshops on how to approach the Bible and Jesus in the light of the new historical scholarship. That would have been classic Bland.

My own acquaintance with Bland came when, searching for a Master's thesis topic, my supervising professor, Roger Graham, said, "McNaught has just done Woodsworth. Why don't you do Salem Bland?" Salem Bland, I discovered in McNaught's A Prophet in Politics, *seemed to be an echo of Woodsworth, critical of church dogma, opposed to the war, and closely linked to farmer and labour movements in the West. He was a professor at Winnipeg's Wesley College. I quickly discovered that he was not an echo but a precursor and mentor, much in demand across the West and in central Canada for his ability as a preacher and public speaker. Moreover, although in the conscription crisis he opposed the conscription of manpower before the conscription of wealth, he was not pacifist. Report has it that at a York University History Department gathering, McNaught and Ramsay Cook engaged in a furious argument on the point. Cook was right. And on the controversial issue of Bland's dismissal from the college in 1917, I came to disagree with McNaught, who saw the move clearly aimed at removing Bland for his radical political views. I argued that the evidence did not bear out that conclusion, and despite Bland's view to the contrary, it was a legitimate*

*response to the financial crisis at the college. I am now inclined to think other-
wise, having found a letter describing an encounter with James Ashdown, chair
of the Wesley board, en route by train from Lake of the Woods to Winnipeg. The
case had become a cause celebre across the West with demands for Bland's reinstatement. Asked about that possibility, Ashdown was adamant. Under no circumstances would Bland be re-employed at Wesley. The other relevant evidence
was the role played by Dr Hughson, pastor of Ashdown's Grace Church, who
was secretary of the college's Committee on Staff. Ever since Bland had delivered
a sermon at Grace denouncing the presence of land speculators, rent gougers,
and financial manipulators among the membership of Winnipeg churches,
Hughson had had it in for Bland. Nothing deterred, Bland of late had been
preaching sermons promoting a transformative social gospel, asking if the church
were up to the task and speculating that, if not, God might move that commission elsewhere. Hughson had sought to bring Bland to "trial" before the General Ministerial Association. After some procrastination, the Association agreed,
but after hearing Bland it refused to condemn him. Hughson, with Ashdown's
evident compliance, took an aggressive role in the public relations of the committee, despite some question as to the legitimacy of the committee assuming a
role more properly the province of the college board. It was Hughson who
released the committee's decision to the press without the courtesy of notifying
Bland beforehand, leaving him to learn the decision in the morning paper. A
year earlier, Woodsworth and Vernon Thomas, who had lost his job at the Manitoba Free Press over his position on the war, wondered how long Bland could
get away with being so outspoken. They were not referring to socialist pronouncements, which the prairie press would later allege as the reason, but
Bland's persistent critique of the church. Socialism was not itself the issue – not
that Ashdown et al were unconcerned about its promotion by faculty. But the
previous year, a newly hired young professor founded Wesley College's first
socialist club. Throughout 1917 Bland was ardently engaged in promoting a
concept of union government as non-partisan people's government but supported the final result in the hope that it would rise above past partisanship. George
Chipman, as editor of the* Grain Growers' Guide, *came to his financial rescue,
giving Bland the opportunity to write a regular column, entitled "The Deeper
Life." Bland, however, needed to be stationed with a Methodist congregation to
receive a full pension from the church's Sustentation Fund. The dismissal controversy had lifted his popularity to new heights across the West, but taking on
a prairie pastorate was not in the cards. The dismissal would turn out to be a
blessing in disguise. With the end of the Western settlement boom, the exciting
prospects of an "ultimate prairie Protestantism" lifting the nation to new heights
of greatness would evaporate and a generation of stagnation would set in in*

Winnipeg and across the West. Continuing at Wesley College would not have offered the kind of challenge on which Salem Bland thrived. He was free, when it came, to accept a call from Broadway Methodist Tabernacle in Toronto, where, despite the controversy that ensued, a new world of public engagement awaited him. Students at the nearby campus of the university were beginning to mobilize to found a new national coeducational student Christian movement, church leaders were eager to deploy him on educational missions, the political scene was compelling, and Joseph Atkinson at the Toronto Star would soon invite Bland to become a regular columnist for the paper. It would become Salem Bland's most prominent "pulpit."

THE NEW CHRISTIANITY IN POST-GREAT WAR TORONTO*

"In a very short time it will be acclaimed from every revolutionary platform ... it will lend to the revolutionary movement an air of religious sanction."[2] It was mid-June 1920. Lieutenant-Colonel C.F. Hamilton, the intelligence and liaison officer of the Royal Canadian Mounted Police, had just read the recently published *New Christianity* by Salem Bland, the stormy petrel of Canadian Protestantism. He sized it up quickly and dashed a letter off to T. Albert Moore, head of the Methodist Department of Evangelism and Social Service, in an attempt to enlist Moore's aid in undermining the public reception of the book.

Hamilton was not alarmed without reason. Unrest was pulsing through the entire Western world, and Canada had been in an unsteady state since the late war years. The conscription crisis triggered a new wave of both agrarian and labour radicalism. Returning soldiers were in a volatile mood, occasionally storming factories to demand jobs. Wartime propaganda utilized the pre-war language of social reform, and many were calling for the redemption of those rhetorical promises, not least of all the churches. In 1918 the Methodist Church called for a "complete social reconstruction" transferring the basis of the economy from competition and profits to co-operation and service. On the other hand, those who saw wartime mobilization of private industry as a temporary measure, only justifiable in a time of national peril, had organized their forces in a

---

* First published as "Introduction" to Salem Goldworth Bland, *The New Christianity, or The Religion of the New Age*, Social History of Canada Reprint Series, ed. Michael Bliss (Toronto: University of Toronto Press, 1973), vii–xxvi. Reprinted with the permission of the University of Toronto Press.

National Reconstruction Association to hasten a return to pre-war conditions of relative governmental non-interference. The clash of forces came in the strikes of mid-1919, the greatest of which had been the Winnipeg general sympathetic strike of May and June. The industrial unionism of the One Big Union had since then split the ranks of labour, but if the cry for direct action had begun to wane a little, labour political militancy was on the rise, and labour churches, devoted to a mixture of Christian, labour, and socialist ideals, were spreading across the nation. The great farm organizations were girding themselves for political action and already, with labour, had taken over the provincial administration of Ontario. To some it seemed that class politics was about to replace the traditional party system. Hamilton could well agree with the powerful metaphor beginning Bland's book, that the Western nations were "like storm-tossed sailors who, after a desperate voyage, have reached land only to find it heaving with earthquakes."

Salem Bland was not a young radical but a seasoned Methodist clergyman, recently a professor at Wesley College, Winnipeg, and now pastor of Broadway Methodist Tabernacle in Toronto. Since his earliest ministry in the St Lawrence and Ottawa valleys, he had been pressing his church forward onto new frontiers. *The New Christianity* was entirely in character. In it, Bland attempted to place the unrest of the times into larger historical perspective and brought social, political, and economic developments in conjunction with the main trends of religion in recent decades. His central theme was that the processes of industrial and social consolidation, the growth of organized labour, and the spread of sociological ideas, especially in the church, spelled the end of the old order of capitalism and Protestantism that had dominated most of Western Christendom for three centuries. In support of this position he described the progressive march of democracy from the twelfth and thirteenth century universities, into religion in the Protestant Reformation of the sixteenth century, into politics in the nineteenth century, and now unmistakably making its way in the world of industry. Allied to democracy was the spirit of brotherhood and sisterhood, planted by Christ in the church, compromised by a "perverse exaltation of dogma and orthodoxy" over the centuries, but now being rediscovered by movements both inside and outside the church and becoming "the master passion" of the day.

The primary impediment to the full realization of democracy, brotherhood and sisterhood, Bland argued, was modern capitalism based on private property rights in industry and motivated by a competitive individualism. The distinctive task of the age, then, was the abolition of capitalism. For

Bland that was as much a religious as a secular objective, for, in keeping with the social gospel he had espoused for over a generation, salvation was not a matter of heavenly reward but the restoration of right human relations here on earth. Industrial combinations, co-operatives, trade unions, public ownership, insurance schemes, industrial councils, and so on all taught people to think socially, and therefore to attack and discredit them was to oppose what Christianity was all about.

The second impediment to a new social order embodying the Christian spirit, however, was the almost absolute attachment of Christians to their respective traditions. None of the prevailing churches was in entire harmony with the needs of the new age, Protestantism least of all. To provide a basis for Christian advance, Bland therefore drew upon recent historical analysis of the changing relationships of Christianity and culture. Devotion to Jesus Christ was the essential kernel of Christianity, he suggested, but the dogmatic and institutional forms of its expression were "subject to the same influences as fashion the changing social order." The chief of those influences were economics and race.

In Western civilization, Bland thought, Christianity had gone through two phases of interaction with the economic order and was now entering a third. The insecurity of life in the feudal period had led to emphases on institutional order and otherworldliness that marked Roman Catholicism. The expansion of every aspect of life, but primarily the economic, in the fifteenth through the seventeenth centuries brought a new spirit into church life reflecting the interests of "freedom-loving, self-reliant, ambitious burghers." They infused into the new Protestant movement a primary concern with the economic virtues of industry, thrift, sobriety, honesty, and self-control, and with the uneconomic vices of indolence, intemperance, licentiousness, and poverty. Humility and compassion fell to a low ebb, and preoccupation with individual character became pronounced.

The new power of labour, Bland suggested, marked the end of bourgeois Christianity and the inception of a labour Christianity dominated by the values of labour, namely the virtue of solidarity, and the duty and right of all to productive labour, to a living wage, and to union or association. To fulfill its destiny, the labour movement would have to broaden itself to include all creative work and recognize its Christian and religious character. To so interpret labour to itself was the prophetic task of the hour. It was equally important to convince the churches of that. Bland was more than a little anxious about Protestantism in this regard, for except in isolated and unofficial cases, Protestant ideology had given little sanction to the struggles of labour. He therefore reserved his strongest criticism for his own Protestant tradition, while he saw a more direct relevance to the new social age in the corporate spirit of Catholicism.

Bland knew as well as anyone that the phrase "bourgeois Christianity" did not express the sum of Protestantism (though he feared it might be its nemesis) and that "labour Christianity" would have to be more than a gloss on an economic movement. He therefore went on to discuss what he loosely called the "racial impact" on Christianity, although by that he meant something less biological than cultural. Jews, Greeks, Latins, Teutons, all had evolved peculiar forms of Christian life. Another form was being added in North America. With the Jewish it would be simple in creed, emphasizing the ethical, but would take a progressive rather than an apocalyptic view of history. With the Greek it would be inquisitive and speculative but would reject later Greek orthodoxy. With the Latin it would show a genius for organization and a catholicity of peoples but would reject a priestly hierarchy for lay leadership and democracy. With the Teutonic it would be free and unceremonious and stress personal dignity without succumbing to individualism. American Christianity would be a social religion committed to keeping the figure of Jesus primary, even when it did not recognize Jesus' divinity.

The chief hope of the future lay in a marriage of Bland's labour Christianity and American Christianity. However, the age was also one of international consolidation, and overarching all of Bland's particular hopes was that of a "Great Christianity" which would accommodate all the older traditions along with those that were emerging in the new world and the African and Oriental missions – a glimmering of the worldwide ecumenical movement of our own time. He was an ardent enough nationalist to hope that the church union movement in Canada would lead the way in breaking out from the traditional structures of Protestant church life. In that he was not wrong, but whether it has been the pathfinder for the substance of his New Christianity is a matter of debate.

The book clearly was not a piece of academic history or theology. Indeed, it could be called Salem Bland's longest sermon, and it had many of the weaknesses of that genre when reduced to print. Nevertheless, it presented a powerful strategic standpoint. It provided Canadian Christians – that is, most Canadians – with the resources necessary for liberation from the tyranny of their traditions. It offered Canadian labour and radical reform all the bulwarks of essential Christianity. At the same time that it gave some sanction to the labour churches, it established perspectives and endorsed objectives that would make those churches unnecessary. Its theoretical dissociation of the essence of Christianity from its cultural expression offered a counterpoise to both the fact and the charges of church domination by the middle and wealthy classes. If it treated Protestantism more harshly than Roman Catholicism, to have softened its criticism would have drawn the stinger for Protestants from the historical scandal Bland was addressing.

The central ideas *of The New Christianity* are no novelty to the later twentieth century, but in 1920 they were "still controversial even in the academic world." There had been considerable discussion of the congruence of capitalism and Protestantism, especially by Catholics and Marxists attacking Protestantism and religion, respectively. To many orthodox Protestants, the espousing of such positions by a Protestant clergyman must have seemed arch-apostasy. To many Protestant social reformers it would be a matter of concern to think that, having exposed themselves to criticism by questioning the capitalist order, they could not consistently seek refuge in traditional Protestant sanctuaries.

Certain of Bland's categories would not be new to informed readers. The idea of a dialectical unity of culture and religion that underlay the book was a product of what has been called the "uniformitarian" cast of mind evolved in the previous century. In various ways Herder, Hegel, Marx, Comte, de Gobineau, Sombart, and Spengler had applied the concept that the collectivities of nation, race, and civilization might have unified "lives" of their own, and Burckhardt had given it classical historical expression in his history of the Renaissance in Italy. That Christianity absorbed much from its cultural setting was a commonplace with George Munro Grant of Queen's University in the 1890s. Bland's characterization of Jewish, Greek, Roman, and Teutonic (Anglo-Saxon) civilization was a long-standing idea used by Josiah Strong in his widely read *The New Era* (1893), an early American social gospel work. That American conditions had bred a democratic spirit in North American Christianity was widely commented on in Methodist circles after W.J. Dawson's lectures to the Methodist Ecumenical Congress in New York in 1891. And Walter Rauschenbusch, the dean of American social gospellers, popularized the idea that labour and Christianity would come into their kingdom together or not at all in his *Christianity and the Social Crisis* (1907). Nor was the title of Bland's work original. Saint Simon, the eccentric grandfather of positivism and sociology, had written a piece under the title of *The New Christianity* a century before, and it is intriguing that Bland's first use of the phrase in 1896 roughly coincided with his first equivocal encounter with the work of Saint Simon's disciple, Auguste Comte.[3]

While Bland's book was not offered with any pretence of originality, it is worth noting that neither Bland nor most of his readers had the benefit of the sophisticated historical analysis of the church's dogma, social teaching and ethos, and economic relations associated with Harnack, Troeltsch, and Weber. Their great turn of the century works remained largely untranslated in 1920. Tawney's celebrated lectures were not given until 1922 and not published as *Religion and the Rise of Capitalism* until 1926; Richard Niebuhr's classic, *The Social Sources of Denominationalism*, was not in print until 1929. Furthermore, in evaluating Bland's originality, it must be borne in mind that the perspectives of *The New Christianity* were largely in his mind in the 1890s and derived from many sources. However, Bland was not writing a treatise for the few but a tract for the many. He was playing the role to which he had called his fellow pastors in 1895, to be popularizers of the new and fruitful ideas of the age. No one could reasonably deny that, whatever the background of the ideas in it, his book was a potent instrument in the context of post-war unrest in Canada.

The New Christianity was one of several books appearing after the war surveying the Canadian scene and urging various reforms. C.W. Peterson's *Wake Up Canada!*, J.O. Miller's *The New Era in Canada*, William Irvine's *Farmers in Politics* (to which Bland contributed the foreword), and W.L. Mackenzie King's *Industry and Humanity* were the chief of these. Bland's work was the most radical in its proposals and implications. With King's book it shares the distinction of being one of that rare breed of attempts to survey Canadian developments in terms of large principles of analysis or historical development. Lieutenant-Colonel Hamilton understood this fact when he wrote Moore that "in this country as a rule there is little discussion of principles." He was therefore concerned that the book would "be given a few eulogistic reviews" and then dropped, and he asked if it would not be advisable "to subject to a reasonably energetic examination a book which declares that Protestantism 'will not survive,' and ignores its work in promoting humanitarian endeavour, and which declares that to criticize public ownership is to commit the sin against the Holy Ghost?"

Moore did his work – a lengthy review in the *Christian Guardian* declared that the book was "not a logical and reasoned advocacy of the rights of Labor; the author apparently aims [rather] to challenge the attention than to convince ... Few of his readers, probably, will agree with all the author's statements, and probably he does not expect them to."[4] Bland noted with disappointment: "not a good word for it. Compare the other reviews." Three months later, however, Ernest Thomas, one of the most able minds in the church, more than redressed the balance in an article in the *Guardian* declaring the book to be an incisive presentation of main currents and indisputable facts.[5]

The book could not fail to be controversial. Father L. Minehan of Toronto thought that its small amount of wisdom had already been given to the world by Pope Leo XIII and the pastoral letter of Catholic bishops of the United States in 1919.[6] The Baptist arch-fundamentalist, Rev. T.T. Shields, thought the book should be very useful to many because "the truth is generally to be found in the opposite of what he [Bland] says."[7] The editor of the *Presbyterian and Westminster*, while disagreeing with much, felt it a very valuable contribution to the debate on social questions.[8] Rev. A.E. Ribourg of St Alban's Cathedral (Anglican), however, was in considerable agreement[9] with many of Bland's arguments.[8] Reactions among Methodists were as diverse as all of these.[10]

The *Toronto Daily Star* on 1 June, however, treated the book favourably as front-page news, but it was in the West that the book was most enthusiastically received. Professor W.T. Allison, writing in the *Edmonton Journal*, thought that parts of the book were brilliant.[11] The *Grain Growers' Guide* concurred and sold the book through its book department.[12] The *Saskatoon Daily Star*, noting that *The New Christianity* was being widely read, reflected that "one reads the book with the feeling that this is just what he has thought all his life, but lacked the power of expression to put it into words ... [It] is a concentrated form of the message which ministers are sending forth from pulpits today."[13]

The book's only adverse reception in the West came from the Bookman in the *Manitoba Free Press*. The *Free Press* had bitterly opposed the general strike and its reviewer thought Bland had entirely misread the character of labour, whose "cruel processes" would hardly further the Christian ethic.[14]

Bland had a warm relationship with a number of labour leaders, like Fred Tipping of the Winnipeg Trades and Labour Council and James Simpson, a vice-president of the Trades and Labour Congress, a leading figure in the Ontario Independent Labor Party, and editor of the *Industrial Banner*. Simpson spoke for such men when he hoped that workers would take the broad concepts of *The New Christianity* to heart and learn to think in such high terms of their mission.[15] In fact, for some time the notion that Jesus and the earliest church were the first socialists had played a role in legitimizing socialism.[16] And it was part of the creed of Marxists like Dr W.J. Curry, a Chilliwack dentist and member of the Socialist Party of Canada in British Columbia, that the religious life of the nation would shift with radical changes in the economic base of society.[17] Bland's book, subtitled *The Religion of the New Age*, was a case in point. It is not difficult to think that the book found its way onto the very platforms the Royal Canadian Mounted Police (RCMP) feared.

Bland considered that it had taken some courage for the publisher, McClelland and Stewart, to issue the book in the first place, but when within a year *The New Christianity* was sold out, suggestions of a second edition were not taken up![18] Had the hand of the RCMP reached beyond the church to the press as well?

Fifty years later, the reprinting of the book is important, not because it was an irritant to the RCMP, nor just because it represents an instance of the social gospel interpreting the post-war crisis in Canada. It is not an especially good indication of the breadth and depth of the mind of its author. Its chief significance lies rather in its intellectual lineage, which is an instructive study in how the highest traditions of evangelical Christianity came into radical conjunction with the currents of economic change, social reform, and political upheaval in Canada in the first decades of this century.

The background of *The New Christianity* begins with Salem's father, Henry Flesher Bland, who had been a minor but expanding Yorkshire woollens manufacturer of mid-nineteenth-century England and was devoted to the twin gospels of education and Methodism. He expected the two "god-like elements of knowledge and love" not only to prepare people for heaven where all distinctions and all the fictitious lines of demarcation on earth would disappear, but also to revolutionize everything absurd in the customs of society.[19] When his business jeopardized his lay preaching, he sold his mills and came to Canada in 1858 to become one of the foremost ministers of the Methodist Church. His belief that children were born in a state of grace stood in sharp contrast to the prevailing views of most church individuals that children were born in original sin; his outspoken preaching, writing, and innovation in church practice on the subject did much to inject a hopeful view of childhood into the Canadian mind, providing, thereby, an indispensable foundation for the later work of social reform![20]

Salem Bland, beginning his ministry in 1880, appropriated these views and soon pressed beyond them. Like his father, he was very much a child of the age of improvement, but he was even more prone to see spiritual and moral significance in the material progress of the age, to preach that personal perfection was possible in this life, and to anticipate a millennial climax to history itself.[21] Already in the early 1880s he was protesting against the doctrine of the dualism of body and soul and asserting that salvation pertained to the whole being, to the restoration of humankind to a fullness of bodily, mental, and spiritual health. He resolved not to preach about heaven but to challenge his hearers to be a genuine people of change, ready to go with Christ "even into exile from heaven, to realize a heaven here."[22] Given the prevalence of the evangelical mind in Canada in the late nineteenth and early twentieth centuries, it is difficult to make too much of the critical relocation of salvation in this transition from the elder to the younger Bland. Implied in the latter's early thought was not only the notion of the body as a living temple, which informed so much of the prohibition, personal purity, and public health movements, but also a thorough – even revolutionary – concept of the need for change in the quality of social life as a whole.

In the early 1880s, Bland's ideal Christian was still the evangelical version of aggressive Protestant individualism. He himself was active in Sabbath and temperance reform. While both reforms could be used to buttress a disciplined commercial ethic, Bland was more prone to use them to flay the idolatry of business values and the rapacity of industrial practices.[23] At mid-decade, however, ten years of profound development began. The writings of Charles Kingsley and Thoreau deepened his appreciation of nature. Principal Grant of Queen's University encouraged him to speak out on subjects of political morality and to reconsider his harsh views of Roman Catholicism. Kingsley again, with Robert Browning, Matthew Arnold, George Eliot, and others, helped him to resolve a lingering conflict over the claims of culture and religion. Religion, he came to believe, concerned not simply an interior transaction between the soul and God, but the awakening of a larger self turned outward to the needs and thoughts of others – and hence embracing the entire range of culture – a position that brought him into direct conflict with the church's restrictive code of discipline.

No sooner was Bland reaching such conclusions than his reading of Ruskin, Henry George, and Tolstoy, as well as the literature of emerging social Christianity in Britain and the United States, broadened the whole social basis of his outlook. His Methodism had never permitted him to adopt the social Darwinism of Spencer and Sumner, but Henry Drummond, Kropotkin, and Benjamin Kidd convinced him of what he already suspected, that the devices and ends of evolution were the social graces rather than competition. It was finally with the aid of Hegel in the mid-nineties that he was able to synthesize his new ideas with a grand concept of the movement and nature of both history and Christianity.[24]

The ideas Bland was wrestling with and bringing to a satisfying resolution were, however, making havoc of the traditional views of many

Christians both in pulpit and pew. In the Christian view the meaning of nature, humanity, and history was given by God. For many that revelation was seen as conveyed in a restricted, often literal and mechanical way, by one individual, Jesus; one book, the Bible; one agency, the Church. Such static conceptions could hardly accommodate the dynamic post-Darwinian world view. For Bland, however, the new outlook fertilized Biblical conceptions. St Paul was peculiarly amenable to reinterpretation and yielded a harvest of new insights. The English philosopher Edward Caird persuaded Bland of the validity of a progressive revelation. The historical critics of the Judeo-Christian Scriptures reconstructed the foundation works of the Old Testament and showed how the great prophetic writings of the eighth century BCE were the foundation of Jewish monotheism and had been the product of long development. The prophets were neither soothsayers predicting the future nor predictors of the figure of Jesus, but heralds of a coming Messiah who would bring in a new age of peace and justice according to God's will for Creation. They were giants of ethical insight who could read the signs of the times and fearlessly propound their political implications. Surely, then, they were the model for those of every age who sought to bring to birth that same justice for their own time. However normative scripture might be, or however representative the history of the Jewish people, revelation had to be sought anew amid the struggles of the contemporary world.

Others were reaching toward similar conclusions, but in the forum where Bland tried out his ripest conclusions in the 1890s, the Queen's Alumni Conferences, he was invariably the most open in his approach to new thought, the most comprehensive in his interests, and the most radical in his applications.[25] In an 1896 sermon on the all-encompassing liberty offered by Christianity, he used for the first time the phrase the "new Christianity."[26] Three years later, before a large convention of Ontario young people, he took the phrase as the title of his address. The "old Christianity" had often sung that "this world's a wilderness of woe," but that was to let the "hope of heaven ... corrupt us, divert us from concern for [the] miserable and oppressed." The "new Christianity" would set aside that strain of escapism and adopt "the idea of conquest." It would not take its Pilgrim out of the City of Destruction but leave him/her there "amid its sins and miseries, starting a college settlement, a mission church, or a Salvation Army Barracks, a Good Government Club or a Municipal Reform Association, resolute to transform the City of Destruction into a City of Salvation." Christians, he concluded, "cannot permanently acquiesce in a society organized on unChristian principles."[27] Bland's address to the young people marked his transformation of the older evangelicalism into an explicitly social faith.

Part of the confidence with which Bland announced the new Christianity of 1899 derived from the expansion of evangelical Christianity in North America throughout the nineteenth century. By 1891 his own church, the Methodist Church in Canada, had become the largest Protestant denomination in the nation, its spirit broadening as it took up an ever-more comprehensive culture-building role.[28] The currents of progressivism were finding their way into the church and, in 1896, in the first of a notable series of social declarations, it pitted the teachings of Jesus against the "heartless combinations" of the age.[29]

By the time Bland left the east for Wesley College, Winnipeg, in 1903, he had become an outspoken advocate of extensive state provision of cultural amenities and social schemes to equalize conditions in society. He was a single taxer, a convinced democrat, and not just a defender of labour's right to organize but an enthusiastic advocate of the coming of a new social solidarity it heralded for society at large. He therefore took a hopeful view of the trend to business combination, believing it would nurture a more social spirit, even among the owners and managers of industry. However, it was the devices of cooperation and public ownership he urged most insistently as more congruent with the trend itself and the ends he had in mind. He had no ties with the agrarian reform movement of Ontario in the 1890s, although he had manifested some sympathy with the American populists of the decade. He had grown up and worked chiefly in the middle-sized industrial and commercial centres of Ontario – Dundas, Kingston, Belleville, Quebec, Cornwall, Smith's Falls, Ottawa – most of them cities deeply affected by the severe depression of the first years of the 1890s. While he saw clearly the profound illness of the great cities he visited, like New York, Birmingham, London, and Paris, he did not react negatively to them but believed that humankind would find its highest fulfillment in the city.[30] He had also lived for a number of years in Quebec and Montreal, and by the 1890s he had developed his sympathies with Roman Catholicism to the point where he opposed the overwhelming majority of his colleagues on the Jesuit Estates and Manitoba schools crises.[31] He had become a proponent of Protestant church union and already was giving voice to ideas that would bring all Christian traditions together regardless of temperament, structure, or doctrine. Heresy did not consist in doctrinal error, he said, for error was necessary to truth. To be heretical was to be possessed of a spirit of faction,[32] an interpretation obviously germane to the social role to which he was calling the church.

Twenty years before the publication of *The New Christianity*, then, Bland had reached all the essential positions expressed in it. He was not, as has been thought, a Western radical, but an Eastern radical who moved West and readily took up its causes, a pattern frequent enough in the Western radical tradition to suggest the need for a more careful examination of its origin, character, and extent. In sixteen years, Bland's role in the West was that of a teacher and popularizer of the new currents of Biblical studies, of liberal theology, and of Christian social thought and action. His students William Irvine, who was instrumental in bringing the United Farmers of Alberta into politics, and William Ivens, who founded the labour churches in the West, were only two of many who were so influenced by Bland that they could not keep themselves or their religion out of the progressive endeavours of the time. Bland, himself, was a revered figure in the prohibition, single-tax, and direct legislation movements, an advocate of free trade, and a leading figure in that shining constellation of Winnipeg reformers that included Nellie McClung, novelist, revered for her tireless efforts to bring women into the political mainstream; Lillian and Marion Beynon, who were the forward-looking women's editors of the *Manitoba Free Press* and the *Grain Growers' Guide*, respectively; Beatrice Brigden, Quaker, who as a "social evangelist" for the Methodist church tirelessly brought sex education to prairie women in the mid-1910s and later worked with A.E. Smith's Labor church in Brandon; Fred Tipping, a president of the Trades and Labour Council; F.J. Dixon, single taxer and eloquent defender of civil rights; S.J. Farmer of the Direct Legislation League and the Farmer-Labor Party; A.W. Puttee, editor of the labour paper, the *Voice*; George F. Chipman, editor of the *Grain Growers' Guide*; A.V. Thomas, editorial writer for the *Winnipeg Tribune*; J.S. Woodsworth of All Peoples' Mission; C.W. Gordon, Presbyterian minister, author (Ralph Connor), prohibition leader, and industrial conciliator; and D.S. Hamilton, the Congregationalist minister who became the first judge of the Manitoba Juvenile Court, to mention only a few.

Throughout his sixteen years in the West, Bland was in constant demand both as a preacher and as public speaker, and he came to be regarded by many as one of the most powerful platform orators in the country. He had great expectations of the cooperative organizations the grain growers were spawning, and by 1913 he was convinced they should enter politics as the core of a new party, even sparking an abortive revolt in that direction at the Saskatchewan Grain Growers' Convention of 1913. Not surprisingly, there had been attempts to rein in so outspoken a figure as early as 1907, and when he was dismissed from Wesley College in 1917 in controversial circumstances, there was a considerable storm across the prairies.[33]

It was symbolic of his position at the end of his period in the West that in the fall and winter of 1918–19 he attended the National Convention of the Trades and Labour Congress in Quebec to gauge the strength of radical forces there; the General Conference of his church in Hamilton, where he was the *éminence grise* behind its advanced social manifesto; and the Saskatchewan Grain Growers' Convention in Regina, where he gave the keynote address, once more calling the farmers to political action. For years some believed he was one of the architects of the Winnipeg general strike of mid-1919, but he had left the West even before the critical Western Labor Conference of March.

It would be easy to press Bland too far to the forefront of the social gospel in Canada, chiefly because he lived so long and associated himself with so many movements of social reform. By 1920, however, there had been a small host of outstanding men and women motivated by Christian social passion. There had been S.S. Craig, the Presbyterian minister who campaigned for Henry George, the great proponent of land reform and the single tax, in the mayoralty contest in New York in 1886, and later established an independent social reform pulpit in Toronto. There was Elliott S. Rowe, the Toronto Methodist minister who was president of the Social Progress Company that published the socialist paper *Citizen and Country* with George Wrigley, an Anglican as editor and head of the Christian Socialist League. There was F.S. Spence, a Methodist and a Toronto alderman, who was a tireless campaigner for prohibition, public ownership, and the rights of labour. Methodist S.D. Chown in 1902 became the head of the first church department anywhere to devote itself to the causes of the social gospel. J.G. Shearer did the same in the Presbyterian Church after creating the church–labour alliance that won the Lord's Day Act in 1907 and went on to form the Social Service Council of Canada.

There was Sara Libby Carson of the Young Women's Christian Association, who, under Presbyterian auspices, and in association with a handful of progressive women like Ethel Dodds, the head worker of St Christopher House, Toronto, flung a network of social settlements across the nation. Men like W.A. Riddell, later Ontario's first deputy minister of labour, and Bryce Stewart, later of the federal Department of Labour, worked under conviction in 1913 for the Methodist and Presbyterian churches as they conducted the first extensive social surveys of Canadian cities and rural areas. F.N. Stapleford and J.S. Woodsworth, both Methodist ministers, had by 1916 become leading figures in the consolidation of social work enterprises.

Then there were church editors like J.A. Macdonnell of the *Westminster* and W.B. Creighton of the *Christian Guardian*, who made their papers agents of the social gospel. Agrarian leaders like Henry Wise Wood, R.C. Henders, and E.C. Drury were not only influenced by the social gospel but active proponents of it. Nor was the labour movement without its contribution to the roster, with Unitarian A.W. Puttee and Methodist James Simpson editing their papers, the *Voice* and the *Industrial Banner*, from a social gospel standpoint.

To review the names is to rehearse the advance of the social gospel in Canadian church and secular life over a generation. Nevertheless, many among the leaders and members in local congregations remained only superficially influenced, and the post-war crisis brought out their latent hostility. *The New Christianity* was written amid a protracted effort by wealthy and prestigious members of Bland's new congregation in Toronto to be rid of the disturber of their peace. He survived, partly because of the strength of his own personality but also because a majority of his congregation stood behind him (a factor that was by no means decisive in such cases). Despite the contention that surrounded him, it was possible for Bland to write with hope, not only because the eye of faith could anticipate the ultimate victory, but also because the Winnipeg and related strikes had not deflected the churches from the social gospel, the labour churches were still expanding, the church union cause was awakening once more, the tempo of farmer and labour political action was increasing, and the Liberal party had adopted an unprecedented social reform program and entrusted its leadership to the chief Canadian exponent of joint industrial councils to bring peace to industry, William Lyon Mackenzie King. Progressive intellectuals were gathering their resources for the establishment of a journal, the *Canadian Forum*, and the Group of Seven had just given its first controversial show. All aimed at clarifying the Canadian consciousness and challenging "the hypnotic trance of a purely industrial and commercial ideal."[34] In one way or another almost all these enterprises had been influenced by the social gospel. Bland had no illusions that an easy path lay ahead for the nation, however. As he wrote, "A new, unquiet, distressful Canada is upon us,"[35] but, equally, the signs had never been more promising.

The immediate constellation of reforms Bland was trying to nurture, however, rose to a peak of influence between the Labour and Progressive victories of 1919–21 and church union in 1925 and did not return in force again for a decade. The social gospel movement sank into a trough of depression, eroded by a post-war recession that put a premium on funds, diverted by the backlash against prohibition and the cross-currents of church union consolidation, and compromised by the failure of the politics of righteousness and the unwillingness of the nation to embrace a more just economic order. Many were simply weary with well-doing. The intractability of social reality forced some into fundamental reconsideration of the mixture of social and religious ideas they had been promoting, while others sublimated their failures in a resurgence of the pacifist crusade. Radicals, who saw the face of power in social and economic relations more clearly, could only hold their ground and await more propitious days. The revolution Lieutenant-Colonel Hamilton feared had not come to pass.

In the meantime Bland had completed his ministry in the church and began a notable twenty-year career as a wide-ranging journalist ("The Observer") for the *Toronto Daily Star*. He threw what additional energy he had in the 1930s into stinging the councils of his church into a more radical stance, flailing Toronto police for harassing reformers, addressing meetings for the new Co-operative Commonwealth Federation, encouraging the Fellowship for a Christian Social Order, and working in united front organizations to counter the spread of fascism and the clouds of war. Many could testify to his ability still to rouse an audience even in his seventies. He died the grand old man of the social gospel and reform in 1950.

It would be easy now to criticize *The New Christianity* on a number of points. It reflects an age of platform enthusiasm with which we are no longer comfortable. The history on which it is based is too sweeping to be altogether plausible. Sociology and anthropology have since badly dated the views of the time regarding relations between race, religion, and society. Bland, himself, was too much a Protestant for us to accept entirely his dissociation of Protestantism from his anticipated new social order. On the other hand, his treatment of Roman Catholicism shows no anticipation of its later tendency to support fascist responses to the problems of capitalism. He was over-sanguine in many of his characterizations of the labour movement, though many who criticized him for it then ignored his qualifications and also his introductory remarks that the agencies of advance might at times be "mistaken, sordid, violent, even cruel." In any case, to read the labour papers of that time is to be impressed by the religious preconceptions behind their anti-ecclesiasticism and their frequent use of Christian touchstones in self-justification.[36] Superficially, the book's small proportion of explicit Canadian content together with a strain of

196

continentalism might make it seem a poor candidate for inclusion in a Canadian social history series, but that would be an unfortunate commentary on the parochialism of the Canadian mind. Bland's introduction makes it clear that *The New Christianity* is aimed at Canadians first, and the book was a product, among other things, of an intensely Canadian – as well as a cosmopolitan – mind.

As far as Bland's primary association of Protestantism and capitalism is concerned, Max Weber's famous argument that the spirit of modern capitalism derived from the Protestant ethic has still to be satisfactorily demonstrated. At least it can be seriously questioned[37] and be proposed that socialism has similar claims to that paternity.[38] Nevertheless, Weber addressed himself to an association of first importance, and, by the same token, so did Bland. He was not wrong that Protestantism and capitalism were in the throes of profound change, but, in contrast to Weber, he believed too deeply in the force of the good in the social movements of the time and appreciated too little the tenacity of the irrationalism of private capitalism.

The new social order has not ensued. The further development of labour, social welfare, and church has been won at the price of accommodation to a system of welfare-state capitalism that has institutionalized poverty, deprived workers of any significant role in industry, and diverted the public with consumerism. It remains as true as in 1920 that an economic system which organizes other individuals for private ends necessarily fractures the community and perpetuates injustice.

Whether one touches the contemporary religious revolution at the point of the occult, the Jesus movement, theological debate, the experimentation in church forms, the ecumenical movement, to say nothing of the cross-fertilization of higher religions, it is evident that traditional Protestantism is at an end. Some might protest that Bland's Christian visions could not have survived in an emerging society of plural values, one which denied the state's allegiance to any single value-system. Undoubtedly, the experience of the last half-century has given the lie to his vision of the righteous state in North America, but the canons of pluralism have problems of their own. Not the least of these is their short-circuiting of meaningful debate on the question of the nature of individuals in society, for pluralist dogma would preclude the application of any given answer to that question in advance, yet that debate is crucial to the ongoing health of society.[39] If *The New Christianity* does anything more than reflect the height of the social gospel and national hope in Canada after the Great War, it is to remind us that the fundamental question of ultimate social hopes remains. Can the vision of social righteousness, the great prophetic hope of a time of peace and justice, be entertained any more as an historical hope at all, or is its function that of a transcendent reality which judges all our temporal constructions? The question is germane to the critique of Bland's book and surely is also crucial to the scale of present action. Should we follow the intimations of pluralism that *The New Christianity* must be relegated to the ghetto of Christian concerns at the end of the Age of Progress? Or should we listen to Bland again when he says simply that "the struggle will not be over religious opinions, or political theories, though both are involved. It will be over what touch individuals ordinarily much more deeply, their livelihood and their profits"?

PART FOUR

Religion and Political Transformation

CHAPTER THIRTEEN

"My Father Was an Evangelist": The Religious Setting of Norman Bethune's Early Years

BACKGROUNDER

Norman Bethune, in his adult years, was not and has not been thought of as a religious person. So why was I being asked to present a paper on the religious background of Bethune's early years at a wide-ranging conference scheduled for 16–18 November 1979 at McGill University? The conference would cap a generation of Bethune studies. Was there a covert assumption that something of a religious background, familial and cultural, would carry on into the later years? The conference would mark the fortieth anniversary of Bethune's death in China on 12 November 1939 from a blood infection he incurred while operating on wounded soldiers of the Communist Eighth Route Army in Yenan fighting the Japanese.

Bethune entered the last decade of his life as an internationally renowned innovative thoracic surgeon treating patients with tuberculosis. Convinced that the endemic poverty of industrial capitalism was a cause of much disease – and tuberculosis in particular – he initiated a campaign to arouse the medical profession to advocate for radical changes in the social order. Following an international conference in Russia in the mid-1930s he seized the opportunity to explore the new experiment in economic organization and social purpose in that country. He returned to quietly join the Communist party. The rise of fascism in Europe alarmed him, and with the military overthrow of the Republican government in Spain in 1936, he was sent to Spain by the popular front League for the Defence of Spanish Democracy, of which Salem Bland was the honorary chair. There he would pioneer the practice of mobile battle-front blood transfusions. Two years later the League, now renamed the League against War and Fascism, sent him to China and supported him there. He became a revered figure promoted by Mao Tse-tung as a model for all Chinese – and in the process endowed all Canadians with a special status in China. Still today Chinese visitors to Canada stand in reverent gratitude before statues of Bethune in Toronto and Montreal.

Bethune was clearly a case of political transformation and an advocate of a radical reformation of the socio-economic order. But, in the terms of this section, had religion played any part in it? Wendell McLeod thought so. McLeod knew Bethune well, was a student in medicine under Bethune, a collaborator with him in social medicine advocacy, and one of the principal conference organizers. In Bethune: An Intimate Portrait (1938), he hints that there was an undercurrent of conflicted but essentially religious drivenness about Bethune. Bethune's father studied for the ministry at Knox College at the University of Toronto when Idealist philosophy, a major feeder of the social gospel, was pushing its way into the curriculum. It is not clear that his father was a social gospel preacher, but he appears to have chosen the rough frontier towns of northern Ontario as his ministerial calling and with his wife involved the whole family in generous-spirited and religiously motivated attentiveness to the needs of families struggling to survive in a harsh economic environment. Bethune's early and persistent belief that it was his destiny to become a great surgeon surely begged for some rationalization as he grew into and out of adolescent self-consciousness. Presbyterian predestination lay at hand. Did that conviction flow forward in some form in the actual career that followed? The doors of perception opened by the family and the influences of the wider religious background of the early years did not simply disappear. He later confessed to having a "love-hate" relationship with his father. Was it the "hate" or the acids of university studies and student debate that dissolved a commitment to formal religion? But what of the love? Where did it lead? As late as his first summer with Frontier College, when he ordered Bibles and hymn books among his supplies, the family faith seemed still intact. The process of religious disengagement itself – and potential re-engagement on deeper foundations – could proceed under such adventurous religious auspices as the Student Christian Movement, to which McLeod alludes, where students of diverse background, including friends of Bethune, gathered to discuss life issues. Did Bethune join them? It is difficult to believe that Bethune, a brilliant, many-faceted personality, torn in many directions, would not, as a student, have found the Student Christian Movement a congenial forum in which to play out the options before him. In 1935 he penned a striking description of the Bethune genealogy that was at once a self-portrait and an uncanny note of foreboding: "I come of a race of men violent, unstable, of passionate conviction ... yet with it all a vision of truth and a drive to [pursue] it even though *it leads ... to their destruction." In the history of Christianity, wrestling with this kind of mental strife has often been a formula for sainthood. To say this is not to claim Bethune for religion, at least not in any formal sense, but in the resolution of his contrary impulses in a decision to pit his life against the mounting threat of fascism as the overarching enemy of the age, there would seem to have been the kind of total commitment to an ultimate cause that was quintessentially religious. For Bethune, evidently, it brought a new sense of peace. These observations were not part of my presentation at the conference. Here they serve in some measure to justify the inclusion of the following essay/paper in a section on religion and political transformation. As such, however, they also offer my own further research and reflections on a remarkable life that continues to fascinate.*

At a personal level, it was not the songs of the Spanish Civil War that I learned in the Student Christian Movement at the University of British Columbia that led me to Norman Bethune. My mother's adopted brother, Frank Reilly, as a young man with a passion for flying and possessing his own airplane, had gone to Spain in 1936 hoping to fly in support of the Republican side but ended up driving a truck ferrying supplies to the front lines of battle. After his return, I learned from him of a chance encounter he had had with Bethune in an isolated location. Bethune was frying blood plasma for lunch! That was my earliest – and at the time rather shocking – bit of knowledge of Bethune. I would come to understand that that was vintage Bethune, for whom taboos were meant to be broken. But there was a further family connection. My father's younger brother, Stanley, was a student-cum-professor-cum-city councillor in Montreal through the 1930s. Stanley had mixed views on the subject of Bethune. And as noted above, our family had a "ringside seat" on the Sino-Japanese War. My father's elder brother was medical director, superintendent, and lone surgeon of the Canadian Hospital in Chongqing, China's wartime capital. He was also in charge of international relief into China during the Second World War. Bethune got mixed reviews within my family. Stanley thought him something of a show-off; Stewart held his peace; while Grandmother Allen resented the attention showered on Bethune, when her own son throughout the entire eight years of the war and five more of the revolution that followed was putting in endless hours at the operating table treating victims of firebombing and wounded soldiers, Nationalist and Communist alike. He offered his services to the new Communist regime, only to find himself imprisoned in solitary confinement for a year for re-education after being convicted in an informal "people's court" of charges of evading new taxes – of which he had no knowledge – on overseas relief supplies.

THE RELIGIOUS SETTING
OF NORMAN BETHUNE'S EARLY YEARS*

"You must remember, my father was an evangelist," wrote Norman Bethune.[1] Obviously he was conscious of the effects of being brought up a son of a zealous Presbyterian minister. However, there appears to be little evidence on which to develop any close correlation between Bethune's youthful development and either the more immediate or the distant religious setting of his upbringing as a son of the manse. This paper is therefore only incidentally biographical, although it suggests that certain of the tensions and conflicts of Bethune's complex personality, such as the contrary pulls of urbane sophistication and the austerity of earnest religious commitment, a certain desire for social success and a deep awareness of basic injustice in society, can in part be seen as intensified reflections of issues endemic in the religious setting of his youth.

Yes, Bethune was aware of the consequence of being his father's son. Indeed, can any child of the ministry forget the intensity of that experience? Which other children in the community have been so publicly committed, especially in Bethune's age, to a clearly conceived style and quality of life? Which other young people listened week in, week out, for years on end to their father's declamations on the central issues of life and faith? In some measure, perhaps, they were saved by grace of also sitting around the breakfast table with him! And there was, thankfully, also a certain common sense in ministers that sometimes escaped the more pious laity. As the most popular Canadian evangelists of Bethune's younger years, Crossley and Hunter, would say, "Many think they need more grace, when it is rest of body or mind, fresh air, sleep or medicine they need."[2] But, tempered as it might be, the effects of a ministerial upbringing were indelible. Particularly was that so for ministerial families that moved often, as the Bethunes did. One could easily learn to be sociable without learning the riches and discipline of enduring relationships among one's peers. The sense that the ministerial family belonged to the congregation – even

* First published as "The Religious Setting of Norman Bethune's Early Years," in *Norman Bethune: His Times and His Legacy*, eds David A.E. Shephard and Andree Levesque (Ottawa: The Canadian Public Health Association, 1982), 22–31. Reprinted with the permission of the Canadian Public Health Association.

to the community – could equally forge a never-to-be forgotten closeness and security or a claustrophobic resentment and bitterness. For the son of the manse at the turn of the century, the heroism that was enjoined in the secular education of young imperialists was compounded by moral earnestness of the Sunday School's singing "Dare to be a Daniel" and marching in a prohibition parade and was further reinforced by a home in which seriousness and commitment lay all around.

Not surprisingly, many rebelled. Indeed, one was almost expected to do so – that was part of the mythology about preachers' families with which one grew up. However, it was not so much simple rebellion as a complex pattern of creative absorption, adaptation, and rejection of the inheritance that marked the careers of such prominent sons of the manse in Bethune's period as, for example, J.S. Woodsworth and L.B. Pearson. But there was also Hartley Dewart, son of the editor of the *Christian Guardian*, who threw over his father's prohibitionism to become the hard-drinking leader of the Ontario Liberal party in 1917; also A.R. Carman, son of the redoubtable general superintendent of the Methodist Church, who abandoned his father's Biblicism to become the cultivated editor in-chief of the *Montreal Daily Star*.[3] Ministerial parents and sons, though, were not usually so prominent, indeed were often quite undistinguished. Two Canadian novels of Bethune's younger years, however, do tell a common story and present an ideal solution. In *Roland Graeme, Knight* (1892) and *The Preparation of Ryerson Embury* (1900), Agnes Maule Machar and A.R. Carman, themselves children of the manse, depict the struggle of their counterparts with the rigid doctrinal and Biblical attitudes and the self-righteousness and irrelevance they perceived in the church. On the brink of putting it all behind them, the heroes are brought face to face, on the one hand with industrial crisis and the working class, and on the other with the "Christ-like" figures of rather solitary, practical clergy, who have given their lives to the urban poor and think of Jesus as a social reformer as well as a personal transformer of individuals. Somewhere in the story, Henry George's influential work *Progress and Poverty* makes its mark, and the heroes set off to establish a cooperative factory and to become a labour lawyer, respectively.[4]

The Protestantism with which the children of the manse, and perhaps sensitive young people more generally, struggled was hardly itself a static entity. Presbyterians and Methodists were, of recent date (1875 and 1884), nationally united denominations with large corps of clergy deployed to realize a long-standing vision of a righteous Canada.[5] The imposing Gothic edifices that dominated church architecture from the Confederation decade onward symbolized not only the openness of a people to divine impression but also the triumph of Protestantism in the mid-century commercial and early industrial city.[6] Between 1841 and 1881, for instance, Methodism in Ontario had increased by more than seven times and Presbyterianism by more than five – increases above that of the general population, which had multiplied four times.

The growth of that period had not come about without strain and stress as the evangelical churches at once accommodated themselves and contributed to an increasingly complex society. An emerging cradle-to-grave Protestantism did much to shape the rhythm of life and the inner discipline of the broad spectrum of new classes from the artisan upward that was created by the burgeoning commercial and early industrial urban order.[7] It was in this period that what came to be known as the Canadian Sunday was established.[8] Camp meetings, revivals, and protracted meetings either declined or took on a more subdued, even sophisticated, tone. Sunday Schools underwent a notable transformation and rapid growth as more optimistic views of childhood prevailed. The machinery of an International Sunday School movement, with standardized lessons and joint denominational efforts in the weekly preparation of Sunday School teachers, spread widely through urban Canada, catering to adults as well as to children.[9] Protestant women's movements, originating in the early 1880s, spread through the churches. Emphasizing the missionary role of the church, women's missionary societies became a way station in the march of the mid-Victorian ideal of true womanhood from the family to the reform movements of the next generation. Even more clearly, the Women's Christian Temperance Union performed that function, though there were many men, apparently, who forbade their wives and daughters to join so activist a body. Constricted in their domestic roles in a double sense – in family and nation – the more adventurous young women began to find in foreign missionary careers a means of bringing feminine ideals to bear on the world of their time.[10]

Men, of course, and especially the more "successful" among the membership, had dominated the general oversight of congregational life, and, as the local, regional, and national church structures expanded, their skills became ever more important in refining methods of ecclesiastical administration. They were not to be left out of the march toward more specialized organizations for themselves. Men's Brotherhoods reaching out to men on the fringe of the church were imported from overseas in the 1890s, to be followed a decade later by the formidable American-based

Laymen's Missionary Movement. As the brilliant biographies of N.W. Rowell and J.W. Flavelle show so well, the men's movements in the church represented the impulses dominating late nineteenth century Canadian Protestantism – a merger of a deeply embedded evangelical ethic, Victorian philanthropy, and metropolitan expansiveness.[11] For men as for women and children, foreign missions were not only an evangelical enterprise, but a projection of their own progressive march toward civilization and a major, if exotic, form of philanthropy.

In short, the Protestantism that Bethune's generation inherited, and against which some choice spirits would rebel, was far from a fossilized institution. Reverberations of old and the sound of new issues still accompanied its advance. Presbyterians had their organ controversies and Methodists were upset about gowns in the pulpit. The more potent controversies over science and religion, which in fact had existed for most of the century, were now keenly debated by a more educated clergy and laity. From early in the century, and through the debate over "Darwin," the essence of their position was that true science and true religion could not conflict, but only pseudo-science and pseudo-religion.[12] Even the most notable Canadian scientist of the nineteenth century, and prominent Presbyterian, John William Dawson, despite his concern to hew as closely to scripture as possible, extended creation days into ages and allowed so much variation by natural selection into species that it has been asked why he did not go all the way with Darwin.[13] As for creation, Principal Grant of Queen's University declared that one only needed now to believe that what had happened at a single stroke occurred rather in succession over a long period of time. And the well-known Presbyterian divine C.W. Gordon (alias the novelist Ralph Connor) recalled his mother reading to him from Henry Drummond's *Natural Law in the Spiritual World*,[14] the thesis of which was that evolution had been presented to the world out of focus. In a revision of Darwin that was to become increasingly popular, Drummond declared that the mechanism of evolution was not the struggle for the survival of self but the struggle for others in the survival of species. That is not to say that young Bethune grew up in a church where the matter was settled. There was indeed intense debate, often between generations and between metropolis and hinterland, as young people went off to college and imbibed the new theories, the better minds among them aware that finally natural selection could not be accommodated to a purposeful universe. Bethune would appear to have been one of them.

The "Old Faith and the New Philosophy" also met on the ground of Biblical "higher criticism." George Munro Grant might take a large view of the matter and publicly support the much-maligned American Presbyterian higher critic, Professor Briggs, and Nathaniel Burwash, the leading Methodist theologian, might push aside his old notes and say "Gentlemen … we now have a new and better method of understanding this material." [15] Nonetheless, though often skilfully contained, controversy raged. In the course of Bethune's youth several Biblical scholars lost their postings in Canadian colleges. In a related doctrinal issue, D.J. Macdonnell, prominent Presbyterian cleric, was harried to an early death in 1896 for questioning the church's doctrine of eternal punishment for unrepentant sinners. [16]

What one might call hinterland revivalism of the Ralph Horner type in the Ottawa valley attempted to hold the line against the new trends in the churches, [17] but revivalism, too, was becoming more urbane, sophisticated – and more sentimental [18] – in the hands of persons like Crossley and Hunter, the famous Canadian revivalists. Crossley, for example, was prepared to revise parts of St Paul in the light of contemporary ideas and advocate women's suffrage. [19] It was not just metropolitan centres but also Western towns that desired their services. The "goods" of the city (if not its vices) were wanted on the frontier. As a plaintiff clergyman at an isolated charge wrote in 1907 to Salem Bland, the urbane Wesley College professor in Winnipeg, "Come, if you can, Doctor, we do not often have college men come out to the frontier points." [20] So undoubtedly it was in the "outback" Ontario of Bethune's youth.

By the 1890s then, the Protestant churches, with their now elaborate "social means of grace," had made a remarkably creative response to the mid-century challenge of the city, and through their urban leadership sat astride the metropolitan network that dominated the Canadian hinterland. But if the sirens of a more cultured Protestantism were calling, the terms in which the quest for a Christian Canada had been established were now put in question by a remarkably rapid process of industrial consolidation. No doubt partly initiated by the severe depression of the early 1890s, in city after city in central Ontario the number of industrial firms decreased sharply, while the workforce remained roughly constant [21] (but see note below†). With the creation of larger, more impersonal units of

---

† Note: Jacob Spelt, on whom this statement relies, ignored the change in classification of industrial units in the 1901 census, thus seeming to reduce their number. The observations that follow must therefore be qualified and the phenomena in question spread over a longer time span.

production came a challenge to the heavily personal form in which the Protestant ethic had been cast, and upon which artisans, the middle class, and entrepreneurs alike relied. Industriousness, sobriety, thrift, and a faithful acceptance of one's lot as divine providence were not enough. Labour spokespersons and local social critics in Toronto and elsewhere petitioned annual meetings of the major Protestant churches in the early 1890s, asking them to raise their voices against a "system of monopoly of land and capital and competition among workers," which was nothing less than "organized robbery." The responses were ambivalent. Replies were warily drafted, suggesting that the influence of "advanced" social critics was already at work among church members.[22]

The problem for those of sensitive social conscience, or who themselves were on the lower rungs of the economic ladder, was not simply the newly aggregated impersonal labour relations. Sheer subsistence, as recent studies have shown, was the lot of the average working individual's family, and working conditions, if not as bad as the most lurid accounts would have it, were a standing affront to a Christian community.[23] It would be pleasing to be able to say that the Protestant churches reacted massively and effectively in response to the twin challenges of the new industrial order: the need for a new social ethic and substantially improved conditions of life and labour for the mass of the population. That was not to be, and perhaps it is too much to expect; but at least it was the direction in which the churches moved.

Principal Grant at Queen's University might reject Henry George, while Albert Carman, superintendent of the Methodist Church, was a firm believer in Georgite solutions,[24] but at mid-decade Grant was promoting annual Alumni Conferences on social problems and related issues, and Toronto Methodists followed suit. Ministerial associations, in Hamilton, for instance, picked up the refrain, and social questions became topical fare in the Protestant press and pulpit. Herbert Casson gave up his Methodist circuit in Ontario to found a Labor Church in Lynn, Massachusetts, and, shortly after, S.S. Craig left his Presbyterian congregation at Oakville to set up a "social reform pulpit" in Toronto. The Toronto Methodist Conference found its way to support a general railwaymen's strike against the Grand Trunk in mid-1899, a year after the General Conference of that church, undoubtedly reflecting the anxiety of small business workers as much as working-class conditions, struck out against "heartless combinations." In the same breath, however, it counselled Methodists not to be too hasty in subscribing to "untried solutions" to the ills of the age.[25]

Canadian Protestantism, however, in the first decade of Bethune's life, was above all preoccupied with ringing up huge majorities in futile efforts to usher in provincial prohibition or with getting a more recently initiated sabbatarian crusade off the ground. Each in its own way was a response to the issues of the new industrialism – problems of urban poverty and social discipline – as broadly middle-class Protestants saw them. For working-class Protestants, arguments of social justice were more to the fore. In short, the 1890s saw the beginning in an organized and systematic way of the Protestant social gospel, a movement reaching into virtually all the agrarian, urban, labour, and social welfare movements of the next generation in English Canada. Hence, it was largely under Protestant church sponsorship that the first major national congress on the social ills of the nation was held on the eve of the Great War.[26] An analogous movement of social Catholicism was likewise in its beginnings in English and French Canada at the same time, but it has little significance for the background to Bethune's life.

By the turn of the century, for Presbyterians as for Methodists, the impact on their traditions of a tumultuous period of development was severe. All the developments sketched above ground the edges off distinctive positions. Furthermore, the encounter of evangelicalism and Calvinistic predestinarian theology heavily modified the latter's emphasis on the distance of a sovereign God in favour of the nearness of God's love. Methodism, in turn, was pressed further toward Arminian free will.[27] The need of such a time was for an integrating philosophy. In Canada, as elsewhere in the English-speaking world, that was found in a form of the idealism fostered by T.H. Green, of Oxford, and Edward Caird, of Glasgow and Oxford.

In Canada, John Watson, of Queen's University, became the leading spokesman of this movement, ably seconded by George Paxton Young, of Toronto, and T.B. Kilpatrick, who taught at Knox College when Malcolm Bethune was studying there. All were Scottish Presbyterians. Stressing an essential Christianity and the final unity of all things in the divine mind, idealism appeared for a time to charm away the niggling difference between denominations, the tension between urbane culture and religious commitment, and the contentions of religion and science, even while it offered a resolution of the claims of personal and social salvation.[28] Watson and his colleagues considered that art, science, and religion were integrally linked as expressions of human intelligence participating in the divine mind, together working for the realization of a "community of free beings by which the ideal of an organic unity of humanity is in process of realization." By no means did Watson and company carry all of Canadian Protestantism with them, but they provided the reigning philosophy as the churches moved into the era of liberal theology and the social gospel.[29]

On the fringe of all this moved the spokespersons of the nascent labour movement. They, too (and how many of their followers?), constituted an important part of the religious background of the age. T. Phillips Thompson, editor of the *Labour Advocate*, attacked the church for submitting to the insidious influence of wealth. With notable exceptions, he thought, the ministry had become "the servile tools" of "rich men's social clubs and Sunday opera companies."[30] But Thompson was a Quaker turned Theosophist, and, with most of the labour newspaper editors of the generation from 1880 to 1910, he saw his task in a religious light.[31] That was not surprising for, quite apart from whether they had been subject to formal church influence (most had), they were spokespersons for an artisanal class whose lodges depicted work as a meaningful activity in a world made by a divine artificer and moving toward his ends through the agency of willing human collaborators.[32] The labour movement was the contemporary vehicle of God's spirit, realizing a world of human brotherhood and social justice. This conviction was not just a subscription to the "undying ethics of Jesus" but entailed a potent millennial and immanent theological conception. In its own way, it too, could – and did – claim to be essential Christianity. There was, after all, a common intellectual base for Thompson and Watson, and it was on that base that G.W. Wrigley at the turn of the century attempted to woo clergy into his Christian Socialist League.[33] Such ventures were just successful enough to be small straws in the wind.

It was in the Protestant youth movements, however, arising in the mid-1880s that these notions of an essential Christianity with a contemporary social and intellectual bias came most readily to the fore. The Ontario Christian Endeavour Convention of 1899 listened intently as the young reformist preacher Salem Bland urged members to abandon the pessimistic world view of their elders and sound the note of Christian triumphalism by working wholeheartedly at municipal reform.[34] In the same year the student YMCA at Wesley College, Winnipeg, urged students to involve themselves in social solidarity with their stricken brothers because "strictly speaking, there is no longer any such thing as individual salvation."[35] There was clearly a certain caricature of the old as young people of Bethune's youth reached out for a new world. It was, after all,

Matthew Arnold of their fathers' generation whom their English professors thrust at them: culture, Arnold had said, was not realized in any until
it was realized in all. Imperialism or prohibition might still be a means of
rising above self, but when members of the Methodist Epworth League
rallied around James Simpson, the perennial and successful Toronto
labour-socialist candidate for civic office, something new was brewing.
Just how far their new social impulses and intellectual conceptions would
carry these pre-Great War youth and students was not yet clear at the time
of Bethune's career as an undergraduate at the University of Toronto.
Eager to do more than read Jenk's *Jesus and the Social Question*, they followed the example of British students and founded university settlement
houses[36] or followed a Canadian innovation and became, like Bethune,
the labourer-teachers of Frontier College.[37]

Then came the war, a heightening of social-religious idealism, and the
radical aftermath – the 1920s, and the crisis at once of the older moral
reform movement (prohibition) and the newer social gospel. Reform was
in crisis, smitten by disillusionment and outright skepticism.[38] But a more
realistic and radical Christian social ethic was being fashioned by young
Canadians of Bethune's age or slightly younger, often veterans of the war,
studying now in Oxford, or at New York with Reinhold Niebuhr and
Harry F. Ward. Early in the Depression these young intellectual Protestants formed the Fellowship for a Christian Social Order, and in 1936 they
published a volume entitled *Towards the Christian Revolution*,[39] which
John Strachey, the British Marxist, praised.[40] Perhaps its most provocative
statement was from the pen of Eugene Forsey: "This generation seeketh
after a sign, and there shall be no sign given it but the sign of the prophet
Marx. Until Christians learn to understand and apply the lessons of marxism they cannot enter into the Kingdom of Heaven – nor, probably, can
anyone else."[41] Agnes Machar's Roland Graeme, Knight, had taken a large
step since 1892! New sons of the manse and their colleagues were finding
a Christian frame of reference that would comprehend a Norman Bethune,
whether he accepted it or not. They were hardly a majority among Protestants of the 1930s, but they were among the more notable voices of that
decade. Like Bethune they were alarmed at the spread of the fascist menace. They picketed scrap-iron shipments to Japan, joined hands in support
of the Committee for the Defence of Spanish Democracy, and, whether
they liked him or not, they were ready to second his efforts as he went
about his historic task in those momentous years.

CHAPTER FOURTEEN

Toward a Materialist Christianity: "Reasoning Otherwise" in the 1930s[1]

BACKGROUNDER

In 1991, nine years into a political career that found me Minister of Colleges and Universities in Ontario's NDP government, I was asked to deliver the three annual Chancellor's Lectures at Queen's Theological College. It was the 100th anniversary of the lectures, which in 1892 effectively initiated the Queen's Theological Alumni Conferences. These were an early marker of the advance of liberal theology and the social gospel in Canada, which, in various publications, I had done much to bring into play within the mainstream of modern Canadian "secular" historiography. In the lectures, I chose to discuss aspects of the role of religion in the processes of political transformation in Canada. The first lecture rehearsed the place of religion in workers' associations, lodges, institutes, and assemblies in the nineteenth century. It drew on the thesis of Michael Gauvreau's just-published Evangelical Century *that, in Canada, the historical theology that dominated instruction in Protestant colleges nurtured an accommodating spirit that kept religious debate in Canada from running to the extremes experienced in the United States. In that country, preoccupation with Darwin and natural theology had divided Protestant religion into bitterly warring camps. I argued a derivative thesis that, if that were so, a spillover into Canadian political culture might go some distance in explaining the ongoing accommodation of third-party politics in Canada. The second lecture reviewed emergent political groupings encouraged, at least in part by this culture from the 1880s to the 1930s, culminating in the arrival of the Fellowship for a Christian Social Order (FCSO) and their classic work,* Towards the Christian Revolution *(1936).*

I had first read Towards the Christian Revolution *in the summer of 1950. It made a profound impression on me. I had found it ethically and theologically clarifying, politically challenging, and the most definitive to date on the Judeo/Christian/Marxist interface. It was also deeply symbolic. That year was my last experience of being* en famille *before leaving for studies at the University of Toronto. It was symbolic in that I had found the book in my father's library. It was a sort of final formative imprint before leaving home – even if my father had never mentioned Marx in my presence. At the time I was sweating it out at the Brick Works in Haney, just east of Vancouver on the lower Fraser River, where my father was stationed as the local United Church minister. The Korean War was then in progress. I was reading* The Hidden History of the Korean War, Washington Post *editor I.F. Stone's stunning journalistic exposé. I was making occasional sallies into Vancouver for a Chinese meal with Stephen Endicott, also from a China missionary family. His father, J.G. (Jim) Endicott, was then head of the Canadian Peace Congress. Steve (who my father worried was having an inordinate influence upon me) was a friend from the 1948 European junket and now the* BC *organizer for the National Federation of Labor Youth, the youth wing of the communist Labor Progressive Party.*

I would later occasionally return to Towards the Christian Revolution *and put it on the reading lists of my senior Canadian history seminars on the progressive tradition in Canada. A companion piece of that summer's reading was Scottish philosopher John Macmurray's* Creative Society *(1936), an urgent and thoughtful promotion of a communist social order as providing the conditions in which creativity and freedom of the human spirit could best flourish. It was not until after the Queen's lectures that I discovered among my deceased uncle Stanley Allen's effects a lengthy typescript of Macmurray's lectures and the discussions at a graduate Student Christian Movement conference at Belleville, Ontario, in 1936. Attended by most of the leading figures of the* FCSO *and the League for Social Reconstruction (*LSR*), the conference made me recognize the extent and nature of Macmurray's influence among Christian and some secular left intellectuals in depression Canada. The transcript was prepared by Harriet, wife of Eugene Forsey, and circulated by Stanley Allen as literary convenor of the* FCSO. *Since then, my friend John Costello's biography of Macmurray (2002) and Frank Milligan's intellectual biography of Eugene Forsey (2004) have done much to illuminate the Macmurray connection and have led me to recast the original Queen's lecture to one on the interplay of the* LSR *and the* FCSO *and the complementarity of their respective landmark books of the mid-1930s,* Social Planning for Canada *(1935) and* Towards the Christian Revolution *(1936), described by Keith Fleming in his intellectual biography of King Gordon (2015) as "two of the pivotal and controversial books published in Canada at the time." My original lecture at Queen's can be found in* From Heaven Down to Earth: A Century of Chancellor's Lectures at Queen's Theological College *(1992), edited by Marguerite Van Die.*

TOWARD A MATERIALIST CHRISTIANITY

"There is no cheap solution of the problem of social reconstruction. There is no escaping the cross. The devil of social injustice goeth not out but by grappling with fundamental issues. This generation seeketh after a sign, and there shall be no sign given it but the sign of the prophet Marx. Until Christians learn to understand and apply the lessons of Marxism they cannot enter the Kingdom of Heaven – nor, probably, can anyone else."[2] A bold new venture, "Radical Christianity," was announcing its manifesto amid the economic wreckage of the Great Depression of the 1930s. International capitalism appeared to be in terminal collapse. A new constellation of Radical Christians was offering a trenchant analysis of the root economic problem that confronted Canada and the world, but not just economic analysis was called for. The religious malaise of the time, the philosophical quandaries, and the political confusion all demanded bold new thought across a broad front of issues and an agenda for action. The manifesto addressed all that and proposed in great detail the shape of a prospective new social/economic/religious order and a framework for political action rooted in Christian premises. The writer, Eugene Forsey, having abandoned earlier plans to study for the Christian ministry at McGill University, had returned in 1929 from three years at Oxford University to become a sessional lecturer in economics and political science. Not just a brilliant young economist but a dedicated and articulate Christian socialist, Forsey, with fellow Christian socialists such as J. King Gordon at McGill's United Theological College, along with others of a more secular bent, were founding members in 1931 of the LSR in Montreal. Forsey and Gordon, but especially the former, played major roles in the writing of the landmark LSR publication, *Social Planning for Canada*, which would dramatically chart new directions for Canadian social and public policy.[3]

Secular in its focus and language, the work contained a deceptively brief section entitled "Religion and Capitalism."[4] Its authors, familiar with Max Weber's *The Protestant Ethic and the Spirit of Capitalism* and R.H. Tawney's *Religion and the Rise of Capitalism*, launched a blunt critique of Canadian churches – especially Protestant – charging that, in the nineteenth century, the churches had promoted industrial virtues as the hallmark of Christian character, nurturing the urban middle class, elevating models of successful capitalist enterprise, and obligating themselves to wealthy donors for church enterprises. The churches, it was argued, provided charity, but at the same time, despite occasional prophetic voices of protest, they were quick to blame the poor for their plight. In recent decades, however, the authors had perceived a growing social consciousness throughout the churches, resulting in a widespread "revolt against the spirit and practices of capitalist society." The League, therefore, thought it not impossible "that radical Christian thought and action might play an important part in the coming period of social reconstruction."[5] That thought was not entirely new. Ernest Thomas, a bridge figure from the earlier social gospel and a member of the LSR, in a recent pamphlet had voiced a similar hope.[6]

That such a hope could be expressed in the mid-1930s was not just the upside of deep depression-generated criticism of existing social and economic institutions. Western Christendom had been badly scarred by the Great War. The philosophical idealism and its more generalized popular expressions that had fueled pre-war church progressivism and Christian social activism appeared to be a spent force. In Canada, after a brief period of Reconstruction optimism, a surging social gospel had faltered, and it went into crisis as its various expressions struggled with intractable realities and contradictory moods of the 1920s.[7] It was against such a background that Forsey and Gordon had gone to Oxford and found an intellectual culture deep in inquiry over a civilization that appeared to have lost its way. Socialism and Labour party politics infiltrated academic studies and extracurricular life. Forsey would return marked forever by three years in which the Scottish philosopher John Macmurray, week in week out, was his tutor.[8]

Macmurray was a member of a group of graduates of the British Student Christian Movement (SCM) known as the SCM Auxiliary or SCMAux, disenchanted with the church, but seeking ways to bring their Christianity to bear on a crisis that appeared to have overtaken every aspect of Western culture. For Macmurray, the modern West was caught in the contradiction of the mechanism of its early period and the vitalism of the nineteenth century. Rationalist and Idealist dualisms were bankrupt. Wrestling with recent currents of realism on the one hand, and exploring the nature of personality and its roots in shared community on the other, Macmurray was also, on the basis of the early works of Karl Marx, seeking a rapprochement of Christianity and Marxism. The Christian doctrine of an incarnating God, Macmurray insisted, led logically and inevitably to a Christian materialism in which theory and practice were one. To believe was to act; profession of belief without action was sheer sentimentalism.[9]

For his part, Gordon, on returning to Canada, had not given up on his ministerial ambitions, and shortly put himself under the tutelage of New York's Union Theological Seminary professors, especially Reinhold

Niebuhr and Harry F. Ward, both of whom, like Macmurray, had been working out a marriage of Christian social thought and Marxist historical materialism. Ward and Niebuhr involved their students in direct action with the poor in New York and joining workers striking against exploitive employers.[10] Ward continued to be Marxist in his social outlook, while Niebuhr was in transition from his Marxism of the twenties, though it left its mark in the variety of Christian realism for which he would become famous.[11] Their goal was to forge a more potent attack on an industrial capitalist economic order whose fundamental assumptions, motivations, and practices they considered morally repugnant, socially unjust, and utterly contrary to essential Judeo-Christian teaching. Under their mentoring Gordon would encounter the Fellowship of Socialist Christians and bring it to Montreal.[12] With mounting alarm over the extent of social distress, the regional Conferences of the United Church, of which Forsey and Gordon were members, were now calling for action. The Montreal-Ottawa and the Toronto Conferences called for the creation of a Christian social order, with the Toronto Conference in 1933, after a spirited address by Salem Bland, narrowly passing an outright condemnation of capitalism as unChristian. Local groups like the League for Christian Social Action in British Columbia were springing into action. In the wake of the Toronto resolution, a day-long conference was convened, resulting in the creation of a Movement for a Christian Social Order under the leadership of John Line, professor of the history and philosophy of religion at Victoria College.[13] At the national level, a special commission on Christianizing the Social Order was created under President Robert Falconer of the University of Toronto and including, among others, LSR members, economist Irene Biss, and Harry Cassidy, head of the Toronto School of Social Work. Reporting to the 1934 General Council, the commission's proposals were "warmly appreciated" and its publication in pamphlet form was authorized for "the widest possible circulation and study" throughout the church. How vigorously local congregations may have responded is not clear. Important as the report was, it carefully avoided the language of class struggle and proposed an absolute ban on politics in the pulpit. Falling short of the radical Christian critique of the social and economic order that Forsey, Gordon, Line, and others across the country were now making, it lacked the "edge" needed to provoke spirited action.[14]

Nonetheless, by 1933 a convergence of forces had become evident. With LSR publications now seeing the light of day, and "the book" near completion, it was time for the formation of a cognate organization to the LSR, grounded on the new Christian materialist realism being scouted among *avant garde* philosophers and theologians on both sides of the Atlantic.

The result was the founding conference of the FCSO in Kingston on 23–25 April 1934. The conference was no precipitous, spur-of-the-moment affair. A dozen members representing the Montreal, Kingston, and Toronto groups met in the fall of 1933 in Toronto's Church of All Nations, where they were led in their devotions by Salem Bland. They set up a formal series of groups across the region to bring forth statements of purpose and organizational proposals for consideration at a founding conference. Over three days, twenty-three clergy and a few laity (including one woman) pooled their ideas under the chairing of R.B.Y. Scott, professor of Old Testament literature at United Theological College in Montreal, and shared in devotions under the leadership of Gregory Vlastos, professor of philosophy at Queen's University in Kingston.[15]

The FCSO quickly spread across the country, incorporating other Depression-spawned groups like the Fellowship of Socialist Christians in Montreal and Kingston, the Movement for a Christian Social Order in Toronto, the BC League for Christian Social Action, the Alberta School of Religion, and Warwick Kelloway's Christian Commonwealth Youth Movement. It found a ready ally in the SCM, which at the time acted as the *de facto* national organization of university students. The FCSO stimulated the organization of other denominational initiatives like the Anglican Fellowship for Social Action. Some ranking figures of the United Church became members, like *New Outlook* editor W.B. Creighton, Secretaries of Evangelism and Social Service, Ernest Thomas and J.R. Mutchmor, and most important, past moderator Richard Roberts who in his British past was well acquainted with Macmurray and would write a foreword for the FCSO's first book and manifesto.[16] Ministers and members of other denominations were invited. By 1937 there were 265 members enrolled.

There was a large overlap of FCSO and LSR memberships, with many on both sides having shared SCM roots. Most of the early leadership of the FCSO were founders of the LSR and as such were party to its alleged role as the brains trust of the emerging CCF party, the Co-operative Commonwealth Federation.[17] When the board of United Theological College, concerned over Gordon's teaching and socialist activism, but pleading financial difficulties, dismissed him from his post as professor of Christian ethics in 1934, he became travelling secretary for both the LSR and the FCSO.[18]

Two years later, in 1936, Gregory Vlastos joined hands with R.B.Y. Scott to edit the Fellowship's book-length manifesto – or "tract for the times" as they put it – *Towards the Christian Revolution*.[19] This was a serious, substantial, and, despite the editors' modest claims, intellectually challenging work and a worthy companion piece to *Social Planning for Canada*. Chapters ranged across the FCSO's philosophical background, its theological principles, ethical foundations, Biblical basis, the economic problem and the proposed new economic order, the political task, the church's role, the Marxist challenge, and the coming new society. Some of the best young minds of church and university, like John Line, Eugene Forsey, J. King Gordon, E.A. Havelock, Edis Fairbairn, J.W.A. Nicholson, and Martyn Estall, in addition to Scott and Vlastos, were the contributors. All were members of the LSR and several had been contributors to *Social Planning for Canada* – especially Forsey, who had written a third of it.[20]

With editions published in the United States and England, *Towards the Christian Revolution* was widely reviewed. It was an alternate choice in the Gollancz Left Book Club in Great Britain, and it was hailed by the prominent British Marxist theorist John Strachey in Great Britain as the best piece yet published by the churches on the current crisis. On the other hand, Reinhold Niebuhr, at Union Theological Seminary in New York, disappointed the authors by viewing it as yet another outcropping of the social gospel. This it was not, as will be shown later in the chapter. The book was one of the most important Canadian publications of the 1930s. It remains the classic statement of Christian socialism in Canada, one of the best of that genre, as well as an important primary document for Canadian intellectual, social, and political history in twentieth century Canada. Unlike other notable original works of Canadian social Christianity, such as J.S. Woodsworth's *My Neighbor* and Salem Bland's *New Christianity*, the book was not reprinted in the Social History of Canada reprint series in the 1970s. Unfortunately, when a belated second edition was published in 1989, its introduction by Roger Hutchinson was so badly mangled by the printers as to defy readability.[21]

Until recently, the Radical Christianity of the Great Depression in Canada has only gathered sporadic and incidental attention in published works. To understand the boldness and originality of *Towards the Christian Revolution* in the context of Christian social thought in Canada, one must go back to the pledge made by the twenty-three who two years previously had gathered at Kingston to found the FCSO: "Believing as we do that there are no distinctions of power and privilege in the Kingdom of God, we pledge ourselves in the service of God and to the task of building a new society in which all exploitation of man by man and all barriers to the abundant life which are created by the private ownership of property shall be done away."[22]

Once more, the dilemma addressed by Henry George in the 1880s was upon the world, only now, not private ownership in land but in capital was the issue. Despite enormous technological progress and industrial productivity, poverty stalked the land.[23] An unplanned profit-driven system was failing the very purpose of the economy – providing for the material sustenance of its people. The times called for new forms of social, political, and industrial organization and fresh attitudes and orientations of public, philosophical, and religious reflection. In this the FCSO was part search and part solution. Its leaders believed that Christianity "has revolutionary resources for this crisis." They acknowledged that "religion has often functioned as an opiate … but we see within religion the same dialectic of reaction and revolution that marks other phases of the social process. We affirm the faith of the prophets and of Jesus as a disturbing, renovating force." The question was how to articulate this in the contemporary context, how to achieve the needed changes in thinking and living, in philosophy, theology, ethics, economics, politics, preaching, and worship that would "constitute repentance for the coming Kingdom."[24] That was the search. The solution lay in transforming society on the basis of a "Radical Christianity." The FCSO insisted that the bond between human beings and God was the same bond that united men and women into a society whose common life embodied the justice and mercy of its God.

Although on the surface there might seem to be a similarity, this new presentation of Christianity was quite different from the earlier social gospel. On this the authors were clear. The revelatory nature of the crisis of the 1930s was driving a new generation toward a more profound grounding of hope and action. Radical Christianity, the authors maintained, rejected the mechanical formula of "evangelism and social service" that had emerged in the wake of the pre-war social gospel with its ties to liberal progressivism. Sin was real and was at one and the same time individual and collective. An individual's redemption, therefore, was "unattainable without fundamental spiritual re-orientation," which would "involve in their very beginning [both] the regeneration of the individual spirit and the recreation of social life." FCSO leaders believed that in this they were restoring the deep-lying concerns of evangelicalism, while at the same time expanding "the range of religious redemptive action." Radical Christianity would thus be "more comprehensive than Evangelicalism" and would "far exceed liberal modernism [and the social gospel] in inwardness and depth."[25]

In moving beyond converting the capitalist to do good, and in offering an analysis of the collective state of the people, which religion addresses, the FCSO was decidedly entering new terrain. The problem was now seen to lie not in the individual *per se* but in the structure of power, and without appreciable change in the structure, things would go on as before. Somehow, a system based on a competitive individualism that undermined both community and the economy needed to be transformed to one based on cooperative structures, with social controls on the means of production and the distribution of wealth. This might entail state ownership in limited areas, but other cooperative and decentralized means of democratic planning and ownership could avoid the bureaucratic dangers of state capitalism. None of the foregoing would be accomplished without an encounter with those who currently wielded economic power, however much one might wish otherwise. Because they wanted to avoid "pious nebulosity," FCSO leaders insisted, therefore, on embracing what they considered hard-headed economic solutions, despite the controversy these might entail.

At the same time, as will be evident in a brief summary of its densely constructed chapters, the arguments of *Towards the Christian Revolution* went far beyond economics. As an attempt to articulate a Christian response, the writers, each in their own way, were cumulatively even more persuasive.

Towards the Christian Revolution

PHILOSOPHICAL AND THEOLOGICAL FOUNDATIONS

"Now as at all times," John Line wrote in the opening chapter, "the greater human issues are moral and religious."[26] The choice of Line to author the two introductory chapters was an inspired one. Professor of the history and philosophy of religion at Victoria College in the University of Toronto, and founder in 1931 of the Movement for a Christian Social Order in Toronto, he had a reputation for clear thinking. In confident and elegant language, he sketched the driving elements of modernity, the reigning philosophies, and the corrupting influence of the commercial revolution on Protestantism. Along with this he outlined the alternative religious responses to the contemporary spiritual crisis in the West: the older but still present options of evangelicalism and liberal-modernism, and the newer and more relevant Barthian crisis theology, neo-Thomism, and Whitehead's Process Theology. Line believed Whitehead to be especially helpful in the dialogue with "unrepentant empiricists." All of these options had strengths and weaknesses, he observed, before moving on to outline the nature of the "Radical Religion" that the Fellowship was advocating.

A time of crisis called for a reassertion of religious categories of sin, judgment, and repentance. In this, Line felt that Radical Christianity was addressing deep-seated concerns of evangelicalism and adding depth to liberal modernism and the social gospel, while casting both in more comprehensive and radical terms. For Radical Christianity, sin was not fundamentally individual acts of commission or omission, but a crucial fact of life, a pervasive disorientation, at once interactively individual and collective. Judgment was not an act of divine intervention in human affairs, but the inevitable disorder that came in the absence of love, in the abuse of power, in the denial of economic justice, in class division, in the abuse of nature, and in the systematic denial of full participation in the way society was organized. Out of such perversions arose the forces of nature and human history that seemed to defy human control. Divine judgment was thus, as the Hebrew prophets had so forcefully proclaimed, built into the very nature of things when the mercy and justice of God were ignored or denied. Accordingly "the strategy of a revolutionary Christianity ... will clearly include alignment with the forces that arise to accomplish the next stage of [human] deliverance."[27] Line had doubts that this would be accomplished through gradual processes. Discontent was rising in many quarters and events were moving swiftly. The "coming of the Kingdom" might well entail violence as Radical Christianity strove to restructure society based on "the dictation of love."

BEYOND IDEALISM: THE MATERIALIST ETHICS OF JESUS

Gregory Vlastos followed Line with a truly impressive chapter, "The Ethical Foundations," in language that established the dominant theme of "material Christianity" that preoccupied the authors. Making a case for the revolutionary nature of the ethics of Jesus, he urged the fundamental importance of material considerations in ethics. Unlike Plato's preoccupation with the education and rule of aristocrats in *The Republic,* Jesus was concerned about the plight of poor widows, workers' wages, political prisoners, their overseers, the helpless, the blind, and the despised. Instead, Jesus called for a reversal of the priorities and power structures of the world of his time. As with Marx, the critical point was to change the world. The Messianic age, the Kingdom of God, in which the disinherited would inherit the earth, was at hand; decision and action were urgent.

Jesus' command to love was not a matter of speculation, an appeal to sentiment or consciousness. Of course, love entailed feeling, but the true test of love was a material one: "If love exists at all," Vlastos insisted, "it exists as a material activity: the material interaction of separate beings recognizing each other's interests and seeking common fulfilment."[28] To enjoy spiritual values outside the context of cooperative community was sentimentalism, and to pursue material values apart from cooperative community was crass materialism. Material things were not themselves a problem; they needed only to be brought within the context of love.[29]

This issue of "materiality" in ethics led Vlastos into the concept of "mutuality," which, he declared, would have revolutionary consequences for civilization. "Mutuality" was the ground of healthy personhood and genuine community. In the dialogue of real life, in the interplay of individual and society, individuals became persons and society became a community. As an example, a worker might say, "'We haven't got a personality unless we organize.'" At the factory they were little more than "adjuncts to the machine." Organized in a union, on the other hand, they became equals cooperating in securing each other's material well-being. They now had personality and community. Mutuality, as a groundbreaking approach to a new social order, was the nemesis of all divisions of status, class, wealth, or power.[30]

It was on this ground that Line and Vlastos took aim at the totalitarianism that had emerged in the interwar years as a response to the growing rootlessness of the masses under liberal democratic capitalism. Fascism in the form of the corporate state in Italy and Germany aimed at resolving the social malaise by cultivating a mystical bond with the state. This was a cover to leaving intact corporate ownership and the subservience of labour under the tutelage of the state. Not unity but uniformity was the result – and the suppression of all dissent.

Vlastos agreed with Line in his description of how God "took sides" via the play of social forces. God was the love, the cohesive, person-nourishing spirit, without which human beings could not live, and thus was the key to the future. "The present crisis," Vlastos concluded, "is the tension between a lingering divisive society of economic classes and new possibilities of co-operative community in a classless society … [Christianity] does not counsel a revolution. It announces it."[31] Vlastos' chapter is as fresh and relevant today as on the day it was written.

THE BIBLE:
PROPHETS AND PROPERTY, COVENANT AND CLASS

For the idea of a Christian revolution to have legitimacy, it was not enough to establish a philosophical background, theological principles, and ethical foundations. Jesus was the son of a people whose history was critical to understanding him. The Hebrew and Christian scriptures were keys to that history and, whether well understood or not, had provided the normative centre of different expressions of Christianity over the centuries. It fell to R.B.Y. Scott to establish a basis for Radical Christianity in the Biblical record. Scott was eminently equipped for the task. Probably the ablest of Canada's younger Biblical scholars, he was well versed in the latest research and keenly interested in the Jewish prophetic tradition. He began his teaching career in 1928 at Union Theological College in Vancouver, moved to Montreal in 1931 to become professor of Old Testament language and literature at United Theological College, and became the first dean of the new Faculty of Divinity at McGill University, eventually moving to Princeton University as the head of its new Department of Religious Studies. He published several important works on Old Testament themes and was among those engaged in deciphering the Dead Sea Scrolls. Perhaps even more than for his scholarship, he was widely known for his hymns celebrating the social Christianity he so ardently advocated.

Scott was quick to point out that there was no plan in the Bible for a social order that could be readily appropriated and applied. What the Bible offered was a record of a people's struggle with issues of social order. Keys to the nature of this struggle came from knowing their nomadic past and their experience of having been freed from slavery in Egypt by a liberating God. This God they came to believe "was a Being of majestic holiness, merciful, just, and true, controlling the processes of nature and the destiny of humanity."[32] Their "dealings" with this majestic Being had been as tribe and family, and, once tribes were consolidated, as a people. With agriculture and commerce came property, class division, and slavery; with national development came temple worship, a priestly hierarchy, kingship, and extravagant wealth and luxury. The prophetic protest against court immorality, corrupt judges, the accumulation of estates, and exploitation of the poor provided the basis for the elaboration of Jewish law. Such concepts were not easily put aside. Tradition had sanctified them as part of the law said to have been given to Moses by God. They signalled that "the divine purpose [was] to be fulfilled ... not in some heavenly world, but in the land of Israel and among the nations."[33] Such thinking informed the concept and content of the Messianic Age, and it was also the subject of Jesus' announcement of his mission.

Central to this Biblical record was the concept of a Covenant in which God entered into a fellowship with the people, intending them to live in harmonious relationship with one another and with God. Given the atomistic individualism of *laissez-faire* capitalism and the evangelical heritage of personal religion, it was important for Scott to note that the Covenant was not with individual people. Individuals gained full personhood as part of a covenanted people. From this Scott derived an organic concept of "persons-in-community," a powerful reinforcement of Vlastos' notion of mutuality. He then went on to underscore Vlastos' emphasis on the material nature of the love relationship by challenging the soul-body dualism that had distorted Christianity since its immersion in a Greek world, and which had become such a boon to the rationalization of capitalist values. The Jewish belief in the resurrection of the body in the final judgment was a concept that placed an ultimate value on material existence. As in the modern holistic concept of "psycho-soma," the true test of love, which after all was the very heart of the Covenant, was in the reciprocal involvement of "persons-in-community" in their material exchanges.

Here, to say the least, was high ground from which to launch a Christian revolution to overcome the twentieth century heresy of possessive individualism. Like his Jewish ancestors, Jesus, Scott insisted, was also a "person-in-community" and "works with these same basic conceptions of God, Man, and Covenant Community, though deepened, enriched and unified as never before."[34]

THE NECESSITY OF SOCIALISM

If capitalism was bankrupt and fascism worse, was socialism the only alternative for humanity? The public in the mid-1930s confronted a bewildering menu of panaceas on offer from many quarters: moral rearmament, technocracy, social credit, cooperativism, new dealism, anarcho-syndicalism, communism, and fascism, not to mention varieties of socialism. It might have seemed curious that when Eugene Forsey came to write his chapter on "A New Economic Order" he began by assessing the merits and, in particular, the demerits of the cooperative movement. Vlastos' and Scott's master concepts of "mutuality" and "persons-in-community" may have seemed to bend the discussion in the direction of cooperativism – and hence Forsey's cautionary words.

Forsey was not in principle opposed to cooperatives and readily recited their formidable achievements. In Great Britain, with a membership of over 7,000,000 and net earnings of 25,000,000 pounds, they were "the largest single distributive business in the country and the only business which grew steadily throughout the depression." Cooperatives were the world's largest buyers of Canadian wheat, owned over 200 mills and factories, and dominated the country's life and accident insurance business.

The problem was that cooperative enthusiasts were conveying the mistaken notion that the movement could give rise to a "free democratic economy" that would gradually supplant capitalism – a "painless substitute for socialism" without having to engage in the messy business of politics. Cooperatives would play a "valuable part in the change to a new order and within the new order." However, they did not have the power to replace the class nature of a society. Notions of "harmonizing" or "balancing" the interests of capital and labour were illusory. Labourers could achieve real freedom and security and a full return on the value of their labour only by displacing the owners of capital and gaining control of the means of production. Since "two classes could not control the same thing at the same time," the conflict between capital and labour was irreconcilable. Intermediate groups like cooperatives must either join the socialist political struggle to eliminate capitalism or become irrelevant.[35]

Only with the development of class-consciousness, Forsey argued, would the fact of class come to an end and, echoing Vlastos and Scott, "real community, mutuality, genuinely personal relationships on a universal scale" be possible.[36] Here, once again, Forsey was betraying the influence of his eminent tutor at Oxford, and who, as recently as late June 1936, had, as theme speaker, led a Student Christian Movement Graduate Conference at Belleville, attended by most of the LSR/FCSO leadership.[37] The cooperative movement as such had no answer to the problem of class, but it was of value in demonstrating the workability of a non-capitalist economy and in initiating the public into the "mental and emotional attitudes" of the new economic order. It was, however, in grave danger of being co-opted by business interests and thus would fail to realize its own aims.

As a result, rather than the limited contribution of cooperatives, socialism was of necessity the way out of the great crisis that had befallen humanity under capitalism. Forsey demurred, however, from attempting a full description of the new order, referring readers to *Social Planning for Canada*, G.R. Mitchison's *The First Workers' Government* [in Britain], and the Webbs' *Soviet Communism*. Along with Gordon, he had visited the Soviet Union in 1932 and was impressed by the progress made there in socialist planning. The Soviets had avoided the Depression, kept workers employed, and improved the standard of living, all under a regime of broad equality. He was concerned, however, about the lack of political democracy and civil liberties but expected that to change in time.[38] Forsey, in his *A Life on the Fringe*, gives few useful details of the trip.[39] His companion, King Gordon, was rather more forthcoming and historical in his observations. The Soviet regime was more Russian than socialist, having developed outside the democratic tradition in a country with a population generally backward, illiterate, and used to Tsarist dictatorship. The dictatorship in Russia, Gordon thought, was different than that in Germany and Italy. Stalin, as secretary to the Central Executive of a Communist Party of two million, had limits to his personal power. The party was guided by "a philosophy and practice of social reorganization" and as industry and education advanced and counter-revolutionary danger waned, the prospects for democratic freedoms would grow.

Forsey's chief concern in ending the chapter was to disabuse readers of the many misconceptions that were abroad about socialism. The socialization of property pertained only to private property in the means of production, which was exploitive, but not to personal property, which was not. Socialism was not "state-capitalist public ownership," which entailed a "perpetual tribute to the former private owners." There would be no confiscation but compensation based on "prudent investment" so as to be fair to all shareholders. Along with this would be graduated taxes to recover from the rich what they had improperly appropriated. Socialist planning would leave the land tenure of farmers intact. Socialized industries would not be run by politicians or public servants but by autonomous boards of directors responsible to a national planning commission, which, in turn, would be responsible to parliament.

But would not government and public enterprises still be corrupt? In response Forsey noted that capitalism made its appeal to greed among business people and to fear among workers. However, by nature, the individual was not "a low money-grubbing animal," different from other human beings. If that were the case, "we may as well give up preaching the gospel of Christ." Ordinary men and women would inhabit the socialist society, but they would be unburdened of "the restrictions which capitalism places upon the spontaneous creative activity which is natural to human beings."[40] The question was how to get there. Careful study was a necessity, Forsey cautioned, lest Radical Christians end up in blind alleys and fall into traps set for them. A bold but astute politics was the order of the day.

THE POLITICAL TASK OF OUR GENERATION

It fell to King Gordon to address the political task, and he did so with the characteristic directness and intelligence that were the hallmark of his later brilliant career, and indicated in the present that the FCSO/LSR were in good hands: "The political task of our generation is that of preventing the rise of the totalitarian state in the remaining democratic countries of the world, and of saving civilization from the devastation of war brought on by the desperate imperialist excursions of the fascist states." This could only be done by building a state, so organized as to provide economic security and maintain individual liberty.[41]

In its attempt to provide a rich context for understanding the necessity and direction of political action, his chapter on the political task was remarkably comprehensive and insightful. He organized his argument under three heads: "Fascism and Liberal Democracy," "The Socialist Alternative to Fascism," and "The Church and Social Action." In a wide-ranging survey of economic history he demonstrated the impact of the current Depression in plunging the business enterprises and middle and working classes of all the Western countries into desperate straits. He warned that the urgency of dramatic intervention by governments to rescue both businesses and the masses provided fertile ground for the totalitarian/fascist phenomenon. To understand the latter, he moved onto the new ground of social psychology and religion. People might turn to radical social action, but, disillusioned and desperate, they could just as easily be attracted to questionable panaceas and self-serving saviours, and to scapegoat groups, as with the Jews in Germany. Combined with "the lack of understanding of social and economic phenomena," a fertile field was available for the forces of reaction to consolidate their economic and political power and suppress democracy.[42]

Here the churches had a role. Although Gordon did not expect the church, given its disparate denominations, to become overtly partisan in politics, the issue between democracy and fascism was crucial for its very *raison d'être*. Fascism was, in actuality, not simply a political movement. With its myths and symbols, its promotion of paganism, its demand of total allegiance, its persecution of outsiders, and its national mission, it was also a religion. Though the Christian religion had often been otherworldly in the face of evil, it had also shown examples of positive cooperative action, especially more recently: in nineteenth century Britain, for example, commendable Christian efforts at social justice initiatives, the inspiration of workers' education, promotion of trade union membership, and encouragement of Labour party activity. Walter Rauschenbusch in the United States had brought the social gospel firmly into socialist territory by recognizing the fact of class struggle and the revolutionary nature of Jesus' life and teaching in his classic work, *Christianity and the Social Crisis* (1907). Others had followed, including Gordon's teachers at Union, steadily sharpening economic and political reasoning from a Christian left perspective and maintaining solidarity with the working class. The result in Britain and North America, Gordon thought, was a more congenial relationship of the church with labour and the radical movement than was the case in European countries. In Canada and the United States, socialist leaders J.S. Woodsworth and Norman Thomas were both former Christian ministers. Churches had, however, generally stopped short at passing resolutions. But now, Gordon thought, "the rapidity of economic change ... [and] the need for a new intelligence ... provide an opportunity for organized religion to play an important role in averting fascism and assisting in the process of social transformation."[43]

There were three principal ways in which the churches could do this: they needed to establish clearly the unethical basis of the prevailing economic system, study in the most scientific way the fundamental causes of economic distress and maldistribution of wealth, and understand the most effective means of promoting the establishment of a just social and economic order. Second – and here Gordon came back to an issue to which he would devote a large part of his later life – the church urgently needed to address the increasing threat of international war, the causes of which were manifold. The world had been turning from the League of Nations to a set of competing alliances that had precipitated the Great War. Public opinion was confused – and non-existent where it mattered most, in the fascist states. Pacifism was not an option. The church needed to do all it could to reinforce a faltering system of collective security, even if it meant supporting sanctions and the use of force, all the while remaining wary against becoming trapped into some new imperialist crusade.[44]

Thirdly, it followed that the church must give all possible assistance to "those forces that are making for a more democratic society ... to promote the highest economic and cultural well-being of the mass of the people. Christians could not simply ignore the realities of a world where the stark choices were now between good and evil. To evade the hard choice was simply to leave the field to the enemy. Echoes of Niebuhr's classroom were obvious – and of John Macmurray. A small group of Christian socialists prepared to join the secular radical movement would be in "a position to urge the movement beyond tempting compromises." As such they could mitigate violence and provide a "channel of understanding between secular forces and intra-church groups." And when radical action faced "the inevitable disasters and setbacks ... an active Christian minority could demonstrate that faith in the ultimate victory of righteousness which in their own tradition finds triumphant expression in the cross."[45]

Gordon was here trenching on the next chapter examining the role of the church, but clearly he wanted to have his say. For him personally the choice was clear. Three years earlier he and Forsey had been among the drafters of the Regina Manifesto of the CCF party. The political task was to establish the new democratic socialist order that would arrest the danger of fascism and avert the looming threat of war.

It was a prescient piece, and Gordon was alone among the authors to confront the threat of war. The Spanish Civil War was now underway, with its International Brigade – including a Canadian Mackenzie-Papineau Battalion, fighting to preserve Spanish democracy against General Franco's fascist insurgency. The response of the church and of pacifism to the prospects of war dominated his final section. While appreciating pacifist ideals, Gordon rejected that course of action because "absolute pacifism suffers from the defect of all absolutisms in a world governed by dialectical principles." It was a notable observation, reflecting as it did a certain relativism in moral decision making and the realistic counsels of his teachers in New York. To read Gordon's chapter is to discover the strong threads of religion, moral commitment, and intellectual energy that would weave together his subsequent career as editor of *The Nation* magazine, as advisor to the Human Rights Secretariat of the United Nations, in his various missions under the United Nations in Africa and the Middle East, and later as professor of international relations at the University of Alberta.[46]

THE CHURCH AS PROPHETIC COMMUNITY

It might have seemed odd for the editors to assign this chapter to three separate authors, but each was eminently qualified to present the three crucial marks of the FCSO's vision of the church as gathered Christian community: it must be prophetic; it must exhibit, as well as announce, the good news of the reign of God; and it must develop a "cultus" or drama by which the gathered faithful rehearsed their reason for being. J.W.A. Nicholson, the United Church minister at Bedeque, Prince Edward Island, would do the first; R. Edis Fairbairn, who had come to Canada from British Methodism via Newfoundland and was now the United Church minister at Canfield, Ontario, would do the second; and R.B.Y. Scott, who we have met above, would do the third.

Nicholson, something of a prophet in his own right, saw the core of prophetic teaching and practice to lie in the organic unity of the community's consciousness of God. He shared with Vlastos and Scott concepts of mutuality and persons-in-community grounded in the exchange of life's material necessities. "Intimacy with God" separate from the equal rights of all to God's providence was a denial of God. The experience of God was not the property of a select, congenial group, but, as a God of love and justice, was fundamental to the concept of church as inclusive fellowship.[47]

Edis Fairbairn, in his radical rendition of the concept of the Kingdom of God, carried forward Nicholson's "voice of prophecy." An ardent pacifist of the 1920s and a carry-over from the radical wing of the earlier social gospel, Fairbairn was a man who felt the anguish of the times deep within his own self. He coped with this by prolific writing of thoughtful, trenchant articles for religious and secular publications. In 1927 he published a book entitled *The Appeal to Reality*, and its argument became the tenor of his remarks on "the Evangel [Good News] of the Kingdom."[48]

An "evangel" called for evangelism, a word, he noted that had become unpopular, conjuring up memories of old-style revivalism and "visions of professional teams of high-pressure salesmen of emotional and often freakish religion." He reminded his readers that communists, fascists, and Nazis used their own aggressive brands of evangelism to work a revolution of religious proportions for their absolutist, mystical, and messianic creeds. In the face of this, radical religion in its conception of the Kingdom of God could provide a meaningful Christian norm for social reconstruction. As was now being more widely recognized, Christianity was not a personal religion with social implications, but a social religion with personal implications. This recognition was, in itself, a revolutionary development, he argued, and its application would require "revolutionary energy and action." It was from the collision of such new ideas with tradition and the existing order of things that radical changes in thinking and acting happened. In short, Fairbairn was bringing the negative and positive attitudes to change together to a single point where collaboration would be possible. In the present context, the mutuality of the Kingdom ethic required the churches to embrace the anger, the resentment, and the revolt of the masses. With a large minority of ministers seized by this new evangel of the Kingdom, "religion may erupt in a new, volcanic energy, the pessimistic prognostications of social realists may be disproved, and Christianity may become effective for social transformation *sans* bloody revolution."[49] As always, Fairbairn's language flared with urgency. Churches that passed resolutions on Christianizing the social order were under moral obligation to act. If they "hang back, irresolute and afraid, they will have no right to condemn more forthright movements which do not hesitate to use bloody violence to blast a way through the resistance of the privileged."[50]

Completing the trilogy on the church's role in the great crisis of the time was R.B.Y. Scott's piece on the unlikely subject of "The Cultus of the Community." By "cultus" Scott meant the panoply of ritual in which an intentional community embodies in story, rhetoric, symbol, song, and ceremony its message and *raison d'être*. Scott was frank about the seeming irrelevance of religious celebration in the face of "flagrant human suffering and evil." It could well be seen as merely offering people an "imaginative escape into an ideal world ... and diverting their moral energies from the task of overcoming and transforming the real world of daily life."[51] However, at its deepest level, religion was an expression of human yearning for meaningful community, a yearning that implied a desire for fellowship with some "Ultimate Reality." Human communities everywhere were riddled with ritual, often observed semi-consciously at best. As flagrant example, he pointed to the use of ostentatious ritual by totalitarian movements. It was the business of religion "to create and enact a vision of the world." The good news of the Kingdom of God as understood by radical Christianity was such a vision. It was not a program or an idea; it was "a vital belief and an incipient experience" within the fellowship of faith. The function of religious celebration was to embody and exhibit "the meaning of Christian culture ... at points of peculiar importance for [the] life" of individuals and society.[52]

There was, he emphasized, a stark contrast between the symbols of fascism in Italy and Germany and those of the church. The former served as a definition of inauthentic community: symbols of state power, military might, and national/racial triumph, not symbols of authentic common life. Those of the church – bread, wine, water, and a cross – were symbols at once of dependence on one another and on nature, and of suffering and triumph over suffering. The rites of fascism were "an assault on our common humanity"; the Christian rites, properly understood, nourished the shared life of a common humanity and, by the same token, committed the church to the task of radical social reconstruction. "None need the steadying strength [of the cultus] more than those most aware of the dangerous tensions and disintegrating forces in contemporary society," Scott concluded.[53]

THE CHALLENGE OF MARXISM

Any reader scanning the chapter titles of *Towards the Christian Revolution* would realize that the argument of the book would come to a climax with chapter nine, "The Marxist Challenge." Marx had surfaced in various references along the way, in the company of others such as Whitehead, Macmurray, Polanyi, Laski, and Rauschenbusch, but here was the name that most threatened the defenders of capitalism. Marx, at last, had arrived in the lexicon of social Christianity in Canada as a social theorist worthy of serious consideration. To be sure, the more radical social gospel clergy, especially in Western Canada, had already encountered Marxism in their contacts with the religiously hostile Socialist Party of Canada and the Social Democratic Party. And in the turn-of-the century crisis of George Wrigley's Christian Socialist League in Ontario, some had peeled off in that direction. That a serious discussion of Marxism was still dangerous, however, was evident in the mysterious pseudonym that shrouded the identity of the author of the chapter, "Propheticus," latterly known as Martyn Estall, Vlastos' colleague in philosophy at Queen's. University presidents, boards of governors, and not least the Royal Canadian Mounted Police (RCMP) were keeping a watchful eye on professors with radical social and religious views. Gordon had just been fired; Forsey was under surveillance and would shortly be forced out of McGill. Underhill (another original member of the LSR) was in trouble but survived at Toronto, and a few years later, Stanley Allen, a member of the LSR and the FCSO, a Montreal city councillor, and one-time president of the Quebec CCF, would be dismissed from the faculty of Sir George Williams College.

Estall had some misgivings about the title of the chapter because it implied a "deep-rooted antithesis" between Christianity and Marxism. Both, he contended, had suffered "the fate or the fulfillment of all ideas, beliefs, programs, movements ... overlaid with legend, tradition, precedent, and institutionalized."[54] What was Marxism? It was threefold: Marx's original ideas and social program; the subsequent history of those ideas and program; and the significance of that history for the future. Estall cautioned that, while Marxism, like Christianity, could be considered as "living things [with] a power to affect the lives of men and women," both Marxism and Christianity were living persons and actual fellowships of people, as in political parties and churches. One might belong to one or the other, or leave the one and join the other. What happens in that process? "In becoming one, must one cease to be the other? That is the ultimate question of this chapter."[55]

Marx, like Jesus, had recognized and declared that what mattered was action: "The philosophers have only interpreted the world in various ways; the point is to change it."[56] Estall then went on to explain in detail Marx's celebrated concepts of the materialist economic interpretation of historical change, the division of labour, and the formation of classes, and how a phenomenon of class struggle had emerged that drove history forward to a final conflict. What gave Marx's theory great interpretive power, however, was not just his "dialectical" process of historical change. Important was his explanation of how in every era the economic system of production and exchange "forms the basis upon which is built up, and from which alone can be explained, the political and intellectual history of that epoch." That, of course, put the axe to the root of prevailing idealist philosophy by grounding all values in economics, and, at least on the surface of it, denied the primacy and even the legitimacy of all religion, including Christianity. Suggestively – and perhaps mischievously – Estall inserted in his text Jesus' response to followers when they fearfully asked Jesus about the coming end of the world: "Who hath warned you to flee the wrath to come? ... He that hath two coats let him impart to him that hath none; and he that hath meat let him do likewise." The material act carried value for Jesus. For Jesus also the axe was laid to the root of class.

Though Estall went at some length to nuance Marx's definition of class to include the plight of North American farmers (a perplexing problem for the drafters of the CCF's Regina Manifesto in 1933), he emphasized that the fundamental common element in all of Marx's categorization was an attack "directed against the exploitation of one group in the community by another." It mattered little therefore that he may have been wrong in some technical details.[57] The revolutionary social change that Marx predicted and sought required carefully calculated and intensive political action. Did Marx's dialectic of historical change, however, inevitably imply violence? Was gradualism an option? Jesus had held out different options regarding the coming Kingdom of God: "It cometh not with observation" and "It suffereth violence and men of violence take it by storm." Historical context was crucial. Lenin had put it well: "To attempt to answer 'yes' or 'no' to the question of a definite means of struggle, without examining in detail the concrete situation at a given moment ... means to depart altogether from the Marxian ground."[58] Hence, various means were available, including party organization, activism on the labour front, and latterly popular front organizations like the League Against War and Fascism.

In seeking to correct popular misconceptions of Marxism, Estall noted that it was not intent on eliminating culture, but wanted an enriched indigenous culture in place of the class-based culture of capitalism. It did not advocate the abolition of the family, but wanted "to do away with the status of women as mere instruments of reproduction." Class struggle was not invented by Marx but was rather a reality he discovered, much like Darwin had discovered natural selection as the means by which species originate and progress.

Like other contributors to the book, Estall saw fascism as the principal menace of the hour, and in much the same terms. Like them, he was loathe to lump fascism and communism together as manifestations of totalitarianism. In theory, at least, fascism "explicitly glorifies and absolutizes the state [while] communism envisages its ultimate abolition." Marx-ists were right in their estimate of the menace of fascism and the need to rally popular support opposing it. Marxism did have its flaws, including its assumption of rationality among the proletariat in choosing their appointed destiny. "Modern techniques of propaganda masquerading as education" readily persuade us "to accept the shadow for the substance." Such flaws, however, only suggest that no one is infallible. Nevertheless, given the danger of the present world situation, Marx had to be numbered among those who in his own words "have raised themselves to the level of comprehending the historical movements as a whole." In so doing he was among the "men and women who have somehow risen above their immediate interests." By so doing these individuals "have won the only sure protection against the beguilements of emotionally-toned appeals to prejudice and love of power." And this position, Estall emphasized, is "essentially religious."[59]

And so the chapter came to a short, pointed concluding section entitled "The Challenge to Christianity." Marx was not, Estall noted, "the only political theorist to deal seriously and antagonistically with organized Christianity." Hobbes and Rousseau also had done so (he might have included Comte), but they, unlike Marx, thought religious sanctions were necessary to secure the authority of the state. Marx saw religion as super-stition, buttressing the state with supernatural sanctions. These presump-tions were at once right and wrong. Hobbes and Rousseau were right that sooner or later Christianity would have to oppose the nation state. Marx was right in believing that for Christianity to function as a rationale for political power in an unjust social order it was indeed "the opium of the people" and an unnecessary anachronism. But they were wrong in think-ing that religion could be artificially created and superimposed or that it could be excised from the life of humanity. Religion was "the integration of the whole of life; its function was social as well as consolatory, and these two may and must be harmonized realistically."[60]

Here Estall came to the crux of the matter and put a stern test to Chris-tians. "Fascism appeals to supernatural, mythical sanctions in an effort to maintain a social order and outlook essentially fragmentary, lacking equi-librium, productive of international tension and internal oppression. Com-munism rejects all such sanctions and hence becomes the inveterate foe of all religion. Can the Christian rightly discriminate friend from foe ... [and discern] the genuineness of his own religion?" To rest content with con-ventional ecclesiastical institutions, to ignore existing injustice and allow the hope of heaven to obscure social vision, would be to reduce Christianity to a pseudo-religion. Joining the Communist party, however, was not an option if one treasured one's faith. What then to do? Estall's response, citing John Macmurray, was to "attack pseudo-Christianity in all its forms in the name of real Christianity. The religious revolution is the immediate and special task of the Christians. Unless we can vindicate the material reality of our religion we are powerless to do anything effective. There must be war to the death between real and unreal religion, even if it should cleave organized Christianity in two and destroy all its existing forms."[61]

In short, the Marxist challenge to Christianity was to make real its own gospel. Were Christians to fail at that, there was Jesus' warning to the religious leaders of the time that the Kingdom of God would be taken from them and "given to a nation bringing forth the fruits thereof."[62]

THE NEW SOCIETY

Towards the Christian Revolution might well have ended with the Estall/ Macmurray challenge. But Eric Havelock's chapter, "The New Society," was still to follow. Associate professor of classics at Victoria College in the University of Toronto, British by birth, Havelock had studied classics with distinction at Cambridge. He had taught at Acadia University briefly before coming to Victoria College in 1929. He was among the founders of the LSR, joined the CCF party, and, with Frank Underhill, became the centre of socialist activism among the faculty, protesting police abuses of civil liberties and the suppression of striking workers. All of this led to tensions with university officials and calls from the business community for his dismissal. He survived and would go on to chair classical studies at Harvard and Yale and to develop influential, if controversial, theories about Greek intellectual history. His interest in politics would continue in his promotion of the study of rhetoric as a way to resist business propaganda.

Forty years before *Towards the Christian Revolution*, Salem Bland had given a much-repeated public address, "Four Steps and a Vision," in which, on the basis of evidence in biological evolution of symbiosis and mutual aid, he had projected a future socialist society that would meet the criteria of Christian ethics and open the doors to a full life for all. Havelock's chapter might well have been subtitled "Five Steps and a Vision." It was based on the evidence of technological evolution whereby a world of scarcity and acquisitive individualism would be eliminated. A new leisure society would be ushered in where the life of the spirit for which Jesus had yearned might thrive. In a way the vision reflected the subtext of all science since the time when Francis Bacon in the sixteenth century had argued that in teasing out nature's secrets, humanity's struggle to over-come nature would finally end, and the millennium of Christianity would follow.[63] To this, Havelock added the riches of his own immersion in classical history and recent activism in socialist politics.

In the 1930s while people were starving and crops were being ploughed into the ground for want of a "market," technocracy was proclaiming that the resources of the earth assured abundance for all. A vision for a future new society had to be persuasive, securely grounded, and not simply a matter of wish fulfillment. Havelock's proposed steps to attain it were offered under five headings: (1) The Cost of Private Ownership, (2) Religion's Search for a Socialist Commonwealth, (3) The Failure of Early Communism, (4) The Vital Need for Social Change, and (5) Life and Leisure in the New Society. His brief sketch of the settlement of North America was a story of emigrants from Europe searching for the wealth and equality the class system of old Europe had denied them. What followed was an analysis and critique of a society that had grown morally bankrupt, illogical, and subversive of human nature. At the same time, however, it was important also to rehearse the human struggle throughout to keep alive the claims of the spirit – in effect, the long search for a socialist commonwealth.

That search began for Havelock at the "beginning" with the "garden Utopia" of Eden where the author of the Book of Genesis had the genius to perceive that it was only in such circumstances of ease and leisure that humanity could reach its "full stature [and] converse with God." The central problem faced by the author of Genesis, why human beings were subsequently expelled from the garden and condemned to days full of care and accumulation, was addressed in a new way by Jesus, "the last prophet of the Jews and the founder of Christianity": "Do not be troubled about what you to eat or drink, nor about what you will put on your body ... Surely life means more than food, and the body more than clothes." Jesus had gone on to point to the wild birds who do not gather grain in granaries, and to lilies of the field who neither toil nor spin, yet are looked after. "O men, how little you trust God." Anxious accumulation was the work of a pagan spirit. The gospels, on the other hand, were full of condemnations of the pursuit of wealth as a futile effort to secure what ultimately offered no security. Citing extensively, Havelock made the most of these texts. There was no room here "for the pious doctrine of the stewardship of riches." But if the much-admired rich were not acceptable in God's kingdom, for whom was it possible? In response Jesus had pointed to children, carefree in their play. In doing so, Jesus was proclaiming a reversal of values, "Who would be greatest must be a servant." And a society "where all are servants is a classless one in which there is no privilege of private property to distinguish the few from the many."[64]

It was not the role of the religious mind, Havelock noted, to develop a detailed plan of the material organization required to sustain such a life. Still, Jesus seemed to have thought that, even in an economy of scarcity, a shared community was possible. Havelock noted that after Jesus' death, Jesus' first followers set out in that direction. Although part of their impetus came from a belief in the imminent coming of the Kingdom and Jesus' return, the communism of the first church was also a clear reflection of this teaching. Havelock observed that "wherever the life of fellowship, the life of the mind and the spirit, has flamed intensely – as among such sects as the early Pythagoreans, the original Epicureans, the Franciscans, and the religious communities of the East or in Gandhi's ashrama – there is also found the necessary condition of economic communism which forms the material basis of such religious experience."[65]

Such initiatives and organized communities had not lasted because they were associations of consumers dependent for income on the private property based economies of the time. Two conditions still had to be met: a secure supply of goods produced with a minimum of toil, and secondly, collectivist production and distribution without competition or gross inequality. Both conditions awaited the advance of science. Because the industrial revolution and the machine age were still so near, Havelock noted, people had missed its profound significance, namely that the long centuries of scarcity had ended and that the ethics of the Garden of Eden were now within reach. In an organized way over the last three centuries, first through applied agricultural science and then by the application of machinery to the production of goods, "man has tamed the earth at last" and "laid the material foundations necessary for [Jesus'] Sermon on the Mount." For Havelock the "garden" was no longer a lush verdant Eden. It had become a modern machine-age society.

The large task of organizing a collectivist economy had at last become technically possible. All the elements were now, or potentially now, in place: the ability to administer production, rapid communications, and transport, the capacity to gather statistics of all kinds including supply and demand, and above all a literate, knowledgeable, and responsive citizenry, and a large civil service capable of managing "the vast proportions and immense capacities and relationships of the socialist state."[66] As with the private ownership of the means of production, the physical and moral costs of class war, and its correlate in international warfare, had become intolerable, not only in itself, but to the increasingly educated conscience of an enlightened population.[67]

Here Havelock finally came to describing his vision of life and labour in the new society. Quite deliberately he plunged into offering a brief sketch of the new economic state – brief because the LSR's *Social Planning for Canada* had already detailed the big picture. The new economy would be structured under "a series of state trusts, self-managing public corporations which in their general policies receive direction from the central organs of government." Money would remain the means of exchange, with goods bought and sold under market conditions. Receipts from sales would be returned to the community in wages and salaries, with the surplus going to the state bank for further investment or public services. With social organization of the machine age economy, ideals and values would change. The gospels of hard work and thrift would gradually disappear. With economic planning none would be without work; all men and women would work, but their work would be valued as an asset, not as a cost. But once basic security had been assured, would striving for worldly success, privilege, and power persist? The answer was that people would probably remain competitive in any social order, but in a socialist society, success would lie more in achievements in the social realm.

The professions, "our contemporary aristocrats," would become the model; "the teacher, the doctor, the writer, the technician, and the public servant are the forerunners" of the new possibilities for the good life. In an economy of abundance, there would be leisure to pursue adult education, now a painful process in the jaded hours after work for the few who attempt it. Government might be reborn, much like the Greeks comprehended it. Opportunities for enjoying the movies, sporting events, and family outings in the countryside would be plentiful. The damnable practice of charity would end, and the gospel of hard work and thrift would gradually disappear as people began to see leisure as a way to develop their creative forces.

Throughout, while insisting on the primacy of the life of mind and spirit, Havelock took the materialist view that the patterns and values of a society would be shaped by the technologies of production and their related structures of ownership and dependency. To talk of the abundant life and denounce the evils of the present order would otherwise be futile. He was, therefore, under no illusion that *Towards the Christian Revolution* would not be read by some who would see their way of life under attack. To them, the message was not utopian but stern. Social and economic trends in North America were duplicating the class-ridden European pattern. Amid widespread poverty and unemployment, faced with the growing protest of the masses and feeling their own security threatened, the middle class could well decide to suppress this protest. That would be the end of democracy, for it was democracy that guaranteed the right to protest. Some of the European middle classes had already taken the fatal road to dictatorship and drawn the multitude after them. In North America it could be different. Here in a greater proportion of the middle class, "there still glowed the embers of a Christianity not yet dead."

And so a sombre Havelock concluded:

We are all hopelessly divided between the capitalist ethic of acquisition ... and the Christian ethic of the Garden. But most of us have at some time caught a little inspiration from Christ even when we are unwilling to acknowledge it. There is now precipitated in our minds a death struggle between the old ethic and the new ... [Of the] three times the Gospels record that Jesus wept ... twice the tears [were] shed over his city of Jerusalem. How significant it is that his bitterest sorrow should have been inspired by the spectacle of a whole society ... over whose destiny he yearned. Whether we, nineteen hundred years later, shall better recognize where lies our peace is yet uncertain. Our children's children may arrive one day at the socialist state only through an avenue of strife and destruction. Or we may learn in time, nor give him cause to weep again over us.[68]

The FCSO, 1936 to 1944

In the years subsequent to the publication of *Towards the Christian Revolution*, the FCSO would continue to maintain informal links with a number of networks. Many of its members had come out of the Student Christian Movement and still had contact with it. Membership also overlapped to some degree with the cooperative and labour movements and the overworked social service professions. These included the founders of the Canadian Broadcasting Corporation and, in particular, producers of such influential pioneering public affairs programs as Citizens' Forum and Farm Radio Forum. It also spun off from its ranks such later groups as Harold Toye's Religion Labour Foundation. King Gordon as travelling secretary kept local FCSO and LSR units and associated individuals and groups in touch with each other. As literature convenor, Stanley Allen, from his base at Sir George Williams University, regularly toured Central and Eastern Canada, setting up book displays for any conference or group that would have him. Both men established close ties with progressive Catholic priests like Jimmy Tompkins and Moses Coady at St Francis Xavier University's adult education department and founders of the Maritime Credit Union movement and Fishermen's Co-ops. Various members also ran for public office under the CCF banner.

The coming of the war brought complications to an organization that, by 1939, was beginning to feel the need for renewal. The FCSO's members had divided views on pacifism, and the growing threat of war saw some division of energies with the pacifist Fellowship of Reconciliation. The war itself, however, did not blunt the central message. Vlastos and his colleagues had long been arguing that "we live in a world that breeds war." In a new publication entitled *Christian Social Action*, undertaken by the FCSO as the war broke, Vlastos declared the war "a judgement of God visited upon us for our sin."

In their social and economic structures, all Western nations had denied "the way of life, of community, of love, [and] the way of destruction, of isolation, of fear" was the result. But, Vlastos insisted, if love is more than sentiment, if it is real, it is possible to see God in times of death and destruction as well as in life and progress: "The lights may have gone out in Europe, but God has not." During the war years, the FCSO continued to struggle with internal divisions, now between communist sympathizers and those on the democratic socialist left. It met its demise in 1944–45.[69]

Reflections and Analysis

There are several lines of reflection that arise out of this review of the FCSO and their mid-thirties manifesto. The first, briefly, is the analytical depth, expository clarity, intellectual boldness, even literary elegance, of the leaders and authors involved. The second is their profound conviction that religion, and Christianity in particular, was not a separate stream of "salvation history" but an integral part and parcel of the gritty life and multifarious history of human beings. To be otherworldly was not an option for Christianity, either in its institutional expressions or its teaching, unless by that was meant a world conceived, restructured, and lived on radically different premises. Out of that observation arise two others.

First, it needs to be noted that in several ways the Radical Christianity of the Great Depression, despite its protestations, was at one with the prior social gospel in taking its place in the larger story of social Christianity in the Western world in the course of the nineteenth century. Some elements of language and Biblical reference remained the same – a preference for

historical rather than speculative reason, the concept of covenanted community, monotheism, the Jewish prophets, the Kingdom of God, the
teaching of Jesus, the centrality of the cross – however differently they
might be nuanced. Gone, however, was the moralism that had hung
around the earlier movement. Gone, too, was the philosophical idealism
that clothed a social service mystique and would continue to dominate
most of the social activism of middle-class liberal Protestants and the
social welfarism of the next decades. Both movements showed the same
evidence of immersion in the North Atlantic world of intellectual reflection, politics, culture, and religion. As I have cautioned elsewhere, the idea
of progress in late nineteenth and early twentieth century Canada was not
the simple concoction of linear inevitability and inherent meaning
alleged by its later critics.[70] Nevertheless, the Radical Christianity of the
Great Depression effectively challenged the Christian legitimacy of any
form of progressivism. The progressivism associated with an advancing
capitalism was hardly adaptable to a time of global economic crisis that
had apocalyptic overtones. The language of crisis that the 1930s engendered was, of course, consonant with historical Biblical and evangelical
thought. The language of crisis had also figured in social gospel rhetoric
– witness Walter Rauschenbusch in the United States and Salem Bland in
Canada – but the FCSO leadership felt that the social gospel generally had
underplayed its own radical implications. In re-emphasizing this they preserved important links with those evangelicals who would later embrace
social justice concerns, a point that has generally gone unnoticed.

What principally marked the FCSO, however, was its readiness to blend
the new realism of the twentieth century with core elements of the Judeo-
Christian perspective on the human condition. Mediating that process had
been seminal figures: R.H. Tawney, whose book, *The Acquisitive Society*, lent
that phrase to the FCSO's characterization of capitalism; Reinhold Niebuhr,
whose *Moral Man and Immoral Society* fashioned a new Christian realism
that decisively put idealism and progressivism behind it; John Macmurray,
who, with Karl Polanyi in Britain, had recently published *Christianity and
the Social Revolution*, which broached the concept of a "New Materialism"
and a "materialist Christianity"; and Alfred North Whitehead, whose philosophy, recently elaborated in *Process and Reality* (1929), cast the new realism in strikingly novel terms blending new science and religious reflection. John Line, in particular, was impressed by Whitehead's Process
Theology, whose "Principle of Concretion" suggested that every existing
entity contained the whole of existence. This was the immanence of God
within both the individuality and the totality of things; and the power that

animated and motivated all things, of necessity being separate from that which it motivated, represented the transcendence of God.

The major, though not the only, deposit of these influences within the FCSO leadership was Marx's down-to-earth historical materialism and dialectical method, a development that opened the possibility of a belated conversation and variegated engagement with Marx that had begun in Canada with workers in labour political formations and self-taught left intellectuals in the years before and during the war of 1914–18. Under Marx's inspiration, "matter in motion" in the 1930s became at once a tool of historical analysis and a vehicle of spirit for the FCSO, shedding new light on central Christian teachings about incarnation, the workings of God in nature and history, atonement, personal and social morality, the place of humans within and over nature, and the relationship of Christianity and modern science. Marx, however, did not go unqualified. Macmurray's "New Materialism" questioned the primacy of hunger over love in human motivation, did not deny ideals but sought the material conditions under which they might best be realized, and critiqued Marx for cutting short the dialectical process. Whitehead dubbed the old view of matter as a case of "misplaced concretion" in a world in constant flux. Both he and Macmurray gave a great deal of thought to the nature of personality in such a world, viewing it not so much as a character one possessed as a shared spirituality reflecting the constant flow of overlapping "events" experienced in the course of life and labour in community.[71] Such notions lent sophistication to FCSO reflection on the nature of class and the compact nature of persons in society, again a key Biblical concept.

In so positioning itself, the FCSO moved into a much more substantial and radical theological territory than that occupied by the mainline of Canadian Protestant theology and the social gospel in Canada.

As such, *Towards the Christian Revolution* was a significant defining point in Canadian intellectual history, and the FCSO leadership evidence of a new generation of Canadian Christian intellectuals.

It has been observed that the paramount issue facing Canadian Protestant theology and social thought in the 1920s and 1930s was the relativism of the new social sciences that undermined the reliance of the Canadian evangelical tradition on the fixed universe of Baconian science, resting, as it did, on the certainties of direct recorded observation and the conclusions drawn therefrom.[72] The FCSO leadership, among whom was the immediate past moderator of the United Church, Richard Roberts, represented a new generation of Christian intellectuals who, accepting that they and all Christians – indeed all people – lived in a world of relative knowledge and values, frankly and confidently believed they could "master the perplexing, but ultimately creative, tensions between transcendence and immanence [of God], evangelicalism and evolution, Christian and modern thought."[73] In that respect dialectical reasoning, with its concept of the interpenetration of opposites, was an invaluable asset. They were at home in a relativistic world. Their ethic of mutuality, a relativistic concept itself, contained a rigorous moral orientation freed of the moralistic dogmatism to which the earlier evangelicals were prone. And their politics recognized the relativity of motive and action to economic status and social class. Amid all the relativities, however, they continued to sound the ancient clarion call, "Choose this day whom you will serve." Radical empiricists might object that there was no ground on which to chart a pathway through the wilderness of the relativist dilemma. But life had never been possible suspended on the horns of a dilemma. Only in decision could one resolve the ambiguities of a world of relative values. In the absence of absolute knowledge, decision was risky, but not to choose, in daily life, in politics, as in anything else, was in fact to side with the prevailing power.

Radical and contemporary as they were, the reflections of the FCSO leadership exhibited a remarkable catholicity that reminds one of the accommodating temper Michael Gauvreau claims to have found among an earlier generation of evangelical theologians in Canada (see "Backgrounder" above).

If there is still a disposition on the part of some to regard the Radical Christianity of the FCSO as an isolated subset of intellectual high culture, Christo Aivalis' impressive article, "In Service of the Lowly Nazarene Carpenter: The English Canadian Press and the Case for Radical Christianity, 1926–1939"(2014), should serve as a ready antidote. Aivalis documents no fewer than 195 articles in four mainline labour journals between 1926 and 1939 that echoed the FCSO's materialist Christianity in pursuing their labour's quest to be free of capitalist bondage. As one such article put it: "A theology which teaches that God is Mammon's silent partner would necessarily be suspect in an age of folk upheaval … Property needs not God to protect it. It is the people who need a divine protector. Jesus announced 'Good News'[: N]amely that Heaven is passionately on the side of the people against the despotic tendencies of property; and under that leadership a messianic passion for men is announcing itself."[74]

Aivalis bears out for organized labour what I argued in *The Social Passion* and more explicitly in "The Social Gospel as the Religion of the Agrarian Revolt" (above) that such apparently secular social and political movements may not be fully understood in their inception, course, culmination, and crisis unless they are viewed as religious phenomena seeking to embed ultimate human goals in the social, economic, and political order. This should not be surprising, given the ubiquitous presence of spirit, and hence of spiritual yearnings among human beings. To make such a claim in no way contradicts Christian materialism as the FCSO understood it; nor does it deny explanations on other grounds in terms of the play of social, economic, or political interest; only that the disciplined employment of religious categories can be equally appropriate in their own right as explanatory tools.

The collaborative relationship of the LSR and the FCSO is a case in point, if somewhat different in its elements. Michiel Horn, in his excellent study of the LSR (1980), noted the striking disinterest of Canadian scholarship in the FCSO and the important role its leadership played in the founding and work of the LSR both before and after the FCSO was itself founded.[75] The overwhelming interest of Canadian historiography, sociology, and political science in the LSR's pioneering work in producing *Social Planning for Canada* has mistakenly left the impression that this was yet another purely secular – even secularist – event in the progress of Canadian positivism.

The close association of the two bodies was not all at the leadership level, nor confined to the initial formal activities of the LSR and the publication of *Social Planning*. Horn cites local LSR and FCSO groups meeting together. Forsey and Gordon participated hand in glove with others of the LSR as an alleged brains trust assisting hands-on in the drafting of the CCF's Regina Manifesto in 1933. When the CCF Members of Parliament and the LSR met in 1936 in the wake of the violent RCMP suppression of the On-to-Ottawa-Trek of the unemployed in Regina to confer on and scout solutions for the massive unemployment that still plagued the country, Forsey, Gordon, and Scott were among the LSR executive invited to attend. As it turned out, three of the seven-member CCF caucus were associated with the FCSO: Coldwell, Douglas, and Woodsworth.[76] And in 1944 it would be Douglas who, as premier of Canada's first democratic socialist government in Saskatchewan, would set about instituting the LSR's principles of social planning, creating in the process what became recognized as the finest public service Canada had known.

The striking implication of these particulars is that the LSR and *Social Planning* were as much religiously as secularly motivated. This is not to say that *Social Planning* was a religious tract in disguise, but that *Social Planning* and *Towards the Christian Revolution* need to be read together for either of them to be fully understood and appreciated. Both must be read against their socio-economic and their religious background to understand their full significance for Canadian social, political, intellectual, and religious culture. It is gratifying that the recent works of Milligan, Janzen, and Fleming give full recognition of that, and in the words of the latter and latest, view *Social Planning for Canada* and *Towards the Christian Revolution* as among "the pivotal and controversial books of the time."[77]

The words that Forsey penned at the opening of this essay were typical of the crisp, biting prose Canadians came to expect from him. In time these particular lines occasioned some grief for him when the Canadian Labour Congress, for which he had become director of research, became locked in battle with communist-led unions like the Mine, Mill, and Smelter Workers. His uneasiness may be the principal reason why the reprinting of *Towards the Christian Revolution* was so long delayed. But it is important to understand what Forsey meant, what his statement signified in the onward march of Christian social and political reflection in Canada, and what it implied for Christian political action.

Others among his fellow authors and the FCSO membership, whether or not they used Forsey's precise language, would have insisted on the main point. It was not enough to take up good causes in a spirit of goodwill in a generalized hope or belief that the good would triumph. The liberal progressive Christian view that currents of divine altruism would link up such efforts in the upward march of improvement toward a Christian moral order may have served middle Canada in an age of economic expansion. It served also to conceal the deep rifts in Canadian society, the scandalous contrasts in reward for economic effort, and the extent to which countless numbers were *systematically* rendered powerless. Not to understand the mechanisms by which inordinate power and wealth were won, consolidated, and expanded was to be ineffectual in efforts to realize a more Christian social order. Not to be aware of divergent class interests, of the conflict built into the organization of work, was to have no rational or consistent strategy of social action. To respond to the needs of the poor and the marginalized, and not to stand with the movements that struggle to change the very structures that made and kept them poor, was to indulge in religious sentiment perhaps, but it was neither prophetic religion nor the religion of Jesus.

To think that one could work significant change while keeping politics at arm's length was likewise a sentimental delusion. The time for making choices was at hand (as always); there were no cheap solutions; there was no escaping the cross of political alliances and political struggle.

The Fellowship for a Christian Social Order clearly marked a turning point in the rationalizing of Christian social and political thought and action in English Canada. The persistent incompatibility of religious vision and the secular structures of entitlement in Canada found a classic response in the materialist Christianity of *Towards the Christian Revolution*, and, by association, in *Social Planning for Canada* as well.

CHAPTER FIFTEEN

"The End of History"
— And Hope in a Time of Cold War and After

BACKGROUNDER

As indicated in the backgrounder for chapter 14, I gave the Queen's University Chancellor's Lectures in 1991. This chapter is a slightly revised version of the third of those lectures. The previous two lectures had dealt with issues that were a matter of history. In this third lecture I addressed issues that were very contemporary: the world of the late 1940s into the 1990s, climaxing in the dramatic collapse of Soviet power and the end of the Cold War. The story thus became more personal and subjective. Those times were stressful times dominated by a tenuous superpower nuclear standoff of apocalyptic proportions, appropriately dubbed MAD *(mutually assured destruction). Whatever hope there was, political or religious, was the hope of my own generation, not anyone else's. In that respect, what follows may be seen as memoir, but it also serves to expand the history of the social Christian movement in Canada as it moved into the post-war world and perhaps to illustrate its influence on the politics of a new era in our country – at least in the short term.*

As noted below, it was Francis Fukuyama's The End of History and the Last Man, *first published in 1989 as the Cold War was ending, that prompted the train of thought opening the lecture and the reflections that followed. The book was widely read and its striking thesis the subject of extended commentary, both pro and con. To be fair to Fukuyama, it is important to note that, within a decade, disillusioned by the experience of the two Bush presidencies in the United States, he would dramatically change course and confess how wrong he was. In various works, notably in* America at the Crossroads: Democracy, Power, and the Neoconservative Legacy *(2006), Fukuyama conceded that the future was open after all and fundamental socio-political debate necessary – to which he would go on to make a notable contribution, arguing, among other things, that a strong state was the best guarantee of democratic freedoms.*

THE END OF HISTORY*

The End of History?

When the Berlin wall came down, with the Eastern European regimes collapsing before popular revolt, and the Soviet empire disintegrating, an
official in the American State Department, Francis Fukuyama, wrote a
much-reprinted and widely discussed book proclaiming the end of history. This was not premillennial apocalyptic. His argument in *The End of
History and the Last Man* (1989) was that, now that liberal democracy and
the free market had triumphed in the world struggle with Soviet communism, the dialectic of world history had come to an end. There were no
ideological competitors left in the field; in principle all problems were
solved, with those outstanding requiring only the practical application of
an appropriate technology. The long debate about the nature of the good
society was over. Life from here on might be less interesting and less
adventurous, but it would also be less risky, individually and collectively.
This might not be the New Jerusalem, but at least we could "cease from
mental strife" and "let our swords sleep in our hands." In its modern version, the notion that history would culminate in an end time has been a
prominent feature of various lines of thought deriving from Friedrich
Hegel and Karl Marx. Liberated from ideological controversy (Hegel) or
class struggle (Marx), humanity could get on with the full free development of the human spirit.

Talk of the end of history has to make us nervous in the postmodern
world. In the Hegelian/Marxist universe, the end time held great promise of
universalization – that is, until one concretizes it in a real historical context.
Hitler's Nazis talked of an end of history and the thousand-year reign of the
Third Reich that would begin with the triumph of Germany, as the vanguard of the Aryan race, over its enemies – communists, the Jews, the dis-
abled and mental defectives, Jehovah's Witnesses, the liberal democracies,
and dissidents in general. The bold Russian experiment in creating a classless socialist society "in one country" fell victim to a Stalinist regime of
secret police, purges, and gulags. Both created the insidious category of "enemies of the state" that justified a holocaust of millions. We also heard from
those standing in the wings of Ronald Reagan's America who were pre-

---

*   Lecture three of the Chancellor's Lectures, delivered at the celebration of the
     100th anniversary of the Chancellor's Lectures at Queen's University, 1991.

pared to welcome a nuclear holocaust as the Biblical battle of Armageddon that would bring historical time to an end, separating God's righteous ones from the unrighteous ones, and inaugurating the millennial reign of Christ.

All these had hope, very political hope; who can deny it? And their hope was linked to a linear view of time and an unfolding historical process that would reach some fulfillment. But what horrors and terrors were they prepared to contemplate – and perpetrate – to reach their promised land!

Beside all that, Fukuyama seems positively benign. So benign, indeed, that we appear almost to have passed beyond the need even of hope itself. Until we probe beneath the surface.

Fukuyama takes us back to the start of our lectures. Like Tory providentialism he seems to talk of a stationary world, where, at least in principle, everything is once more in its proper place and relation. But in its proper place and relation relative to what? For Tory providentialists, the static conceptions of the great chain of being sanctified the dominance of a privileged aristocracy. Fukuyama's "end of history" sanctifies the dominance of a powerful, super-wealthy oligarchy growing richer by the minute, with its foundations in the privacy of capital and primacy of the "free" market. Liberal democratic institutions hover loosely around and above all that, compromised, however, by interventionism abroad (Chile, Nicaragua, and anti-colonial insurgencies) and the forces of an industrial military complex at home.

In another respect, however, Fukuyama represents the extension, even the fulfillment, of the idea of progress. Gone, however, is any hint of religious foundations. Only the gods of the market survive. Progress, whatever other freight it carried, as Christopher Lasch reminds us in his book, *The True and Only Heaven*, was at bottom a matter of technological innovation driving a constant expansion of goods and services.

Let me make it clear that I do not deny the remarkable accomplishments of the Western so-called free-market economies in their ability to mobilize and deploy an amazing array of goods and services for the larger part of their populations. And I am under no illusions that government can run business better, though there is little evidence that it would do worse. Like François Mitterand, the current president of France, and a number of recent British authors, not to mention our premier, Bob Rae, I consider myself a market and pluralist socialist. But that the end of the Communist challenge precludes any challenge to traditional free-market ideology, I would strongly contest.

Indeed, there is a huge irony in Fukuyama's claim, idolizing as it does the ultimacy of free-market consumerism as a democratic indicator of the general will. Wasn't the Cold War, Americans – and the rest of us – were told, a contest between American "In God We Trust" democracy and a godless materialistic Communist totalitarianism?

What rules Fukuyama's claim out of court, however, is that the free market does not now, and will not in future, meet the needs of the vast majority of the world's peoples. Given the environmental impact of the current scale of international energy and resource exploitation by the "developed world" for its own uses, it is impossible to imagine the rest of the world being able to access the level of American, European, or Japanese consumption without wholesale ecological collapse. Not only would the biosphere not permit that scale of consumption, but capitalism has not shown any capacity to instigate the restraint in consumption that might bring demand into harmony with ecological principles.

Both at the production and consumption ends of the free market, growth is the operative word. Business people tell you frankly that they cannot manage reduced or steady-state operations on an ongoing basis.

The triumph of the free market on those terms, then, can only be coincidental with the assumption of American or G7 pre-eminence. Since their level of consumption cannot be universalized for the world's peoples, the language of the "triumph of the liberal democracy and free market capitalism" and the "end of history" can only serve its present beneficiaries. If the equitable distribution of goods and services in a world of finite resources were to require, as it will, the allocation of resources, regulation of production, prioritization of services, etc., then the market could no longer properly be described as free and some other overriding value must prevail! To draw such a conclusion, however, is to deny that there is anything but the most momentary triumph of capitalism or anything qualitatively changed about the course of world history. The conditions congenial to competing interests and ideologies as to what constitutes the good life remain – and *require* that we renew that debate with unprecedented vigour.

The best evidence, closer to home, that the debate may not be over is the repeated astonishment and crude claim by *Wall Street Journal* editors and journalists that despite the collapse of Soviet communism there has been a recrudescence of the same phenomenon with the election of a New Democratic Party (NDP) government in Ontario! Imagine the apoplexy as that was then followed by NDP victories in Saskatchewan and British Columbia! The simple mindedness of the civil religion of an otherwise great nation is in my view one of the greatest obstacles to hope in the world today. But the reaction to those electoral victories is one small sign that Mr Fukuyama is wrong. History has not come to an end even if George Bush is in some sense president of the world.

A Stranded and Bracketed Hope

For those of us who came to maturity in the immediate post-war years of the latter 1940s, hope was at first writ large. Victory in war fuelled high expectations. Soldiers returned to found families; suburbs expanded; the economy boomed. Veterans flocked to universities where political clubs, United Nations clubs, civil liberties clubs, and religious clubs thrived as never since. Some of us went off to help in rebuilding the new post-war Europe. We sang, "As sure as the sun greets the morning / And rivers run down to the sea / A new world for mankind is dawning / Our children shall live proud and free."

But who could forget the recent past? We recalled the pre-war struggles to halt the fascist tide sweeping Europe and sang the songs of the Spanish Civil War. We remembered the horrors of the holocaust, the concentration camps, and the forced labour:

Far and wide as the eye can wander
Heath and bog are everywhere;
Not a bird sings out to cheer us,
Oaks are standing gaunt and bare.
We are the peat bog soldiers,
We're marching with our spades to the bog.
Up and down the guards are pacing,
No one, no one can go through:
Flight would mean a sure death facing,
Guns and barbed wire greet our view.

On one side our hope was bracketed by horrors unspeakable but about which one had to speak. Too soon our hope was bracketed on the other side by the outbreak of Cold War hostilities and the daily escalation of the nuclear threat. Winston Churchill gave his famous 1946 "Iron Curtain" speech at Fulton, Missouri, and the preoccupying enmity of the pre-war years between Russia and the West returned to take over our lives. Historians are still debating who started the Cold War. I recall meetings of international student organizations where we desperately tried to maintain the early post-war unity of young people worldwide. We failed – and it was never clear whose leading strings unravelled the cloth – the Comintern or the US State Department. Both were no doubt complicit.

It was a difficult time to keep hope alive. For some of us, protest became almost a way of life, a way of projecting our hope mixed with foreboding onto the surrounding universe. As we married and had families we schooled our children in the arts and crafts of protest as well. Only late in our lives did we get confirmation from studies of children's reactions to talk about nuclear annihilation that our instincts were right. One little boy, queried about all that, said, "It's alright; my Dad is working on it." Our children viewed their futures more positively than others because we were doing something about it. And in fact we were moved by some distant hope, or else why would we have voiced any protest at all?

In some respects, the nuclear protests and the disarmament campaigns were the least of our challenges. The threat was clear and direct, the object defined, and the action precise. But how did one understand this crazy post-war world where wars kept occurring, famine continued to ravage, and third-world development encountered obstacle after obstacle? For what kind of human future could one hope and how could one bring it to pass? What were the resources we could depend on in the traditions on which we had been brought up? In particular, was the religion of our youth relevant to such a time? What, finally was the grounding of whatever hope sustained us?

Religious Quest and Political Hope

The forum in which I worked out my own early approaches to those questions was the Student Christian Movement of Canada, the SCM. In its heyday, no student organization on Canadian university campuses did more to stretch the minds of students than the SCM. It was sometimes considered to be a university within the university. Always there were study groups on the nature of the university, ways of knowing, the records of the life and teaching of Jesus and the Prophets, Christianity and economic values, faith and politics, Christianity and science, and, of course, love, sex, and marriage. The SCM, conceiving of itself as an arena where faith and reason met, held agnostics weekends and welcomed all those earnestly enquiring into "the meaning of it all" and searching for a foundational faith for their lives. And there were regional and national conferences with stimulating and often provocative speakers at the leading edge of their fields, like George Grant.

Always there were books tempting us beyond the boundaries of our formal studies: Arthur Koestler, *Darkness at Noon*; C.S. Lewis, *The Problem of Evil*; Denis de Rougemont, *Love in the Western World*; Herbert Read on modern art; Edmund Carpenter on Eskimo sculpture; J.W.N. Sullivan, *Beethoven, A Spiritual Biography*; Marshall McLuhan, *The Mechanical Bride*; Karl Heim, *The Transformation of the Scientific World View*; Norbet Weiner, *The Human Use of Human Beings*; Ortega y Gassett, *The Revolt of the Masses*; Edmund Wilson, *To the Finland Station*; Paul Tillich, *Love, Power, and Justice* and *The Shaking of the Foundations*; Oscar Cullman, *Christ and Time*; Albert Camus, *The Rebel*; Jean-Paul Sartre, *No Exit*; George Orwell, *Animal Farm* and *1984*. Of the reading of books there was no end! Much of it was stimulated by Bob Miller, study secretary of the SCM of Canada, who carted wide-ranging book displays around the country's university campuses and would go on to found in Toronto what was probably the best intellectual bookstore in its time in Canada.

We spent whole summers working and studying social and ethical issues with other students in agriculture, mental hospitals, and industrial work camps. The Student-in-Industry work camps I attended were the most radical of these, with leaders like Lex Miller, author of *The Christian Significance of Karl Marx*, and Bob Miller, fresh from advanced theological studies and early ventures in social and spiritual renewal in post-war Europe. We came from well-ordered middle-class homes where life was reasonably secure, but the burden of the twentieth century was on our shoulders. We read Helmut Gollwitzer's *Unwilling Journey*, an account of his being conscripted into the German army and imprisonment as a prisoner of war in the Soviet Union and his growing disenchantment with Marxism. We read Maisie Ward's *France Pagan* and followed the growth of the French Priest-Worker movement with a fascination and admiration that led some of us, most notably Dan Heap, into extended periods of industrial work. I recall clearly my devastation on learning that the French Catholic hierarchy, concerned that the priests were in turn being radicalized by their experience, repudiated that heroic attempt to renew the religious instincts of the French working class.

Somehow the historic conflict between capital and labour had to be overcome. We read Joseph Fletcher on property and re-examined Biblical views of property relations implied in such concepts as the year of Jubilee when all property was to be redistributed. Max Weber and R.H. Tawney schooled us on the intimate links between the Protestant ethic and the spirit of capitalism. We concluded that the solidarity inherent in the labour movement, imperfect as it was, was a better and more Biblical ethic with which to approach industrial renewal than the ideology of the North American business class.

Such conclusions were not simply couched in Marxist terms, however. For one thing, none of Fletcher, Weber, or Tawney were Marxist. Anglicans in the McGill unit of the SCM had introduced some of us to Hastings Smythe's Society of the Catholic Commonwealth, which taught us to see in the elements of the bread and wine of the Mass/Communion the labour and struggle of working people whose lives, too, were being given for us, often in a daily crucifixion of body and spirit in their workplaces. For others of us for whom such notions were too exotic, there was George Macleod of Iona whose Scottish Presbyterian linkage of work and worship in *Only One Way Left* put a simple question, "How could we offer up in worship to a god of love and justice the products of an economy where some organized the labour of many for private ends?"

Clearly there was a carry-over in the post-war SCM from the pre-war years. There was evidence of the intimate association with the Fellowship for a Christian Social Order. It showed also in the continuation in some places of the Sharman studies of the records of the life of Jesus, which had been so popular during the generation between the two world wars. A preference for the religion of Jesus in the Gospels as against a Pauline religion about Jesus was still strong, but there was also a growing recognition that the quest for the historical Jesus was no simple matter. Albert Schweitzer stood as a towering witness to that. The dilemmas of the quest could only be overcome in the decision to follow – as Schweitzer did at Lambaréné in Africa – only then would one know truly who Jesus was. Both Sharman and Schweitzer, however, reinforced our restiveness within our own church traditions.

The post-war successes of the World Council of Churches gave hope that the denominational captivity of the Christian spirit would be overcome and that the Western domination of the church would fade away. The SCM reversed the flow of Christian missions and brought young leaders of third-world churches like K.H. Ting from China, "V.J." from India, and Arturo Chacone from Chile to live and work among us. Church union projects at home and abroad, like the Church of South India, aroused great interest, but the true excitement was the potential liberation of the Christian spirit to engage the issues of the modern world. Inevitably we were pressed beyond Christian ecumenism to comparative religion and were unwittingly being prepared for the Canadian diversity of faiths that lay just ahead in the future. In the course of it all we developed an enormous respect for the pluralism of our planet.

It was clear we were at the end of an age, but what was around us did not feel like the dawn of another. Paul Tillich had no difficulty persuading us that we stood at the end of the Protestant era. But it was the return of Bob Miller from the Ecumential Institute in Basel, Switzerland, and work with the Evangelical Academies in Germany that confronted us with the hard reality of our time as manifested in contemporary European art, literature, philosophy, and theology.

The crisis of depression, war, nuclear confrontation, and industrial society took on new proportions as part of the larger crisis of civilization in the West. The distortions of modern art, the language of the absurd in literature, the abandonment of idealism, and the rejection of the notion of the divine as in any sense the extension of the human in philosophy and theology, even the separation of religion as a human work from the wholly otherness of God all bore in on us. In what, indeed, could one hope? Gone finally were all the vestiges that lingered from our liberal progressive past. Had even the radical Christianity of our immediate depression forebears been too sanguine in its hopes? Where could one begin to build again?

Deitrich Bonhoeffer in his *Letters and Papers from Prison* observed how we had reached a time of radical irreligion, where people were no longer afraid of death. If God was not the hope that beckoned where our human powers left off, could God be found again in the very midst of life itself? Not, to be sure, in the "divine immanence" of liberal progressivism, and not in what Bonhoeffer described as the "positivism of Karl Barth's dogma of wholly otherness," but within the drama of lives lived out, others and one's own, personally and collectively where discipleship could be costly.

Then Bishop Robinson wrote *Honest to God*, and the death of God movement was upon us. Tillich sensibly argued that, in reality, God was whatever constituted our ultimate concern or concerns. But all ultimate concerns were not of equal weight, as Tillich well knew. Did Martin Buber's *I and Thou* offer the key to the awareness of a God, not hidden in the believer's conscience, not a prisoner of the church, nor the *deus ex machina* who rescues us at our extremity, but the inexplicable mystery that visits us in moments of awe, of interpersonal communion, in the compassion of vicarious suffering, moments so qualitatively different that they ring with authenticity, with an all-inclusive exclusiveness that reorients all our temporal values? But if this was a, or the, key, what did it mean for someone like myself brought up in the social gospel belief in a politics of the Kingdom of God conceived as a social order?

Was Buber saying that meaning and hope were confined to a series of solitary epiphanies, momentary revelations of no significance to our larger lives in communities and nations? No, because such experiences were always relational and implied the inherent value of the other and pulsed with the wholeness of a universe. Such experiences instigated an expanding élan of love even as they evoked the conviction that one had discovered one's true self. This, we believed, was the ultimate foundation of any enduring social ethic or politics. It was, of course, possible to build ethical and political systems on other foundations, but to the extent that they ignored the love that we knew we owed each other, they would not satisfy and would not last. Almost instinctively, we knew this was the "pearl of great price" at the heart of Jesus' teaching.

Ellen Flesseman, a Dutch Jewess who saw Christianity as an extension of her Judaism, reinforced by Suzanne de Dietrich's *The Witnessing Community*, taught us to link Buber's I-Thou to the binding covenant of the Jewish people with the God solely known as "I am," to the visions of the prophets of the eighth century BCE, and their insistence that "I am" did not require religious ritual but clean hands, a pure heart, and dealing justly. The covenant was with a people and therefore involved the public sector as well as the private, as we would say, and that carried over into the new covenant, even though the dispersion of the new "witnessing community" within the greatest empire the world had yet seen made the public implications of the I-Thou often seem more implicit than explicit.

But did that mean that a particular social order was implied and that it could be realized in time? We wrestled with Paul Tillich and Oscar Cullman on Greek and Hebraic conceptions of time. For the Greeks, time was a kind of captivity in "natural" cycles from which one had to escape to find one's true end; for the Hebrews time was linear, in which God, respecting the conditions of a good creation and the freedom offered humankind, struggles to keep the ways of justice before an erring humankind as their true destiny. The implications of each held vastly different meanings for personality as for politics. The Greeks partitioned the person into body and soul, with only the soul destined to immortality outside of time. The Hebrews dealt holistically, symbolically destining the entire person to resurrection at the end of time. The Greeks practised a practical politics subject to fate and fortune, while the Hebrews expected an earthly Messianic rule and Christians prayed for the Kingdom of God to come on earth. If time began in a garden, it would end in a city, the "new Jerusalem."

The question of just what to expect at the end of time, however, has been a matter of great confusion for us Christians. We've had our premillenialists and our post-millenialists. C.H. Dodd talked of a "realized eschatology," i.e., that the kingdom had already come in Jesus Christ and we now lived in the context of that reality. Reinhold Niebuhr, one of my predecessors in these lectures, caught between the polarities of moral individuals and immoral society, counselled that the struggle for the Kingdom of God had to be undertaken afresh in every generation. Rudolf Bultmann proposed an existential eschatology that imported the end of time, demythologized, into the present experience of the believer. And Donald Meyer, in high Niebuhrian style, addressed the difficulties confronting the politics of hope. Neither the pure end nor the pure means were proper to politics, which dealt with the limitations and dilemmas inherent in the actual choices available in the processes of history. These were all important issues to deal with but it was easy to forget that the point of it all was not whether politics could somehow evoke and institutionalize unending love or perfect justice. The only question at the "final judgment" is, "Have you cared for the poor?" And the answer was equally the answer to that other question, "Have you cared about God?"

So where at the end of the day, in our search for grounds for hope, did we find ourselves: The transcendent experiences we all knew were, à la Buber, profoundly relational; the covenant of God is with a community and is part of a strategy for the restoration of humankind to their true nature, the sign and seal of which is living humbly and dealing justly. Although the freedom God accords does not *guarantee* perfect fulfillment in time, *the conception and the hope are in terms of fulfillment in time* and not outside of time. And the political question about arrangements made to end the inequity – and the iniquity – of poverty and the religious question about faithfulness to God turn out to be one and the same. Social order and economic structure stand under the judgement of Buber's "I-Thou."

These are all propositions of enormous political consequence. Clearly they repudiate Fukuyama's view of the end of history, if for no other reason than that the bastion of capitalism whose triumph he celebrates houses a higher proportion of children in deep poverty than any other industrial country. Those who have dipped into Kevin Phillips' *The Politics of Rich and Poor ... in the Reagan Aftermath* will readily see how the triumph of free-market forces in the United States itself has promoted the transfer of wealth from the poor and the working middle classes in the United States to the rich. (In case you do not know, Mr Phillips was the chief political analyst for the Republican presidential campaign and wrote the political bible of the Nixon era.) Is this the "end of history" the world should covet? At the very least it is inconsistent with the political and economic hope of "disinherited" peoples and with Judeo-Christian expectations. When Kevin Phillips predicts that the social and economic consequences of the Reagan era will provoke an era of political transformation in the United States, however, we can only say, "The world is waiting for that sunrise!" The real debate about the future of the world, unencumbered by a Cold War, is about to begin. Far from being sidelined at the "end of history," Christians and people of all faiths are called again to mental strife and political action for a just world order. And far from the election of new governments in Ontario, British Columbia, and Saskatchewan being a curious recrudescence of a dying political option, it represents the possibility of a new politics in North America and the hope that this can be brought to the marginalized and oppressed everywhere.

Social Gospel and Social Democracy

It is important at this juncture in our history – and in this lecture – to ask where the new vigour of social democratic politics in Canada has come from. It is partly a matter of political disenchantment, of anger with Ottawa over free trade. In Ontario, it was disillusionment with Liberal inaction after the highly popular performance of the NDP/Liberal Accord. It was bitterness over the constitution and taxes. Elements such as these, however, have more opened the gate than determined what could pass through it. It is relevant to recall that during the free trade debate, the prime minister was forced time and again onto the defensive regarding the potential impact of free trade on social programs. Viewed as a referendum, that election confirmed, in fact, that a majority of voters chose to protect social programs rather than to promote free trade. And recall that amid the neo-conservative years of the '80s, Ontario launched itself into the most progressive social assistance reforms proposed anywhere in North America, in fact, running against the stream of most jurisdictions.

There has been a new political culture developing in Ontario and Canada amid the seemingly paralyzing years of Cold War. Partly it is the long-term result of what we can broadly call social democratic platform-building going back over a century. Partly it is the force of European immigrants who, since the war – but also going back to the early century – have brought more progressive attitudes and social policies from their home countries. But what has gone unnoticed and certainly un-researched and publicly unreported has been the impact of ecumenical church coalitions and the new force of progressive Catholic social thought and action in the development of political attitudes over the past two decades. Significant as this was, it was not all gain.

If there was a date when the radical Christianity of the depression gave way to a new post-war social gospel, it was when the Religion-Labour Foundation was scuttled in the early 1960s to make way for the Interchurch Committee on Industrial Society. A condition of Catholic membership was that management had to be equally involved, and that meant that the Religion-Labour Foundation had to be put aside. The Poverty Conference in Montreal in 1968 furthered the coalition strategy and compensated for that loss by establishing the Coalition on Development. With the dramatic increase in Canadian International Development Agency (CIDA) dollars for non-governmental organizations in the early seventies, coalition activity sprang ahead. On the international front there was the Interchurch Committee on Development and Relief, which sponsored the well-known annual Ten Days for World Development program; the Interchurch Committee on Refugees; the Interchurch Committee on Human Rights in Latin America; the Canada Asia working groups; and Project Ploughshares on peace and disarmament issues. On the domestic front, there was Project North focusing on aboriginal issues and the economic exploration of the North; the Church Council on Justice and Corrections; and the Coalition on Corporate Responsibility. The latter was especially effective in its research, its perseverance in pursuing specific issues within the corporate world, and its public activity around such matters as changes to the Bank Act and the third-world debt crisis. In all, over some twenty years, about forty such instruments of church social action were fielded, some with more effect than others. Taken together, they would seem to raise questions about theories of secularization of Canadian society.

For two decades the coalitions kept justice issues before church congregations and parishes and communities across the country. They and the groups they interacted with sensitized people to the structural problems that lay behind endemic poverty at home and abroad. Many local churches learned how business and international finance were complicit with some Western governments in upholding unsavoury third-world governments and frustrating democratic movements. The coalitions had no specific party affiliation and took on a more refined and targeted style than their counterparts in the 1930s, and their rhetoric was more restrained. That their impact was felt upon all parties cannot be doubted, but overall their activities and arguments were most congenial with the social democratic left, and they did an enormous amount to set the stage for the latest advance of social democratic politics in Canada.

While there was considerable Catholic participation in the foregoing coalitions, there had been over the years increased levels of Catholic social thought and action since the mid-seventies associated with names like William Ryan, Gregory Baum, and Bishop Remi De Roo, whose progressivism furthered social democratic politics in Canada. The early Co-operative Commonwealth Federation (CCF) had come largely out of a Protestant, sometimes secular, and sometimes Jewish background. Although the early CCF leadership quoted Papal encyclicals like *Rerum Novarum* and *Quadragesimo Anno* to good effect, they had little impact on the Catholic community, with the possible exception of Saskatchewan, where a progressive community of German settlers from Wisconsin were tutored by liberal-minded monks at Muenster who published an influential weekly called the *Prairie Messenger*. By the end of the thirties, the Saskatchewan CCF was receiving its share of the Catholic vote. In most of the rest of the country Catholics were simply warned by their bishops about supporting the CCF, but in May 1933, the Quebec bishops formally banned participation, going beyond their British and European counterparts in condemning all forms of socialism and declaring their support of capitalism. Ironically, the CCF stimulated the Jesuit-sponsored École Sociale Populaire to produce a manifesto, "*Pour la restauration de l'ordre sociale*," which had some similarities to the CCF program and became the basis of a new party, Action libérale nationale (ALN). The ALN won twenty-six seats in the 1935 election but was outmanoeuvred by Duplessis in 1936.

This religiously inspired program anticipated many of the initiatives of the Quiet Revolution of the 1960s. Father Moses Coady in the Maritimes in the 1930s promoted a radically co-operative vision of economic life that went beyond anything in Catholic social thought at the time, but despite a quite remarkable social impact, contacts with the Fellowship for a Christian Social Order (FCSO), and the affiliation of some Catholics with the CCF, especially in Cape Breton, his work had no direct impact on party formation in the region. In 1971, however, when Pope Paul VI formally opened the gates to Catholic participation in democratic socialist politics, the Catholic Church in Canada "refined its critique of contemporary capitalism" as Baum puts it and moved significantly to the left.

This shift to the left in the Catholic social action movement in Canada was part and parcel of the ecumenical coalitions described above and a reflection of Canadian Catholic involvement in the third world, especially Central and South America. Many Catholic laity, priests, and bishops readily absorbed the new Liberation Theology of the Latin American Church and the pronouncements of the Canadian Conference of Catholic Bishops became increasingly radical after 1975, culminating in "Ethical Reflections on the Economic Crisis" published at the end of 1982.

This new Catholic social activism penetrated widely and deeply into the population at large. In the latter 1970s I recall the entire Hamilton-Wentworth Catholic school system writing letters to Washington in the wake of Oscar Romero's assassination, demanding the withdrawal of American support for the El Salvadorian government. Pupils were being politicized early; they are voters now. In 1987, the Catholic bishops and the United Church worked with unions, farmers, women, and the poor to produce a call for a people-oriented economy, "A Time to Stand Together, a Time for Solidarity" – shortly after which Pope John Paul II issued his *Encyclical on Social Concerns* assailing liberal capitalism and Marxism alike. The constant cycle of Catholic laity and clergy into Latin America and back, their work with refugees and the poor in urban and rural Canada, their witness on issues of peace and war, constantly reinforced the political force of the democratic left in Canada. And it must also be said that, in the Reagan era, the American Catholic bishops were among the few outspoken opponents of American military strategy, and the churches in general were the principal American critics of Reagan's Latin American policies. There, too, the church was fulfilling its mission as the principal institutional base for an alternative vision of society. Is it too much to hope – and it may be – that in the Republic to the south, religion will inspire the new politics of transformation of which Kevin Phillips spoke, as it did in the civil rights movement of the 1960s under Martin Luther King?

The potent force of Latin American Liberation Theology in Canadian Catholic social thought and action in the 1970s and 1980s gave it an immediate link with the Protestant and political heirs of the Radical Christianity of the Great Depression and the earlier social gospel. I, for one, was at first shocked by the unequivocal vigour with which the term "social gospel" was not just embraced but brandished by the new Catholic activists as a slogan. Like some others, I was too familiar with the weaknesses of classic social gospel progressivism to be altogether comfortable with such contemporary uses of the term. But when American sympathizers, meeting Gustav Guttierez, one of the principal liberation theologians, bemoaned the lack of a liberation theology in America, Guttierez, according to Robert McAffee Brown, pointed immediately with great enthusiasm to the works he had just been reading: *Christianity and the Social Crisis, Christianizing the Social Order, Theology of the Social Gospel,* and

Prayers for the Social Awakening – all by Walter Rauschenbusch, who died in 1917 but, like the radical wing of the social gospel in Canada, was not afraid to speak of class struggle, and socialism as a spiritual quest. In Canadian terms, the best answer would have been the FCSO and the authors of its book, *Towards the Christian Revolution*, who had a similar perspective on the ways in which social structure, class, social and religious values, and access to political power were conditioned by where one sat in the hierarchy of economic life. Perhaps that is because living conditions for many in Canada in the 1930s momentarily resembled those in large parts of Latin America!

The prosperous post-war decades of the fifties and sixties had distanced the Canadian population from the depression years. The compromise between capitalism and Keynesian economics seemed to be working to the advantage of business and public alike. The CCF, and after 1961 the NDP, seemed to dangle on the political vine, a "protest movement becalmed," especially outside Saskatchewan and Manitoba. Economic nationalists failed to halt the Americanization of the economy. The social gospel and the radical Christianity of the 1930s were in a state of suspended animation. Little was to be done but to pen a lament for the nation.

There are many who date their renewed commitment to Canada to George Grant's little book, but it is only part of an expanding story. The trigger, however, which would ultimately give the confluence of new forces on the left an expanded political presence was the American loss of status as a creditor nation as it moved into the 1970s and the ongoing difficulties of the British economy, both of which led to the breakdown of the business/Keynesian accommodation and the subsequent emergence of the neo-conservative agendas, supply-side economics, and the scaling back of social programs, all allied to a new surge of heroic individualism promoted by authors like Ayn Rand. The net result, however, was to call into political battle all those who rejected the reimposition of nineteenth century economic values on late twentieth century post-industrial society.

That, and the appalling decision of the World Bank and the International Monetary Fund to turn the screws on indebted third-world economies they had lured into debt in the first place, provided the context for the emergence of the ecumenical coalitions and Catholic social activism.

With a much broader base of socially conscious electors than the older social gospellers or radical Christians could provide, the horizons of social democratic politics in Canada have dramatically expanded. Everyone will not agree, but I take that as a sign of great hope.

Conclusion

Fukuyama, then, is wrong on a number of counts. Economic conditions and the environmental challenge at home and abroad continue to provide the conditions that have led to challenges to free-market ideology over many decades. The issue of the nature of the good life, the ongoing requirement of a public agenda for our life together, and the persistence of religious and intellectual engagement nurturing political hope all ensure that of challenges to free-market ideology there will be no lack.

As to Fukuyama according a twin triumph to liberal democracy, one can only gasp at the immensity of the illogic. If there is one thing liberal democracy rests upon, it is the legitimacy – even the necessity – of dissent and debate between competing options as to what constitutes the good life. In Fukuyama's world where dissent is no longer seen to be necessary, liberal democracy is implicitly dead and we are back to all intents and purposes to a one-party state like the fascists and communists who had just been defeated!

We must hope that, with the Cold War over, we can truly begin to think freely again. Indeed, we only have hope to the extent that we are free to imagine and to think. One of the great ironies of our situation as Christians is that while statues of Marx are being toppled in Russia and Eastern Europe, the Christian dialogue with a much renovated post-war Marxism has been a very creative force in European and Latin American theology. While it is impossible to embrace the totality of the old Marx, if I can put it that way, Eugene Forsey was right that we ignore his central insights at our peril.

Imagination, the religious quest, political hope, the preferential option for the poor (we are all poor because at any given time we are all beggars before God and only a fraction of our real selves) – all of these are but different forms of the transcendent experiences out of which we live and without which we are not truly human. Politics, too, participates in transcendence, and the struggle to create a qualitatively new order of social and economic relations is perhaps the most demanding burden that hope, imagination, true religion, and conditions of the poor place upon us.

I do not think that means repudiating all the works of capitalism, but capitalism is hardly a viable or sustainable economic model for the future of planet earth. There are around us remarkably structured systems of production and distribution, available services, expertise of all kinds for which we can be thankful. Far from efficiency and profit being incompatible with social justice, quite the reverse is actually the case. The ultimate questions are who profits and efficiency for what ends? An economic system that squanders a vast pool of unused and underused available talent is hardly efficient or optimally profitable. A capitalism that promotes endless economic growth on a finite planet and takes no account in its books of resource depletion is not efficient, moral, or even sane. A politics that demonizes the public sector and privileges the private, when there is no substantiating evidence, only ideology, yet aspires to government, may lay claim to shell game expertise but hardly deserves our respect.

Only if we give up on our imaginative capacity, or shrink from our instinct for compassion, or wall ourselves off from the transcendent in the midst of our lives, need we ever feel bereft of political hope. We can still say with Rosemary Radford Reuther in *The Radical Kingdom*, "Whether or not there will be an actual historical fulfillment of the prophetic vision of the nations coming together in peace, harmony, and equity on "God's holy mountain," it is in the midst of that struggle – and perhaps only fully there – that one can lay hold of this vision as the deepest moral certitude of our lives."[1] Pace Mr Fukuyama, the end of history still beckons from afar and calls us into present action.

CHAPTER SIXTEEN

Max Weber and the "Iron Cage of Capitalism": The Debate Continues, 1960–2016

BACKGROUNDER

What follows is more a combined report/review than an essay. It is a sequel to chapter 3, "The Great Protestant Ethic Debate," covering the years 1904/05 to 1960. Concluding, as that essay did, with Kurt Samuelsson's population study in Religion and Economic Action, *I was impressed, no doubt with Samuelsson, that his study spelled* coup de grace *for both Weber's thesis and hence the controversy. I was wrong on both counts. This further exploration makes it clear, among other things, that Samuelsson made a methodological error on the basis of a common careless reading of Weber's text. Weber carefully confined the period of effective popular impact of his thesis to the late sixteenth and seventeenth centuries. A later survey, after the model of the ascetic neo-Calvinist ethic had spread into surrounding populations, was thus, by definition, invalid. Not only was Samuelsson's methodology faulty[1] but he was among those who grossly misconstrued Weber, charging that Weber taught that Reformed theologians of the period preached "free-for-all capitalism" and, quoting another (Lecerf), taught, "You doubt your election [to salvation]? Enrich yourself and you will be sure of the love of God." He also stands accused of being among those who have redefined Weber's terms and then declare him mistaken.[2]*

One effect of the parade of errors was to prompt a growing public fascination and engagement of contributors across a broad interdisciplinary front. The Weber thesis controversy, in its classic period, running into the early years after the Second World War, had featured a number of alternative propositions regarding the emergence and nature of modern capitalism as though that was the nub of Weber's thesis – which it was not. The debate to date had been dominated by historians of various stripes challenging the empirical foundations of Weber's thesis and theologians questioning Weber's rendition of Calvinist doctrine. The post-war period, however, saw a rapidly expanding interest in Weber's

*proposition as philosophers, psychologists, a growing interest in interdiscipli-
nary studies, and new interpretive postures broadened the range of discussion.
To boot, post-war activity around issues of third-world development naturally
gave a new relevance to theories of economic takeoff in the West. Inevitably,
the question and Weber and his Protestant ethic argument engaged the interest of journalists and entered the realm of public discussion. By the 1980s, the
literature had become so diverse and the arguments so divergent that professors and students in the humanities and social sciences, not to mention the
literate public, were in need of a map to find their way through a minefield
of controversy.*

*This chapter cannot review in detail a further half century of debate. Extend-
ed reviews of four rather different books, however, may go some distance in illuminating the contours and content of a continuing discussion. Gordon Marshall's* In Search of the Spirit of Capitalism *is a carefully argued, thoroughly
documented, brilliant analysis of the issues in debate as of 1982, including a
forthright statement of his own positioning on the big picture issues. William
Swatos, Jr, and Lutz Kaelber in* The Protestant Ethic Turns 100: The Centenary of the Weber Thesis, *published in 2005, offer an unusually rich collection of essays that, while not avoiding controversy, rather explore in some
depth such relevant matters as Weber's family background, his early career, his
responses to critics, his American experience, the "grand narrative" of his historical philosophy, and the relevance of his thesis to political discussion in the
United States. Philip S. Gorski, in a notable study in 2011,* The Protestant
Ethic Revisited, *shifts the "ascetic neo-Calvinist" argument onto the ground of
state formation, not to oppose Weber but to add another, more empirically
demonstrable, argument supporting Weber, namely, that the new, orderly, more
democratic, socially responsive polity fostered in the Calvinist congregations
facilitated methodical capital accumulation and hence added to an already
existing "spirit of capitalism" the intensification that was the ascetic neo-
Calvinist contribution to the uniquely aggressive "spirit of modern capitalism."
Finally, as a conclusion, I review James Livingston's slim book* No More
Work, *where he assails in the same breath the Protestant work ethic of the
Reformation and the promotion of full employment policies in a world of
disappearing work.*

*But see also the discussion in chapter 9 of the Protestant ethic as the spirit of
socialism in the thought of Salem Bland and the later work of Thelma McCormack (1969).*[3]

MAX WEBER AND THE IRON CAGE OF CAPITALISM

1. In Search of the Spirit of Capitalism

When colleagues asked Gordon Marshall, a historical sociologist at the University of Exeter, to write a paper to help their students cope with the growing complexity of the debate, he ended up with a 236-page book, *In Search of the Spirit of Capitalism* (1982). Marshall was well equipped for the task, having just completed an impressive study of Calvinism and the development of capitalism in Scotland.[4] Marshall would go on to a stellar career in his field and university administration.

A major problem that had plagued the debate, Marshall said, was the common readiness of critics to leap into the discussion of Weber's work in complete ignorance of its context in a growing scholarly debate in Germany over the origins of modern capitalism and Weber's reasons for joining in the discussion. This problem was exacerbated by another, Marshall would later explain, namely the practice of taking their clues as to Weber's motives for writing the essays from his latter writings.

The principal determinant of economic interest and scholarly concern at the time was the actual state of industrial development in Germany compared with that of Great Britain where the theorists of the classical school of political economy, Smith, Ricardo, et al., articulated their industrializing experience in the abstract, rational terms of the natural sciences that, in turn, defied notions of government intervention. Late German industrial development, however, called for government intervention and hence for the investigation of the historical factors at play in economic development that might guide public policy. While there were those in Germany who followed the British classical school, a German Historical Economic School arose deeply committed to empirical studies and the quite different criteria necessary to the study of social and cultural phenomena, involving as they did considerations of value. Critics who ignored this context and saw in Weber's *Protestant Ethic* a monocausal idealist argument inevitably misunderstood and misconstrued his work. It was in the context of this "controversy [between the classical and historical schools] over the nature of modern capitalism and the appropriate framework within which to analyze it," Marshall advised, "that Weber began to write about capitalism, about the principles of concept formation in the social sciences, and to study the writings of his colleagues."[5] In *The Protestant Ethic*, working within the context of the historical school, Weber was wrestling "not with the ghost of Marx, but ... with that of Adam Smith."[6]

Marshall then narrowed the focus, first to note that in Weber's doctoral dissertation and early writings, Weber was already "according historical primacy to non-economic factors [thus denying] a strictly economistic approach to social evolution,"[7] and second by citing the three scholarly colleagues of the historical school who provided the immediate stimulus – and provocation – for Weber's concept of "the spirit of capitalism": George Simmel, Werner Sombart, and Heinrich Rickert. Recovering in 1902 from a nervous breakdown of four years duration, Weber simultaneously found the ethical perspective, historical grounding, and methodological reflections that would feed the core of his argument. Simmel, in *The Philosophy of Money* (1900), argued that while avarice was common to every age and attitudes toward the singular pursuit of wealth varied culturally, only under modern capitalism had money's value as a means crossed the boundary into an absolute value in itself, with the result that the "consciousness of purpose in [money] comes to an end."[8] Weber thought this part of Simmel's argument brilliant and readily built it into his chapter on economic ethics, but when Simmel moved on from the social and economic arena to metaphysical questions of "meaningfulness" and the disintegrating effects of money culture on the self, Weber was not prepared to follow. Under modern capitalism, he observed, the "honest man of recognized credit" followed a creed of maximizing profit and increasing capital as a moral duty without compunction. Something more than the philosophy of money was required to explain this unusual and untraditional attitude.[9]

Werner Sombart's *Modern Capitalism*, published in 1902, recounted the history of the modern spirit of capitalism from its tentative beginnings in thirteenth century Italy and forward across 600 years and three stages of capitalist development to its triumph in latter eighteenth century Europe. Each stage had its own distinctive culture. A self-sufficient handicraft economy, an intermediate stage of commercial capitalism, and finally "high capitalism" were each described under three headings: basic values from which goals and rules were derived; procedures for organizing productive activity; and the technology, methods, and knowledge available to pursue economic goals. Despite significant differences, the first two stages, however, were essentially traditional in their manner of accessing natural resources and in maintaining a balance between meeting stable basic necessities of life on the one hand and the temptations of unlimited acquisition on the other. That was to say, a balance between the traditional and the rational. The modern capitalistic system, Sombart argued, differed radically in each of his three system-defining categories. Its techniques and technology had advanced to a qualitatively new level of productivity; organizationally and system-wide, it broke with tradition in combining owners of capital who managed operations and a "formally" free, but property-less class of workers, and most important, in terms of system ethos, it combined "unlimited material striving" and a sober "calculating rationality." This, for Sombart, was the "spirit of modern capitalism." Sombart credited a number of other causal factors such as the stimulus of precious metals from the Americas, double-entry bookkeeping, and the arrival of the modern state, but the centrepiece of all was the new ethos, the "spirit of capitalism." Sombart's work attracted numerous critics. One large issue was that at the heart of Sombart's work was a major ambiguity. Sombart claimed that the "spirit of capitalism" was "simultaneously the (or a) causal element in generating capitalism and a unique feature of capitalism itself."[10] But if the former was the case, the spirit of capitalism pre-existed modern capitalism and could not then be unique to it. Further, if a cause, Sombart had not established the historical origin of this spirit. The next year, in response to critics, Sombart published *The German Economy in the Nineteenth Century* and tackled that further question, attributing the spirit of unlimited accumulation to the marginalization of the Jewish Diaspora in Europe that drove them into trade and finance. That, in turn, was legitimated by an ancient Jewish law prohibiting Jews from charging interest on money loaned to fellow Jews but permitting them to do so with non-Jews. Weber, himself, however, had become convinced that the spirit of capitalism was both of more recent vintage and rooted in the ascetic Protestantism of the Reformation. There were other difficulties. Weber felt that Sombart's characterization of the spirit of capitalism as combining a spirit of restless and ruthless adventurism with a rational calculating pursuit of unlimited accumulation was mistaken, first, because adventurism was not unique to the modern era and, second, because the two attributes were mutually contradictory. Weber was thus seized of the necessity of publicly entering the debate.

Marshall makes it abundantly clear that Weber's argument in *The Protestant Ethic and the Spirit of Capitalism* was set firmly in the German Historical School. Marshall does so for two reasons, first to answer later critics that Weber, in rooting the uniqueness of modern capitalism in an idea – the spirit of capitalism – was working within a Hegelian idealist framework. Second, it was important to distinguish Weber's emphasis on the uniqueness of modern capitalism from the universal postulates of the Classical school of political economy. Weber was neither idealist nor rationalist. As Marshall explains, to argue historically that attitudes derived from the world view of an age meant that "any explanation of the particular ethic that prevails in a given historical situation must ... relate economic beliefs and actions to the ... non-economic conditions in which these are located."[11] Both Simmel and Sombart had argued in that vein, and Weber followed suit, but, while he accepted the empirical structure of Sombart's argument, he found it necessary to contest salient details of the account. One of those details was Sombart's confusion around questions of value and, still more particularly, around the origins of the "value" that lay at the heart of the "spirit of capitalism." In adopting a historical approach, Weber, with others of his generation, had to wrestle with the value issues and subjectivism that inevitably arose in the context of disciplined investigation of social and cultural subjects. This issue would lead directly into Weber's innovative concept of the "ideal-type." Enter Heinrich Rickert and "value-relevance."

Rickert, Marshall says, is critical to any attempt at understanding Weber's "ideal-type" approach and to assess the merit of criticism levelled against it. It was in the name of this method that Weber made the unusual and, for many, puzzling choice of Benjamin Franklin as the singular exemplar of the spirit of capitalism. Rickert was a prominent neo-Kantian philosopher and member of a group that met periodically to consider the issue of conceptualization in the natural and social/cultural sciences. Weber appears to have read Rickert's two-volume *Limits of Conceptualization in the Natural Sciences* shortly after the second volume appeared in 1902.[12] While he by no means agreed with Rickert on all points, he was seized of the potential in Rickert's idea of "value-relevance" for resolving the issue of achieving objective knowledge in social and cultural subject matters.

Rickert contested the reigning view that reality was clearly divided into separate realms of "nature" and "human spirit," each requiring different methods of investigation: "generalization" in the case of nature where "laws" defined the behaviour or described the characteristics of massed groupings of phenomena; "individualization" in the case of human phenomena, where issues of morals, values, and spirit in self-aware subjects (e.g., historical persons) required a depth of individual analysis. Rickert rejected the presumption that investigation in either field could yield certain knowledge of reality. Reality was "indivisible, infinitely complex, and conceptually unknowable" in its completeness. Generalization and individualization represented the extreme ends of a continuum of approaches to "the problem of attaining objective knowledge" in any science. A principle was needed by which to "reconstruct the data of direct experience, or abstract from reality, on a basis that is not arbitrary." For Rickert, that principle was "value-relevance."[13] Generalization was still appropriate to natural phenomena where opinions or values and the like were not complicating factors. However, where the quest for significance reigned and "intersubjectivity" prevailed, "value-relevance" opened the door to objective knowledge.

Weber was too deeply grounded in the historical school to follow Rickert into neo-Kantian expectations of an ultimate resolution of conflicting values and notions of a valid universal history. Despite the ever-changing nature of opinions and values, Weber concluded that "value-relevance" made objectivity in the historical sciences possible. By establishing the value underlying the cultural phenomenon or historical person in question firmly at the centre of investigation, testing its explanatory power against empirical evidence, this "one-sided objectivity" would yield reliable knowledge. If not, at least it might be the means of discovering a more relevant value for the research project. The next step for Weber in this process of conceptualization in the cultural sciences was to locate the value in a representative "ideal-type" so that, in this case, "the spirit of modern capitalism is a historic individual," or "what the modern capitalist Weltanschauung would look like were it ruthlessly systematized" in terms of the underlying value of the dutiful pursuit of material wealth as an end in itself.[14]

As Marshall tells us, the jury is still out on Weber's "ideal-type" methodology. There was reason, however, for his choice of Benjamin Franklin as his ideal-type. Not only did Franklin explicitly teach the unqualified duty of diligent ongoing pursuit of money-making as an end in itself, but, ringed round with repressive counsels against self-indulgence, represented an economic regime unprecedented in human history and, in the light of tradition, entirely irrational and evidence of turpitude. Moreover, living, as Franklin did, in the primitive economic conditions of colonial Pennsylvania, it could not be said that he represented the superstructural product of an advanced economic base, as Marxists would argue.[15] This was not to oppose Marx, however; rather to preserve the focus of Weber's intent in *The Protestant Ethic* that even economist arguments needed to take account of non-economic elements in the culture at large.

At this point, however, Marshall argues that Weber has accumulated two problems of "Herculean" proportions to resolve: how to empirically establish the source of the underlying value or spirit of modern capitalism and, second, how to avoid the tautological trap that Sombart fell into viewing the "spirit of capitalism" as both a pre-existing source and a unique feature of modern capitalism. Weber had done significant early research on the changing economic attitudes of Silesian farm labour, which he drew on to illustrate the contrast between traditional and modern in their views of compensation in relation to consumption and an inherited and acceptable lifestyle. Similarly, but more as anecdote, he contrasts the convivial transactions of medieval capitalists – "putters-out" in the textile trades – with the cool, calculating rationality of modern capitalists. Again, repudiating Sombart, Weber scores the suggestion that "restless adventurism" in any way characterizes the rationalist ethos of modern capitalism. While Weber occasionally allows that economic ethics and economic ethos may develop separately, generally, Marshall observes, he describes them as having "an adequacy" for each other and that under changing circumstances tend to change together. Weber was clear that his study was provisional; the scouting of the ideal-type would need more definitive empirical demonstration. However, that left an open door for criticism, and Marshall concludes his chapters on the "spirit of capitalism" with half of Weber's equation, saying, "The truth is that Weber offers little or no independent evidence concerning the motives and worldview of either modern or medieval businessmen and labourers." While commenting that Weber's case remains "empirically unverified," Marshall suggests that "possibly, in practice, [it is] unverifiable."[16] And so Marshall moves on to the Protestant ethic, the discussion of which may have consumed the larger part of debate over the adequacy of the Weber thesis, but in which, in Marshall's view, Weber is more convincing than his critics.

Faced with the barrage of criticism from almost every conceivable angle levelled at Weber's argument, the lay person, Marshall observes, "will probably conclude that Weber's interpretation of Protestant doctrine is erroneous, or, more charitably, that the whole question … is simply so complicated that it is best left to the theologians and to the faithful themselves." He insists, however, that this is "the most straightforward and strongest part of Weber's discussion."[17]

For Weber, the two key components of the Protestant ethic were the concepts of a "calling" and the doctrine of "predestination." He quickly eliminated Luther from the discussion, even though Luther's concept of work in the world as a "calling" of equal sanctity to Catholic holy orders was revolutionary and a hugely important part of the generalized Protestant ethic – especially when buttressed by Luther's equally revolutionary teaching of the priesthood of all believers. However, as Marshall points out, for Luther the "call" was also to be faithful in the station of life to which one was called, and that was clearly traditional and devoid of the social dynamism of the modern. Moreover, Luther held a rather soft view of predestination, while Calvin taught a ruthlessly logical version of it and was entirely comfortable with social mobility. Hence Weber quickly ushered Luther to the wings and placed Calvin at centre stage.

Marshall offers a helpful summary of the doctrine in which its salient features stand out: all were hopelessly bound in sin and could plead no merit; God, in God's sovereignty and in God's grace, elected some to salvation, leaving others damned; this remained one's eternal fate and one could not know who was of the elect or of the damned. One's purpose on earth was to simply glorify God, "living out on earth a life filled with apparently godly behaviour and good works."[18] Recognizing the psychological crisis this doctrine created for followers, later Calvinist and neo-Calvinist pastoral theologians taught that it was "the absolute duty of the individual to assume himself or herself to be chosen"; and more, that any doubts about this were a sign of imperfect faith.[19] Weber's reading in the neo-Calvinist literature convinced him that this pastoral turn converted the Calvinist movement into the dynamic force it became.

Marshall helpfully lists the most common criticisms of Weber's description of the Protestant ethic from his own time forward: that he "misrepresents Calvin's doctrine of 'calling,'" that he "overplays the importance of predestination in Calvin's theology," that all the elements of the Protestant ethic are also to be found in medieval Catholic theology, that "attitudes to wealth and its accumulation" in Calvinism are shared by Catholics and other Protestant groups of the time, and that Weber's treatment of the Puritan movement is so unrepresentative as to "cast doubt" upon his whole characterization of ascetic Protestantism.[20]

Dividing the criticisms into logical errors and empirical issues, Marshall makes short work of these criticisms, giving names and citing chapter and verse. Those, like W.S. Reid, who on various grounds rose to the defence of Calvin, whatever their motive, simply talk past Weber, ignoring his explicit statement that not Calvin, but later neo-Calvinist denominations and sects, including Puritans and Methodists, were his reference groups.[21] Those, like Winthrop Hudson and Samuelsson, who claimed that Weber appeared to be ignorant of the forceful condemnation of avarice and material accumulation among neo-Calvinist and Puritan divines like Richard Baxter have either been careless readers or were incapable of coping with the subtlety of Weber's argument differentiating between ethical teachings and psychological effects.[22]

Others, like H.M. Robertson, who had his own interpretation of the roots of capitalism, accused Weber of entirely misrepresenting Catholic teaching, especially the stricter Jansenists who encouraged "industry, thrift, order, and honesty" and the "Jesuits [who] went even further" in promoting disciplined enterprise and trade. "It would not be difficult," Robertson concluded, "to claim that the religion which favoured the spirit of capitalism was Jesuitry, not Calvinism."[23] Both Tawney and Parsons were quick to repudiate Robertson, who "failed to engage Weber at any point," and the respected Catholic author, James Broderick, systematically exposed the faults of Robertson's argument, accusing him of "systematically distorting Jesuit teachings on economic matters."[24] However, having disposed of the above critics, whose arguments addressed discursive issues, Marshall turned to those who questioned Weber on empirical grounds.

Among the more serious empirical issues, Weber was charged with what was selectivity in his mining of Calvinist and neo-Calvinist texts and in particular of leaning too heavily on the Puritan divine Richard Baxter. The Dutch historian Albert Hyma questioned Weber's conflating of Dutch Calvinism with English Puritanism.[25] Others argued that it was not ascetic Calvinist pastoral theology but the consequences of minority status and discrimination, whether in Britain, Western and Eastern Europe, the Middle East, or India, that forced the pace of capitalist development. Then, Marshall says, there was the "negative causality" argument, that it was persecution itself which should be credited with the stimulus to escalate capitalist development into its modern ethos that Weber was addressing. While all these cases could be tested empirically, Marshall suggests, to meet the terms of Weber's claims respecting the spirit of capitalism may still need to have recourse to theological texts.

Two British scholars, David Little and Michael Walzer, did just that with striking results.[26] While not denying Weber's attribution of "personal anxiety" to the psychological effects of Calvinist predestinarian doctrine, they clearly miss the unique nature of anxiety over salvation when they suggest that anxiety induced by rapid social change, which was obvious in the texts, needed to be part of the mix. Undoubtedly, consulting a broader spectrum of life, as Little and Walzer note, would enrich and expand Weber's central concept without departing from his ascription of its source to ascetic neo-Calvinism. In that respect, both men rightly underlined the importance of the revolutionary concepts of social order held by the Puritans as critical elements to observe in tracking the developing ethos and ultimate character of modern capitalism, parting company only in their emphasis: Little – "[Whatever their differences] all groups ... engendered the principles of voluntary choice, self-initiated behaviour and consensuality, [and] took up arms against the old order that the rule of freedom might replace the rule of necessity"; Walzer – "[The] new spirit of the Puritans can be defined as a military and political work-ethic, directly analogous to the 'worldly asceticism' which Max Weber has described in economic life, but oriented not toward acquisition so much as toward contention, struggle, destruction and rebuilding." Calvinist conscience gave to war and to politics (and if Weber is right to business as well) "a new sense of method and purpose [distinguishing them] from that of medieval men, caught up in their unchanging world ... and also from Renaissance men, pursuing a purely personal ambition."²⁷

As Marshall rightly observes, evaluating "the refutations and recastings of Weber's interpretation of Protestant theology" would be an enormous and tedious task, but a careful reading of the alternative interpretations of the relevant texts "have confirmed Weber's interpretation of the general thrust of pastoral theology as being correct in essentials."²⁸ But if Weber's thesis is plausible, Marshall insists, it requires the empirical investigation of "the attitudes and conduct of the Protestant business and labouring classes. Unfortunately ... for someone who is so explicitly interested in the practical consequences of theology ... [Weber] is strangely unconcerned about documenting these consequences empirically."²⁹ This, says Marshall, is "the heart of the matter" and he devotes an entire chapter with that title to it.

The heart of the matter was the empirical question as to whether evidence to justify Weber's claims regarding the contrast between the attitudes and practice of pre-Reformation capitalists and those of the new post-Reformation capitalists was born of ascetic Calvinism. Setting up a "case for the defence" and a "case for the prosecution" approach, Marshall's rigorous cross-examination of the evidence pro and con is much too detailed to be adequately summarized here, but summoning what was historically known of pre-Reformation capitalists, the evidence cited by the "defence" gave strong support for Weber's description of "traditional" capitalist enterprise:

aggressive profiteering and wealth accumulation in wide-ranging, apparently adventurist economic activity, whether as private merchants or traders, public financiers of various government operations including war, speculation, investment in land; financing joint stock voyages whether of exploration or in search of El Dorado, trade in slaves, and other operations of questionable morality, not excluding outright robbery! Motivation was various, for family prestige, honour, the purchase of political influence and for sustaining a comfortable or opulent life-style. There was unmistakeable evidence, also, of anxiety and guilt, given public attitudes and religious teaching that avarice and the pursuit of wealth put one's immortal soul in grave danger. Relief from such fears prompted substantial charitable giving – even the gift of entire fortunes – usually to religious (Roman Catholic) agencies, especially late in life, to ensure salvation. Alternatively, the conscience-stricken wealthy often sought escape in socially acceptable roles as "in court" public service or as landed gentry. All this was in sharp contrast to Weber's description of the dedicated ascetic neo-Calvinist fulfilling his or her "calling" in rational, systematic economic activity as an end in itself, with profit sanctified by single-minded continual re-investment in his or her "calling," all sustained and endorsed through membership in self-governing religious communities committed to fulfilling God's will in the world.[30]

If the case for the defence seemed secure, Marshall's "case for the prosecution" dimmed the hopes of supporters with three concerns that rendered Weber's thesis "empirically problematic." The first had to do with Weber's recourse to "value reference" and the systematic application of an "ideal-type" to evaluate the empirical reality of the subject under examination. Thus, the apparent irrationality of the multiple "adventurist" pursuits of the traditional pre-Reformation capitalist, viewed from another perspective, could be seen as a rational calculation to maximize profit in an uncertain world rather than an expression of a psychological trait of "adventurism." So considered, the empirical data seeming to confirm the contrast of traditional and modern is rather a consequence of a change in the field of operations, that is, the nature and scale of the available market, and not a difference in the "value" or "spirit" at the heart of economic actions being described.[31]

Marshall proceeds in similar fashion with his other two concerns: "the problem of determining the meaning of economic behaviour for social actors," labourers as well as capitalists, and the problem of tautology, given Weber's practice of defining "his principal variables in terms of each other."[32]

After an exhaustive canvass of critics' allegations of empirical shortcomings under these three headings, Marshall's verdict is that while the defence had done little to vindicate Weber on empirical grounds, the prosecution had left him largely unscathed. The critics (and supporters) were generally guilty of failing carefully to read and digest Weber's tightly written texts; they pursued inadmissible lines of argument on the basis of their own redefinitions of the Protestant ethic and/or the spirit of capitalism; they, like Weber, himself, failed to offer hard evidence pro or con regarding the motives of economic actors; and they resorted to irrelevant anachronistic tests of Weber's thesis outside his specific time frame. Weber's thesis, Marshall insisted, was "in principle falsifiable," but the critics' strategy of avoidance and the "clutter of inadmissible evidence preferred by many of the combatants" left him with many questions. "Serious discussion has barely begun," were his last words as he moved on to his penultimate chapter, "Continuities in a Controversy," and his conclusion.[33]

If "The Heart of the Matter" dealt with matters of logic and empirical evidence, "Continuities" focused attention on three persistent encounters more subtly intellectual and ideological in nature: an "exchange – of sorts" between historians and sociologists, "Weber and Marx" and historical materialism, and "Weberology and teleology," discussing, among other things, "Parsoniansism." The first of these was a rather raw debate – inconclusive as Marshall wrote – over accusations of historians that Weber's argument, in his *Protestant Ethic* essays, ignored a host of evidence that capitalism had long predated the era of the Reformation and therefore invalidated Weber's argument. Although Weber's tightly argued text put such claims out of court, the common response of sociologists was to refer critics to later works of Weber demonstrating his clear knowledge of the long history of capitalism and the multiple causations involved in its development. Both sociologists and historians had failed to give Weber's text the dedicated scrutiny essential to understanding its intent.

The debate over the influence of Marx and historical materialism on Weber's intellectual formation and writing – and in the *Protestant Ethic and the Spirit of Capitalism* in particular – had, by the 1980s, a substantial history, dragging great names like Hegel into the discussion. Was Weber Hegelian, therefore an idealist and anti-Marxist? Or, as an economic historian, was he, with some reservations, intellectually inclined toward historical materialism? Marshall's sixteen pages on the subject offer as intelligent a discussion of the issues involved as one is likely to find in so short a space. The evidence was mixed. Marx and Weber were in general agreement in their characterization of capitalism and capitalists – and of all critics, according to Marshall, Marxists, though persistent, were the most lenient. In the body of his text, however, Weber categorically rejected the Marxist argument that religion was one component of the superstructure of ideas, values, and morals determined in the last analysis by the necessities of the economic base of a society. He could hardly do otherwise and maintain the integrity of an argument that rested on the status of religion as an independent variable in the historical process. Yet, concluding the original essays, his sketch of a future research program included investigation into the influence of economics on religion. And in his later *Sociology of Religion,* he accepted the reality of such influences.

The matter was further complicated by a variety of attempts by some Marxists to move beyond earlier mechanistic views and recognize the independence of consciousness and agency and hence of cultural and related factors. Such revisionists would seem capable of drawing Weber into their orbit. Notwithstanding such efforts in sophistication, however, Marshall observes that the common practice among Marxists was to argue simply that individual capitalists of the time resorted to Calvinist language as rhetoric, legitimating their class interest and economic behaviour. In the big picture, Calvin provided a cadre of ideologists galvanizing a revolutionary bourgeois class, throwing off the trammels of the feudal system. A number of non-Marxists, like Milton Yinger (1967) and Dennis Forcese (1968), joined Marxist Christopher Hill in his classic statement of this position.[34]

However, after all the theorizing, claims, and counterclaims, Marshall says, insurmountable difficulties had, to date, frustrated the critical task of gathering sufficient quantitative and qualitative data to reasonably substantiate "whether the Protestant ethic decisively shaped the capitalist mentality of entire social strata, or the reverse."[35] The qualitative issue of "accessing" the states of mind of professing Calvinist capitalists of the time was to determine whether it was sincerity of belief or sheer rationalization of economic behaviour driven by other motives and interests that was at the heart of their profession. Given the scale of difficulty entailed, he suggests that one is driven back to personal preference based on commitment to one "framework of interpretation" or another, as to whether "ideas can exert an independent influence on social conduct, or that changing attitudes are inevitably, sometimes or never, the result of a change in objective circumstances."[36] But in the complicated world of competing "frameworks," a number of options present themselves, including which Marx or which Weber does one hold in view? Marshall's own view is that, although Weber did not compose his essays to challenge Marx, the two are diametrically opposed, and he cites Weber at his most nuanced in the original *Protestant Ethic* essays to make the point: "I consider the influence of economic developments on the fate of religious ideas to be very important and shall later attempt to show how in our case the process of mutual adaptation of the two took place. On the other hand, those religious ideas themselves simply cannot be deduced from economic circumstances. They are in themselves ... the most powerful plastic elements of national character, and contain a law of development and a compelling force entirely their own."[37] Weber would go on later, Marshall explains, to develop the concept of "elective affinity" to explain "the ways in which different theologies are suited to the respective existential needs and everyday situations of various social strata" showing how "theodicies of dominance, mobility, and escape [respectively] are appropriate to ... elites, the middle classes ... and the disprivileged."[38] And, quoting Weber, "Other things being equal, strata with high social and economic privilege will scarcely be prone to evolve the idea of salvation ... [but] assign to religion the primary function of *legitimising* their own life pattern and situation in the world."[39] Despite this apparent echo of Marx, the two positions remained irreconcilable in Marshall's estimation. Ever ready to accept the influence of other elements in the rise of capitalism and in the accumulation over time of "the spirit of capitalism," Weber's language, especially his early phrase "mutual adaptation" and his later concept of "elective affinity," preserved his insistence that religious ideas arose autonomously and functioned dialectically in the processes of history. Professing an epistemology that strictly separated fact and value and insisting on the irreducibility of competing values, Weber could "have no truck" with a Marxist "epistemology of *praxis*" and a deterministic world view that claimed "to answer scientifically questions about the meaning and objectives of the course of history."[40]

"Weberology and Teleology" may have seemed like a mystifying way to end a chapter entitled "Continuities." At issue was what Talcott Parsons set out to do with the Weber thesis after giving the Anglo-American world its first English translation in 1930. Reading Weber's original 1904–05 essays in the light of their 1920 introduction and the latter works – in other words, reading Weber backwards – Parsons thought he detected indications that Weber was moving toward a general theory of social action. In 1937, he published *The Structure of Social Action*, conflating elements of Weber, Pareto, and Durkheim in a universally applicable theory of social action. Offered as an alternative to Marx, Weber was thus bent in idealist and spiritualist directions that were no part of Weber's intent. The theory would later be wrapped in Parsons' belief in universal elements in evolution that would bring Kalahari Bushmen and American industrial capitalists into the same explanatory frame of reference. But Parsons' idealist and universalist penchant, Marshall points out, led to a total misreading of Weber, whose discreet historical instincts led him to eschew world views and the use of universal laws to explain phenomena. His preferred method was "to identify the 'adequate causes' for historically specific configurations and events."[41] Although, or perhaps because, Weber was remarkably wide-ranging and incredibly knowledgeable historically, world views and generalized applications of evolution to historical events were never part of his stock in trade. This had been part of his difficulty with Marx.

Parsons' popularity as a teacher spread his views widely within the academy and beyond and became one of Marshall's principal "continuities" in the Protestant ethic debate, especially in the United States. Marshall hastens to say, however, that the eight scholars he mentions in his notes as "Parsonian" did not necessarily follow Parsons whole hog and differed among each other.[42] Nevertheless, they were given to universalist and environmental theorizing in a similar vein. The result has been the frequent argument that the *Protestant Ethic* essays were the opening salvo in the development of a general "theory of comparative cultures." In this context, it became "fashionable" to see in Weber's thought an underlying preoccupation with an "autonomous process of rationalization" underway in modern Western culture. Thus, Gabriel Kolko (1959), for example, in a critique of Weber''s philosophy of history, argued that Weber's purpose was to develop "universally relevant historical laws" and, having demonstrated the causal power of the Protestant ethic, he indicates that Weber went on to claim "that the Ethic was not merely a necessary condition of rationalized institutions [in the West] but also a sufficient condition regardless of other factors." To this faulty rendition of Weber's argument, Kolko added a note of condescension, blaming the alleged train of reasoning on the "German philosophical tradition" of invoking a *Geist* (Spirit) as a "prime mover" in historical events![43] In a later, rather more sophisticated fashion, Friedrich Tenbruck (1980) parlayed Weber's interest in the rationalizing process into a grand theodicy, explaining the ways of God to humanity. Tenbruck described an evolution from "the failure of primitive religion to eliminate suffering and misfortune, to successively more encompassing solutions for human ills, each transcending the other, unify[ing] more and more of the isolated events of reality into a systematic worldview capable of explaining all the miseries of the world."[44] In this fashion, the Parsonians viewed religious progress as an autonomous process driven by an inner logic. Thus, Christianity's gradual "de-magnification" of the world culminated in "the ruthless logic of Calvinist doctrine ... [whose] ethos of worldly asceticism [created the spirit of] modern capitalism [and drove] the modern world in non-religious directions."[45] The net result of this misreading of Weber's *Sociology of Religion*, Marshall says, is a "spiritualistic interpretation of the Protestant ethic [thesis] which Weber himself openly repudiated"[46]– just as he repudiated the materialism of Karl Marx. Weber was exploring a specific instance of how the inner logic of a religious idea effected and was affected by the material and ideological interests of a rising class that would go on to dominate civilizational development. He was not proposing a general theory of religious ideological determinism.[47]

Marshall ends "Continuities" with a brief review of "New Directions." Sometimes exciting, often misconceived, they include the significant work of Robert Merton on the Reformation and modern science, Gerhard Lenski and his many followers contesting Comte and Marx on the future of religion as a social force, and the attempts to harness the Protestant ethic model to projects of modernization and third-world development by, for example, attempting to instill an "achievement-oriented" ideology among elite groups and business people. Whether legitimate or outrageous, Marshall effectively disabuses the various proponents of the notion that such projects had anything to do with Weber's thesis in *Protestant Ethic and the Spirit of Capitalism*.[48]

In these latest chapters, Marshall's thesis in *In Search of the Spirit of Capitalism* becomes more explicit. His "broad appraisal" is that Weber's "masterly argument" had rarely been matched in quality by critics. Despite notable weaknesses, Weber presented "a thesis that is sociologically sophisticated, historically specific, and … open to empirical discussion." Often using "bastardized versions" of the thesis, critics would cite "inadmissible data in the wrong times and places," while supporters ignored the empirical issues and treated Weber's impressive achievements as though they authenticated the reliability of Weber's argument in the original essays. After three-quarters of a century, oversimplification, the grinding of partisan axes, failure to read the original essays, reliance on "inaccurate secondary expositions," and a general resort to unhelpful rhetorical devices, have left the issues little advanced beyond the first years of discussion. This damning conclusion, as of 1982, is supported by the hundreds of items in Marshall's bibliography and notes.

The principal gains he can point to reflect the above shortcomings – admonitions about being thoroughly familiar with a text before critiquing it and being honest and modest about the limitations of one's own research. Above all, there are dangers in introducing into such discussions "personal theological or socio-political aspirations and values … [that] serve merely to obscure and mystify the events."[49]

The balance of Marshall's conclusion returns to his earlier observations on the respective roles of historians and sociologists in the debate, as he cites a general absence of theoretical framework among the former and the common evasion of empirical issues among the latter. Using Weber's affirmation of the inseparability of history and sociology in both his methodology and in his practice as a classic case in point, Marshall cogently – but with evident feeling – endorses the movement for their "reunion" that arose in the late 1950s "when the positivistic orthodoxies in both disciplines were explicitly challenged." Not the *discovery* of universal laws of society, but the *uncovery* of "the meaning of social actions and relationships as agents participate in these." Then, comparative analysis can lead to "causal explanations of these actions, of social structures and processes, and of the course of social change in the development of civilizations."[50]

2. The Protestant Ethic Turns 100

Max Weber is to sociology what Einstein is to physics. This striking – and perhaps surprising –analogy is the burden of Charles Lemert's foreword to Lutz Kaelber and William Swatos, Jr's collection of essays, *The Protestant Ethic Turns 100: Essays on the Centenary of the Weber Thesis.*[51] Coincidentally, both Einstein and Weber published their world-changing papers in 1905. Lemert describes Einstein's papers as establishing "the theory of the physical universe as … an indefinite space in time without a stable physical structure … a space vulnerable to time's warping speed." In a close, if not perfect, analogy, Weber's papers pointed to a vast, expanding capitalistic social "cosmos" whose structure rendered it inherently unstable, born as it was of "late-traditional religion" and the modern capitalist impulse for the rational pursuit of unlimited accumulation. The result was a social world of "discontinuous spheres" that could be described but not unified. Hence the great irony: "Economic rationality in this world arose from an other-worldly calculation!" In the upshot, both Einstein's and Weber's universes implicitly placed an "impossible burden" of meaningfulness on the shoulders of solitary individuals.[52]

Lemert was one of the most interesting and engaged social theorists of recent decades. A long-time professor at Wesleyan University in Ohio and author of the much-reprinted sociological text *Social Things: An Introduction to Sociological Life*, Lemert introduced the radical French socio/linguistic theories of Michael Foucault and Jacques Derrida to the American academy.[53] Lemert concludes by commending to his sociological colleagues the rigorous honesty with which Weber faced "the terrible moral contradictions" of modern capitalism.

Kaelber and Swatos assembled a stellar cast of essayists to celebrate the hundredth birthday of the Weber thesis. Unlike Marshall's systematic survey of criticism and response, the contributors to this collection, while not avoiding controversial issues, were more intent on pressing more deeply into the Weber phenomenon – his person, his family, his early works and their relation to the famous essays, their reception, the significance of his American experience, his philosophy of history, his concept of "the iron cage of capitalism," his continuing relevance, and more. Co-editor Kaelber introduces the collection, reflecting on the principal themes addressed in the eight essays that follow and positioning readers on the state of research on Weber and his famous thesis as the twenty-first century opened. He notes that the 1990s saw a burst of activity, measured by the number of papers presented at meetings of the American Sociological Association, and that while the number of papers had since dropped, the number of abstracts reported had never been higher.[54] It needs to be noted that the collection clearly has an American audience in mind but also that most of the contributors are of German origin and specially equipped culturally and linguistically for a finely nuanced understanding of the Weber persona, the scholarly world he inhabited, and the rendering of Weber's extraordinarily difficult German prose.

THE FORMATION AND CONSOLIDATION OF THE PROTESTANT ETHIC

Hartmut Lehmann, who had a distinguished scholarly career as a historically and sociologically engaged theologian in Germany and the United States, had published two significant books on the Weber thesis in the previous decade, the latest being *Weber's "Protestant Ethic": Origins, Evidence, Context* (1993), which he edited with Guenther Roth.[55] Lehmann opens the text proper with a re-examination of Weber's correspondence with colleagues and critics to underline the contingent circumstances of the arrival of Weber's thesis on the intellectual landscape in 1904–05.[56] Entitled "Friend and Foe: The Formation and Consolidation of the Protestant Ethic Thesis," the result is as much an intimate glimpse into the Weber persona as it is insight into the matter of Lehmann's prosaic subtitle. Apparently opposite poles of the Weber personality emerge as Lehmann describes Weber's masterful diplomacy in dealing with colleagues on the one hand and the intemperate severity of his responses to critics. But that is colourful subtext to Lehmann's purpose, which is to show how, in the context of the former, Weber's famous thesis came to be written, and how under the pressure of the latter, a defensive Weber would, at length, amplify the reasoning and the empirical evidence supporting his case. Emerging from his debilitating illness, Weber was now co-editor with Edgar Jaffe and Werner Sombart of the journal *Achiv fur Sozialwissenschaft*. Intent on securing a substantial critique of Sombart's impressive but flawed *Modern Capitalism*, Weber doggedly pursued the eminent economist Lujo Brentano to take up the task but, failing to do so, undertook the job himself. The upshot was the publication of the three papers that constituted the original version of *The Protestant Ethic and the Spirit of Capitalism*. As for Weber's critics, despite the abrupt tone of the replies, Weber was driven to reply at length, offering further evidence and argument. Thus the critics added their "inspiration" to the "consolidation" of Weber's final version of 1920. What is more engaging is Lehmann's attribution of Weber's extreme defensiveness on the one hand to his acute intelligence and confidence in his case and the resources he was bringing to the task and on the other hand to a kind of "canonization" of these first essays, as evidence of his capacity once more to enter the academic lists following his illness and the loss of his professorship.[57]

"DIMENSIONS OF THE PROTESTANT ETHIC"
Martin Riesebrodt, writing his essay "Dimensions of the Protestant Ethic,"[58] confessed to a certain ambivalence about the many interpretations abroad about Weber and his controversial thesis. He proposed to employ various historical contexts "to recover meanings in the text that were obvious to Weber's contemporaries but are no longer evident [today]."[59] Riesebrodt was professor variously of divinity, sociology, and politics at Chicago and Geneva and a specialist on the impact of modernity on traditional religion. In his finely crafted essay, Riesebrodt's first issue concerned Talcott Parsons and Anglo-American publishers, who, in breaking up and separately publishing the various parts of Weber's *Collected Essays* and the *General Economic History*, created a "messy" situation that had taken decades to overcome. It is to this and a lack of close attention to context that Riesebrodt traces many of the misunderstandings that grew up around Weber's work. In particular, because of its similarities to the original 1904–05 text, there was a general failure in reading the 1920 edition of *The Protestant Ethic* against the background of the dramatically changed fortunes of Germany and the world, and the intervening shift of Weber's preoccupation with the grand project of the economic ethics of the world's great religions. A new language of Western "world mastery" and "intra-world mastery individualism" now informed the text.

Riesebrodt goes on to re-examine the contexts of five salient issues with illuminating results. To disabuse Americans of the prevalent view of Weber as a "bourgeois opponent" of Marx and historical materialism, he re-examines Weber's early reading, research, and writing, his teaching, and his associations and affiliations, concluding that Weber rejected both historical materialism and idealism as world views but wholeheartedly accepted them as powerful complementary methodologies in a multi-causal approach to history.[60] To take another example, Riesebrodt questions the prevailing view that Weber's breakdown in 1898 resulted from a violent encounter with his father over the latter's dominating behaviour toward his wife, Weber's mother. Reviewing Weber's early career, his rapid ascent to one of the most prestigious university chairs in economics, the demand for his services as a consultant, the endless requests for his presence on political platforms and at Lutheran assemblies, all point to a more obvious cause. Sheer overwork was the problem. Riesebrodt cites Weber's own self-analysis, that he had laboured ceaselessly to prove that he was worthy of his position, as though work were a kind of "talisman" that would save him from succumbing to – well, he knew not what. Weber vowed never to live like that again. Riesebrodt then links this insight and resolve directly to Weber's priority concern for "conduct of life" issues, which lay at the heart of his *Protestant Ethic* writings. Hence, the papers of 1904–05 were, in one important dimension, a working out of a personal "conduct of life" crisis and, in another dimension, a response to a world that had become a "secularized cosmos" in which a religiously originated work ethic now functioned, absent a ground of meaning, as the duty-bound driving force of capital, professionals, and labour alike.[61]

In the course of such ruminations, Riesebrodt sheds valuable light on Weber's involvements in the vigorous religious and philosophical debate that was a hallmark of German intellectual life of the time. Brought up in a Lutheran family, with a father who viewed church membership from the perspective of social advantage but a mother who was deeply religious and interested in the discussions of Max and his young friends, Weber joined in the public debate at a high level, disagreeing with the political posture of leading Lutheran theologians like Ritschl and Harnack, arguing that Lutheran statism bred a submissive people unlikely to rise to the challenge of democratic social change the way Anglo-American peoples were doing. Not only was traditional religious life becoming impossible, so also was the Renaissance vision of the fully rounded individual. Our fate was now to become specialists in the thoroughly rationalized "social cosmos" of modern capitalism. Nietzsche's "Zarathustra" was ever present in such discussions. Riesebrodt ends with Weber's repudiation of a Nietzschean future of "Ubermenschen," advising that only by taking up the challenge of "autonomy," of heroic individualism, dedicating ourselves not to self-aggrandizement but to a cause as "specialists with a heart," we may salvage something of a "calling" and of personality in the face of the new "mechanistic" order.[62]

"REMNANTS OF ROMANTICISM: MAX WEBER IN AMERICA"

"Weber cannot be understood without an appreciation of his experiences [in America] and America's special path to modernity is difficult to grasp without a substantial dip into Weber's extensive body of writing." Alan Wolfe, in the *New Republic*, was reviewing Lawrence Scaff's *Max Weber in America*. Wolfe also implicitly explains why three of eight chapters in this collection are entirely or largely devoted to this reciprocal relationship: Scaff, himself, on the near legendary visit, editor Swatos on "Contexts of Publication," and Stephen Kalberg on Weber's "iron cage" and the "past, present, and future of America's political culture."

Scaff was professor of political science and sociology at Wayne State University and a leading Weberian scholar. Most recently he has published *Weber and the Weberians* (2014). Although knowledge of Weber's visit to the United States in mid-1904 had long been available in Marianne Weber's biography of her husband, the visit, Scaff suggests, has principally been viewed as another instance of the many "Atlantic Crossings" of members of the North Atlantic intellectual community of the time. Scaff's "'The Cool Objectivity of Sociation': Max Weber and Marianne Weber in America" (1998) seems to have rescued Weber from this cul-de-sac. Even so, Weber's visit to the Oklahoma and the Indian Territories remained something of a sidelight, never fully explored nor its significance understood for its importance in "clarifying Weber's 'thesis' about the 'Protestant ethic'; his conception of the 'spirit of capitalism,' including his well-known imagery of 'the iron cage'; and [his view] of political and social life in the United States."[63] Scaff's masterful reconstruction of that segment of the visit, "Remnants of Romanticism," makes good that lack.

The magnetism of the American experiment was all around Weber in his youth. One branch of the family had succumbed to the lure of this expansive New World society and its burgeoning economy and was now living in New York. Weber, Sr, himself, had travelled across the American West to the Pacific in 1883 with a group exploring business opportunities. Young Max had been given a copy of Benjamin Franklin's *Autobiography* by a political friend of his father, and over time he read widely into American literature, history, and economics, including Alexis de Tocqueville's *Democracy in America* and James Fenimore Cooper's romantic Leatherstocking Tales chronicling the last days of the frontier and Indian culture in New

England and the Eastern states. Max Sering's 1887 book describing the legal, administrative, and technical rationalism that supported the rapid advance of settlement across the continent was a notable influence.[64] Thanks to the intervention of a prestigious Heidelberg colleague, Weber, as yet little known internationally, received an invitation to give a paper on agrarian economics at the Congress of Arts and Sciences, part of the Louisiana Purchase Universal Exposition of 1904 in St Louis. Regardless of invitation, Weber was intent on using the occasion to visit the United States to undertake a wide-ranging survey of American social, ethnic, religious, economic, culture, and gender issues. What had never been clear, however, was whether Oklahoma and the Indian Territory had been part of the original plan. According to Scaff, the first sign of interest appeared at St Louis where the prominent political economist and tax expert Jacob Hollander, having attended Weber's lecture and learned of his keen interest in the sociology and politics of areas under transition from traditional to modern, appears to have made the suggestion. Certainly, Weber wasted no time in securing letters of introduction from Hollander and others, readily gave up a reception with President Roosevelt, and was on his way to Guthrie and Muskogee, the principal cities of the region.

Muskogee especially, a sprawling frontier city of some 12,000, was the legal centre of the region and site of federal government political and service agencies, as well as the executive offices of the Indian Creek Nation. It was here Weber spent the bulk of his time meeting lawyers, editors, local political figures, Indian agents, and representatives of the "Five Civilized Tribes" (Cherokee, Chickasaw, Choctaw, Creek, and Seminole) of the Indian Territory and Oklahoma. Weber's correspondence records the more important names, whom Scaff further identifies, along with others, offering characterizations, responsibilities, and attitudes toward the complex issues developing in the region. J. Blair Schoenfelt, as Indian agent, was in charge of the Union Agency for the Five Tribes, and J. George Wright, his superior, was US Indian inspector for the Indian Territory, appointed in 1898 when, under the Curtis Act, the federal government unilaterally extinguished Indian self-government and collective title to their territorial land. Structural faults and ill-defined responsibilities and reporting relations combined with political appointments on the various federal oversight commissions left the system open to influence peddling, conflict of interest, and insider trading, all of which were under investigation during Weber's visit.

These same conditions allowed Schoenfelt and Wright to expand their roles and activity, though they emerge in Scaff's account as critics of a distant federal government out of touch with local opinion and conditions. Robert Owen, the most important of Weber's contacts, joined them in attempting to shield the "Five Civilized Tribes" from misconceived initiatives. Owen, a member of the Cherokee Nation and a devout Presbyterian, was a former Indian agent, now a prominent lawyer and businessman. His mother, Narcissa Chisholm Owen, was an accomplished painter whose work graced the halls at St Louis as well as a published defender of indigenous culture. Owen was a "progressive modernizer" and a member of the Democratic Party. He would become a Senator for two decades from the new State of Oklahoma and was said to "have written the last chapter in the history of the Indians as a separate nation" in America.[65]

At the time of Weber's visit, Owen was still angry and indignant over the arbitrary suppression of Indian rights and the subsequent consequences for his people. This was a region undergoing forced march from traditional communal landholding, self-government, and a separate national identity to private property ownership and government by a distant bureaucracy, with each Indian – and their former Negro slaves – awarded a new status as American citizens. In all of this, the federal government was acting under the combined pressure of immigration, a "free land for all" movement, industrial and financial interests, railway barons, as well as partisan editors and authors. It was not just the officials Weber met, but various attorneys – whose relaxed shirtsleeve, feet on the windowsill discussions he especially enjoyed – real estate individuals, oil workers, salespeople, and business people, who, with miscellaneous "adventurers, confidence men, Indians and Creek freedmen," jammed Muskogee's hotels and streets.[66]

Scaff's excellent section "The Problems of the Indian Territory" details the complex conditions of rapid change on the frontier Weber was experiencing at first hand. After his train ride to the territory and a first intensive day in Muskogee, Weber wrote that "nowhere else does the old Indian romanticism blend with the most modern capitalist culture as it does here right now ... With almost lightning speed everything that stands in the way of capitalistic culture is being crushed," he wrote. "The next time I come here, the last remnants of 'romanticism' will be gone."[67]

Scaff is at pains to counter the impression left by Marianne Weber's editing of her husband's letters that this was a "sentimental journey" to experience the romance "a la Fenimore Cooper" of the end of Indian ways and the passing of the frontier, let alone to muster votes against capitalism or support for Indian culture. Weber's correspondence, Scaff says, rather, pulsates with the dynamism he observed on every hand driving change at an unprecedented pace. Factory-made houses on stone foundations were mixed with Indian cabins in spaces in the endless brush; crops were being planted in areas between trees in the forest tarred and lit and still smoking; the smell of petroleum from drilling rigs like Eiffel Towers populating the Oklahoma landscape filled the air alike of open prairie and the tent "towns" and "cities" whose "streets" were sprayed with petroleum to keep down the dust. The construction of railways and electric train lines seemed to go on endlessly and telephone and telegraph poles and wires existed everywhere.[68] Although Weber himself mentions Cooper's Leatherstocking Tales in passing, Scaff prefers the works of Cooper's contemporary, Washington Irving (referenced elsewhere in the Weber corpus), with their embrace of "the notion of ascetic Puritanism and the calculating spirit of capitalism"[69] as more appropriate to the tenor of Weber's correspondence from Muskogee.

Thus Scaff emphasizes the subtle thesis working itself out in Weber's fertile mind: "Innerworldly asceticism's mastery of 'the natural' of romance" is the source of the dynamism Weber observes, "but with a gain in the power of the kind of imagination that can master the self and the world."[70] That, Scaff suggests, would be one way to describe Weber's sense of "the historic destiny" of devout Presbyterians like Robert Owen and dedicated Methodist newcomers who had flocked to Muskogee. They would become the "agents of that 'ethical style of life' that was spiritually adequate [for the economic stage of capitalism] and signified its victory in the human 'soul.'"[71]

As for the famous "iron cage" metaphor that Weber borrowed from John Bunyan's *Pilgrim's Progress* to sum up the ultimate spiritual imprisonment that awaited the brave American experiment, Scaff almost prefers Weber's own Eiffel Tower imagery – that "quintessential symbol of the fabulous modern sublime" – to represent the combination of remarkably free, dynamic development and the "mechanization, expropriation, and domination" that was happening in the Indian Territory.

The visit to Oklahoma and the Indian Territory, of course, was not the whole of Weber's journey in America, nor the sum of his conclusions there or the whole of his reflections on the future of the country. Scaff especially notes Weber's admiration of the dominant sectarian form of American church life, with its anti-authoritarian bias, its capacity to nurture personal and political freedom, and democratic progressivism. Paradoxically, the same ascetic Protestantism that was propelling America toward the "iron cage" of capitalism was fostering "processes of sociation that counteracted the corrosive and invasive effects of capitalist culture."[72]

Weber came home from his immersion in Americana primed with reflections, images, and evidence that would appear not just in *The Protestant Ethic* essays of 1904–05 but throughout later works as he refined and expanded his central thesis. As Scaff notes, for Weber, what was happening on the American frontier was the last great opportunity for human beings to freely indulge the dynamic spirit of creativity to fashion a new order of things. The issue, however, was how to live under the stern new dictates it imposed.

"THE CONTEXTS OF THE PUBLICATION AND RECEPTION OF THE PROTESTANT ETHIC"

William H. Swatos, Jr, editor of *The Encyclopedia of Religion and Society* and co-editor of this volume, together with an associate, Peter Kivisto, have cobbled together a chapter that needed one more trip to the chopping block and their title, "The Contexts of the Publication and Reception of the Protestant Ethic," given a tighter focus with the additional words, "in America." Their opening, quoting the acclaim with which Weber's first publication, his East Elbian Studies, was received a decade before the first *Protestant Ethic* essays, was a good, even startling opener, but their first sections offer little that is new. One notable exception is the fact that the oft-cited Rachfahl criticisms were principally directed at Ernst Troeltsch over his publications on the social teachings of the Christian churches and it was only at Troeltsch's insistence that Weber responded at all.[73] Otherwise, we are treated to now well-established perspectives on Weber[74] – none of which are strictly relevant to the story Swatos and Kivisto want to tell: the reception of Weber and *The Protestant Ethic and the Spirit of Capitalism* in the United States, or more precisely, the promotion of Talcott Parsons as "the American Weber" for his translation and publication of *The Protestant Ethic*, its subsequent "canonization" as the benchmark work in sociological studies in America, and a critique of Parsons' own major work, *The Structure of Social Action*.

In this regard, the authors first establish as a foil for their argument and later criticism of Parsons, members of a group of sociologists at the University of Indiana forty years later in the 1970s when revisionist Marxism had found surprising favour in the profession (a note the authors evidently want to steer shy of). Criticisms would include oddities of translation, Parsons' isolation of *The Protestant Ethic* from its larger context in Weber's work, his use of Weber's introduction to the 1920 version of the *Protestant Ethic* to preface his translation of the 1904–05 original, and his muddying of Weberian waters a few years later in *The Structure of Social*

Action, where he argued that a comparative study of leading sociologists, Marshall, Pareto, Durkheim, and Weber, supported a theory of voluntaristic social action. Unfortunately, this creates an unnecessarily defensive tone to the discussion in which the authors appear to be rescuing their "American Weber" before establishing his credentials, which were considerable. To glean estimates of Parson's accomplishment they undertake to examine reviews that appeared within two years of the publication of each of the three works: Parson's translation of *The Protestant Ethic*, his *Structure of Social Action*, and Hans H. Gerth and C. Wright Mills, *From Max Weber*, which span the years 1930 to 1946, a kind of axial period after which "canonization" would presumably follow. The findings are interesting, surprising, and diverse, and while more suggestive than definitive, they appear satisfying for the authors. "Did Parson's 'invent' a particular Max Weber? The answer is [that] we will probably never know," the authors concede. Two subtly different issues appear to be in play: Is Parsons the "American Weber," a stand-in who articulates Weber's thesis *in* America? Or is there an "American Weber," in the sense of a "Weber" who is characteristically "American?" The latter notion would not be alien to Weber, whose thought readily accommodated various mixes of socio-economic and ideo-cultural factors. In fact, both in experience and anticipation, he spoke of a distinctive American example, at least until habituation left behind original religious meanings and moved closer to the European model. The methodology here may yield the former; if the latter, then the authors need to provide content and context for the de-Parsonizers as part of the American mix and not simply antagonists, which they never do. Indeed, despite a title that begins with the word "context," no real context is given to set Parsons and his two works in the particular circumstances of the 1930s – only an unelaborated reference to Parsons' concern about Karl Marx.

Nothing, of course, can deprive the United States of pride of place in the delivery of the first English-language translation of Weber's *Protestant Ethic* essays, nor Parsons the honour of executing the demanding task. But why America? Why Parsons? The first public assessment of Weber's work was an approving essay by the highly respected British theologian P.T. Forsyth in 1910 in *The Contemporary Review* entitled "Calvinism and Capitalism." The authors quietly confine the point to a footnote and suggest that sociology was slow to develop in Britain because of the prominence of Herbert Spencer in the British intellectual community, which left Weber in the hands of historians of religion and economic historians like Richard Tawney. But Spencer was also very influential in the foundations of American sociology. What is left unsaid, at least in this regard, is the remarkable presence of notable German-Americans among the country's academic population resulting from active interchanges over recent years. It was one such, Hugo Munsterberg, a former Weber colleague, then at Harvard, who was a driving force in launching the St Louis Exposition Weber addressed in 1904.[75] It was Heinrich H. Maurer, who, in a little-noticed article in 1924 in the *American Journal of Sociology* – without reference to ethnicity – is given pride of place as author of the first academic review of Weber's thesis in the United States. Maurer's principal merit was a prescient warning against confusing Calvinism and Lutheranism in Weber's generalized use of the phrase "Protestant ethic." The confusion would be the source of much misinterpretation until fully clarified in the latter 1980s.[76] A spate of articles in the latter 1920s and Tawney's publication of *Religion and the Rise of Capitalism* spurred Parsons onto his historic translation, with an introduction by Tawney.

Despite the issues Swatos and Kivisto provoke, their findings in the main body of their essay are worthy of note and appear to endorse Parsons in the face of the assault of the "de-Parsonizers," and there is little doubt that the canonization of Weber the authors speak of or the status of *The Protestant Ethic* as a "benchmark work" in American sociological education are real enough, but Parsons as a fully "American Weber" is hardly borne out, especially given occasional reference to ongoing confusion surrounding the *Protestant Ethic* essays outside a rather confined academic and intellectually engaged community.

It would appear that even the academic and intellectually engaged were slow to warm to Parsons' accomplishment. The stunning news from the authors' survey of professional journals is that none of the five major journals of social research carried a review within the set two-year period. However, in the slim number of reviews located, there was a consistent level of praise for Parsons' work and approval of Weber's argument, whether by German-schooled Howard Becker of the University of Pennsylvania (later Wisconsin) in a review in the *Annals of the American Academy of Political and Social Sciences*, C.D. Burns in the *International Journal of Ethics*, R.M. Fox in the *Nation and Athenaum*, or leading Marxists like Benjamin Ginzburg in the *New Republic* and Sidney Hook in the *Nation*.[77] However, Becker's was the only strictly social scientific review. He was clear-headed enough to recognize that Weber was not undertaking an empirical study but employing the fiction of an ideal-type methodology to wrest understanding from "empirical chaos."[78] Burns offered evidence from the behaviour of successful business people in support of Weber. In his review, Hook brought a sophisticated version of historical materialism to Weber's view that economic factors were susceptible to ideological and cultural influence – despite the views of "vulgar Marxists" who, he said, "reduce the whole of social life to simple economic equations."[79]

Parsons' *Structure of Social Action* did not fare so well, whether in *The New Republic* or the *American Sociological Review* where prominent sociologists George [E.] Simpson and Louis Wirth, respectively, expressed appreciation of the strengths Parsons brought to the subject, especially his understanding of Weber, but were equivocal about the book itself and its singular commitment to voluntary action in the social arena.[80] Simpson, known for his work on Black religions in the New World, was particularly severe. Parsons had wrestled with four monumental figures and "brought forth a mouse" – a theory of social action that "offers no foothold for scientific research."[81] Swatos and Kivisto excuse themselves from exercising any judgment on Parsons' theory by suggesting that the equivocation in the reviews "may hide more than we can unearth today."[82] But *Social Structure* appeared amid Roosevelt's social activist New Deal response to the great crisis of capitalism of the 1930s. Their excuse could hardly fail to be seen by the socially and politically conscious as a political statement.

In *From Max Weber*, Gerth and Mills offered a translation of early empirical studies Weber had done to much acclaim, along with Weber's address in St Louis – which they did not hesitate to re-title to bring it into conformity with Weber's larger thesis. They also included some passages from the celebrated *Protestant Ethic* essays. This time round, specialized and public intellectual journals alike were quick to serve up reviews: Harvard's religious scholar, Harry M. Johnson, in the *Nation*; "Anonymous" in the *American Sociological Review*; Sigmund Neumann in the *Yale Review*; and Paul Honigsheim, notably "a survivor of Weber's Heidelberg circle," in the *Journal of American Sociology*.[83]

None of these saw any inconsistency in the rendering of Weber's line of argument nor in the quality of translation, only praise and some improvement with regard to the clarity of Weber's text. Honigsheim, who professed intimate acquaintanceship with Weber, urged that for Weber, the religious question was always foremost, "not state church or Biblicism, but individualistic Protestantism … Also Weber's political attitude is based on it."[84] So Swatos and Kivisto seize the notion of *The Protestant Ethic* as a "*political* project" (italics theirs) written under the conviction that "Germany and Protestantism were approaching catastrophe."

Political project? Protestant individualism? Voluntarism? As they conclude their section on "The American Weber," they note that in 1946

Weber was for some a myth and for most, outside a small circle of specialists, very much of an enigma. There is no question that, on a read of this chapter, the authors are formidably informed and acquainted with every subtlety of Weber's thesis and the debate it has engendered. And they move on to a brief but informative account of Weber's canonization – though it seems a bit of a leap from the preceding discussion. But why do they leave us with another enigma? Was Parsons' translation and his *Structure of Social Action* also a political project and, as with Weber, "the unfolding of a personality through times that were neither easy nor stable"?[85] And would that offer some legitimacy to "de-Parsonizers" in another difficult, unstable time of the 1970s?

MAX WEBER'S "IRON CAGE" AND THE PAST, PRESENT,
AND FUTURE OF AMERICAN POLITICAL CULTURE

Max Weber's *Protestant Ethic and the Spirit of Capitalism* may have been canonized as a benchmark work in American sociological programs of study in the latter twentieth century, but what of his dire anticipation that American capitalism would eventually become an "iron cage" or "steel hard case" fashioned by a rational, calculating capitalist order where technically driven work in a vast mechanized "cosmos," devoid of the meaningfulness of a personal calling and regulated by a rationally driven bureaucracy of specialists, would become a fate that none would have the power to escape? Given the strength of ascetic Calvinism in American religious life and the freewheeling capitalism Weber observed during his 1904 visit, no other destiny seemed probable, on the basis of the projections of his fictional "ideal-type" methodology. A retreat into the private sphere would become the only means of escape.

Stephen Kalberg, in a tightly reasoned chapter with the overlong title "Utilizing Max Weber's 'Iron Cage' to Define the Past, Present, and Future of American Political Culture," suggests that an inherent dualism Weber recognized deep in American heritage opens the way to a more ambiguous result – one that "both conforms to and deviates from" the iron-cage model.

Kalberg, an associate professor of sociology at Boston University, teaches sociological theory and comparative political and economic cultures. He is affiliated with Harvard's Center for European Studies. At the time of writing, he had published a translation of Weber's *Protestant Ethic and the Spirit of Capitalism* and a number of penetrating studies of Weber and his work. Several books have followed, the latest, a book-length version of the present chapter (2014).

Historically, Weber observed, "'world mastery individualism' had been powerfully qualified in America by 'civic sphere ideals and values' that pulled and guided individuals beyond self-interest calculations and toward the betterment of their communities."[86] Although both of these elements were much weakened by Weber's time, both had religious origins in America's Puritan past, born, in turn, of English and continental ascetic Protestant movements. Drawing heavily from Weber's writings on churches and sects in the United States, Kalberg suggests that the foregoing dualism in American life, in turn, reflected the dualism Weber found in ascetic Calvinist churches and sects: on the one hand, an ascetic lifestyle and worldly economic activism to demonstrate one's salvation, and on the other, membership in a self-governing congregation with a vision of a holy commonwealth rid of evil, whether that meant confronting miscreant persons, mistaken popular opinions and practices, heavy-handed corporations, or corrupt and authoritarian political regimes, and thus to promote "God's humane Kingdom on earth." For the faithful, one's engagement in methodical labour and the resultant prosperity were not personal possessions but dutiful pursuits and products for up-building that Kingdom. Self-governing ethical congregations schooled their members at once in the mastery of self, in community participation skills, in brotherly and sisterly concepts that looked beyond the congregation to the Puritan commonwealth as it grew. Over time, in the contagion of public life, a generalized version of this demonstrably powerful model produced a civic sphere of ideals and practices promoted by "families, neighborhoods, schools, and communities" undergoing varying degrees of secularization.[87]

Membership in a Protestant sect or church became an early sign of trustworthiness in business and other contractual relations, not just with each other but with "outsiders," again a rudimentary model for the "large number of 'orders' and clubs of all sorts" that Weber observed in America, whose members wore "some kind of a badge ... to guarantee [their] 'honorableness.'"[88] In locating the origin of a civic sphere of trust and goodwill in the young republic in a specific religious tradition, Weber, Kalberg says, differed from de Tocqueville, who saw it rooted, rather, in civil associations connected with commerce and politics.

Thus, as "ethical action became diffused across American society's political and economic arenas, in innumerable associations," the consequences for the country's political culture were enormous, not only in the challenge it presented to interest-oriented motivations in the public domain, but also outweighing the state as a force for social integration. For Weber, the American case was most unusual, and not explicable as an evolutionary product of industrialization. The common rootage of both world mastery individualism and civic sphere idealism allowed an "intertwining" through which the latter would moderate the egocentric bias of the former. At the same time, the tension between them "in large part accounted for the dynamism and restlessness of American political culture" and "broke asunder the iron cage."[89]

Weber had feared that the growth of bureaucratization in America would gradually smother the unique dualism of American political culture, to the detriment of civic sphere ideals he himself embraced. "Massive 'ossification' would then proceed and a closed, rigid, and inward-looking society devoid of noble ideals, pluralistic and competing values, and ethical action, would come into being."[90] Since the original religious grounding of work as a "calling" would be eroded and disappear via processes of habituation and secularization, what the future held was an iron cage where work had become an end in itself, a requisite badge of social acceptance. What Weber failed to anticipate, Kalberg argues, is that the decline of ascetic religion would open the gates to two powerful forces contrary to ascetic inner-world mastery individualism and civic idealism alike: a "ubiquitous intense consumer culture and an extraordinarily vibrant entertainment culture."[91] In the face of this threat, Kalberg reminds us that for Weber, deeply rooted cultural components remain available in the social organism and, given the right circumstance and an available social carrier, can re-emerge with new vigour. In the current state of play, then, a "triumvirate" has taken the place of the former dualism: consumer-entertainment industries, world mastery individualism, and civic sphere ideals, which interact with each other in a complex fashion, modifying each other in ways that would seem to defy future American imprisonment in Weber's iron cage model of modern capitalism.

THE PROTESTANT ETHIC AND THE "SPIRIT" OF CAPITALISM AS GRAND NARRATIVE: MAX WEBER'S PHILOSOPHY OF HISTORY

Max Weber, winding up his 1904–05 publication of *The Protestant Ethic and the Spirit of Capitalism*, called for a program of historical research to detail the story of ascetic religion from ascetic monasticism of the Middle Ages to its ultimate "dissolution into pure utilitarianism" in the modern West. Weber was "too modest," Donald A. Nielsen writes in his chapter, "The Protestant Ethic and the 'Spirit' of Capitalism as Grand Narrative: Max Weber's Philosophy of History." Weber, in this very work, he claimed, had already accomplished that for which he wished.

As the founder of historical sociology, Weber had the greatest impact among sociologists, but for Nielsen, he was as much a historian as a sociologist, dedicated, in his own words, to understanding "the manner in which 'ideas' become effective in history." This was not to say that Weber had written a standard developmental or evolutionary account. Nor was Nielsen the first to be interested in Weber as historian; Germany of the nineteenth century was a hothouse of historical research and reflection. Weber's rejection of the concept of a universal history, notions of inevitability, and the idea of a "zeitgeist" as an explanatory device had been commonly noted and the influence of Hegel and Marx widely discussed. But those, like Wolfgang Schluchter, who appeared determined to extract a theoretical system and sequentially staged development in *The Protestant Ethic*, Nielsen argues, simply misunderstand Weber and do a disservice to the subtlety of his undertaking.[92]

The narrative devices Weber uses to describe "an extraordinarily varied set of historical phases," are not developmental, Nielsen says; rather they "proceed through a series of 'fluid' transitions … accomplished through 'inner' processes that are best described as 'spiritual', taking place as they do, within the realm of ultimate values, ideas about salvation, and the ultimate ends of life." For Weber, these "shifting inner experiences" are best explained not in terms of external factors or psychological processes but through religious ideas. "When the inner meaning of economic activity no longer exists, the spirit has fled."[93]

Nielsen is mindful of contemporary suspicion of "grand narrative" history but rightly suggests that without a clear recognition of the grand narrative at the heart of *The Protestant Ethic*, the work "is not only incomprehensible," but easily misread as an "analysis of the linkages between two sets of ideas, the 'Protestant ethic' and the 'spirit of capitalism.'"[94] Nielsen structures his analysis and commentary on Weber's grand narrative through a series of chronological phases that will be familiar to informed readers: "The orchestration of life in the Middle Ages; the religious breakthrough to new forms of consciousness with Luther; the transformation of Reformation teachings effected by Calvin; the religious ethics of everyday life of the seventeenth century Puritan sects; the spirit of modern capitalism in the work of Benjamin Franklin; the transformation of Puritan religious teachings and Franklin's capitalist spirit into a purely utilitarian philosophy; and finally, the emergence of an economic cosmos divided between its inherited, but waning spiritual foundations and the resurgence of social and economic practices reminiscent of an earlier era, ones devoid of any spiritual dimension and encased in the 'steel hard shell' of mechanized capitalism."[95] The text is punctuated with mini-narratives and biographical sketches that, for Nielsen, are engaging in themselves but also serve to integrate the larger narrative that ranges across five centuries of Western culture and the histories of half a dozen countries, with pointed references to Judaism, early Christianity, and classical culture. It is, Nielsen tells us, the most heavily documented of Weber's works, divided almost equally between text and notes.

Nielsen's own presentation of the several phases of Weber's narrative is always illuminating. His final judgment is that, although in his historical orientation Weber rejected the teleological idealism of Hegel and was critical of "Marx's effort to see the history of spirit in light of material social practice, [not to mention Nietzsche's projection of the *ubermensch*], it is with them he is to be compared." Weber developed "in the [*Protestant Ethic and the Spirit of Capitalism*] his own variant of a dialectical philosophy of history, a narrative of the ceaseless, fluid ebb and flow of spiritual reckoning in the inner lives of historical individuals." The notion that the Weber thesis is simply a sociological account of "the relationship of religion and economic action [needs] to die a final death" – and find a resurrection as a life-bearing "grand historical narrative of European civilization's inner life" and the challenges it poses for our own time.[96]

RATIONALISM, TRADITIONALISM, ADVENTURE CAPITALISM:
NEW RESEARCH ON THE WEBER THESIS
In a chapter carrying into the twenty-first century the search for the spirit of capitalism and the role of religion in its spectacular ascendancy in Western and international economies, co-editor Lutz Kaelber subjects contrary positions to a keen "cross-examination." Entitled "Rational Capitalism, Traditionalism, Adventure Capitalism: New Research on the Weber Thesis," the chapter begins with Kaelber citing a large multinational study endorsing religion as "good for the economy" and setting it over against another study that found "little, if any, link between the strength of Protestantism and capitalist development, at least in mid-to late nineteenth century Europe."[97] The problem with such studies, Kaelber says, is that they ignore the fine distinctions and conditions Weber sets; not religion or Protestantism in any time or place, but ascetic Calvinist groups and their prosperity relative to "comparable groups in *similar circumstances* and the *potentially short period* before those other groups, without sharing the same ethical beliefs, could adopt the same economic ethics."[98] These criteria clearly invalidate population studies like those of Samuelsson in *Religion and Economic Action*.[99]

Kaelber helpfully charts the distinguishing features of Weber's typology of economic organizations and motivations to clarify the muddied waters of debate. These charts show how Weber's "spirit of modern rational capitalism" was a separate strand from "state driven political capitalism," "forced exploitation by private robber capitalists," and "irrational speculation by venture capitalists." Drawing on the 2001 work of Guenther Roth, into the intriguing history of the cosmopolitan financial and industrial ventures of the extended Weber family, Kaelber describes how Weber resorted to individual capitalist entrepreneurs in the family lineage to illustrate some of the specific ideal-type capitalists in his study.[100] Weber's depiction of the transformation of a linen export company run in a traditional easygoing manner with the intent of maintaining a comfortable level of activity and lifestyle is a case in point. "Some young man" in the owner's family arrives on the scene and systematically implements employment practices that transform "peasants into workers," develops marketing techniques that expand the business, and reinvests profits in the company, so as to meet and survive the competitive struggle. With this rationalization, a "comfortable old ideal collapsed and crumbled." The account yields two ideal-types: that of the traditional capitalist and the rational, calculating capitalist imbued with the spirit of capitalism intensified by the legacy of ascetic Calvinist ethics. These *dramatis personae* were, however, Weber's grandfather, Karl Augustus and his father's brother, Weber's uncle, Carl David! The real scenario, which does not detract from Weber's purpose, was somewhat different. Carl David fled to the duchy Lippe-Detmold where the company was situated so as to avoid a three-year draft into the Prussian army.[101]

For the ideal-type of the "booty/robber capitalist," Weber chose Henry Villard, who "organized the famous 'blind pool' [of fifty million dollars] in order to stage a [New York] stock exchange raid on the shares of the Northern Pacific Railroad" – whose president Villard then became.[102] Villard, in reality more "venture" than "robber" capitalist, hardly deserved the designation, "grandiose robber capitalis[t]," Weber gave him. Villard was not a "Weber" and Kaelber appears to have introduced Villard to point out that if Weber wanted an ideal-type combined "booty/venture capitalist" he had to look no farther than the founder of the extended family's wealth, the successful worldwide entrepreneur Carl Cornelius Souchay. Of Huguenot origin, Souchay was germane to Weber's thesis. Was Weber embarrassed by his ancestor's trading and banking activities, which apparently included "speculation, carpet baggery, [and] smuggling"?[103]

Kaelber, quite naturally, then turns to four studies that bore on the veracity of Weber's argument. Two of these, which affirm the thesis, focus on colonial America and rural nineteenth century Ohio, while two others assail the entire thesis. Historian James Henretta, in "The Protestant Ethic and the Reality of Capitalism in Colonial America" (1993), documented how four Massachusetts Bay capitalists, despite the opposition of clergy wedded to older communal forms of association, initiated a prolonged period of commercial success. Their "religiously guided" economic ethic expressed itself in "methodical, rational acquisition and enterprise," thus advancing the "spirit of capitalism" that would, in time, dominate the region. Also affirming Weber's argument, Anne Kelly Knowles, in *Calvinists Incorporated* (1997), demonstrated how Welsh farmers of "Calvinist Methodist" persuasion, immigrating to Ohio, "developed into formidable industrial entrepreneurs who resembled Max Weber's ascetic Protestants." Kaelber comments that, in her study, Knowles appears unaware that her study was a "stunning confirmation of Weber's thesis."[104] Although Weber includes Methodists among his ascetic Calvinist sects, they are usually described as Arminian for their rejection of the Calvinist doctrine of predestination. They were, however, methodical and ascetic in their style of life and disciplined in their use of time.[105]

On the other side of the ledger, Kaelber turns to what he describes as "one of the most thorough examinations ... to date" of the "English Puritan experience in the early modern period." In *Protestantism and Capitalism: The Mechanics of Influence,* Jere Cohen brought an important new perspective to the debate, clarifying the two ways – direct and indirect – that the Protestant ethic influenced the development of capitalism. The first "mechanism," as he terms it, was via the religiously grounded personal work ethic implicit in the concept of a "calling" to which Puritans subscribed. The second mechanism functioned indirectly through society as the Puritan example, secularized, became a cultural norm. However, Cohen categorically denied that "a spirit of capitalism" could be found among the Puritan tradesmen he studied, citing Gordon Marshall's work on the economic ethics of early Scottish Calvinist entrepreneurs in support, and he questioned whether "the 'spirit of capitalism' has ever existed as Weber described it." Far from being modern, the Puritans were traditional on key questions of profitability, satisfaction with existing lifestyle, and contentment within their present calling.[106]

Kaelber, who had crossed swords with Cohen previously,[107] however, points Cohen to the evidence noted above of colonial entrepreneurs in New England and the Welsh immigrants in Ohio and cites chapter and verse to demonstrate Cohen's misinterpretation of Weber and his misrepresentation of Marshall. He also faults Cohen's methodology in a number of respects, including selectivity in choice of quotations, reliance on dated and discredited works, and offering as argument what was little more than opinion.

Finally, as a kind of *coup de grace*, Kaelber cites a recent article by Margaret Jacob and Matthew Kadane who triumphantly announced that Weber's long-missing example of a real-life Protestant capitalist had now been found, namely, the English merchant capitalist Joseph Ryder 1695–1768).[108] Dedicated to an ascetic Calvinist calling, the disciplined use of time, and material austerity, Ryder was not only successful in commerce as a clothier, but left behind a 14,000-page spiritual journal in forty-one volumes covering thirty-five years. Ryder's Calvinism, somewhat modified by currents of covenant theology and providentialism, allowed for a less inscrutable God and the possibility of believers discovering and carrying out God's will in practice. While confirming the larger part of Weber's argument, the authors had some questions – for example, whether predestinarianism was the sole source of salvation-anxiety among the Calvinist sects – in response to which Kaelber notes that Weber, himself, had some flexibility on that issue. More importantly, they observed that it was with considerable uneasiness that Ryder walked the line between religion and commerce, leading Kaelber to comment that perhaps "Weber's ideal-typical depiction [of a Protestant capitalist] glosses over the uneasiness with which ascetic Protestant merchants negotiated between the secular and the sacred."[109] Ryder and those like him, of course, were not yet possessed of the "spirit of capitalism" that, unencumbered by religious scruples, would sanction a dutiful, rational, and methodical pursuit of profit as a good in itself.

Satisfied that new research had unearthed clear examples of rational economic pursuit among ascetic Calvinist groups dedicated to their "calling," that Weber's ideal-type Protestant capitalist had been found, and that Weber's preferred focus on rational economic action as distinct from self-satisfied traditionalism and reckless adventure "greed is good" capitalism had been clarified, Kaelber cautioned those who "wish to put an end to Weber worship" not to foreclose on the future too hastily. Future research was especially needed to gather evidence of "the spirit of enterprise among capitalists freshly weaned off their religious ascetic roots or those who continued to combine austere religious traditions with profit maximization long after industrialization."[110] So Kaelber's final advice to "scholars who explore the interface of religion and the economy" is that they await results before deciding to deposit "Weber's thesis in the dustbin of history."

3. *The Protestant Ethic Revisited (Again)*

The second decade of the twenty-first century was barely a year old when the Weber thesis was once again the subject of a significant book. In *The Protestant Ethic Revisited,* Philip Gorski offers qualified complementary support for Weber's argument in *The Protestant Ethic and the Spirit of Capitalism.*[111] The qualification arises from Gorski's concern as a historical sociologist for empirical evidence, the complementary support from his special research interest in state formation in the Reformation and post-Reformation periods in Europe.

Philip Gorski is a graduate of the University of California (Berkeley) who studied under the distinguished sociologist of religion Robert Bellah. Gorski has taught at the University of Wisconsin and, since 2007, at Yale, where he is the co-director of the Center for Comparative Research. He has been the author and editor of several books and many articles.

Gorski is familiar with all the latest research and writing on the Weber thesis. He states quite explicitly that Weber's focus was not the Protestant ethic in general but the neo-Calvinism of the latter sixteenth and seventeenth centuries. On the issue of empirical evidence, Gorski is sensitive to the difficulties surrounding the subject, especially the problem of documenting the religious and psychological states of mind of appropriate neo-Calvinist capitalists of the age. The support he offers Weber, therefore, derives from the more documentable role of Calvinism in state formation in the same period. In his major publication on the subject, *The Disciplinary Revolution: Calvinism and the Rise of the State in Early Modern Europe* (2003), he argued that it was the revolutionary ethic of ascetic Calvinism that provided the conditions for the personal discipline, political order, bureaucratization, and secure property rights necessary to dynamic economic advance. In short, Calvinist state formation was another expression of the same ethic that Weber argued was a critical agent in the emergence of the spirit of modern capitalism.

Addressing the Weber thesis directly in 2011 in a series of carefully argued and documented chapters, Gorski deftly steps from alternative theories of state formation to the case for the Protestant ethic in its Calvinist form as the driving force behind the rise of the leading centres of the commercial revolution – Amsterdam, London, and, with qualifications, Prussia. The book culminates in an extended discussion of the Weber thesis itself and the related issue of secularization.

Gorski's introduction to *The Protestant Ethic Revisited* takes aim at the so-called "Tilly thesis" of the modern "give war a chance" school, which contrarily sums up the process of successful state formation – and hence of economic advance – with the Darwinian formula, "war makes the state and the state makes war."[112] Gorski concedes some points to the "bellicists" for bringing "war, politics and religion" together.[113]

. While Gorski recognizes the complexity of Weber's argument, he is uneasy about the impression of monocausality that Weber leaves in the text.[114] He also has serious reservations about Weber's derivation of a singular devotion to work from predestinarian doctrine and sees his own more documentable work providing backup empirical support for Weber.

This support, however, did not extend to Weber's later concept of the "Great Divergence" of the West. Weber had advanced this "Great Divergence" concept in *The Economic Ethics of the World's Religions*, arguing that the holy worldliness of the Protestant ethic set up personal and social dynamics that contrasted sharply with Eastern religions that were either too world denying or too world accommodating to foster the aggressive entrepreneurial activity that would characterize modern Western capitalism. By 2011, that theory had been put in question in the light of research showing levels and sophistication of economic activity in India and China in advance of the West until the onset of the Industrial Revolution.[115] Citing the research, Gorski, on the basis of his state formation studies, proposed an alternative "Little Divergence" theory among the European states that would be immensely important for the future of Europe itself.[116] In short, the persecution, conflict, and warfare provoked by the rapid expansion and economic success of Calvinist populations led to massive flights of Calvinists to particular states to the north – Holland, England, and Prussia. This redistribution of human capital left southern Europe the more in the hands of a Catholic church dedicated to expanding holy orders, preserving feudal relations, and political absolutism, while in the north, the Calvinist dramatic reduction of saints days, lengthening of the work day, dissolution of monasteries, creation of large estates, and bias for self-government all nurtured a distinctive socio-political ethos and a level of economic prosperity that radically differentiated the northern states from the Atlantic and Mediterranean states. London and Amsterdam, in particular, would lead the way into the commercial revolution of the seventeenth and eighteenth centuries. The socio-political and religio-economic impacts of the dispersion of Calvinist populations have long been well-known. Gorski's innovation was to deploy these demographic data in the form of an alternative to Weber's "Great Divergence" concept.

Gorski is careful not to overstate his argument, not wanting to set up another monocausal deterministic theory. He describes his argument as a proposal for further research.[117] He acknowledges the merit of other attempts to explain the phenomena in question. Was it urbanization? Did the correlation of religion and economics run the other way, as Marx argued? He deplores the continuing overly simple subscription of most current Marxists to the proposition that capitalism arose out of the agricultural revolution and the accidental discovery of the power of steam.[118] He appears to join a gathering consensus that "Weber's goal in writing *The Protestant Ethic* was not to disprove historical materialism; it was to round it out by examining the role of 'ideal factors' in the development of modern capitalism."[119] By the same token, he declares that "the goal of the research program I sketch ... is not to disprove the Weber thesis with its emphasis on the ideational and social-psychological impacts of the Protestant Reformation; rather it is to explore material and socio-political consequences" and to "isolate the multiple waves of [religious] causation ... insofar as they impacted the process of economic development."[120] This, he concludes is more pertinent, since "the great question that defines our time is not so much the rise of the West as it is the return of the East; not the genesis of capitalism, but the preeminence of the West."

4. Conclusion

LOVE AND WORK
IN THE SHADOW OF THE REFORMATION[121]

Like Gorski, James Livingston, in his book *No More Work,* points beyond the initial question Weber asked to another one: After the "iron cage" of capitalism – what?[122] For Gorski, it is the question of the role of religious and/or other ideal and empirical factors as they bear on the "pre-eminence of the West" and its manifold ramifications for the rest of the world. For Livingston, it is the related question of the role of religious and/or other cultural factors in their relation to the meaning and future of work in the latest stage of "iron cage" capitalism as the total "victory of the machine" looms ever closer, threatening an end not just to work but also to the complex of meanings inherent in a work ethic that served so long to justify it. The two come together in the question, What is the image of living and working human beings that drives these phenomena forward? For Livingston, as for Weber, the end of work, as conceived and practised in the context of an evolving industrial revolution, poses far-reaching moral and spiritual questions, including the very meaning of what it means to be human. But, Livingston warns, "We won't have any answers until we acknowledge that work now means everything to us – and in the future it can't."[123]

Livingston is a professor of history who has taught in a number of locales, including prison, but since 1988 at Rutgers University in New Jersey. He has published seven books in a critical social vein. His special interest is in various themes in the interplay of economics, class, and culture in the evolution of American politics and society.[124] *No More Work* is written in a popular style, with a touch of irreverence designed, no doubt, to attract attention.[125] The substance, however, is a serious mix of intellectual history and political advocacy, critiquing proponents of full employment in the name of a basic annual income for everyone. His principal target is the work ethic bequeathed to moderns by the Protestant Reformation.

Livingston's genuinely thoughtful and often brilliant reflections are too wide ranging for a close critique here. Ironically – no pun intended! – in his slim, 100-page volume, Livingston mentions Max Weber only once. But *No More Work* is all about Weber and his famous thesis, at the driving centre of which was a profound concern over the future of life and work in a world dominated by "the spirit of modern capitalism." Weber wrote in German of the "steel hard shell (or cloak)" of capitalism. The "iron cage" was Parson's phrase in his translation of Weber's work; Livingston writes of "the iron grip of capitalism."[126] Variations of the phrase "the conduct of life" that punctuate Weber's pages point to the ethical centre of Weber's argument; Livingston's work pulsates with concern over how a once-meaningful, historic concept of work, overtaken by economic contradictions and moral hypocrisy, now, in its stripped-down form, stands athwart the good life in the present and the creative thinking demanded by the looming prospects of a workless world. Livingston thus offers occasion to pursue the implications of Weber's concern for "the conduct of life" into a time when, with the iron cage cracking under the hammer blows of cyber technologies, new horizons once more open before us for new thought and practice on fundamental questions of human destiny.

In chapters entitled "Labour and the Essence of Man" and "Love and Work in the Shadow of the Reformation," the history of the idea of work from Plato and Aristotle through Luther, Hegel, Marx, and Freud underlines how deeply the idea of the saving value and ennobling value of productive work had penetrated the Western image of what it meant to be human. While Weber's more rigorous ascetic neo-Calvinist ethic became submerged in the process leading to the "iron cage," Livingston sees Luther's more unequivocal ethic of "holy worldliness," expressed through faithful work in one's "calling," a continuing force in an increasingly secularized form in the United States. He thus charges left-wing, liberal, and right-wing advocates of full employment as a solution to the ravages of automation of indulging in a Reformation-bequeathed work ethic by which the work of industrial capitalism became universally accepted as the bedrock of character and the credential of full membership in society.

Livingston reserves his severest criticism for advocates of "craftsmanship" as a solution for the crisis of work – public intellectuals like Hannah Arendt, Richard Sennett, Christopher Lasch, and Lewis Mumford, whose Aristotelian reflections on "work" (in Greek, *poiesis*, or labour as a kind of poetic self-transcendence). Livingston does not deny the value of creative crafting and the importance it may have in a future leisured society, but as a solution to the crisis of work it serves chiefly in the present to "keep us comfortable in the prison house of work."[127] His critique of left advocates of full employment is quite different: people like David Ellermann who defends his leadership in the world of worker's cooperatives by returning to Anglo/American anti-slavery and common law principles that prohibit the ownership of any person by any other person or agency, with their corollary that workers have a right to that with which they mix their labour (John Locke). Or brilliant trade union intellectuals, like Alex Gourevitch and Steve Fraser who write books with titles like *From Slavery to the Cooperative Commonwealth* (2016) and *The Age of Acquiescence* (2015), respectively. Or genuinely progressive journalists like Thomas Edsall in the *New York Times*. All promote their full employment cause with the same arguments that work is of the essence of being a responsible human being and engaged citizen, free from the perils of the dole, and out of the pockets of hard-working middle-class taxpayers. While the views of such progressives reflect historic teaching on the positive virtues of work, they also carry forward what Livingston calls the "ambiguities" of Hegel and Marx, who detected and protested the "slave-morality" entailed in the actual conditions of labour, and Freud, who saw in the current work world symptoms of "repression, perhaps even regression."[128] However, Livingston's progressives sometimes sounded like Tea Party enthusiasts in projecting the language of servility and repression onto government itself. Hence, Edsall, incorporating a quotation of a colleague, that "the economics of survival have forced millions ... to rely on "pity-charity liberal capitalism" ... *consigning* [them] to a *condition of subjugation* – living out their lives on government subsidies like Medicaid, the Earned Income Tax Credit, and now Obamacare."[129] However, to complicate things, the components of Weber's iron cage included distant bureaucracies run by rationally driven functionaries! Livingston pointedly notes that a "full employment policy" also presumes government dependency. He questions the reality of "apologetic" suggestions that such a policy would be short term. Where were the new jobs going to come from when for years employment had stagnated as corporate profits and stock prices soared? And, under an anticipated recovery, would the jobs be part-time with no benefits, and soul-destroying "temp" and contingent work?

The answer, Livingston says, is to separate compensation and work and establish a guaranteed basic annual income for all. Far from inviting debilitating national consequences in a final corruption of the work ethic among the public at large, Livingston offers four grounds for thinking otherwise.

First, he cites long-term experiments with the guaranteed annual income in half a dozen low-income urban and rural populations in the 1960s through the 1980s that detected no decline in the motivation to work among participants. One such study in New Jersey became the basis of the Nixon administration's Family Assistance Program to fix a broken Social Security system. It proposed a guaranteed annual income to all American families in need, proposing to raise incomes above the poverty line, which, in today's dollars, would be $32,000. The Plan passed the House of Representatives in 1970 with a large majority, only to be killed in the Senate. The later studies were quickly shelved, with one done in Dauphin, Manitoba, quietly sidelined by the provincial government despite its positive results.[130]

Second, Livingston cites the answers given in conversations and interviews with almost 200 people from a wide range of occupations to his question, "Why do we want to work?" The uniform answer was some form of, "A reason to live ... to get out of bed and do the right thing while awake ... somewhere to go, a place – more than that actually, an *emotional* destination – that would help them translate their inchoate, inarticulate desires into a coherent, regular, recognizable set of meanings [and] give their humdrum everyday lives some durable shape." It was never "just for the money."[131]

Livingston's third line of defence is that, in fact, in a broken labour market, the separation of work from compensation, in terms of any rational calculation of the real value of inputs and outputs, already occurs on a massive scale. That part-time workers at McDonalds make eight dollars an hour while its CEO is paid 300 times that amount is just an outrageous example of what occurs in workplaces across the nation.

In his fourth line of defence, Livingston takes to the offensive. He asks why, for the sake of an outmoded work ethic, the "no free lunch" crowd wants more work and more production when retail shelves are already overflowing, when economic growth now threatens global ecological collapse and the incineration of human beings off the face of the earth.

So Livingston returns to his central thesis that the crisis of work is not just an economic issue of primary proportions but, at its centre, a moral and spiritual crisis forcing us to ask what being human is all about. Freud, he says, held that the two fundamentals for human fulfillment are work and love that serve to get us out of ourselves and into a relationship where self-transcending action and meaning can be found. The question Livingston has been asking all along has been "whether love can replace work – whether 'socially beneficial labor' the love of our neighbors can replace 'socially necessary labor' as the criterion we use in calculating the distribution of income and the development of character."[132] His answer is that we already do that. Free public education, medical care, social services, and information on the web are just some of the examples of surrogate income for millions. Twenty percent of family incomes in the United States come from government transfers, he says. The socially beneficial labour entailed in conveying such services has no clear market value, but they are of huge moral and social benefit – and profound spiritual significance. The drama and tragedy of the end of work and the working class of the industrial revolution is upon us. We may not have any choice but to find in the labours of love an alternative ethic that inclines us to see the good of our neighbour as equivalent to our own. Are we, or are we not, our brothers' and sisters' keepers?

And Weber?

In 1917, a dozen years after the publication of the *Protestant Ethic* essays, Weber gave two notable lectures on the conduct of life within the "steel hard" confines of modern capitalism. Both were addressed to professionals, those whose "callings" were science and politics, in both of which Weber had a special interest. Both were fields that would later, like all else, be affected by the cyber revolution but not eliminated by it.[133] To the best of my knowledge, he gave no such addresses to industrial workers and unskilled labourers, leaving the impression, perhaps, that one might not be "called" into such work. However, in the course of his advice to scientists, he noted that to fulfill themselves as persons, they needed to pursue a cause. He went on to explicitly extend the advice to others without limit. But it is difficult to imagine elevating riveting in a shipyard or tending the looms in a textile factory as a cause. Joining a union to fight for better wages, hours, and working conditions, yes, but not the repetitive labour in the nation's workshops. In short, it was the human – the humane – dimension of such labour that could constitute a fulfilling cause and create "personality."[134] Weber was fully conversant with the "slave-morality" and the "repression"

Hegel, Marx, Nietzsche, and Freud condemned as inherent in work under the conditions of industrial capitalism. Those elements were also of the essence of Weber's concept of the "steel hard cloak" that, via its multiple components of methodically rationalized conditions of life and labour, was utterly depersonalizing. The "heroic individualism" he commended to scientists can readily be read as applying to workers as well, however difficult their lot. This was not the heroics of a once meaningful Protestant ethic that was now dubbed "inner-worldly ascetic world mastery individualism."[135] Nor was it the heroics of Nietzsche's "last men," the *ubermensch* of *Thus Spake Zarathustra*, whom Weber perceived as lacking both spirit and heart. Scientists were adjured to reject Nietzschean "self-aggrandizement" and grasp what autonomy they had and labour with "heart" in their chosen cause. So, by this showing, were workers for whom the requisite causes would be more hazardous but more fulfilling. There was, apparently, no hope to be found in those religions that had succeeded polytheism but, after a prophetic period, had become routinized. Old "gods" had been resurrected – Wagner and the Ring – but were no match for the new gods, the impersonal forces (aka the spirit of capitalism) that virtually determined the shape and inner character of everything they touched.

Weber seems not to have anticipated or speculated on a rusting, cracking, and ultimate collapse of the iron cage. The difficulty he had with both Hegel and Marx was their erection of a universal system whose inner workings moved to a predetermined goal of a final emancipation of humanity. Weber, rather, saw in history a story of "developmental tendencies and contingencies, of visions, illusions, and reactions to unintended consequences." History was "full of ironies and paradoxes."[136] Perhaps it is one of the ironies of our present situation that an ancient question of Weber's now rationalized and routinized religion should animate a vision of life beyond his predicted iron cage. That would not have surprised Weber, for whom values and visions remained in suspension in religion as though awaiting revival in a propitious time. And perhaps it would be one of those paradoxes that the driving thrust of methodical, rationalized production that has enslaved millions since the ethic of ascetic neo-Calvinism infected the spirit of capitalism – now increasingly, everywhere, being transmuted in the totally impersonal cybernetics of automated industry – would finally break open the iron cage and herald a post-capitalist culture in which economics and ancient vision come together to offer humanity the possibility of a society covenanted to work for each other's well-being. The evidence for this, Livingston insists, has been growing, not without struggle, but growing out there, in the expanding structures of new socio-economics of love.

Myth, Religion, and the Politics of Sacred and Secular

1

Implicit in the title of this book is the issue of the relationship of the secular and the sacred. The various chapters, Canadian and otherwise in content, deal with notable instances of religion crossing a boundary commonly thought to separate the sacred from the secular. Despite the current tendency to depreciate religion, I prefer to refer to the "religious and the secular." The word "sacred" bears a connotation of untouchability, lest whatever deity is being spoken of be profaned. This preference betrays my bias for religion active "beyond the noise of solemn assemblies." I first addressed this sacred/secular question on the last page of *The Social Passion* and more recently at a little greater length in the prologue of *The View from Murney Tower*, where I expatiated on the paired term, "secular." I noted how profoundly Judaism, the Jewish inheritance of Christianity, was concerned with the secular as the context, matrix, arena – as you will – even the substance, in and through which "the religious" could properly be expressed and even find fulfillment. And I called attention to the importance of the Protestant ethic for this discussion, with the elevation of the realm of worldly activity we denote as "secular" and early steps into modernity. Here, in a ruminating postscript that touches some of the above themes, I want to consider the sacred and the secular in the context of mythologies out of which they separately arose, and their significance for religion and political thought and action. I suggest not just that they thus have some fundamental features in common in those respects, but that they actually need each other. I am aware that, as composite terms, "sacred" and "secular" catch up a multiplicity of related phenomena that may not always be consistent. In the discussion that follows, the frame of reference is limited to the religion, myth, and politics in the Western tradition.

2

Myth. For two centuries Christian theology has been in crisis. At the crux of the crisis is the mythology woven in, through, and around the varied literatures –historical, poetic, legal, ritual, wisdom, prophetic – of the Judeo-Christian scriptures, the Bible. So says Gary Dorrien in his typically insightful book, *The Word as True Myth: Interpreting Modern Theology* (1997). Dorrien, who has been described as the most rigorous as well as the most readable historical theologian working today, is Reinhold Niebuhr Professor of Social Ethics at Union Theological Seminary in New York. In my experience, he is one of the ablest interpreters of modern Christian thought, both of its philosophical and theological foundations and of its social and political expressions. The legacy of the Enlightenment and the rise of modern science, having put in question the mythological elements of Judeo-Christian religion, precipitated a debate that has left few academic disciplines untouched and sent Biblical scholars, theologians, and apologists, Christian and Jewish, and numerous related commentators, scurrying to rework the faith in terms that speak to generations schooled in the ethos of modern science and technological rationality. Dorrien's discussion of how three successive theological movements, liberal/idealist, crisis/neo-orthodox, and liberationist/postmodern, sought to resolve the issue, leaves no question as to the seriousness of the issue of myth for any discussion of the sacred and the secular.

Seven decades earlier, in works like *Symbol, Myth, and Culture* (1926), the prominent German philosopher, Ernst Cassirer, laid the foundations of twentieth-century explorations into the nature and power of myth as he struggled to understand the profound crisis for the politics of the modern nation state entailed in the rise and power of Nazi mythology of state and race in Germany. In his posthumous classic, *The Myth of the State* (1946), Cassirer attributed the power of myth to two critical elements: its capacity to heighten awareness of self and society and the binding force it was capable of exerting over its followers. It is instructive that the two roots of the word "religion," we are told, precisely follow Cassirer on myth: to heighten awareness and to bind together. Taken together, these two features of myth and religion explain their power to mobilize whole societies for common endeavour – for good or for ill. The crises of religion and politics in the twentieth century appear to share a similar basis, though with radically different consequences. For Christianity, and for religion more generally, a declining power of the mythical, and for the state an escalation, even to the point of enabling a new (ancient?) pseudo-religion of the state. Aspects of these inter-related phenomena are further explored in chapters four, fourteen, and sixteen. The fates of the religious and the secular, as two encompassing dimensions of human culture(s), are seldom unrelated.

Cassirer's approach to myth through the symbolic nature of language offers a key to the nature – even the necessity – of myth in articulating important aspects of human experience. Language is probably the greatest gift human beings possess. Language is a vast and intricate system of symbols, reflecting an even more vast, intricate, and awesome universe. As far as we know, we are the best symbolists in the universe, but all that reminds us of what we easily ignore – that, however refined, our articulated thoughts remain at best one step removed from the objects and subjects of observation and communication. How much more is that the case when we move into the realm of religion where we grapple with how to understand and explain our farthest and deepest apprehensions of the nature of existence, the meaning of life, and moments of transcendent experience. When it comes to the God-language of religion, the issue becomes a mind bender. How does one speak of a "reality" that does not "exist" in the strict meaning of the word, but is, nonetheless, the stuff of experience and demands to be spoken of?

Historically, myth and its associated literary devices, simile, metaphor, analogy, and allegory, have not just been an appropriate language of religious discussion; they have been the *sine qua non* of religious communication. There are other languages. In philosophy, this is the realm of metaphysics, that which is beyond the order of reality capable of scientific demonstration. And there is theology, reasoning that systematically pursues the logical implications of various God-beliefs or "theisms." Myth is different, attempting as it does to respond to the foregoing apprehensions and experience in a grand narrative of beginnings, exploits, and destiny of a people or the entirety of humankind on earth. With great imaginative power, myth molds stories of heroes and heroines and historical events to its purpose, and, in a cosmological setting, it engages God and/or gods in an ongoing dialogue with its human subjects. Myth does not seek to prove the "existence" of God, it assumes it, aware, apparently, that to do so is, so to speak, to range God with other known things. To know in that way elevates the knower above God, the implications of which are obvious.

A central feature of language is naming some thing or being and the interrelationships among them. To name something is to bring it into that utilitarian realm where we can exercise power over it. But to approach gods or God, who are neither things nor beings, in those terms, either in reason or faith, however much humans have stooped to it, is obviously absurd. The Christian Cappadocian Fathers of the sixth century of the Common Era refused to employ a "God language" for those very reasons and initiated what is called the *apophatic* tradition in Christianity. Their Jewish antecedents were chary of naming God and held it to be a sacrilege to use "the Lord's name in vain" – that is to puff up one's vanity; they preferred to use four unpronounceable consonants for the purpose.

For the Hindu seeking a "beatific vision" and reunion with Brahma beyond the transmigrations of soul, or the Buddhist committed to a spiritual journey toward a pure subjectivity, emancipated from and oblivious to the cares, passions, delusions, and sufferings of the external world, this was *Nirvana*, or "no-thing-ness," and being "no thing" was beyond naming.

It is a widely held misconception that the secular domain, in contrast to the religious, is somehow free of such allegedly anachronistic modes of thinking and expression, being governed, it is claimed, by rational, fact-based, pragmatic considerations. Such claims are used to wall the religious off from the secular public issues of state, politics, and economics and to relegate religion to the realm of personal spirituality. But in the Judeo-Christian-Islamic inheritance, God covenants not with individuals but with a whole people. It is their corporate ethos and structured life together that is primary. In the creation story, whatever else one makes of it, God sees that "Adam," – the primordial human – as individual, is a mistake; humanity is binary, sexual, co-creative in love – in the spirit of this God. Family results, a people and nation. It is in the culture of family, however conceived, and community that, born individual, full personhood evolves in solidarity with others to play its part in the human/divine drama. This is all relational and, indeed, political. Ultimately, it presages a city, kingdom, empire where the power of love and justice heals all hurts.

The notion that religion is inherently divisive, especially in view of the increasing pluralism of our societies is, on balance, mistaken and the actual sources of divisiveness need in many, perhaps most, instances to be sought elsewhere. To exclude religion from the public square short-circuits the work necessary to turn our new multi-faith and multicultural circumstances into an asset in public life in the form of enriched social criticism and the public aspirations of diverse new communities in our midst. Or is that why some fear the presence of the religious in the public domain? The mythology, however, has its own explanation of where the problem lies. In the arrival of self-consciousness in "the garden" of human development, consciousness of the other is also born, and with it, the ethical quandaries, the spiritual perversions, and the psychic traumas that afflict humanity – the perennial temptations of status and power over the other, idolatries of tribalisms – ancient and modern, the pursuit of institutional advantage, the preferential option for competitive enterprise over cooperative effort and equitable sharing of "the fruits of labour." The "history" incorporated into the myth is graphic in telling that story – of persons, social relations, economics, politics, and religion, all being bent out of shape in the process The mythology is clear. The "knowledge of good and evil" can assume bewildering – even terrifyingly – complex forms within our very psyches and our collectivities. In any case, it does not require acute observation to note that public issues are quite capable of arousing intense conflict in their own right. That, too, underscores the wisdom of myth, properly understood. It is too easy to shoot the messenger and think the problem is solved. As sceptic John Gray reminds us in *Black Mass: Apocalyptic Religion and the Death of Utopia* (2007), religion, given the pervasive human issues it addresses, cannot be isolated from the public square.

3

It was the revolutionary work of the Jewish prophets of the eighth century BCE to transform the violent tribal ethos of a warrior people and their God that did not hesitate to command the complete annihilation of the men, women, children, and domesticated animals of a hostile tribe into one of the world's great mythologies, monotheistic, universal in its declaration of the unity of humankind, ethically oriented and justice driven. The prophets were not the originators or the sole proponents of monotheism in the ancient world, however. The Egyptians had precedence with Osiris, and the Roman Stoics would later follow in that path, but the conception for both of these was of an "imperial monotheism" that sanctified an empire resplendent in power and glory. For the Prophets, the one God over all was a defender of the poor and a liberator of slaves and the disinherited. It was a "monotheism of the oppressed." Among the three mythologies that lay at the base of western civilization, the Greek, the Nordic, and the Judaic, the last was distinctive in the singularity of its God who self-identified simply as "I am that I am." This God originates a good creation, chooses as a founding figure for a new people one Abraham, who welcomes strangers into his tent and feasts them rather than killing them, as was the custom. Abraham's descendants fall into slavery, but "I am" stages a dramatic liberation that becomes the centrepiece of this new people's identity. By repeated conquests and exile by surrounding empires, this God is said to be disciplining them for the task of bringing warring nations together in a future era of peace, justice, and well-being for all peoples. Depending on current circumstances, this mission would now be confidently seen as the work of the nation itself, now in the apocalyptic intervention of God. All of which, Judaic and later, by inheritance, Christian, was told in a mix of vivid literary imagination and historical renovation. It was an epic encompassing past, present, and future.

Under the impress of this self-understanding, an elaborate legal code was developed, flawed by the prevailing patriarchalism and residual barbarism but providing protection for widows, orphans, slaves, strangers, and beasts of burden. A "Year of Jubilee" was projected – though possibly never implemented – when, in every fiftieth year, all debt would be cancelled, land redistributed, and slaves freed. The myth anticipated the coming of a messianic figure who would bring Israel's mission to fulfillment, culminating in a final judgment graphically emphasizing the ethos of life lived in God's kingdom. The Christian Scriptures elaborate this myth with a Jesus as the awaited messiah, who embodies the myth[1] and a future New Jerusalem, whose gates would be opened wide for all to enter and where provision would be made for their sustenance. There would be no more need of religion because the "light of God was in its streets" and the spirit of the law given by God would be "written upon their hearts" (the Christian Scriptures, "The Book of Revelations"). Over time the figure of Jesus is further mythicized and philosophized: the "Word" that was "in the beginning with God and was God," the "light of every person coming into the world"; the creative power of God invested with all the archetypes of the created world; the Son, "begotten not created, of one substance with the Father," and so on – with a rather skeletal historical Jesus hidden away, for centuries it seemed, in church cupboards. Much ink has been spilled over millennia spiritualizing this Jesus as an otherworldly figure. But when Jesus declared that his "empire was not of this world," the world he was rejecting was not the world itself but the world of Roman imperial power, validated by the divinity of its emperors. When Jesus said, "My peace I give unto you, not as the world gives," the peace of this world he had in mind was the *pax Romana* maintained by marching centurions, brutal repressions, and mass crucifixions. His counter-cultural reversal of accepted categories and norms – the "Sermon on the Mount" with its blessings *and its maledictions*, was not a rejection of the secular world as such but of the profoundly mistaken priorities that governed the existing social and religious order.

An otherworldly Jesus would have been flatly contrary to his Jewish prophetic inheritance and Jewish law, the driving ethical and spiritual centre of which he was determined to recover for this world for which he cared so deeply. The prophets who, it is now clear, were the inspiration of the Jewish law, the Torah, had written their political screeds and engaged in social protest, but, by the same token, were possessed of incredibly imaginative narrative ability and great poetical powers. The records clearly suggest that Jesus self-consciously followed in their steps – and observed how often they met their end at the hands of the religio-political authorities in Jerusalem.

It would be too much to suggest that this understanding of the great Judaic mythology was not recognized and embraced before the Protestant revolt against Rome. Various outbreaks of social revolt over the centuries were inspired by it. Franciscans and what is called the left wing of the Reformation were full of it. But in replacing the Pope with the Bible as the authority in all matters of faith, in translating the Bible into the language of the people, and in making the "preaching of the Word" and a communal meal the centre of worship in the place of the mystery of the Mass, the Protestant revolt – with the help of Gutenberg and his printing press – offered up the myth of Jewish prophecy for public consumption. All was not gain, however, as a suffocating bibliolatry would overtake large sectors of Protestant belief, promoting various bizarre versions of misunderstood myth.

The Judeo-Christian mythology, however, was very different from the Nordic and the Greek mythologies whose gods and goddesses, apparently, were happy to be named, and whose maverick ways were the despair of the "presidents" of their respective Pantheons, Odin and Zeus. Plato is said, with some justification, to have dismissed Greek mythology as a pack of dirty stories about lively gods and goddesses who, in their intimate relations with human beings, sometimes appeared more interested in breeding a race of demi-gods and favouring warring heroes than fulfilling their appointed roles vis-à-vis their human wards and their world. There was Demeter, goddess of fertility, Athena, goddess of wisdom, Aphrodite, goddess of love, Mercury, god of war, Neptune, god of the sea, celebrated in Homer's *Iliad* with one of the most magnificent passages in all of Western literature, and so on. It fell to Greek philosophy, Socrates and Plato in particular, and lawgivers like Solon, to address the political issues of governance and the nature of a just society. And incorporated in Greek mythology were instructive "mini-myths": Cassandra and her ominous box containing all the ills of the world, Sisyphus, rolling his stone repeatedly to the mountaintop, only to have it plunge again to the under-brush below; Procrustes, on whose dreadful bed all were condemned to be cut or stretched to one size; Prometheus, chained high in the Cauca-sus Mountains, his liver being perennially eaten, for having given the gift of fire to human beings, bestowing divine powers that might rival those of the gods. Ulysses, in the *Odyssey*, homeward bound from the Trojan wars, had his encounters with seductive Sirens and the one-eyed giant, Cyclops. In the developing culture of the modern West, Greek mytholo-gy fascinated young and old alike. For scholars, visual artists, poets, and novelists the *Iliad* and the *Odyssey*, and the entire cast of gods and god-desses, were a treasure trove of archetypal figures and events available for creative recasting for contemporaries. But for Karl Barth, the twentieth-century founder of "crisis theology," this panoply of divinities inhabiting and interacting with humans in one world was so contrary to the "whol-ly otherness of God" that he saw in the Judeo-Christian tradition that, when it came to the "mythology" of the Bible, he insisted on using the alternative term "sagas"!

4

The difference was, indeed, stark: For the Graeco-Roman, as in all the ancient empires, the emperor, the head of state, was divine; for the Jew, it was sacrilege to represent God with any earthly image or being. The sign of God's presence with and for them, but not God's self, was the Ark of the Covenant, hidden behind the great veil in the temple. This was the nub of what made the Jews and the early Christians the most difficult people for the Romans to govern in the entire empire. This, of course, was also the nub of what separated Christian and Jew when the destruction of the Temple in Jerusalem in 70 CE brought on a struggle between rival options as to how the worship of the one and only God could continue.

Given the differences, the Graeco-Roman, Nordic, and Judeo-Christian mythologies seemed at one level in the mainstream of Western culture to cohabit in uneasy tension, now as complement or counterpoint, now as competitor or rival, even while on the margins and within the main-stream itself the continuing vile calumnies of Christians about Jews as "Christ killers" smouldered, flamed into the open in horrific pogroms, and ultimately exploded in the Nazi "Kristallnacht" of 9–10 November 1938 and the "Final Solution" of the Holocaust that followed. The power of myths of racial purity and national glory were on full display when pious Protestants and Catholics in high places in Canada refused entry to shiploads of Jewish refugees seeking asylum in Canada. Had the shared Judeo-Christian prophetic mythology sunk so low?

5

In 2013, John Robinson's *Honest to God* (1963) was reprinted to celebrate the fiftieth anniversary of what had become the most widely read theological book of all time. Translated into seventeen languages, it was read around the world by people of diverse faiths. Myth was very much at the centre of *Honest to God* as Robinson brought together the demythologizing work of Rudolf Bultmann, the "religionless Christianity" proposed by Dietrich Bonhoeffer in his *Letters and Papers from Prison* (1952), and the "God beyond God" – the "ground of being" of Paul Tillich's *Systematic Theology* (3 vols, 1951–63). All were reaching for a God-language that would break away from ancient cosmologies and mental images of God as some kind of Super Being who, however, had failed to derail the growth of a new quasi-religious "paganism." All three, Bultmann, Bonhoeffer, and Tillich, were wrestling with the existential crisis brought on by the momentous issues that had led to a second world war in a generation. Practically, the task was twofold: first, to make the Christian gospel more accessible to a generation steeped in the ethos of modern science, and second, to bring a new maturity of reflection about the identity and role of a Christian community uneasy over the growing secularity of the world around them. Bultmann demythologized the concept of eternal life in the Gospel of John to mean a quality of life lived here and now in the spirit of Jesus, not an eternal life after death with God and other departed faithful in heaven "up there." Bonhoeffer counselled seeking God in the midst of life and not on the margins of the continually dissolving frontiers of the unknown. Tillich, seeking a new absolute on which to ground belief, found it in the "God beyond God" whose ultimate unknowability opened onto a "courage to be" engaged, "correlated" in new ways to secular culture.

In popularizing such views, Robinson ignited widespread interest and, of course, intense controversy. To speak of a "God beyond God" – beyond, that is, the conventional, domesticated God who was easily named – was that to join the Cappadocians without a God-language, or even to fall in with Nietzsche and the death of God? Current revisionist work on Nietzsche took some of the sting out of that. Nietzsche's dead God was the God of the submissive, pious, middle-class Lutheran congregations in which he had grown up. And perhaps Nietzsche's "ubermensch" needed to be re-examined in light of his confession that Jesus was the greatest human to have walked the earth. To say these things, however, was still an offense to many, but it had to be said. It was clear in *Honest to God* that if myth was a problem, analogy was not, to which Tillich's *"ground* of being" bore witness. Some years later in the new millennium, the Irish theologian Richard Kearney would propose a systematic analogical God-language in *Anatheism: Returning to God after God* (2010). However, from a certain perspective, there was something curious in Robinson's association of Bultmann and Tillich. Despite their common existentialism, Tillich disagreed with Bultmann's demythologizing project. Myth, for Tillich, was neither an inferior form of expression nor simply pre-scientific. As a complex set of symbols, myth was the essential language of human beings as they confronted their "ultimate concerns" in life. It was the essential language of faith in its encounter with the sacred, just as it was the necessary mode of scientific expression as science undertook to draw its findings into the realm of unifying theory. To negate myth was to negate faith and to leave science in a chaotic miscellaneous state.[2]

Meanwhile, with the publication of *The Hero with a Thousand Faces* (1949), Joseph Campbell was carving a name for himself in the interpretation of myth. Employing a modified version of Carl Jung's concept of the collective unconscious with its universal archetypes, and driven by his independent explorations, Campbell found remarkable similarities in the mythologies of diverse cultures, which convinced him of the unity of humankind. He became convinced that myth was profoundly therapeutic, conducive to both a happy life and social well-being. With the remarkable public response to the now-legendary interviews with Bill Moyers on public television and their publication as *The Power of Myth* in 1988, Campbell's articulation of myth for a world passing from modernism to the post-modern was a sign of the times.

It was against this background of demythologizing and remythologizing that Gary Dorrien, after writing important studies of the renewal of social Christianity in the United States, the origins of neo-conservatism, and the intellectual roots of the new American imperialism, undertook to address the issue of mythology and the crisis of Christian theology.

As Dorrien completed his finely nuanced and thoroughly documented argument, he expressed his surprise at the appreciation he felt for the strength of the positions he had been critiquing – and especially for the "evocative appeal of process theology, Jungian spirituality, and … ecofeminism." They offered an ethical and spiritual vigour and "an awareness of the cosmic context [that escaped] much of mainstream Protestantism." He did not want their new ways of recovering and reconfiguring their "sense of sacred relation to the whole" lost to Christianity. There were, however, insurmountable problems for Dorrien in the theology of immanence on which they all were grounded, namely, the problem of all monistic systems, where God, Spirit, or gods are identified with the "All," the whole of existence. Identified with that "All," of which human beings and their deepest concerns were a constitutive part, the power of these divinities to effect any significant change in human circumstances was implicitly limited, if not entirely vitiated. As Dorrien concluded, "If God is not free from us in some way that makes God's power transcend the world, God cannot be free for us in our suffering and mortality."[3] Dorrien thus joined Karl Barth and Paul Tillich in affirming the "wholly otherness" of God, while chastising Barth for wholly lacking in appreciation for what the immanentists were trying to accomplish.[4] It is on this contrast in the implications of immanence and transcendence in theology that Dorrien comes to his distinction between a true and an illusory mythology.[5]

Dorrien's nomination of the mythology of the "Word" in the Gospel of John as "true myth" recalls Cassirer's work on the symbolic power of language and its transcendence of the reality to which it points – and in some sense "creates" – for the thought processes of conscious minds. Analogously, the expressive power of the eternal "Word" creates, enlightens, and, as the Christ, enters into the psychics of personality and the processes of history to reconcile and make new. In the freedom of its transcendence of the created order, Dorrien says, the "Word" cannot be known in itself, but only apprehended in the narrative of myth, including its mythicized version of historical experience.[6]

For Dorrien, the contemporary political implications of this "true myth" were consistent with the prophetic mythology of the Judeo-Christian tradition, with its monotheism of the oppressed, and found expression in close association with Michael Harrington in the Socialist party and the left wing of the Democratic party. In recent decades, as a noted public intellectual, he would accept up to 200 invitations a year, compellingly expounding and promoting a politics at once secular and sacred with three primary objectives: first, the urgency of economic democracy to resolve the alienating consequences of capitalist economics for workers and their families; second, the importance of valuing the contribution differences of gender, race, and religion bring to public and religious debate; and third, the necessity of bringing an end to the 1,600-year reign of Christendom and the Roman imperial monotheism that has been its hallmark, a version of which continues in the present as justification and sanctification of the American empire.[7]

6

"Myth," however, is a rather slippery word in contemporary parlance, generally signifying an assertion or belief, whether in capsule story form or extended narrative, that purports to explain a certain train of thought, course of action, or set of circumstances, which, though superficially persuasive, do not, on examination, accord with reality – in short, a fabrication or a falsehood, whether intended or not, but often advanced for purposes of self-promotion or intended to defame. Myth, in this sense, is a prolific phenomenon of partisan politics. Over the past generation neo-conservative and neo-liberal ideologues have insidiously and shamelessly embellished traditional free enterprise mythology with beguiling stories of "trickle-down economics" and "rising tides that lift all boats." These "mini-myths" of supply-side economics have not infrequently been accompanied by an exotic mythological concoction of Ayn Rand heroic individualism and crypto-anarchistic views of the evils of government. In reality, over the past few decades, the net result of these "applied mythologies" has been a reversal of several decades of progressive income redistribution and the creation of an obscene, socially disintegrative level of income disparity where top corporate executives make as much on the first day of the year as the average wage worker will earn in an entire year. Unfortunately, political myths die hard, especially when accompanied by seductive lies that across-the-board tax cuts in a progressive taxation system will treat everyone fairly when, in reality, they further line the pockets of super-rich oligarchs and further entrench their power.

Perhaps the greatest irony in this whole discussion of the play of the religious "beyond the noise of solemn assemblies" is that the politics of the modern, secular, territorial nation-state, like the religious, rests on a foundation of myth – indeed, on a succession of myths. The social contract theory that has dominated the political thought of the modern West is based on what can only be described as State of Nature myths describing a hypothetical original condition of human beings as a starting point for equally mythical social contracts intended to resolve a state of disorder that has overtaken humanity. Three men, writing between 1651 and 1762, laid the foundations of social contract theory. Thomas Hobbes, in his monumental *Leviathan or the Matter, Forme, and Power of a Common-Wealth Ecclesiastical and Civil*, the State of Nature was one of individuals waging a "war of all against all," perhaps in some measure reflecting the troubled post-Reformation times in which he wrote. In Hobbes' account, the solution to this intolerable situation comes with individuals ceding their powers to an absolute "sovereign" who would impose peace, thus bringing to birth an orderly society out of primordial chaos. Hobbes' Social Contract was quite compatible with that older myth of the divine right of kings, the latest English claimant to which, Charles I, had lost his head at the hands of the Puritan Commonwealth. With the latter's defeat in 1660, his successor, Charles II, advised his people that they were not to trouble themselves with public affairs; that it was his responsibility. Francis I of France went so far as to substitute himself for the "Host," the Christ, under the canopy in the Corpus Christi parades.

It was to repudiate that doctrine that John Locke wrote his *Essay Concerning the True Original, Extent and End of Civil Government*, in which he proposed a State of Nature very different from that of Hobbes. Humanity was not individual but familial, not engaged in perpetual warfare but enjoyed the liberty of a people who assumed that all were equally created by God. This importation of Christian myth was not surprising from one who also wrote on "the reasonableness of Christianity." Property and human labour were important in Locke's account. A natural "right to that with which one mixed one's labour" was a buttress to that same equality. War was unlikely but could result from envy and property offences, especially as population grew and life became more complex. Once started, conflict was bound to spread and was an important reason for coming together in a formal social contract to found a civil order of society committed to maintaining original liberties.

Jean-Jacques Rousseau, a century later amid the ferment of the French Enlightenment, wrote not one, but two, social contract myths. The first offered his views on the "fall" of humanity from an original State of Nature, and the second described his ideal or "normalized" social contract to maintain original freedom under modern social conditions. His famous opening sentence in *Du Contrat Social* (1762), "Man was born free and is everywhere in chains," encapsulates the burden of his imaginative political myth-making. Sparse in numbers, well provisioned by nature's bounty, and sympathetically disposed, the conditions were conducive to free and peaceful association. Multiplication and social progress brought comparisons of ability, status, and lot, which in turn brought envy, competition, and conflict. Private ownership of property led to increasingly deep divisions between the propertied and the propertyless, with further subservience for the latter as the propertied instigated government and won protection of property rights. This constituted Rousseau's first social contract and the need for a second.

For Rousseau the way to restore the benefits of lost freedoms under the new conditions was to create a new people by gathering all the individual wills into a "general will." How would this general will be mobilized and expressed politically? Rousseau's preferred agency appears to have been periodic assemblies of the whole people. Agreements so arrived at did not admit of dissent, since that would be to repudiate the freedom newly gained. The impracticability of Rousseau's ideal solution, however, led to much ink being spilled on alternatives. Was there one general will or many discordant ones? Would an assembly of representatives of the people serve? Or plebiscites enacted by a national figurehead? Or was the general will a quasi-mystical concept, intuitively sensed by a self-proclaimed charismatic who would lead the nation toward its predestined end? Social contract mythology has been used to justify each of these. And the feminist criticisms that social contract myths have dealt hardly on minorities are no doubt correct.

Nineteenth-century political mythology seemed to run off in all directions, at once religious and secular, and yet managing, incongruously, to cohabit within the dominant progressive mythology of the age. The *laissez-faire* mythology of nineteenth-century political economy was rooted in French Physiocracy, which taught that society, like the Newtonian understanding of the natural world, functioned on the basis of inherent natural law and constituted a self- regulating system. Hence, *laissez-aller, laissez-faire, car le monde va par lui-même*. What the Physiocratic myth, somewhat bastardized, served to promote, however, was the economic, and therefore the political, interests of the new entrepreneurial classes and an aspiring upper middle class. Their politics aimed at severely limiting the state so it would not "restrain trade," that is, the merchants, landlords, and capitalists. Physiocracy gave economic voice to the prevalent Deism of the age, a theology that argued that God had created the universe complete at the beginning, and thereafter it would operate on the basis of pre-established law. Scottish economists further postulated a "hidden hand" that would convert self-serving motives into public good, thus relieving the emerging business classes of ethical concerns that might impede their economic activity. Ironically, the notion of the hidden hand was taken by rising non-conformist Protestants to be the hand of Divine Providence, thus projecting a benign religious aura over all. The classical *laissez-faire* political economy of Ricardo and Spencerian "survival of the fittest" theory added their weight to an amoral system that implicitly precluded the intervention of the state on behalf of the working classes and other marginalized groups.

Two further political myths of the century, however, would, in different ways, promote the positive uses of the state with social reformist and revolutionary ends in view. Auguste Comte, one of the principal founders of modern sociology, offered his pioneering work in the context of a three-stage historical myth in which humanity had reached a third, and presumably final, scientific stage, having outgrown earlier stages in which preoccupation with religion and then philosophy prevailed. The ultimate questions with which religion and philosophy dealt were meaningless, incapable of resolution. A new social science would discover the general laws that governed the social behaviour of human beings and pave the way for positive uses of the state, the rise of a new cult of the expert, and a vast expansion of bureaucracy. Major intellectuals like John Stuart Mill were influenced, and under leading figures like Frederic Harrison, Positivism became an impressive intellectual movement among a diverse and widespread congeries of progressives – socialists, ethical societies, social liberals, labour leaders, and even social Christians – protesting *laissez-faire* doctrine as a coldly rational system, devoid of human feeling, and lacking any concern for ethics and social justice. While Comte's "positivism" was thoroughly secular with respect to traditional religion, Comte found it necessary to invent a substitute "religion of humanity" to bind and motivate his projected new social order. Ironically, he was doing so at the very time religious revival was sweeping the Western world!

It fell to Karl Marx and Friedrich Engels to craft what, by late century, had the makings of a triumphant mythology among working classes celebrating the imminent arrival of a new international social order. History as human beings had known it was about to come to an end. Just as an original primitive communism had given way to a millennia-long period of division of labour and class struggle, now, the industrial proletariat would rise to end capitalist exploitation. In doing so, as the vast majority of humankind, it would end class struggle and set the stage for new era of fulfillment for the human spirit. The myth was translated into the inspirational hymn sung by socialists of the time, *The Internationale*. It sang of "prisoners of starvation [and the] wretched of the earth" arising in a "final conflict," for "justice thunders condemnation, a better world's in birth." Pitting itself against the warmakers in the years leading up to the Great War of 1914–18, its vision was trumped by national mythologies that, in the upshot, proved more powerful.

The concept of history developing in three stages had a long history dating from the work of Joachim of Fiore in the twelfth century CE. Joachim was a monk who is credited with conceiving the first Christian "philosophy" of history. Based on Judeo-Christian scriptures, and patterned after the Christian Trinitarian doctrine of God, Joachim's scheme divided history into three ages, an Age of God the Father (Creator), the Age of Christ (Redeemer), and the Age of the Spirit when, with the indwelling of the Spirit, people would live freely with no need of the constraints of church and state. Popularized by the Franciscan order, it went underground when condemned by the Papacy and the Franciscans disbanded. Under the name of "the eternal gospel" it underwent something of a revival in the nineteenth century as a component of the progressive thought of the time.[8] More myth than philosophy, the secular adaptations of Joachim would themselves be dubbed "secular religions" by later scholars.

7

All political parties in Canada have come to share in various ways a multiplicity of traditions and associated mythologies that deserve more attention than they have received. It has not been my purpose here to attempt such an investigation. Rather, I have wanted to offer a modest background of argument and evidence around the emergence and significance of the secular arising out of a context of religiously articulated mythology and to show that, as for religion itself, myth lies at the base of secular movements of modern political thought and action.

Pragmatism and rationality are, of course, crucial to evidence-based public policy formulation, political action, and the process of political implementation in government but, *pace* Bismarck, pragmatic politics is not just "the art of the possible." It is the art of the most *desirable* possible. There are, after all, few political issues that admit of only one alternative course of resolution. And a rational politics that succumbs to the dictum that "perception is everything in politics" is surely *en route* to a politics of deception and the proliferation of more "myths" to trap the unwary. Politics does not originate its own values, which properly arise from the community at large, and not least of all from religion and its mythologically articulated apprehensions of the nature of God and what it means to be human. Myths, whether religious or secular, as I have argued above, understood in their classic form, and given the subject they address, have legitimate claims to a rationality of their own. This is not, of course, to advocate the resurrection of ancient cosmologies as competitors of modern science and claimants for the allegiance of post-moderns. Rather, it is to underline the true meaning and function of myth. The universality at which the religious and secular myths aim, however, is too often subverted by literalist bibliolators, tribalists of all kinds, ancient and modern, self-serving charismatics and psychopaths, and economic predators, separately or in common, with consequences that are sad, tragic, and even horrifying. Either way, to dwell on the role of myth is not to depreciate or subordinate, let alone ignore, the explorations and enduring insights of the humanities and social sciences, the remarkable findings of the biological sciences, or the revelations of physics, astronomy, and cosmology about the origins, evolution, and functioning of the universe as a whole, which are at once exciting and challenging.

To argue that the secular and the sacred need each other is not to advocate the reinsertion of institutional religion into the formal affairs and structures of the state. The separation of church and state is a necessity in the equitable governance of populations and especially of modern pluralistic societies, and is an accepted fact in all liberal and social democratic polities.

The matter under discussion here is a rather more subtle question than the separation of church and state. Religion, with its mythological God-language, does not need to be reticent about claiming its place in public debate alongside the competing or complementary sciences and secular mythologies of our time. It is out of such a dynamic process that our politics develops its provisional postures, its interim regimes, and its overall direction. The corollary of that for the religious, however, must be that, in the name of the great mystery that it celebrates and the unity of humankind that it professes to nurture, it put aside all pretension to absolute knowledge of the nature of God and God's will for humanity and the universe, and throw itself, with all the seriousness and richness of resource of which it is capable, into the open and creative dialogue essential to life together. Perhaps it will then realize its true self, and the sacred and the secular will meet in mutual embrace and together find a fresh understanding of prophetic religion that the secular is where the sacred really happens – the signs of which will surely be "mountains and hills of privilege being brought low, valleys of poverty and despair raised up, all wrong dealing rectified, and the rough places of life made smooth."[9]

Notes

CHAPTER THREE

1 Max Weber, "Die protestantische Ethik und der Geist des Kapitalismus," *Archiv fur Sogiolwissenschaft und sogialpolitik*, 20 and 30 (1904–05); reprinted and somewhat revised in 1920 as the first study in *Gesammelte aufsätze zur Religiousoziologie*, from which the English translation was made in 1930 by Talcott Parsons, American sociologist.

2 R.H. Tawney, "Foreword," in Max Weber, *The Protestant Ethic and the Spirit of Capitalism* (New York: Charles Scribner's Sons, 1958), 4.

3 Albert Salomon, "Max Weber's Methodology," *Social Research* 1, no. 2 (May 1934): 147. Weber was once proposed as chancellor of the German State.

4 Max Weber, *The Protestant Ethic and the Spirit of Capitalism* (New York: Charles Scribner's Sons, 1958), 90–1, for the limitations that Weber placed on the significance of his subject.

5 Although Weber does not cite the statistics or the source, the source is given in Kurt Samuelsson, *Religion and Economic Action* (Stockholm: Svenska Bokförlaget, 1957), 2.

6 Weber, *The Protestant Ethic*, 159.

7 Ibid., 182–3.

8 Salomon, "Max Weber's Methodology," 161.

9 Weber, *The Protestant Ethic*, 181–2. The attitude also reflects Weber's own state of mind as a believer in the fundamental importance of values and spirit but who is unable to commit himself to any ultimate value.

10 F.L. Nussbaum, "The Economic History of Renaissance Europe," *Journal of Modern History* 13, no. 4 (December 1941): 537.

11 These comments are derived from Samuelsson, *Religion and Economic Action*,

8–11, and Ernest Troeltsch, *The Social Teaching of the Christian Churches* (2 vols London: George Allen and Unwin, 1931), vol. 2, 916–7.

12 Lujo Brentano, *Anfäge des modernen Kapitalismus* (1916), cited in Samuelsson, *Religion and Economic Action*, 12–3.

13 Werner Sombart, *The Quintessence of Capitalism* (New York: E.P. Dutton, 1915), *The Jews and Modern Capitalism* (London: T. Fisher Unwin, 1913). The first is a translation of a work that preceded Weber and from which the idea of a "spirit of capitalism" derived. The second is one of a series of unilinear studies that, when woven together in Sombart's later multivolume work, suggested a different thesis than they did separately. See Nussbaum, "Economic History," 531.

14 Troeltsch, *Social Teaching*, vol. 2, 643.

15 Ibid., vol. 2, 646.

16 Roland H. Bainton, "Troeltsch Twenty Years Later," *Theology Today* 8, no. 1 (April 1951): 70–96.

17 Karl Holl, *The Cultural Significance of the Reformation* (New York: Meridian Books, 1959), 32–5; first published in German just after the First World War.

18 Ibid., 87–8

19 Ibid., 89.

20 Ibid., 182–4.

21 P.T. Forsyth, "Calvinism and Capitalism," *Contemporary Review* 97 (June 1910): 728–41; 98 (July 1910): 774–87.

22 Herman Levy, *Economic Liberalism* (London: Macmillan, 1913), 92.

23 W. Cunningham, *An Essay on Western Civilisation in its Economic Aspects* (2 vols Cambridge University Press, 1904), cited in Samuelsson, *Religion and Economic Action*, 20.

24 W. Cunningham, *Christianity and Economic Science* (London: J. Murray, 1914), 58–69.

25 George O'Brien, *An Essay on the Economic Effects of the Reformation* (London: Burns, Oates and Washbourne, 1923).

26 No endnote given.

27 Samuelsson, *Religion and Economic Action*, 16.

28 R.H. Tawney, *Religion and the Rise of Capitalism* (London: John Murray, 1926).

29 Ibid., 84

30 Ibid.

31 Ibid., 249.

32 Max Weber, *General Economic History* (New York: Greenberg Publishers, 1927).

33 Kemper Fullerton, "Calvinism and Capitalism," *The Harvard Theological Review* 21, (1928): 163–95.

34 Talcott Parsons, "Capitalism in Recent German Literature. Sombart and Weber," *Journal of Political Economy* 36, no. 6 (December 1928): 641–61 and 37, no. 1 (February 1929): 31–51.

35 F.H. Knight, "Historical and Theoretical Issues in the Problem of Modern Capitalism," *Journal of Economic and Business History* 1, no. 1 (November 1928): 119–36.

36 Earl. J. Hamilton, "American Treasure and the Rise of Capitalism," *Economics* 9, no. 3 (November 1929): 338–57.

37 Samuelsson, *Religion and Economic Action*, 23.

38 Ibid.

39 Amintore Fanfani, *The Origins of the Capitalist Spirit in Italy* (Milan: University of the Sacred Heart, 1933).

40 Samuelsson, *Religion and Economic Action*, 23.

41 Christen T. Jonassen, "The Protestant Ethic and the Spirit of Capitalism in Norway," *American Sociological Review*, 12, no. 6 (December 1947): 676–86.

42 Georgia Harkness, *John Calvin: The Man and His Ethics* (New York: Henry Holt, 1931), chaps 8 and 9.

43 R.N. Carew Hunt, *Calvin* (London: The Centenary Press, 1933), 130–3.

44 Wellman J. Warner, *The Wesleyan Movement in the Industrial Revolution* (London: Longmann, Green and Co., 1930), chaps 5 and 6.

45 Isabel Grubb, *Quakerism and Industry before 1800* (London: Williams and Norgate, 1930), cited in Samuelsseo, *Religion and Economic Action*, 28.

46 H. Richard Niebuhr, *The Social Sources of Denominationalism* (New York: Henry Holt, 1929), 79.

47 H. Richard Niebuhr, *The Kingdom of God in America* (New York: Harper and Brothers, 1937), 86.

48 Ibid., 84.

49 Ibid., 85.

50 Amintore Fanfani, *Catholicism, Protestantism and Capitalism* (London: Sheed and Ward, 1935). The other major contribution by a Catholic to the discussion is J.B. Kraus, *Scholastik, Puritanismus und Kapitalismus* (1930), cited in Samuelsson, *Religion and Economic Action*, 21. Kraus' argument is apparently similar to that of Tawney.

51 H.M. Robertson, *Aspects of the Rise of Economic Individualism* (Cambridge: Cambridge University Press, 1933), 16.

52 J. Broderick, *The Economic Morals of the Jesuits* (London: Oxford University Press, 1934).

53 Talcott Parsons, "H.M. Robertson on Max Weber and His School," *Journal of Political Economy* 43, no. 5 (October 1935): 688–96. The last point is the one

R.W. Green uses as the key contribution of Robertson to the debate: *The Weber Thesis and Its Critics* (Boston: D.C. Heath, 1957), xi.

54 Albert Hyma, *Christianity, Capitalism and Communism* (Ann Arbor: George Wahr, 1937), chaps 3–7.

55 Gordon Walker, "Capitalism and the Reformation," *Economic History Review* 8, no. 1 (November 1937): 1–19.

56 Nussbaum, *Economic History*, 537.

57 Ibid., 539.

58 Ephraim Fischoff, "The Protestant Ethic and the Spirit of Capitalism: The History of a Controversy," *Social Research*, 11, no. 1 (February 1944): 53–77.

59 Benjamin N. Nelson, *The Idea of Usury: From Tribal Brotherhood to Universal Otherhood* (Princeton: Princeton University Press, 1949).

60 Roland H. Bainton, "Troeltsch Twenty Years Later," 89.

61 W. Stark, "Capitalism, Calvinism and the Rise of Modern Science," *Sociological Review* 43 (1951): 95–104.

62 Milton Yinger, *Religion and the Struggle for Power* (Durham, NC: Duke University Press, 1946).

63 Harold J. Grimm, *The Reformation Era* (New York: Macmillan, 1954), 578–81.

64 Roland H. Bainton, *The Reformation of the Sixteenth Century* (Boston: Beacon Press, 1952), 244–56.

65 Winthrop S. Hudson, "Puritanism and the Spirit of Capitalism," *Church History*, 18, no. 1 (March 1949): 3–16.

66 John T. McNeill, *The History and Character of Calvinism* (New York: Oxford University Press, 1954), 222, 419–21.

67 Winthrop S. Hudson, "The Weber Thesis Re-examined," *Church History* 30, no. 1 (March 1961): 88–99.

68 Leo Strauss, "Comment," *Church History*, 30, no. 1 (March 1961): 100–2.

69 Samuelsson, *Religion and Economic Action*.

CHAPTER FOUR

1 Carl J. Friedrich, ed., *Totalitarianism*; Proceedings of a Conference held at the American Academy of Arts and Sciences, March 1953 (Cambridge: Harvard University Press, 1954), 373–5.

2 Eric Voegelin, "The Origins of Totalitarianism," and Hannah Arendt's reply in *The Review of Politics* 15, no. 1 (January 1953): 68ff.

3 Eric Hoffer, *The True Believer* (New York: The New American Library, 1951); and Else Frenkel-Brunswick, *The Authoritarian Personality* (New York: New Harper and Brothers, 1950).

4 J.L. Talmon, *The Origins of Totalitarian Democracy* (New York: Frederick A. Praeger, 1960), 11.

5 Hannah Arendt, *The Origins of Totalitarianism*, 2nd enlarged ed. (Cleveland: The World Publishing Co., 1958), 459.

6 Voegelin, "The Origins of Totalitarianism," and Arendt's reply.

7 Eric Voegelin, *The New Science of Politics* (Chicago: University of Chicago Press, 1952), 132.

8 Hannah Arendt, "What was Authority?" in *Authority*, ed. C.J. Friedrich (Cambridge: Harvard University Press, 1958), 82–112.

9 Voegelin, "The Origins of Totalitarianism," and Arendt's reply.

10 Erich Kahler, *Man the Measure: A New Approach to History* (New York: George Braziller, Inc., 1956), 568–9.

11 Ibid., 640.

12 Ibid., 596, quoting Juenger.

13 Karl Löwith, *Meaning in History* (Chicago: University of Chicago Press, 1949), 207.

14 Arendt, *The Origins of Totalitarianism*, 299.

15 Voegelin, *The New Science of Politics*, 1.

16 C.J. Friedrich and Z.K. Brzezinski, *Totalitarian Dictatorship and Autocracy* (Cambridge: Harvard University Press, 1956), 17–26.

17 Friedrich, ed., *Totalitarianism*, 336 and 341.

18 Arendt, *The Origins of Totalitarianism*, 373–5.

19 Ibid., 367.

20 Ibid., 395, quoting Roberts, 72

21 Ibid., 402–3.

22 Jerzy G. Gleksman, "Social Prophylaxis as a Form of Soviet Terror," in *Totalitarianism*, ed. C.J. Friedrich, 60–74.

23 Peter F. Drucker, *The End of Economic Man: A Study of the New Totalitarianism* (New York: The John Day Company, 1939), 149–56.

24 Friedrich and Brzezinsky, *Totalitarian Dictatorship and Autocracy*.

25 Arendt, *The Origins of Totalitarianism*, 418.

26 Ibid., 417.

27 Ibid., 395

28 Ibid., 394, quoting Hitler's warning to jurists in 1933.

29 Ibid., 468–74.

30 Ernst Cassirer, *The Myth of the State* (New York: Doubleday, 1946), 55–7.

31 Robert Tucker, *Philosophy and Myth in Karl Marx* (London: Cambridge University Press, 1961), 218–32.

32 C.J. Friedrich and Brzezinsky, *Totalitarian Dictatorship and Autocracy*, 293.

33 Drucker, *The End of Economic Man*.
34 Ibid. Both Drucker and y Gasset, from different perspectives, see the central
    problem of the alienation masses in traditional capitalism, both in work
    relationships and access to knowledge, by establishing genuine community
    with the culture of order it would generate as against organization and con-
    trol (Peter Drucker, *The Future of Industrial Man* [New York: John Day, 1941],
    205.
35 See Dietrich Bonhoeffer, "Outline for a Book," in *Letters and Papers from
    Prison* (London: Fontana Books, 1953), 165.
36 Voegelin, "The Origins of Totalitarianism."
37 C.J. Friedrich, and Z.K. Brzezinsky, *Totalitarian Dictatorship and Autocracy*,
    247–63; Franklin H. Littell, "The Protestant Churches and Totalitarianism,"
    in *Totalitarianism*, ed. C.J. Friedrich, 108–19.
38 Albert Camus, *The Rebel* (New York: Alfred A. Knopf, 1954), 27.

CHAPTER FIVE

1 S.F. Wise, "Sermon Literature and Canadian Intellectual History," *The
   Bulletin*, United Church Archives, no. 18 (1965): 3–18; "God's Peculiar Peoples," in *The Shield of Achilles*, ed. W.L. Morton (Toronto: McClelland and
   Stewart, 1968); Goldwin French, "The Evangelical Creed in Canada," in *The
   Shield of Achilles*, ed. W.L. Morton (Toronto: McClelland and Stewart, 1968);
   Gordon Stewart and George Rawlyk, *A People Highly Favoured of God* (Toronto: Macmillan, 1972), especially chap. 9; William Westfall, "The Dominion of
   the Lord: An Introduction to the Cultural History of Protestant Ontario in
   the Victorian Period," *Queen's Quarterly*, 83 (Spring 1976): 47–70; *Salvation!
   O The Joyful Sound: Selected Writings of John Carroll*, ed. John W. Grant
   (Toronto: Oxford University Press, 1967), especially "Getting Religion,"
   130–59; and John S. Moir, "The Upper Canadian Roots of Church Disestab-
   lishment," *Ontario History* 60 (December 1968) are readily accessible samples
   of this literature.
2 A useful outline of the evolution of the idea of Providence can be found in
   James Hastings, *Encyclopaedia of Religion and Ethics* (Edinburgh: T. & T.
   Clark, 1908–26).
3 The best known example is Mgr L.-F.-R. Laflèche, "The Providential Mission
   of the French Canadians," available to English readers in Ramsay Cook,
   French-Canadian Nationalism (Toronto: Macmillan, 1969), translated from
   *Quelques considerations sur de la rapports de la societé civile avec la religion et la
   famille* (Montreal: Eugène Senécal, 1866), 37–62.
4 John Beverly Robinson, *Canada and the Canada Bill* (London, 1840), 13–80.

5 For glimpses of Strachan's views, see Wise, "Sermon Literature," but for a systematic treatment of his views, see Norma MacRae, "The Religious Foundations of John Strachan's Social and Political Thought as Contained in his Sermons, 1803–1866" (unpublished MA thesis, McMaster University, 1978). See especially for Strachan's views on: chain of being, 22–3; God's Providence, 27–34; man's earthly lot, 35–7, 52, 71, 97–8; practicality of Christianity, 43–7; class and subordination, 69–71; and the British as a chosen nation, chap. 5, and in particular, 80, 100. Further to the "chain of being" question, MacRae, ch. 1, references Terry Cook, who too quickly downplays its significance (Cook, "John Beverly Robinson and the Conservative Blueprint for the Upper Canadian Community," *Ontario History* 44 [1972]).

6 One of the clearest expositions of this Tory–Old Whig mindset can be found in Samuel H. Beer, *British Politics in the Collectivist Age* (New York: Alfred A. Knopf, 1965).

7 MacRae, "Religious Foundations," 73–4; Cook, "John Beverly Robinson," 82–4, 90–1.

8 Stewart and Rawlyk, *A People Highly Favoured*, chap. 9.

9 French, "The Evangelical Creed in Canada," and "Egerton Ryerson and the Methodist Model for Upper Canada," in *Egerton Ryerson and his Times: Essays on the History of Education*, ed. Neil McDonald and Alf Charlton (Toronto: Macmillan, 1978), 45–58; also, Neil McDonald, "Egerton Ryerson and the School as an Agent of Political Socialization," in *Egerton Ryerson and his Times: Essays on the History of Education*, eds Neil McDonald and Alf Charlton (Toronto: Macmillan, 1978), especially 95–104.

10 Bishop Mountain, quoted in H.H. Walsh, *The Christian Church in Canada* (Toronto: Ryerson Press, 1956), 137. See also Bishop Strachan, "A Sermon on the Death of the Late Bishop of Quebec, 1826," quoted in William H. Elgee, *The Social Teachings of the Canadian Churches, Protestant, The Early Period Before 1850* (Toronto: Ryerson Press, 1964), 15, on the similarity of outlook among the three, Wise, "Sermon Literature."

11 Anthony Rasporich, ed., *William Lyon Mackenzie: Selected Writings* (Toronto: Holt, Rinehart and Winston, 29172), 66.

12 William Westfall, "The Dominion of the Lord," 52.

13 See Westfall, "The Dominion of the Lord," whose excellent study too sharply distinguishes the secular and the sacred in mid-Victorian business and religion (see Neil Semple, "The Impact of Urbanization on the Methodist Church in Central Canada, 1854–1884," [unpublished PhD dissertation, University of Toronto, 1979]; and Peter Hánlon's forthcoming MA thesis on the late Victorian Protestant lay elite in Hamilton [McMaster University]).

14 Both pieces are included in the University of Toronto Social History Reprint

series, T.C. Keefer, *The Philosophy of Railroads* (Toronto: University of Toronto Press, 1972). See especially 7–11, 83–9, and H.V. Nelles' excellent introduction.

15 See for example, Elgee, *Social Teachings*, 182–3.

16 Excerpt in B. Sinclair, N.R. Ball, and J.O. Peterson, *Let Us be Honest and Modest, Technology and Society in Canadian History* (Oxford University Press, 1974), 108–9.

17 William Leiss, *The Domination of Nature* (Boston: Beacon Press, 1972), 48–54.

18 J.C. Galway, "The Claims of the Mechanics' Institutes" (1844). Excerpt in Sinclair et al., *Let Us Be Honest and Modest*.

19 See for example the frequent testimony of skilled trades workers before the Royal Commission Relations of Labor and Capital. Greg Kealey, ed., *Canada Investigates Industrialism The Royal Commission on the Relations Labor and Capital, 1889* (abridged) (Toronto: University of Toronto Press, 1973), 115, 118, 120, 155–7, 244–5.

20 Some elements of this transition are sketched in Bryan Palmer, *Culture in Conflict* (Montreal: McGill-Queen's University Press, 1979), chap. 4, "Reform Thought and The Producer Ideology," especially 98–100. The providential dimension of the work ethic and its bifurcation are evident in Stanley Kutcher, "John Wilson Bengough: Artist of Righteousness," (unpublished MA thesis, McMaster University, 1975), chap. 4.

21 The most accessible, brief review of the religious dimension of late century labour and socialist movements in Toronto is Gene Homel, "Fading Beams of the Nineteenth Century: Radicalism and Early Socialism in Canada's 1890's," *Labour/LeTravailleur* 5 (Spring 1980), especially 13–32. Homel portrays an alliance of labour leaders and socialists who wanted to apply "Christianity's social message" and radical clergy concerned to "redeem Christian ethics." The religious enthusiasm fades with the dying century, says Homel, while the ethics live on. MA research papers surveying labour and socialist papers from 1872 to 1914 make it plain that the core conviction of both groups was that God, however understood, was working to assure a future of justice and brotherhood in history, and that this view persists at least until 1914 unabated (Jim Stein – 1974; Joan Sangster – 1976; Katherine O'Conner – 1980; Edgar Rogalski – 1981). Even the most radical editor, W.A. Cotton, writes in 1909, "The new spirit of Christ, the Socialist movement sweeps on and is fought by the churches," *Cotton's Weekly* (25 March 1909). See Phillips Thompson, *The Politics of Labor* (New York: Bedford, Clarke and Co., 1887), University of Toronto Social History Reprint Series, 210, but see the entire final chapter. Thompson's views on the destiny of labour cannot be separated from his theosophical convictions as to the evolutionary force of an

indwelling universal spirit. His views of the common individual also link him with W.L. Mackenzie (see above, 6).

22 As cited in R.J. Taylor, "Darwin's Theory of Evolution: Four Canadian Responses" (unpublished PhD dissertation, McMaster University, 1976), 12.

23 *Footprints of the Creator* (1847) and *Testimony of the Rocks* (1857).

24 Taylor, "Darwin's Theory of Evolution," 268–73.

25 Ibid., 268.

26 Ibid., 271–2.

27 The following account of Dawson's views is based principally upon Charles F. O'Brien, *Sir William Dawson: A Life in Science and Religion* (Philadelphia: American Philosophical Society, 1971), especially chaps 2–5. On Dawson, Miller, Providence, see 39–59, 65–6. For the most popular and readable of Dawson's many books, see *The Story of Earth and Man* (London: Hodder and Stoughton, 1874), especially the last four chapters.

28 See H.J. Reimer, "Darwinism in Canadian Literature," (unpublished PhD dissertation, McMaster University, 1975), which deals, among others, with Charles G.D. Roberts, Archibald Lampman, and Wilfred Campbell.

29 See for example the notes for Salem Bland's evolutionary socialist lecture, "Four Steps and a Vision," Bland Papers, no. 19 (1898), United Church Archives. Also C.W. Gordon, *Postscript to Adventure: The Autobiography of Ralph Connor* (New York: Farrar and Rinehart, 1938).

30 As this applied to children in particular, see Neil Semple, "The Nurture and Admonition of the Lord: Nineteenth Century Canadian Methodism's Response to Childhood," *Histoire Sociale/Social History* 14 (May 1981), 157–76.

31 See Taylor's excellent treatment of Watson (Taylor, "Darwin's Theory of Evolution"). For a wider ranging treatment of Watson and also the backlash to the influence of his disciples, see A.B. McKillop. A *Disciplined Intelligence* (Montreal: McGill-Queen's University Press, 1979), 181–203. For other idealist intellectuals of the time, see S.E.D. Shortt, *The Search for an Ideal: Six Canadian Intellectuals and their Convictions in an Age of Transition* (Toronto: University of Toronto Press, 1976); Brian Fraser, "Theology and the Social Gospel among Canadian Presbyterians: A Case Study," *Studies in Religion/Sciences Religieuses* 8, no. 1 (1979), 34–46; and Morton Paterson, "George Blewett: A Forgotten Personalist," *Idealist Studies* 8, no. 2 (1978), 179–89.

32 John Watson, "The Outlook in Philosophy," *Queen's Quarterly* 8 (April 1901): 251.

33 Terry Cook, "George Parkin and the concept of Britannic Idealism," *Journal of Canadian Studies* 10 (August 1975): 15–31.

34 William Osborne, *The Genius of Shakespeare and other Essays* (Toronto: W. Briggs, 1908), 68–70.

35 For a treatment of this idea found in various of Blewett's writings see Morton Paterson, "Divine Encounter in Blewett," *Studies in Religion/Sciences Religieuses* 6, no. 4 (1976–77), 397–404. Blewett taught at Wesley College, Winnipeg, and at Victoria College, Toronto.

36 Fernand Dumont, *The Vigil of Quebec* (first English ed.; Toronto: University of Toronto Press, 1974), 130–1.

CHAPTER SEVEN

1 John H. Hallowell. *Main Currents in Modern Political Thought* (New York: Henry Holt, 1950), 651.

2 These reactions of the church press are cited in Stewart Crysdale, *The Industrial Struggle and Protestant Ethics in Canada* (Toronto: Ryerson Press, 1961), 18–9. It is not unlikely that among the strikers and those who rallied to their support were some who were not prepared to accept the editors' opinions as to their Christian duty (see Doris French, *Faith, Sweat and Politics* [Toronto: McClelland and Stewart, 1962]). For a fuller account of the social stance of Methodism and Presbyterianism in these years, see Marion Royce, "The Contribution of the Methodist Church to Social Welfare in Canada" (unpublished MA thesis, University of Toronto, 1940), and E.A. Christie, "The Presbyterian Church in Canada and its Official Attitude Towards Public Affairs and Social Problems, 1875–1925" (unpublished MA thesis, University of Toronto, 1955).

3 Crysdale, *The Industrial Struggle*, 22.

4 C.D.W. Goodwin, *Canadian Economic Thought* (Durham, NC: Duke University Press, 1961), 32–8; *Toronto World*, 7 February 1898; *Grain Growers' Guide*, 21 November 1917, 32–3.

5 United Church Archives, Toronto, reading lists in the Bland Papers.

6 Bland Papers.

7 C.H. Hopkins, *The Rise of the Social Gospel in American Protestantism, 1865–1915* (New Haven: Yale University Press, 1940), 110–5.

8 For an expression of this transition, see the introduction to General William Booth, *In Darkest England and the Way Out* (London: International Headquarters of the Salvation Army, 1890).

9 The distinction was between bringing the message and creating the social reality. For an illuminating discussion of this process, see Donald B. Meyer, *The Protestant Search for Political Realism, 1919–1941* (Los Angeles and Berkeley, 1960), chap. 1.

10 United Church Archives, Toronto, J.B. Silcox, *Social Resurrection*.

11 C.S. Eby, *The World Problem and the Divine Solution* (Toronto: William Briggs, 1914).

12 W.S. Ryder, in a paper presented to the Pacific Coast Theology Conference, 1920; *Western Methodist Recorder*, September 1920, 4–5. See also David Summers, "The Labour Church" (unpublished PhD thesis, University of Edinburgh, 1958).

13 *Kingston Daily News*, 14 February 1894, 13 February 1896, 20 February 1896, 11 February 1897; *Queen's Quarterly* 5 (April 1898), 316–8; 6 (April 1899), 314–16; 7 (April 1900), 332; 8 (April 1901), 388.

14 Robert Sandall, *The History of the Salvation Army*, vol. 3, *Social Reform and Welfare Work* (London: Thomas Nelson and Sons, 1955), 80.

15 Alexander Sutherland, *The Kingdom of God and Problems of Today* (Toronto: William Briggs, 1898), xiii.

16 Bland Papers, Salem Bland, Sermon at St James Bond United Church, 31 October 1937.

17 Summers, "The Labour Church," 427ff; Hopkins, *The Rise of the Social Gospel*, 85–7; French, *Faith, Sweat and Politics*, 129–30.

18 *Social Welfare* (October 1923): 14–15; W. Ward, *The Brotherhood in Canada* (London: The Brotherhood Publishing House, 1912). See also F.D. Leete, *Christian Brotherhoods* (Cincinnati: Jennings and Graham, 1912).

19 J.F. McCurdy, *The Life and Work of D.J. Macdonnell* (Toronto: William Briggs, 1897), 23–4, 289–309; Minutes of the Toronto City Missionary Society of the Methodist Church, 29 December 1894, 10 December 1895. For the less well-known Scottish side of the story, see Stewart Mechie, *The Church and Scottish Social Developments, 1780–1870* (London: Oxford University Press, 1960).

20 *Social Welfare* (February 1929): 113. *The Social Service Congress of Canada, 1914* (Toronto: Social Service Council of Canada, 1914), 134–6.

21 *Canadian Student* (October 1919): 16–20; *Social Welfare* (February 1929): 113; and Murray G. Ross, *The YMCA in Canada: The Chronicle of a Century* (Toronto: Ryerson Press, 1951), 215–32.

22 Kenneth McNaught, *A Prophet in Politics* (Toronto: University of Toronto Press, 1959), chap. 4.

23 *Social Service Congress of Canada*, 307.

24 Methodist Church of Canada and Presbyterian Church in Canada, *Reports of Investigations of Social-Conditions and Social Surveys*, 1913–14: Vancouver, Regina, Fort William, Port Arthur, London, Hamilton, Sydney. United Church Archives, Toronto.

25 *Voice* (8 December 1916): 8; *The Nutcracker* (17 November 1916): 8.

26 Moral and Social Reform Council, *Minutes of the Annual Meeting*, 5 September 1913. United Church Archives, Toronto.

27 See H.H. Walsh, *The Christian Church in Canada* (Toronto: Ryerson Press, 1956).

28 A.E. Smith, *All My Life* (Toronto: Progress Publishing, 1949), 33.

29 Ibid.

30 W.E.S. James, "Notes on a Socialist Church," in Summers, "The Labour Church," 690–6.

31 For an able discussion of these factors in their British context, see Stanley Pierson, "Socialism and Religion: A Study of their Interaction in Great Britain, 1889–1911" (unpublished PhD thesis, Harvard University, 1957).

32 *Canadian Annual Review*, 1908, 101; 1909, 307; 1910, 315; 1912, 277.

33 Ibid., 1909, 306.

34 Ibid., 1910, 315–6.

35 Ibid., 1908, 99.

36 Paul Fox, "Early Socialism in Canada," *The Political Process in Canada*, ed. J.H. Aitcheson (Toronto: University of Toronto Press, 1963), 89.

37 Methodist and Presbyterian Churches, *Report of a Social Survey of Port Arthur* (n.p., 1913), 10.

38 Thomas Voaden, *Christianity and Socialism* (Toronto: Methodist Book Room, 1913).

39 Methodist and Presbyterian Churches, *Report of a Limited Survey of Educational, Social and Industrial Life in London, Ontario* (n.p., 1913), 43.

40 *Ottawa Free Press*, 2 March 1914; *Ottawa Evening Journal*, 3 March 1914; and the record of the conference proceedings cited above, *Social Service Congress of Canada*, 1914.

41 Charles Stelzle, "Capturing the Labour Movement," *Social Service Congress of Canada*, 35–8.

42 *Canadian Men and Women of the Time*, 1912.

43 Canadian Brotherhood Federation, *Constitution* [and list of officers and General Council], c. 1916. United Church Archives, Toronto.

44 *Canadian Men and Women of the Time*, 1912; *Canadian Forum* (November 1938), 229; Summers, "The Labour Church," 690–6.

45 *Social Service Congress of Canada*, 1914.

46 McNaught, *A Prophet in Politics*, 79–85. For a detailed discussion from another point of view, see A.R. Allen, "The Crest and Crisis of the Social Gospel in Canada, 1916–1927" (unpublished PhD thesis, Duke University, 1967), chap. 2.

47 See for instance the early reactions of the Methodist Church, *Journal of Proceedings of the General Conference*, 1914, 404–6; 1918, 290–3.

48 Presbyterian Church in Canada, *Acts and Proceedings of the General Assembly*, 1916, appendix, 13–14.

49 *Canadian Annual Review*, 1918, 598. *Social Service Council of Canada, Minutes, Annual Meeting, January 1918.*

50 See the first issues of *Social Welfare*, beginning October 1918; *Methodist Journal of Proceedings*, 1918, 290–3; Statement of the Presbyterian Board of Home Missions and Social Service, *Presbyterian and Westminster*, 10 April 1919, 351.

51 *New Republic*, 8 February 1919.

52 *Hamilton Spectator*, 12 October 1918; *Western Methodist Recorder*, March 1919, 5–6.

53 *Voice* (Winnipeg), 19 April 1918.

54 Ibid., 21 June 1918; 5 and 12 July 1918.

55 Summers, "The Labour Church," 379–80.

56 *Edmonton Free Press*, 10 May 1919; *Industrial Banner*, 10 October 1919; *Youth and Service*, August 1919, 114–5; *Western Methodist Recorder*, October 1920, 3; *Alberta Labor News*, 25 September 1920; *Christian Guardian*, 30 July 1919, 2, quoting John Queen of the Winnipeg strike committee.

57 *Canadian Churchman*, 28 November 1918, 763.

58 See William Ivens' euphoric mixture of prophecy, platform rhetoric, and industrial tactics in *Western Labor News*, Special Strike Editions, e.g., no. 3, 19 May 1919.

59 For more extensive discussion of the Labour Churches in Canada, see McNaught, *A Prophet in Politics*, Allen, "The Crest and Crisis of the Social Gospel," Summers, "The Labour Church," and D.F. Pratt, "William Ivens and the Winnipeg Labor Church" (unpublished BD thesis, St Andrew's College, Saskatoon, 1962).

60 Editorial, "I Was Hungry," *Christian Guardian*, 27 November 1918, 6.

61 *Christian Guardian*, 5 March 1919, 5.

62 *Canadian Churchman*, 27 February 1919, 133; 10 April 1919, 234–5.

63 *Canadian Churchman*, 29 May 1919, 344; 10 July 1919, 441.

64 *Western Methodist Recorder*, June 1919, 8.

65 *Presbyterian and Westminster*, 22 May 1919, 497; 29 May 1919, 518–9; 5 June 1919, 549–50.

66 *Social Welfare*, 1 August 1919, 266–70; *Christian Guardian*, 28 May 1919, 5; 4 June 1919, 4–5; 11 June 1919, 3; 18 June 1919, 4; 25 June 1919, 4.

67 For a detailed discussion of the more general church reaction, see Allen, "The Crest and Crisis of the Social Gospel," chaps 6, 7.

68 *Western Methodist Recorder*, June 1919.

69 McNaught, *A Prophet in Politics*, 118.

70 *Christian Guardian*, 25 June 1919, 2; *Toronto Daily Star*, 12 June 1919, 1, 8.

71 See for instance United Church Archives, Toronto, Bland Papers, Salem Bland, "Four Steps and a Vision."

72 *Social Welfare*, 1 November 1919, 39; 1 December 1919, 75; *Christian Guardian*, 1 October 1919, 6.

73 *Canadian Baptist*, 1 May 1919, 4; 31 July 1919, 3; *Presbyterian and Westminster*, 19 June 1919, 603; 25 December 1919, 594; *Christian Guardian*, 15 October 1919, 22.

74 *Christian Guardian*, 30 June 1920, 18–9.

75 *Western Methodist Recorder*, October 1921, 4.

76 *Social Welfare*, 1 September 1919, 287; 1 August 1920, 316–7; 1 August 1922, 235.

77 See A.R. Allen, "The Crest and Crisis of the Social Gospel," chap. 11.

78 *Christian Guardian*, 25 March 1925.

79 *Social Welfare*, August 1927, 483; August 1929, 242.

80 "The Christianization of Industry," *Social Welfare*, 1 August 1927, 488–9; see also United Church, Department of Evangelism and Social Service, *Annual Report, 1924–5*, 10.

81 See Creighton's reflections on this possibility, *New Outlook*, 12 January 1927, 19.

82 *Grain Growers' Guide*, 14 and 28 August 1909; 30 September, 6 October 1919.

83 McNaught, *A Prophet in Politics*, 74, n74.

84 *Grain Growers' Guide*, 7 June 1916; 20 December 1916.

85 Moral and Social Reform Council, *Minutes*, 10 September 1909; Social Service Council of Canada, *Minutes*, 5 September 1913; Manitoba Conference of the United Church, *Minutes*, 1932, 42.

86 *Canadian Annual Review*, 1913, 578; Manitoba Conference, *Minutes*, 1929, 60; *The Single Taxer and Direct Legislation Bulletin* (Winnipeg) 3, no. 8 (1916).

87 See his Circulars nos 9 and 10 for United Farmers of Alberta Sunday, 27 May 1917, Bland Papers, United Church Archives, Toronto.

88 *Grain Growers' Guide*, 29 January 1917, 4 December 1918.

89 *Christian Guardian*, 17 March 1920, 25; 15 December 1920, 14.

90 For further elaboration of this suggestion, see A.R. Allen, "Salem Bland and the Social Gospel in Canada" (unpublished MA thesis, University of Saskatchewan, 1961), chaps 5 and 6.

91 *Presbyterian Witness*, 23 June 1921, 10–1.

92 The documentation for this is too diffuse to be suggested through a few citations but may be found in A.R. Allen, "The Crest and Crisis of the Social Gospel," chaps 14–16.

93 Ibid., chap. 10.

94 See correspondence between Moore and Hamilton from 25 May 1920 to 25 April 1922, Papers on Methodist Industrial Relations, 1920–2, United Church Archives, Toronto.

95 A.E. Smith, *All My Life*, 76–7.

96 United Church, Department of Evangelism and Social Service, *Annual*

Report, 1927, 24–5, 27–9; *New Outlook,* 21 March 1928, 2; 8 January 1930, 46; Dobson Papers, Union College Library, B.C., Hugh Dobson to L.C. McKinney, 30 April 1929.

97 *New Outlook,* 22 December 1926, 5; 8 January 1930, 31, 44.

98 In 1926 the Canadian Association of Social Workers was formed, and in 1928 the Canadian Conference of Social Work held its first national meeting. The immediate shrinkage in size of the Social Service Council's annual meetings indicated the impact of these developments on the stature of the council. For an expression of the rationale upon which the council was founded, see *New Outlook,* 10 June 1925, 23. For expressions of the new social worker's outlook see J.D. Ketchum, "Judge and be Judged," *Canadian Student,* November 1925; *Social Welfare,* June–July 1926, 189–90; and for a warning about the dangers of a social work that had lost its sense of God, see United Church, Department of Evangelism and Social Service, *Annual Report 1927,* 25. The social gospel's stress upon the immanence of God, of course, abetted the very secularism about which some of them were now concerned.

99 See for instance *Canadian Student,* January 1924, 99; *Christian Guardian,* 20 February 1924, and issues of subsequent months for discussion of the subject; *Social Welfare,* April 1923, 137–9; *New Outlook,* issues of July through December 1925; *Canadian Churchman,* 21 January 1926, 36.

100 *New Outlook,* 12 August 1925, 5–6; 12 February 1930, 153; *Canadian Student,* March 1925, 163; March 1926, 165–6. Student Christian Movement Archives, Minutes of the General Committee, 24–26 September 1926.

101 [Ernest Thomas] *Fellowship Studies* (Toronto: United Church Department of Evangelism and Social Service, 1927 or 1928); *Canadian Student,* March 1926, 168; Dobson Papers, Dobson to Armstrong, 14 May 1928.

CHAPTER EIGHT

1 *Manitoba Free Press,* 5 October 1903, 7.

2 W. Sparling, "The Church's Call to the Students," *Canada's Missionary Congress* (Toronto: Canadian Council Layman's Missionary Movement, 1909), 272–3.

3 A.G. Bedford, "The Sunlit Way: A History of the Founding Colleges of the University of Winnipeg" (unpublished manuscript), 65, 98, 136. I am indebted to Professor Bedford of the University of Winnipeg for allowing me to read his manuscript. Needless to say, apart from one or two incidental references, the following is based upon my own research in the University's sources and in the reform movement in general. See also *Minutes of the*

Manitoba and North-West Conference, 1903, 51–3; *Vox Wesleyana*, 6, no. 2 (1901); 16, no. 2 (1911), College advertisement inside cover.

4 Bedford, "The Sunlit Way," 59, 88–9, 91–2.

5 Ibid.

6 Wesley College Faculty Minutes, 27 November 1903; 5 January 1904; 29 January 1904; 1 December 1911; 12 January 1912.

7 Ibid., 8 May 1905.

8 Ibid., 2 November 1906; 5 November 1906; 6 November 1906.

9 Faculty Minutes, 9 May 1913.

10 Ibid., 3 April 1903; 28 April 1903; 13 November 1903.

11 *Manitoba Free Press*, 12 March 1904, 4.

12 *Vox Wesleyana* 4, no. 8 (1900): 129–32.

13 *Manitoba Free Press*, 2 November 1903, 3.

14 Ibid.; Wesley College Faculty Minutes, 9 May 1913.

15 Wesley College Executive Minutes, 1896–1914, 1–4, *Vox Wesleyana* 13, no. 4 (1909): 99; 15, no. 6 (1911): 49.

16 Ibid., 16, no. 4 (1912): 22–24.

17 Faculty Minutes, 26 January 1906.

18 Ibid., 4 March 1904.

19 *Vox Wesleyana*, 8, no. 5 (1904): 118. R.O. Joliffe was a brilliant Toronto graduate and gold medallist in Classics (*Minutes of the Manitoba and North-West Conference*, 1904, 49–51).

20 See David R.L. Howarth, "An Appreciation of our Faculty," *Vox Wesleyana*, 14, no. 6 (1910): 32–3.

21 *Manitoba Free Press*, 10 October 1903, 8.

22 Report of the Committee on Temperance and Moral Reform," *Minutes of Manitoba Conference*, 1905, 66–7; *Journal of the Manitoba Conference*, 16 June 1908, 132–3.

23 Methodist Church of Canada, *Journal of the General Conference*, 1906.

24 See his "Suggestions for the Young Preacher," *Vox Wesleyana*, 16, no. 1 (1911): 8–9; see also *Manitoba Free Press*, 10 October 1903, 8.

25 *Vox Wesleyana*, 12, no. 4 (1908): 77; 13, no. 1 (1908): 10; *The Gleam*, 1, no. 3 (1914): 18; 1, no. 4 (1914): 33.

26 *Vox Wesleyana*, 2, no. 6 (1898): 178.

27 Ibid., 6, no. 6 (1902): 120–1; *Wesley College Executive Minutes*, 7 December 1909, 133–4; *The Gleam*, 1, no. 2 (1914):22–4.

28 *Vox Wesleyana*, 4, no. 1 (1900): 7–8; 5, no. 6 (1901): 110.

29 Ibid., 3, no. 4 (1899): 74.

30 Ibid., 13, no. 1 (1908): 10.

31 Ibid.

32 Ibid., 13, no. 5 (1909): 113-5.

33 See for example W. Ivens, "The Social Content of a Religious Education," *Vox Wesleyana* 15, no. 1 (1910): 11-2; "Theological Student and Sociology," *Vox Wesleyana* 15, no. 5 (1911): 12; "Relation of the Church to some Social Problems," *Vox Wesleyana* 15, no. 5 (1911): 23-4; and H.D. Ranns, "Is Religion in the Melting Pot Today," *Vox Wesleyana* 16, no. 2 (1911): 13-5.

34 *Vox Wesleyana*, 4, no. 1 (1899): 4-5.

35 Ibid., 1-2.

36 Ibid., 5, no. 2 (1900): 19-21.

37 Ibid., 7, no. 6 (1903): 106; 13, no. 4 (1909): 84.

38 Ibid., 12, no. 3 (1908): 47-8.

39 Ibid., 13, no. 2 (1908): 1.

40 Ibid., 17, no. 2 (1912): 2-4.

41 Ibid., 4, no. 1 (1899): 1-2.

42 Ibid., 4, no. 5 (1900): 73; 5, no. 3 (1900): 47.

43 Ibid., 4, no. 3 (1900): 39-40; 4, no. 4 (1900): 55-6; 4, no. 8 (1900): 135.

44 Ibid., 12, no. 1 (1907): 1-2.

45 Ibid., 7, no. 2 (1902): 26-8; also "YWCA Notes," Ibid., 6, no. 5 (1902): 101.

46 Ibid., 6 (1902): 100-1.

47 J.S. Woodsworth, *Strangers Within Our Gates* (Toronto: Missionary Society of the Methodist Church, 1909), 323-6.

48 *Vox Wesleyana* 17, no. 2 (1912): 22; 17, no. 6 (1913): 46; 19, no. 5 (1916): 29-30. The settlement was located at first at Sutherland Avenue and later at 156 Austin Street.

49 Ibid., 16, no. 1 (1910): 7-9; see also Alfred Fitzpatrick, *The University in Overalls*, (Toronto: Press of the Hunter-Rose Co., 1923).

50 *Vox Wesleyana* 15, no. 4 (1911): 11-12.

51 Ibid., 12, no. 1 (1907): 19-20.

52 Ibid., 14, no. 5 (1910): 12-14.

53 Ibid., 13, no. 2 (1908): 24. The only unequivocally alarmist article was one by Rev. Wellington Bridgman apparently solicited to present another view alongside an article by Woodsworth 13, no. 3 (1908): 62-6.

54 Ibid., 4, no. 1 (1899): 1-2.

55 Ibid., 4, no. 3 (1899): 39-40; 4 (1900): 55-6.

56 Ibid., 4, no. 8 (1900): 135; 7, no. 4 (1903): 71-3; 12, no. 1 (1907): 21.

57 Ibid., 6, no. 2 (1901): 25.

58 *The Gleam* 1, no. 3 (1901): 40.

59 *Vox Wesleyana* 20, no. 5 (1917): 32.

60 Ibid., 12, no. 3 (1908): 48.

61 Ibid., 13, no. 1 (1908): 11.

62 Ibid., 12, no. 4 (1908): 69–70.

63 Ibid., 13, no. 1 (1908): 3; *The Gleam* 1, no. 3 (1914): 51–2.

64 *Vox Wesleyana* 13, no. 6 (1909): 178; 16 (1911): 15; 17 no. 1 (1912): 30–1.

65 Ibid., 13, no. 1 (1908): 11.

66 Ibid., 16, no. 5 (1912): 9.

67 Ibid., 6–8.

68 Ibid., 14, no. 3 (1910): 25.

69 Bedford, "The Sunlit Way," 98.

70 Ibid., 114.

71 See *Vox Wesleyana*, Convocation Numbers; Faculty Minutes, passim; articles on the Woodsworth Boys, in *Christian Guardian*, 10 May 1922; 14 June 1922; 7 May 1924.

72 B.Y. Card, *The Expanding Relation: Sociology in Prairie Universities* (Regina: Canadian Plains Research Centre, 1973); *Vox Wesleyana* 16, no. 1 (1911): 28–9; 16, no. 3 (1912): 16–9; Faculty Minutes, 8 October 1909; 21 January 1910; 7, 9 March 1913; 16 October 1914; *The Gleam* 1, no. 4 (1914): 8–9.

73 *Vox Wesleyana* 15, no. 1 (1910): 11–2.

74 Ibid., 15, no. 5 (1911): 12. Fewster, like Ivens, was of British background and was president of the student body in 1912–13 (ibid., 17, no. 6 [1913]: 29).

75 B.Y. Card, *The Expanding Relation*.

76 See lists of Church and individual subscriptions, *Minutes of the Manitoba and North-West Conference*, 1902, 1903, 1904. The Massey family had given the college large support in the first decade, especially, and of $246,575 pledged to the new endowment, $130,000 was from four individuals. University of Winnipeg Administrative Collection, "Old Documents of Interest" file.

77 Executive Minutes, June 1900; 25 October 1901.

78 Allan Artibise, "The Urban Development of Winnipeg, 1874–1914" (unpublished PhD thesis, University of British Columbia, 1971), 9, 34, 136ff.

79 *The Gleam* 1, no. 3 (1914): 18; 1, no. 4 (1914): 33.

80 See extension of Bland's weekly student conferences to include Varsity and Wesley YWCA, *Vox Wesleyana* 20, no. 3 (1917): 48, and "Appreciation of our Faculty," ibid., 20, no. 5 (1917): 33.

81 Letter to the editor, *Toronto Daily Star*, 21 March 1931. *Minutes of the Board of Directors*, April 9 1918, in University of Winnipeg Administrative Collection, Miscellaneous finance file, 1915–18.

82 J.P. Haryett to the board of Wesley College, 25 May 1918; E. Loftus to J.P. Haryett, 29 May 1918; William T. Brady to the board of Wesley College, 29 May 1918.

CHAPTER NINE

1 Thelma McCormack, "The Protestant Ethic and the Spirit of Socialism," *British Journal of Theology* 20, no. 3 (September 1969).

2 It is quite understandable, of course, that he is treated so in such works as: David Jay Bercuson, *Confrontation at Winnipeg* (Montreal: McGill-Queen's University Press, 1974), 5–7; Ramsay Cook, "Introduction," Catherine Cleverdon, *The Woman Suffrage Movement in Canada* (Toronto: University of Toronto Press Reprint, 1974), 47–8; A. Ross McCormack, *Reformers, Rebels and Revolutionaries: The Western Canadian Radical Movement, 1899–1919* (Toronto: University of Toronto Press, 1977), 87, 134; John Herd Thompson, *The Harvest of War: The Prairie West, 1914–1916* (Toronto: McClelland and Stewart, 1978), 31, 38, 105, 126, 135.

3 *Manitoba Free Press*, 17 September 1903, 3.

4 See Salem Bland Papers, no. 428, "Echoes of the Conference of 1903," United Church Archives, Toronto.

5 Educational address, 14 March 1903, Salem Bland Papers, no. 23, United Church Archives, Toronto.

6 *Methodist Magazine and Review* 56 (July–December 1902): 377.

7 *Manitoba Free Press*, 29 September 1903, 16; *Manitoba Free Press*, 30 September 1903, 16.

8 See Irene Spry, "The Great Transformation: The Disappearance of the Commons in Western Canada," in *Man and Nature on the Prairies*, ed. Richard Allen (Regina: Canadian Plains Research Center, 1976).

9 *Canadian Men and Women of the Time*, 1912.

10 See W.L. Morton, *Manitoba, A History* (Toronto: University of Toronto Press, 1957), chap. 9.

11 *Manitoba Free Press*, 14 June 1904, 8; *Manitoba Free Press*, 31 October 1904, 6.

12 *Manitoba Free Press*, 29 June 1904, 10; *Vox Wesleyana* 8 (November 1903): 34–35.

13 *Telegram*, 5 October 1903. See also *Manitoba Free Press*, 21 November 1903, 5.

14 *Vox Wesleyana* 2, no. 6 (1898): 178.

15 The Needfulness of Fellowship," 1 August 1896, Salem Bland Papers, no. 342, United Church Archives, Toronto.

16 *Vox Wesleyana* 8 (November 1903): 35.

17 *Manitoba Free Press*, 10 October 1903, 5; *Vox Wesleyana* 7, no. 6 (1903): 106; *Vox Wesleyana* 16, no. 6 (1912): 1–5; "Thoughts on Art," 7 December 1907, Salem Bland Papers, no. 43; "Talk on Reading," November 1906, Salem Bland Papers, no. 37, United Church Archives, Toronto.

18 Paul's Greatest Prayer," 15 June 1903, Salem Bland Papers, no. 417, United Church Archives, Toronto; *Vox Wesleyana* 10 (November 1905): 10–12.

19 Ibid.

20 Christian Perfection," 4 December 1880, Salem Bland Papers, no. 243. See also Richard Allen, "Salem Bland: The Young Preacher," *The Bulletin* (United Church Archives), no. 26 (1977): 82.

21 See the citations in Morton Paterson, "The Mind of a Methodist: The Personalist Philosophy of George John Blewett in its Historical Context" (paper presented to the World Methodist Historical Society, Toronto, 1977).

22 Minutes of Methodist Ministerial Association, 1903–1913, United Church Archives.

23 Ibid., 14 October 1907.

24 *Western Methodist Bulletin* [later *Western Methodist Times*], December 1904. Thirteen issues of the paper exist spanning December 1904 to July 1906, all in the Salem Goldworth Bland collection, United Church Archives, Toronto.

25 *Manitoba Free Press*, 28 June 1904, 4.

26 These views of Bland's are scattered through such frequently delivered addresses and sermons as nos 1, 2, 10, and 381 in the Salem Bland collection, United Church Archives, Toronto.

27 The Saints for the Age," Salem Bland Papers, no. 16; "Four Steps and a Vision," Salem Bland Papers, no. 18.

28 The Social Ideal," 13 February 1905, Salem Bland Papers, no. 28.

29 Journal of Manitoba Conference, 9 June 1905, 21; 13 June 1905, 38–9; Minutes of Manitoba Conference, 1905, 66–7, UCA-MNO.

30 *Manitoba Free Press*, 4 December 1905, 13; *Manitoba Free Press*, 9 December 1905, 13; "Winnipeg Politics," 3 December 1905, Salem Bland Papers, no. 33.

31 *The Voice*, 1 December 1905, 6.

32 Journal of Manitoba Conference, 9 June 1905, 23; 13 June 1905, 36; 11 June 1906, 62; 12 June 1906, 65; 16 June 1908, 129, United Church Archives.

33 See reading lists, Bland collection, United Church Archives, Toronto.

34 The Place of the Kingdom of God in the Preaching of Today," 12 February 1906. Salem Bland Papers, no. 235.

35 See title page with date of delivery, "Four Steps and a Vision," Salem Bland Papers, no. 18.

36 The upshot for Bland was probably more a radicalizing and historicizing of idealism than a full turn to empiricism as laid out in S.E.D. Shortt, *The Search for an Ideal* (Toronto: University of Toronto Press, 1976).

37 Adolf Harnack, *What is Christianity?* 4th ed., trans. Thomas B. Saunders (New York: Williams and Norgate, 1923); and Salem Bland, "The Place of the Kingdom of God in the Preaching of Today," 12 February 1906.

38 Ibid.

39 *Manitoba Free Press*, 9 March 1907, 3.

40 Lane to Bland, 3 May 1907, Salem Bland Papers, no. 885, miscellaneous correspondence.

41 Ibid., Whittaker to Bland, 13 February 1907.

42 William H. Brooks, "Methodism in the Canadian West in the Nineteenth Century" (PhD dissertation, University of Manitoba, 1972), 327, 340.

43 See such sermons and addresses as: "The Contribution of the College Man to the National Life," 24 April 1904, Salem Bland Papers, no. 431; "The Spell of Jesus," 11 December 1904, Salem Bland Papers, no. 436; "Christianity a Spirit rather than a Creed," June 1907, Salem Bland Papers, no. 441; "Study of Comparative Religion," 27 November 1907, Salem Bland Papers, no. 442; and "The Duty and Difficulty of Preserving Unity in the Church," 20 March 1896, Salem Bland Papers, no. 339.

44 *Selkirk Weekly Record*, 21 October 1910, 1; see also *Crystal City Carrier*, 24 December 1903, 1; *The Western Prairie*, Cypress River, 4 March 1904, 4; *The Neepawa Press*, 13 November 1906, 1; *The Holland Observer*, 1 November 1907, 1; *Carberry News*, 21 January 1910, 1; *The Stonewall Argus*, 4 May 1910.

45 *The Killarney Guide*, 19 November 1914, 1; and 25 November 1914, 5.

46 *Grain Growers' Guide*, 26 February 1913, 7, 10.

47 *Christian Guardian*, 8 July 1908, 9–10.

48 G.N. Emery, "The Methodist Church and the 'European Foreigners' of Winnipeg, the All Peoples' Mission, 1889–1914," paper read before the Historical and Scientific Society of Manitoba, series 3, no. 28 (1971–72): 85–100; *Vox Wesleyana* (December 1908): 62–3; Faculty Minutes, 15 January 1919, 304.

49 *The Voice*, 2 May 1910.

50 14 January 1911, Salem Bland Papers, no. 449.

51 Signs of the Times," 26 February 1911, Salem Bland Papers, no. 450.

52 *Manitoba Free Press*, 21 November 1903, 5.

53 Winston Churchill, *The Inside of the Cup* (New York: Macmillan, 1914); "Winston Churchill's *The Inside of the Cup* or Religion No Substitute for Justice," 3 August 1914, Salem Bland Papers, no. 455. It is instructive to compare the Rev. Frederick DuVal's treatment of the same book as reported in the *Manitoba Free Press* (4 August 1913). DuVal holds the issue at arm's length and gives the congregation an easy out. See also *Grain Growers' Guide*, 6 August 1913, 847.

CHAPTER TEN

1 J.S. Woodsworth, *Strangers Within Our Gates* (Toronto: Missionary Society of the Methodist Church, 1909), 255.

2 For this information, for incidental items below, and for many valuable per-

spectives, I am much in the debt of Paul Rutherford, Department of History, University of Toronto, who provided me with a copy of his paper presented to the Canadian Historical Association, 1971, 'Tomorrow's Metropolis: The Urban Reform Movement in Canada, 1880–1920.'

3 See *Canada Year Book*, 1913, chap. 3, Tables 6–8, analysis, 57, based on towns and cities of over 5,000.

4 Ibid., Table 15, 69.

5 Ibid., Table 21, 79.

6 See United Church Archives, Stephenson Collection, "Search Guide"; C.C. Love, *Frederick Clark Stephenson* (Toronto: Ryerson Press, 1957); and F.C. Stephenson, *The Young People's Forward Movement for Missions* (Toronto, William Briggs, 1897).

7 The percentages are too large even when the populations of all Canadian towns and cities are included in the calculation. Woodsworth uncritically reproduced the chart (see below, 17). The rest of the chart and Woodsworth's own statistics seem generally reliable.

8 United Church Archives, Stephenson Collection, Minutes, General Board of Missions, 5 October 1907, 389.

9 Ibid., Stephenson to T.E.E. Shore, 26 June 1911.

10 *Canadian Epworth Era*, September 1912, 214.

11 See the program lists and outlines published regularly in the *Epworth Era* and the *Missionary Outlook*.

12 Public Archives of Canada, J.S. Woodsworth Papers, scrapbooks (hereafter cited as Woodsworth scrapbooks), vol. 29, leaflet containing reviews.

13 *Missionary Outlook*, January 1912, 11.

14 Woodsworth scrapbooks.

15 *Manitoba Free Press*, 11 November 1911; *Telegram*, 17 October 1911.

16 The foregoing reviews are found among undated cuttings in Woodsworth scrapbooks, vol. 29. Oddly enough, the wide-ranging *Review of Historical Publications Relating to Canada* reviewed neither Woodsworth book.

17 Many were quite moved by the book. "It filled me up so," wrote Dr C.T. Scott of Brantford, that "I had to preach on the theme on Sunday" (*Missionary Outlook*, May 1912, 107). For additional comments on the book see *Canadian Epworth Era*, October 1911, 224–5; *Christian Guardian*, 4 October 1911, 14; 18 October 1911, 26; and *Nurses Alumnae Journal*, August 1912, 13–14.

18 United Church Archives, Letters to C.B. Sissons, 28 August 1907.

19 See especially the personal statement of his perceptions of urban life on pages 11–12.

20 *Weekly Free Press and Prairie Farmer*, 11 July 1913.

21 Woodsworth scrapbooks; *North Ender* (Winnipeg), 23 March 1911; also "Social Perfection," *Christian Guardian*, 23 April 1913.
22 Apologies to Plato, *The Republic*.

CHAPTER ELEVEN

1 W.L. Morton, "The Social Philosophy of Henry Wise Wood," *Agricultural History*, (April 1948): 116.
2 22 February 1919.
3 United Church Archives, Salem Bland Papers, letter, 17 April 1919, in Wood to Bland, 18 April 1914.
4 *Presbyterian Witness*, 23 June 1921, 10–1.
5 *Leader* (Regina), 22 February 1919.
6 *Grain Growers' Guide*, 12 January 1916.
7 *Christian Guardian*, 17 March 1920, 25.
8 For example, Rev. J.M. Douglas, the Independent Liberal who won the federal seat of Assiniboia in 1896 with Patron backing, followed later by R.C. Henders and W.R. Wood, Thomas Beveridge, the editor of *The Melita New Era* in Melita, Manitoba.
9 *Presbyterian and Westminster*, 8 May 1919, 457–8.
10 Interviews, F. Passmore, 13 December 1960; W. Irvine, 14, 15 May 1961.
11 19 June 1920.
12 8 January 1913.
13 7 June 1916.
14 28 August 1909.
15 Ibid., 14 August 1909.
16 Ibid., 30 September, 6 October 1919.
17 W.K. Rolph, *Henry Wise Wood of Alberta* (Toronto: University of Toronto Press, 1950), 9–10.
18 See "Organization for Democracy," *Grain Growers' Guide*, 4 December 1918, 39; "The Prince of Peace," *Grain Growers' Guide*, 23; "Mr. Pepys in the West," *Grain Growers' Guide*, 8 January 1919, 47; UFA convention address, *Grain Growers' Guide*, 29 January 1919; also W.L. Morton, "Social Philosophy," and Rolph, *Henry Wise Wood*, 9–10, 63–6.
19 Minutes, Board of Directors, SGGA, 30 March 1917, Saskatchewan Archives; *Grain Growers' Guide*, 6 June 1917, 10.
20 UFA Circulars nos 9 and 10, 14, 18 April 1917.
21 22 May 1920, 6; also *Grain Growers' Guide*, 6 June 1917.
22 *Grain Growers' Guide*, 4 December 1918, 41.
23 *Grain Growers' Guide*, 5 November 1919, 8.

24 *Nutcracker*, 10 May 1917.

25 *Leader* (Regina), 21 February 1919.

26 *Grain Growers' Guide*, 5 November 1919.

27 See Thomas Flanagan, "Political Geography and the United Farmers of Alberta," *The Twenties in Western Canada*, ed. S. Trofimenkoff (Ottawa: National Museums of Canada, 1972), 138–47.

28 *Morning Leader* (Regina), 19 February 1919.

29 Leo Courville, "The Saskatchewan Progressives," (unpublished MA thesis, University of Saskatchewan, Regina Campus, 1971), 59.

30 J.H. Thompson, "The Prohibition Question in Manitoba, 1892–1928," (unpublished MA thesis, University of Manitoba, 1969).

31 Guy J. Cyrenne, "The Saskatchewan Grain Growers' Association: Their Educational and Social Aspects" (Honours paper, University of Saskatchewan, Regina Campus, 1973), 20, 25–6; "First Ukrainian M.P. Dies," *Leader-Post* (Regina), 23 April 1973, 41 (Michael Luchkovich).

32 John MacDougall, *Rural Life in Canada: Its Trends and Tasks* (Toronto: Westminster Company, 1913).

CHAPTER TWELVE

1 Richard Allen, *The View from Murney Tower: Salem Bland, the late Victorian Controversies, and the Search for a New Christianity* (Toronto: University of Toronto Press, 2008).

2 United Church of Canada Archives, Toronto, Papers on Methodist Industrial Relations, 1920–22, C.F. Hamilton to T.A. Moore, 12 June 1920. All other references below to Moore and Hamilton vis-à-vis *The New Christianity* derive from the small body of correspondence in this collection. For more on Hamilton, see Public Archives of Canada, Papers of Charles Frederick Hamilton; also Carl Berger, *The Sense of Power: Studies in the Ideas of Canadian Imperialism, 1867–1914* (Toronto: University of Toronto Press, 1969), 248, 253. On Bland, see Richard Allen, "Salem Bland and the Social Gospel in Canada" (MA thesis, University of Saskatchewan, 1961); and on the details of the context of *The New Christianity*, see Allen, *The Social Passion: Religion and Social Reform in Canada, 1914–28* (Toronto: University of Toronto Press, 1971).

3 United Church of Canada Archives, Toronto, Salem Bland Papers, 838, "Comte," November 1897.

4 16 June 1920.

5 1 September 1920.

6 *Toronto Daily Star*, 2 June 1920.

7 *Globe*, Toronto, 17 June 1920.

8 *Globe*, 10 June 1920.

9 *Globe*, 17 June 1920.

10 *Toronto Daily Star*, 2 June 1920.

11 19 June 1920.

12 8 September 1920.

13 19 June 1920.

14 10 June 1920. The Regina *Leader* simply reprinted the review in the *Guardian*.

15 11 June 1920. The Toronto *Labour Leader*, 4 June 1920, followed this approach, while the *Hamilton Labor News* like the *Western Labor News*, Winnipeg, reproduced the introduction to the book, which had the same effect.

16 See, for instance, the editors of the two early Canadian socialist papers, George Wrigley in *Citizen and Country*, 11 March 1899, 1, 3, and W.A. Cotton in *Cotton's Weekly*, as reported in J.C. Hopkins, ed., *Canadian Annual Review of Public Affairs, 1909* (Toronto: Canadian Annual Review, 1910), 306.

17 *B.C. Federationist*, 12 July 1918.

18 S.G. Bland, "A Great Convention Hears Prophetic Words," *Toronto Daily Star*, 10 October 1942.

19 United Church of Canada Archives, Toronto, Henry Flesher Bland Papers, "The Substance of an Address delivered in the Odd Fellows Hall, Addingham, Feb. 20, 1844, to the First Annual Festival of the Mechanics Institute," which he had organized there.

20 See his *Universal Childhood Drawn to Christ* (Toronto: W. Briggs, 1882), based on his sermon of 27 November 1875 (Henry Flesher Bland Papers).

21 Salem Bland Papers, 243a, "Christian Perfection," 4 December 1880; 252b, "The Twin Revelations of God," 10 December 1881; and 251c, "The Ultimate Triumph of Christianity," 22 October 1881.

22 Ibid., 245a, "Significance of Conversion Cry," 19 February 1881; 258b, "Farewell Sermon on Cataraqui Circuit," 17 June 1882.

23 Ibid., 249c, "Religion and Business," 27 August 1881; also 243c, "Joshua's Covenant," 1 January 1881; 244c, "Isaiah's Vision," 29 January 1881; 252c, "Character," 17 December 1881.

24 Ibid., "My Intellectual Pilgrimage," ms. of address, 16 May 1939.

25 See, for instance, the conference reports in the *Daily British Whig*, Kingston, 11 February 1897, 16 February 1899, 12 February 1901; *Kingston Daily News*, 20 February 1896, 11 February 1897.

26 Salem Bland Papers, 343, "Man and the Word Glorified in Christ," 11 September 1896.

27 Ibid., 20, "The New Christianity," address to C.E. Union, Brockville, 8 November 1899.

28 See W.H. Magney, "The Methodist Church and the National Gospel," *Bulletin*, United Church Archives, Toronto, xx, 1968.

29 Methodist Church of Canada, *Journal of the General Conference* (1894): 300.

30 Salem Bland Papers, 1, "Human Nature," 1885–6; 2, "Men Needed," 1892; 381, "Sermon to the Independent Order of Foresters," 16 June 1900; 419, "The Canada of the Morrow," 31 July 1902.

31 Henry Flesher Bland Papers, Scrapbook 2, clippings 1888; "Journal of the Montreal Methodist Conference," 6 June 1896, 26–7.

32 Salem Bland Papers, 351, "Discipleship Open to All Temperaments," 28 August 1897; 909, "A Study of Christian Churches and of the Church of the Future," December 1900; 910, Normal School lectures, 1900–1; 386, "Some Signs of the Times," 23 February 1901.

33 See references in Allen, *The Social Passion*.

34 F.B. Housser, *A Canadian Art Movement: The Story of the Group of Seven* (Toronto: Macmillan, 1926), 156.

35 The Greatness of Times of Change," *Grain Growers' Guide*, 23 July 1919, 28.

36 Canadian labour papers merit a study like that of H.G. Gutman, "Protestantism and the American Labor Movement: The Christian Spirit in the Gilded Age," *American Historical Review* 72, no. 1 (October 1966).

37 There is an enormous literature on the subject, which has so far not resolved the issue definitively. For a recent critique, see Kurt Samuelsson, *Religion and Economic Action* (London, 1961).

38 Thelma McCormack, "The Protestant Ethic and the Spirit of Socialism," *British Journal of Theology* 20, no. 3 (Sept. 1969).

39 For an introduction to that issue, see the Epilogue in Donald B. Meyer, *The Protestant Search for Political Realism, 1919–1941* (Los Angeles and Berkeley: University of California Press, 1961).

CHAPTER THIRTEEN

1 Cited in Roderick Stewart, *Bethune* (Toronto: New Press, 1973), xiv.

2 H.T. Crossley, *Practical Talks on Important Themes* (Toronto: William Briggs, 1895), 33.

3 See Margaret Prang, *N.W. Rowell, Ontario Nationalist* (Toronto: University of Toronto Press, 1975), 74, 180.

4 For a discussion of these themes in the books see Mary Vipond, "Blessed Are the Peacemakers; the Labour Question in Canadian Social Gospel Fiction," *Journal of Canadian Studies* 10, no. 3 (1975).

5 John S. Moir, *Enduring Witness: A History of the Presbyterian Church in Canada* (Toronto: Presbyterian Publications, 1975), chap. 7, "An Age of Unions"; and

J. Warren Caldwell, "The Unification of Methodism, 1865–1884," *The Bulletin of the United Church Archives* 19 (1967).

6 William de Villiers Westfall, "The Dominion of the Lord: Victorian Protestant Ontario," *Queens Quarterly* 83 (Spring 1976).

7 William Magney, "The Methodist Church and the National Gospel, 1884–1914," in *The Bulletin* 20 (1968).

8 For the emergence of the Canadian Sunday and the struggle for its defence see Sharon Meen, "The Battle for the Sabbath: The Sabbatarian Lobby in Canada, 1890–1912," chaps 1, 2 (unpublished doctoral diss., University of British Columbia, 1979).

9 An extended account of the transformation of urban Methodism is contained in Neil Semple, "The Impact of Urbanization on the Methodist Church in Central Canada, 1854–1884" (unpublished doctoral diss., University of Toronto, 1979).

10 Christopher Headon, "Women and Organized Religion in Mid and Late Nineteenth Century Canada," *Journal of the Canadian Church Historical Society* 20, no. 1–2 (1978); and Susan Walma, "Alma College and the 'Women Question': 1877–1899" (unpublished Master's research paper, McMaster University, 1978).

11 See Magney, "The Methodist Church," 48–50; Richard Allen, *The Social Passion: Religion and Social Reform in Canada, 1914–1928* (Toronto: University of Toronto Press, 1971), 7, 11, 231; Prang, *N.W. Rowell*, 64–7; and Michael Bliss, *A Canadian Millionaire, The Life and Times of Sir Joseph Flavelle, Bart., 1858–1939* (Toronto: Macmillan, 1978), especially chaps 4–7.

12 Charles F. O'Brien, *Sir William Dawson, A Life in Science and Religion* (Philadelphia: American Philosophical Society, 1971), chap. 2; D.C. Masters, *Protestant Church Colleges in Canada: A History*, (Toronto: University of Toronto Press, 1966), e.g., 34, 89–90; and Robert J. Taylor, "The Darwinian Revolution: The Responses of Four Canadian Scholars" (unpublished doctoral diss., McMaster University, 1976).

13 O'Brien, *Sir William Dawson*, chap. 5, esp. 123.

14 From original draft of Gordon's autobiography, *Postscript to Adventure*, New York, 1938, C.W. Gordon Papers.

15 Masters, *Protestant Church Colleges*, 90–1; and Prang, *N.W. Rowell*, 74.

16 Masters, *Protestant Church Colleges*, 133–135; J.C. McLelland, "The Macdonnell Heresy Trial," *Canadian Journal of Theology* 4 (1958); and W.L. Grant and C.F. Hamilton, *Principal Grant*, (Toronto, 1905), 151–61.

17 Brian R. Ross, "Ralph Cecil Horner: A Methodist Sectarian Deposed, 1887–1895," joint issue of *The Bulletin* and *Journal of the Canadian Church Historical Society*, 19, 26 (1977), 1–2 (1977).

18 Semple, "The Impact of Urbanization," chap. 5.

19 Crossley, *Practical Talks*, 83–5.

20 John E. Lane to Salem Bland, 3 May 1907, Salem Bland Papers, no. 885, miscellaneous correspondence, United Church Archives.

21 Jacob Spelt, *Urban Development in South Central Ontario* (Toronto: Carleton Library reprint, 1972), 176–86.

22 Ramsay Cook, "Henry George and the Poverty of Progress in Canada," *Historical Communications/Communications Historique* 12, no. 1 (1977): 150.

23 See Terry Copp, *Anatomy of Poverty, The Condition of the Working Class in Montreal* (Toronto: McClelland and Stewart, 1974), esp. chap. 2; Greg Kealey, *Working Class Toronto at the Turn of the Century* (Toronto: New Hogtown Press, 1973), esp. 14–23.

24 Cook, "Henry George."

25 Allen, *The Social Passion*, chap. 1.

26 Ibid., chap. 2.

27 Those were the tendencies of Anglo-American theology, and the signs were not lacking in Canada. Robert E. Chiles, *Theological Transition in American Methodism: 1790–1935* (New York: University Press of America, 1965).

28 Masters, *Protestant Church Colleges*, 91–2; and Brian Fraser, "Theology and the Social Gospel among Canadian Presbyterians: A Case Study," *Studies in Religion/Sciences Religieuses* 8, no. 1 (1979). On the role idealism played for cultured evangelicals in a time of turmoil, see Melvin Richter, *The Politics of Conscience: T.H. Green and His Age* (London: Weidenfeld and Nicolson, 1964).

29 Taylor, "The Darwinian Revolution," 202–8; but see especially Brian McKillop's masterful recent work, *The Disciplined Intelligence* (Montreal: McGill-Queen's University Press, 1979).

30 T. Phillips Thompson, *The Politics of Labor* (Toronto: University of Toronto Press, 1975; reprint of 1887 edition), 172.

31 Jim Stein, "Labour and Religion in the Canadian Labour Press, 1872–1891" (unpublished master's paper, McMaster University, 1975); Joan Sangster, "Religion and the Prairie Labour Press, 1900–1910" (unpublished master's research paper, McMaster University, 1976).

32 This note keeps cropping up in the new studies of Canadian working class culture by Gregory Kealey, Wayne Roberts, Russell Hann, Bryan Palmer, and others.

33 See especially the early issues of Wrigley's reform journal, *Citizen and Country*.

34 Salem Bland Papers, no. 20, "The New Christianity," 8 November 1899.

35 *Vox Wesleyana* 2, no. 6 (1898): 178.

36 Allen, *The Social Passion*, 11–12.

37 See the following paper by Marjorie Robinson in this collection on the subject of Frontier College, 32–9.

38 This general trend of development is recounted in Allen, *The Social Passion*, but for a briefer treatment see Richard Allen, "The Social Gospel and the Reform Tradition in Canada, 1890–1928," *Canadian Historical Review* 49, no. 4 (1968).

39 Wendell MacLeod has provided an interesting brief account of the background to these developments as part of the setting of Bethune's Montreal years (Wendell MacLeod, Libbie Park, and Stanley Ryerson, *Bethune: The Montreal Years* [Toronto: James Lorimer, 1978], 25–9, 65–6). The larger story of this new wave of radical Protestantism is told in Roger Hutchinson, "The Fellowship for a Christian Social Order" (unpublished doctoral diss., University of Toronto, 1975).

40 See his review, *The Left News*, May 1937, 369–71.

41 R.B.Y. Scott and Gregory Vlastos (eds.), *Towards the Christian Revolution* (Chicago: Willett, Clark, 1936), 139.

CHAPTER FOURTEEN

1 Ian McKay has been characteristically gracious in allowing me to borrow these words from the title of his impressive "reconnaissance" of the first phase of the history of socialism in Canada, *Reasoning Otherwise: Leftists and the People's Enlightenment in Canada, 1890–1920* (Toronto: Between the Lines, 2008).

2 R.B.Y. Scott and Gregory Vlastos, eds, *Towards the Christian Revolution* (Chicago: Willett, Clark and Co., 1936), 139.

3 See the relevant parts of Eugene Forsey, *A Life on the Fringe: The Memoirs of Eugene Forsey* (Toronto: Oxford University Press, 1990); Frank Milligan, *Eugene A. Forsey: An Intellectual Biography* (Calgary: University of Calgary Press, 2004); Michiel Horn, *The League for Social Reconstruction: Intellectual Origins of the Democratic Left in Canada, 1930–1942* (Toronto: University of Toronto Press, 1980); Eileen R. Janzen, *Growing to One World: The Life of J. King Gordon* (Montreal: McGill-Queen's University Press, 2013); and Keith R. Fleming, *The World is our Parish: John King Gordon, 1900–1989, An Intellectual Biography* (Toronto: University of Toronto Press, 2015). Forsey claims to have written a third of *Social Planning for Canada* in *A Life*, 49.

4 League for Social Reconstruction, *Social Planning for Canada* (Toronto: University of Toronto Press, 1935), 37–8. On the LSR, see Horn, *The League for Social Reconstruction*.

5 The League for Social Reconstruction, *Social Planning*, 38n1.

6 Ibid.

7 Richard Allen, *The Social Passion: Religion and Social Reform in Canada, 1914–1928* (Toronto: University of Toronto Press, 1971).

8 Milligan, *Forsey*, 50–64.

9 John Costello, *John Macmurray: A Biography* (Edinburgh: Floris Books, 2002), 87–93, 100–3, 130–6, 189–99, 226–37.

10 Janzen, *Gordon*, 64–76.

11 The best expression of this in the 1930s and one of Niebuhr's most widely read books is *Moral Man and Immoral Society: A Study of Ethics and Politics* (New York: Charles Scribner's Sons, 1932).

12 Author's interview with Gordon, 4 May 1972. See also Janzen, *Gordon*, chap. 10, "Christian Socialist."

13 Horn, *League*, 62–3; "The Fellowship for a Christian Social Order," *New Outlook*, 9 May 1934, 345.

14 Phyllis Airhart, *The Church with the Soul of a Nation* (Toronto: University of Toronto Press, 2015), 90; United Church of Canada, Proceedings of General Council, 1934, 30; and *Christianizing the Social Order*, UCC Pamphlet, PAM.BV4-520 U5, United Church Archives. Horn, *League*, 63, errs in stating that General Council rejected the commission report.

15 "The Fellowship," *New Outlook*, 9 May 1934, 345.

16 Horn, *League*, 63.

17 Horn, *League*, 62–3.

18 See Janzen, *Gordon*, chap. 7, especially 103–10 for the details of the dismissal and the offer of travelling secretary for the FCSO, which naturally grew to incorporate the LSR.

19 Scott and Vlastos, eds., *Towards the Christian Revolution*, Preface.

20 Horn, *League*, 62–3.

21 See Hutchinson, "The Fellowship for a Christian Social Order: A Social Ethical Analysis of a Christian Socialist Movement" (PhD thesis, Toronto School of Theology, University of Toronto, 1975).

22 *New Outlook*, 9 May 1934, 345, cited in Horn, *League*, 62.

23 Henry George, *Progress and Poverty* (1879). Reprint, New York: Robert Schalkenbach Foundation, 1960. George's book was an international best seller and ranks with Marx in terms of readership and reprintings.

24 Scott and Vlastos, eds, *Towards the Christian Revolution*, Preface.

25 John Line, "Theological Principles," in *Towards the Christian Revolution*, eds Scott and Vlastos, 40.

26 Ibid.

27 Scott and Vlastos, eds, *Towards the Christian Revolution*, 48.

28 Ibid., 59.
29 Ibid., 59–61.
30 Ibid., 62–9.
31 Ibid., 74.
32 Ibid., 79–80.
33 Ibid., 80.
34 Ibid., 82.
35 Ibid., 134–5.
36 Ibid., 136.
37 Forsey's wife had attended and taken notes. This information is in the possession of the author.
38 Scott and Vlastos, eds, *Towards the Christian Revolution*, 139. Horn, *League*, 85, notes that Leonard Marsh, Frank Scott, and Graham Spry of the LSR also visited Russia and that in the LSR's next book, *Democracy Needs Socialism*, feared that continued dictatorship would jeopardize "the real gains of the last twenty years."
39 Forsey, *Life*, 52–3.
40 Scott and Vlastos, eds, *Towards the Christian Revolution*, 143–4.
41 Ibid., 146.
42 Ibid., 153–4.
43 Ibid., 165–7.
44 Ibid., 171.
45 Ibid., 172–4.
46 Author's interview with Gordon, 4 May 1972. For the full story, see Janzen, *Gordon*.
47 Scott and Vlastos, eds, *Towards the Christian Revolution*, 179–80.
48 See Allen, *Social Passion*, 324–7, 62; and Scott and Vlastos, eds, *Towards the Christian Revolution*, 182.
49 Scott and Vlastos, eds, *Towards the Christian Revolution*, 183–8.
50 Ibid., 190.
51 Ibid.
52 Ibid., 193.
53 Ibid., 196.
54 Ibid., 199–200.
55 Ibid., 201.
56 Ibid., 201, quoting Marx's eleventh thesis on Feuerbach.
57 Ibid., 205–7.
58 Ibid., 216, citing Julius F. Hecker, *Moscow Dialogues*, 142.
59 Ibid., 220–2.
60 Ibid., 222–3.

61 Ibid., 223, from Macmurray, *Creative Society*, 147.

62 Ibid., 224.

63 Francis Bacon, *The New Atlantis* (1627). See also T.C. Keefer, *The Philosophy of Railroads* (1842; reprinted in H.V. Nelles, ed., *The Philosophy of Railroads and Other Essays* [Toronto: University of Toronto Press, 1972]).

64 Scott and Vlastos, eds., *Towards the Christian Revolution*, 233.

65 Ibid., 234-5.

66 Ibid., 238-40.

67 Ibid., 241.

68 Ibid., 251; Luke 19:2.

69 For this later development, see Hutchinson, "The Fellowship for a Christian Social Order."

70 See above, chap. 5, "Providence to Progress."

71 Costello, *Macmurray*, 12, 137, 317 for example, but passim throughout chap. 10, "Discovering the Personal," and chap. 15, "Fighting for the Humanities." Costello notes that in the Dunning Lectures, given at Queen's University, Ontario, in January 1949, and published as *The Conditions of Freedom*, Macmurray significantly advanced his thinking on this subject.

72 Michael Gauvreau, *Evangelical Century* (Montreal: McGill-Queen's University Press, 1991), 220-22, 257-8, sees this issue developing in the decade before the First World War and assuming crisis proportions in the twenties and thirties.

73 Hutchinson, "Fellowship," 45.

74 Christo Aivalis, "In Service of the Lowly Nazarene Carpenter: The English Canadian Labour Press and the Case for Radical Christianity, 1926–1939," *Labour/Le Travail*, 73 (Spring 2014). The quote is from *The Trades and Labour Congress Journal* (July 1930): 38.

75 Horn, *The League for Social Reconstruction*, 62–3.

76 Ibid., 123; and Thomas H. and Ian McLeod, *The Road to Jerusalem* (Edmonton: Hurtig, 1987), 304–5.

77 Fleming, *Gordon*, 4.

CHAPTER FIFTEEN

1 Rosemary Radford Reuther, *The Radical Kingdom* (New York: Harper and Row, 1970), 288.

CHAPTER SIXTEEN

1 Kurt Samuelsson, *Religion and Economic Action* (New York: Basic Books, 1961).
2 Gordon Marshall, *In Search of the Spirit of Capitalism* (London: Hutchinson, 1982), 84, 123, 139, hereafter cited as Marshall.
3 Thelma McCormack, "The Protestant Ethic and the Spirit of Socialism, *British Journal of Sociology* 20, no. 3 (September 1969).
4 Marshall, *Presbyteries and Profits: Calvinism and the Development of Capitalism in Scotland, 1560–1707* (New York: Oxford University Press, 1980).
5 Marshall, *Spirit of Capitalism*, 30.
6 Ibid., 33.
7 Ibid., 31.
8 Ibid., 34, n38.
9 Ibid., 36.
10 Ibid., 39.
11 Ibid., 40.
12 Ibid., 34.
13 Ibid., 45–52.
14 Ibid., 50–1.
15 Ibid., p. 54.
16 Ibid., 67–8.
17 Ibid., 69.
18 Ibid., 74
19 Ibid., 75.
20 Ibid., 82.
21 Ibid., 83 and 190n34 citing W. Stanford Reid, *Skipper from Leith: The History of Robert Barton of Over Barnton* (Philadelphia: University of Pennsylvania, 1962), 91.
22 Marshall, *Spirit of Capitalism*, 84 and 190 n38 citing a dozen references including Kurt Samuelsson, *Religion and Economic Action* (London: Heinemann, 1961), 31–2.
23 Marshall, *Spirit of Capitalism*, 87 and 190n47; and Robertson, *Aspects of Rise of Economic Individualism: A Criticism of Max Weber and his School* (Cambridge: Cambridge University Press, 1933), 28, 164.
24 Marshall, *Spirit of Capitalism*, 87–8, 190n48–50; Broderick, *The Economic Morals of the Jesuits: An Answer to Dr. H.M. Robertson* (London: Oxford University Press, 1934).
25 Marshall, *Spirit of Capitalism*, 90, 191n57.
26 Ibid., 91–2, referencing David Little, "Max Weber Revisited: the 'Protestant

Ethic' and Puritan Experience of Order," *Harvard Theological Review* 59 (1966): 415–28; and Michael Walzer, "Puritanism as a Revolutionary Ideology," *History and Theory* 3 (1963): 59–90.

27 Marshall, *Spirit of Capitalism*, 91–2, 191n60–3, especially the extended commentaries in 192n63–4.

28 Ibid., 92, 191n62.

29 Ibid., 95.

30 Ibid., 102–13.

31 Ibid., 112–3.

32 Ibid., 106, and Samuelsson, *Religion and Economic Action*.

33 Marshall, *Spirit of Capitalism*, 122–3, 129–31.

34 Christopher Hill, "Protestantism and the Rise of Capitalism," in *Essays in the Economic and Social History of Tudor and Stuart England in Honour of R.H. Tawney*, ed. F.J. Fisher (Cambridge: Cambridge University Press, 1961). See also Christopher Hill, *The World Turned Upside Down* (New York: Viking Press, 1972). Tawney had anticipated the above argument in his own classic work, *Religion and the Rise of Capitalism* (New York: Harcourt, Brace, 1927) arguing that the spirit of capitalism effectively stripped Puritanism of its strong commitment to social obligation.

35 Marshall, *Spirit of Capitalism*, 149.

36 Ibid., 150.

37 Max Weber, *The Protestant Ethic and the Spirit of Capitalism* (Reprint, London: Unwin, 1971), 277–8.

38 Marshall, *Spirit of Capitalism*, 154–5.

39 Max Weber, *Economy and Society* (3 vols, New York: Bedminster Press, 1968), 491. Italics in the original.

40 Marshall, *Spirit of Capitalism*, 157.

41 Ibid., 158.

42 Ibid., 159 and see 205ns71–3, especially the extended commentary in n72.

43 *Ethics* 70 (1959): 24–5.

44 Marshall, *Spirit of Capitalism*, 159; see Tenbruck, *British Journal of Sociology* 31 (1980): 316–51.

45 Marshall, *Spirit of Capitalism*, 160 and 205n72.

46 Ibid., 161.

47 See the entirety of Marshall's carefully nuanced argument, *Spirit of Capitalism*, 159–64.

48 Marshall, *Spirit of Capitalism*, 164–7.

49 Ibid., 168–9.

50 Ibid., 171.

51 William H. Swatos, Jr, and Lutz Kaelber, *The Protestant Ethic Turns 100: Essays*

on the Centenary of the Weber Thesis (Boulder and London: Paradigm Publishers, 2005). Published in a series, Great Barrington Books, edited by Charles Lemert.

52 Ibid., ix–xii.

53 Lemert is prominently associated with various high-level research centres. Now retired but still teaching, he has published ten books in the last ten years. A graduate of Andover Theological College, he recently published *Why Niebuhr Matters*.

54 Swatos and Kaelber, *The Protestant Ethic Turns* 100, xxxii.

55 Hartmut Lehmann and Guenther Roth, eds., *Weber's "Protestant Ethic": Origins, Evidence, Context* (New York: Cambridge University Press, 1993). In addition to various teaching positions in Germany, Australia, and the United States, and various visiting professorships, including at the Institute for Advanced Studies at Princeton/Harvard, Lehmann has been a director of the Max Planck Institute for History at the University of Gottingen and has been honoured with the degree "Theol.h.c." by the universities of Basel, Lund, and Helsinki.

56 Ibid.,1–22.

57 Ibid., 22.

58 Martin Riesebrodt, "Dimensions of the Protestant Ethic," in Swatos and Kaelber, *The Protestant Ethic Turns* 100, 23–51.

59 Ibid., 24.

60 Ibid., 30–8.

61 Ibid., 42–8.

62 Ibid., 48–50.

63 Lawrence A. Scaff, "Remnants of Romanticism: Max Weber in Oklahoma and Indian Territory," in Swatos and Kaelber, *The Protestant Ethic Turns* 100, 77–110; and Scaff, "The 'Cool Objectivity of Sociation': Max Weber and Marianne Weber in America," *History of the Human Sciences* 11 no. 2 (May 1998): 61–82.

64 Scaff, "Remnants of Romanticism," 87 and 87n21.

65 Ibid., 94, citing "Senator Owen and the Halo of Romance," *Current Opinion* 56 (1914): 350.

66 Ibid., 93, citing Clarence B. Douglas, *Territory Tales: Oklahoma in the Making from the Twin Territories* (El Reno, OK: El Reno American, 1951), 28.

67 Ibid., 102.

68 Ibid., 103 and 103n58 citing Max Weber Papers, 28 September 1904.

69 Ibid., 105–6 and 106n65, and Weber, *Protestant Ethic*, 127, 261, 275.

70 Ibid., 106.

71 Ibid., 106 and 106n66; Weber, "The Second Reply to Fischer," in *The Protestant*

Ethic Debates; Max Weber's Replies to His Critics, ed. David J. Chalcraft and Austin Harrington (Liverpool: Liverpool University Press, 1998), 50.

72 Ibid., 108.

73 William H. Swatos, Jr, and Peter Kivisto, "The Contexts of the Publication and Reception of the Protestant Ethic," in Swatos and Kaelber, *The Protestant Ethic Turns* 100, 112–37. William H. Swatos, Jr, ed., *The Encyclopedia of Religion and Society* (Walnut Creek, CA: AltaMira Press, 1998), 119.

74 Swatos and Kivisto, "Contexts," 111–3.

75 Scaff, "Remnants of Romanticism," 78–9.

76 Swatos and Kivisto, "Contexts," 120 and 120n30–2.

77 Ibid., 124–9.

78 Ibid., 125.

79 Ibid., 129.

80 Ibid., 130–2.

81 George E. Simpson, "Individual and Social Action," *New Republic* 96 (28 September 1938): 223; Swatos and Kivisto, "Contexts," 131n47.

82 Swatos, *The Encyclopedia of Religion and Society* (Walnut Creek, CA: AltaMira Press, 1998), 131. The language suggests a direct lift from a public address.

83 Swatos and Kivisto, "Contexts," 132–4.

84 Paul Honigsheim, "Review of *From Max Weber*," *Journal of American Sociology* 52 (January 1947): 376–8.

85 Swatos, *The Encyclopedia of Religion and Society* (Walnut Creek, CA: AltaMira Press, 1998), 134 and 134n55.

86 Stephen Kalberg, "Utilizing Max Weber's 'Iron Cage' to Define the Past, Present, and Future of the American Political Culture," in Swatos and Kaelber, *The Protestant Ethic Turns* 100, 191–208. Stephen Kalberg, translation of Max Weber's *The Protestant Ethic and the Spirit of Capitalism* (Los Angeles: Roxbury Publishing Company, 2002), 194.

87 Kalberg, "Utilizing Max Weber's 'Iron Cage,'" 194–7, 200–1.

88 Quoting Weber, "'Churches' and 'Sects' in North America: An Ecclesiastical Socio-Political Sketch," *Sociological Theory* 3 (1985a): 10.

89 Kalberg, "Utilizing Max Weber's 'Iron Cage,'" 204.

90 Ibid., 206.

91 Ibid., 206.

92 Wolfgang Schluchter, *The Rise of Western Rationalism: Max Weber's Developmental History,* ed. Guenther Roth (Berkeley: University of California Press, 1981).

93 Donald Nielsen, "Max Weber's The Protestant Ethic and the 'Spirit' of Capitalism as Grand Narrative: Max Weber's Philosophy of History," in Swatos and Kaelber, *The Protestant Ethic Turns* 100, 53–77.

94 Ibid., 54, 56.

95 Ibid., 55.

96 Ibid., 75.

97 Lutz Kaelber, "Rational Capitalism, Traditionalism, and Adventure Capitalism: New Research on the Weber Thesis," in Swatos and Kaelber, *The Protestant Ethic Turns 100*, 139–63.

98 Ibid., 140, original italics.

99 Kurt Samuelsson, *Religion and Economic Action* (New York: Basic Books, 1961).

100 Guenther Roth, *Max Weber's deutsch-englische Familiengeschichte, 1800–1950* (Tubingen: Mohr Siebeck, 2001), 145n8.

101 Kaelber, "Rational Capitalism," 147 and 147n10; Weber, *The Protestant Ethic*, 28–9.

102 Ibid., 144, referencing Weber in the text without citing the source.

103 Ibid., 146–7.

104 Ibid., 149–53; Henretta, in Hartmut Lehmann and Guenther Roth, eds, *Weber's "Protestant Ethic"* (New York: Cambridge University Press, 1993), 327–46; and Anne Kelly Knowles, *Calvinists Incorporated: Welsh Immigrants and Ohio's Industrial Frontier* (Chicago: University of Chicago Press, 1997).

105 See also Marshall's critique of Weber's inclusion of the Methodists for its distorting effect on his time frames, *Spirit of Capitalism*, 130.

106 Kaelber, "Rational Capitalism," 154.

107 Ibid., 153 n18.

108 Margaret C. Jacob and Matthew Kadane, "Missing, Now Found in the Eighteenth Century: Weber's Protestant Capitalist," *American Historical Review* 108 (2003): 20–49.

109 Kaelber, "Rational Capitalism," 161.

110 Ibid., 163; 163n41 citing *Protestant Ethic* (2002b), 119, and 183n248, and giving as an example, David J. Jeremy, ed., *Religion, Business and Wealth in Modern Britain*.

111 Philip S. Gorski, *The Protestant Ethic Revisited* (Philadelphia: Temple University Press, 2011).

112 Ibid., Introduction, 1, 2.

113 Ibid., 2, 17–24.

114 Ibid., 209n56. Gorski in *The Protestant Ethic Revisited* notes that Weber would later qualify his apparently monocausal argument in the *Protestant Ethic*. Gorski refers to Weber's *General Economic History*, 354: "In the last resort the factor which produced capitalism is the rational permanent enterprise, rational accounting, rational technology and rational law, but again not these alone. Necessary complementary factors were the rational

spirit, the rationalization of the conduct of life in general and a rationalistic economic ethic."

115 Ibid., 207, n6. Among others on this subject, Gorski in *The Protestant Ethic Revisited* cites Kenneth Pomeranz, *The Great Divergence: China, Europe and the Making of the Modern World Economy*, (Princeton, NJ: Princeton University Press, 2000), and N.K. Chaudhuri, *Asia before Europe; Economy and Civilization of the Indian Ocean from the Rise of Islam to 1750* (Cambridge: Cambridge University Press, 1991).

116 See chap. 5, "The Little Divergence," in Gorski, *The Protestant Ethic Revisited*, 187–209. This chapter had been included in Swatos and Kaelber, *The Protestant Ethic Turns 100*. I have deferred its consideration so as to place it in this larger context of Gorski's work.

117 Gorski, *The Protestant Ethic Revisited*, 189.

118 Ibid., 208, n32, identifies the source of this frequent Marxist argument as Robert Brenner, The Agrarian Roots of European Capitalism," in *The Brenner Debate: Agrarian Class Structure and Economic Development in Pre-Industrial Europe*, eds Trevor Ashton and C.H.E. Philpin (Cambridge: Cambridge University Press, 1987).

119 Ibid., 205–6.

120 Ibid., 206.

121 I have taken this title of one of Livingston's chapters as the title of this review of his book to indicate the thrust of my use of his book as a conclusion to this chapter.

122 James Livingston, *No More Work: Why Full Employment Is a Bad Idea* (Chapel Hill: University of North Carolina Press, 2016).

123 Ibid., 11–2.

124 His first work was *Origins of the Federal Reserve System: Money, Class, and Corporate Capitalism* (Ithaca, NY: Cornell University Press, 1986). In 2009 he published *The World Turned Inside Out: American Thought and Culture at the End of the 20th Century*.

125 Livingston's preferred title was *Fuck Work!* – perhaps to attract attention to a small book easily overlooked among a flood of publications, or to appeal to a masculine working-class audience that needs to hear its message of hope – or the generally disenchanted – but his publisher mixed the suggestion. Despite his strong words on a gender- and racially driven labour market (9–10), Livingston makes few concessions to gender-neutral language, perhaps for the same tactical reason.

126 Livingston, *No More Work*, xi.

127 Ibid., xx.

128 Ibid., 45.

129 Ibid., 46ff.
130 Ibid., chap. 1, "The Family Assistance Plan and the End of Work," 13–28.
131 Ibid., 81
132 Ibid., 96.
133 I am relying here on Riesebrodt, "Dimensions of the Protestant Ethic," 48–51.
134 Note that this was a time of growing interest in personalist philosophy.
135 See Kalberg, "Utilizing Max Weber's 'Iron Cage,'" 100, 194ff.
136 Riesebrodt, "Dimensions of the Protestant Ethic," 28–9.

POSTSCRIPT

1 John Spong, *Biblical Literalism: A Gentile Heresy. A New Christianity for a New World; A Journey into Matthew's Gospel* (San Francisco: HarperOne, 2015).
2 Gary Dorrien, *The Word as True Myth: Interpreting Modern Theology* (Louisville, KY: Westminster John Knox Press, 1997), 118–9.
3 Ibid., 229.
4 Ibid., 235–6.
5 Ibid., 229–30.
6 Ibid., ch. 6, "Dialectics of Word and Spirit: Christ as True Myth," 229–39. See also Spong's illuminating interpretation in *The Fourth Gospel: Tales of a Jewish Mystic* (San Francisco: HarperOne, 2014). Among other works, Dorrien went on to publish the widely hailed prize-winning *The Making of American Liberal Theology* (Louisville, KY: Westminster John Knox Press, 1998–2006) in three volumes: *Imagining Progressive Religion, 1805–1900*; *Idealism, Realism, and Modernity, 1900–1950*; and *Crisis, Irony, and Postmodernity, 1950–2005*.
7 See Dorrien's recent book of essays, *Economy, Difference, and Empire*, Columbia University Religion and Politics Series (New York: Columbia University Press, 2010).
8 Marjorie Reeves and Warwick Gould, *Joachim of Fiore: The Eternal Gospel in the Nineteenth Century* (Oxford: Clarendon Press, 1987).
9 This is my demythologized rendition of this frequently cited passage from Deutero (Second) Isaiah 40:4. The Book of Isaiah is considered to comprise the writing of three different authors over two centuries, beginning with the first written about 742 BCE in response to threatening expansion westward of the Assyrian Empire. This passage comes in the first chapter of Deutero Isaiah, which is more confident of Israel's future and its renewing mission under God of bringing together all peoples in a time of peace, justice, and prosperity on an earth jubilant over the restoration of true order.

Index